D1005434

THE DEFINITIVE GUIDE

Archaeology

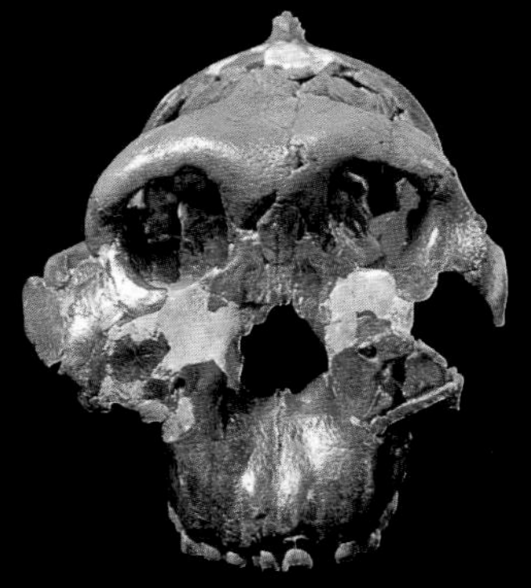

THE DEFINITIVE GUIDE

Archaeology

Consultant Editor

Paul G. Bahn

Published in 2003 by Fog City Press
814 Montgomery Street
San Francisco, CA 94133 USA

FOG CITY PRESS
Chief Executive Officer: John Owen
President: Terry Newell
Publisher: Lynn Humphries
Managing Editor: Janine Flew
Coordinating Designer: Helen Perks
Editorial Coordinators: Sarah Anderson, Tracey Gibson
Editorial Assistant: Kiren Thandi
Production Managers: Helen Creeke, Caroline Webber
Production Coordinator: James Blackman
Sales Manager: Emily Jahn
Vice President International Sales: Stuart Laurence
European Sales Director: Vanessa Mori

WELDON OWEN PUBLISHING
Publisher: Sheena Coupe
Creative Director: Sue Burk
Project Editor: Jenni Bruce
Designer: Clare Forte
Picture Research: Jo Collard

Color reproduction by Colourscan Co Pte Ltd
Printed by Tien Wah Press Pte Ltd
Printed in Singapore

ISBN 1 876778 86 5

Library of Congress Cataloging-in-Publication Data is available

A Weldon Owen Production

Contents

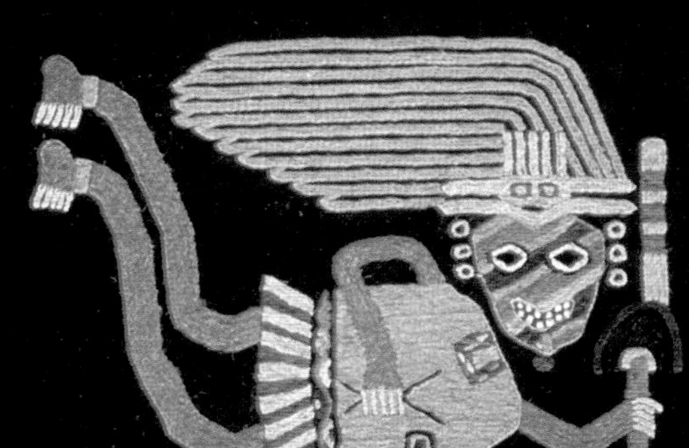

Introduction

Why bother with archaeology? Isn't it just about long-dead people who are no longer relevant to us? Well, for starters, archaeology can be a lot of fun. Even if you don't want to play an active role in the field, almost everyone has some interest in the past, be it their immediate ancestors or a stone or bone they have found somewhere.

Archaeology can also be a source of immense pleasure through its varied and beautiful treasures, its lost cities and tombs, its digging and detective work. Archaeological tourism has become a major phenomenon, as increasing numbers of enthusiasts travel to visit exotic sites and cultures.

From a more academic viewpoint, archaeology is the only subject that can tell us about our origins and our remote past. It is also crucial to our future, because it is only by knowing our "trajectory"—what has happened to us so far—that we can hope to assess where we are going.

I hope this book will provide a useful and stimulating introduction to the world of archaeology, and entice you to delve further into this enthralling subject.

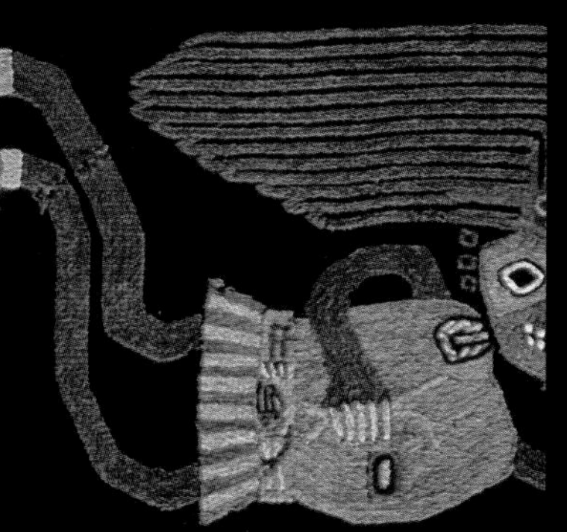

Paul G. Bahn

How to Use This Guide

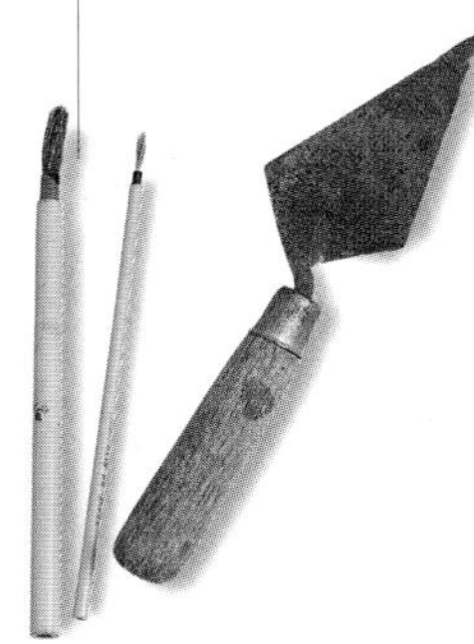

With this Definitive Guide, you can explore the fascinating world of archaeology and understand how its detective work is gradually revealing the story of the human past.

This Guide is divided into two main parts. Part One, *Exploring Our Human Past,* delves into the science of archaeology—from its earliest beginnings to its current methods and sub-disciplines—and provides an overview of the ages of humankind that archaeology sheds light upon—from the appearance of the first humans to our recent industrial past. Part Two, *A Guide to Sites and Treasures,* provides a survey of the world's most significant archaeological finds—from the first camps and oldest cremations to the intricate artifacts and astounding monuments of the great civilizations.

THE HISTORICAL PAST

The Sculpture of Greece and Rome

Monumental Greek sculptu
the 7th century BC onwar
to be used as dedications in sanctuar
and as grave markers. Some
earliest types were the nak
(kouroi) and draped won
(korai). Roman taste fo
sculpture has meant tha
the lost Greek bronze sc
of the 5th and 4th centuries BC

INTERPRETING THE REMAINS

The Art of the Past

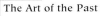

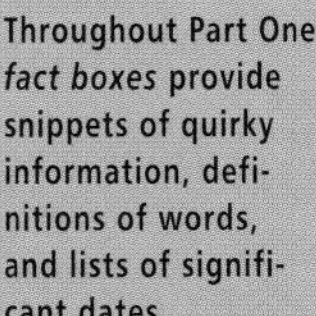

Status Symbol
Art can be an indication of wealth and power: opulent mosaics decorate the huge villa built by the emperor Hadrian in AD 125–34 at Tivoli near Rome.

Ancient Tradition
Aboriginal cave paintings at Kakadu National Park, Australia, belong to the world's oldest continuous art tradition, which dates back at least 40,000 years. These examples were painted in the 1950s.

Art is something that exists in every present-day human society and that seems to have existed in every ancient one, too, back to at least 40,000 years ago, and probably beyond.

Because it encompasses such a vast variety of activities and products, art is notoriously difficult to define. Furthermore, in many cultures it is not seen as a distinct entity, but simply as an inherent aspect of normal social or religious life, with no clear boundaries between the aesthetic and the practical. For example, in most Australian Aboriginal cultures, there is no word for "art" as such, and all their aesthetic manifestations—paintings, carvings, musical instruments, song, dance—are simply considered extensions of the cultural and natural environment. For archaeological purposes, however, the best approach is probably to see "art" as a deliberate visual communication, a message expressed in durable form.

ART ON THE ROCKS

Rock art—paintings and engravings on rocks, shelters, and cave walls—exists in virtually every country in the world, and extends back to at least 40,000 years ago in some areas. One of those areas is Australia, where some Aboriginal groups still produce rock art today, making it the world's longest continuous art tradition. Rock images probably have innumerable functions, serving as narratives, territorial boundaries, memory triggers, myths, rites of passage, and tribal secrets and laws, and fulfilling many other religious and secular roles. Portable art also extends far back. In Australia, for example, the Mandu Mandu Creek necklace of perforated shells is about 32,000 years old.

THE EARLIEST ART
Dated to at least 230,000 years ago, a pebble of volcanic rock found at Berekhat Ram in Israel may be the earliest known art object. The pebble's natural shape resembles a woman, but grooves have been added to create the neck and arms.

Throughout Part One, *fact boxes* provide snippets of quirky information, definitions of words, and lists of significant dates.

112

DECORATION

Art has had a huge rol
ology. Ceramics and m
which dominate the a
logical record of many
have been classified ac
their shapes and decor
The concept of style h
ferentiate the products
and areas, since artifact
ration are often produ
tinctive ways that are s
community or culture
pottery, for example, h
reveal the colonization
pattern of the Pacific is

CONVENTIONS OF REPRESENTATION

All art styles employ conventions, especially regarding depictio
representation of beings or objects in the real world. For examp
ancient Egyptians (above) drew humans with the head in profil
eye seen full-face, the shoulders were shown full-width from th
but the rest of the body was in profile. The major personage—
pharaoh or tomb-owner—was drawn bigger than the other fig
which were often arranged in horizontal rows, set one above th
Similar sets of conventions are known in every corpus of ancien
from Ice Age art, which shows mostly adult animals drawn in p
no ground lines and few scenes, to recent art in every part of t

EUROPE

Delphi

- Famous oracle in Greece
- Dated from Archaic to Roman, 7th century BC–4th century AD
- Excavated by the French School in Athens from the 1880s
- Finds include bronze sculpture, sculptured reliefs
- On public display; finds in Delphi Museum, Delphi

One of the most important sanctuaries of the Greek world was located at Delphi, on the slopes of Mount Parnassus in central Greece. Its popularity was based on the presence of an oracle that was consulted by leaders throughout the Mediterranean. At the heart of the sanctuary lay the Doric Temple of Apollo. After a devastating fire in the 6th century BC, the temple was rebuilt with marble figures placed in the triangular pediment at the eastern end; the Greek historian Herodotus records that the work was paid for by an Athenian family who had been in exile.

A sacred way led up to the temple. Along its route, various cities of the Greek world erected treasuries to house their dedi-

Temple and Theater
The Greeks believed that Delphi was the center of the world. Today, the ruins of the Temple of Apollo can be seen in front of the remains of the theater, which was used mainly for theatrical performances during the great festivals of the sanctuary

309

Discus Thrower
This Discobolos (below) is a Roman marble copy of the bronze original by the Athenian sculptor Myron, c. 450 BC. The form of the discus thrower displays the mastery of anatomy developed in Greek sculpture.

Draped Figure
Inspired by Egyptian art, early Greek sculptors created korai, statues of draped maidens. Appearing from about 660 to 500 BC, the form gradually became more naturalistic. This terracotta kore dates to the 6th century BC.

The Farnese Herakles
The Farnese Herakles (below) was created by the 3rd century AD Athenian sculptor and copyist Glycon. It is a copy of a colossal bronze work by Lysippos, a 4th century BC Greek sculptor renowned for the naturalism and slender proportions of his figures.

THE ART OF THE PAST

eligion and Art
rt was often used to orify the gods of the ncient world. This statue the Greek god of the a, Poseidon, is dated 450 BC and was possibly eated by Kalamis.

113

Part Two pages focus on particular sites and treasures. Entries are presented in five chapters arranged according to geographical location.

Graphic *feature pages* are scattered throughout Part One of the Guide to highlight topics of particular interest and visual appeal.

Part One pages provide an overview of archaeology and the human past. The entries are arranged into three sections and six chapters.

Stunning *color photographs and illustrations* are accompanied by substantial captions that expand on the information in the main text.

Feature boxes in Part One provide additional detail on a fascinating individual or a specialized aspect of the topic discussed on the page.

A Timeline of Archaeology

Pre-18th Century

6th century BC ■ Nabonidus, King of Babylon, excavates early temple ruins.
5th century BC ■ Herodotus documents the Greek–Persian Wars and becomes the "Father of History."
AD 1092 ■ Antiquarians of the Song Dynasty in China document bronzes and jades from earlier dynasties.
15th century ■ Renaissance ushers in a new interest in the classical world.
1586 ■ William Camden's *Britannia* lists archaeological sites in England.
17th century ■ John Aubrey conducts long-term field studies of Wiltshire monuments, including Stonehenge.
1666 ■ Roger de Gaignière publishes *Antiquité des Gaules.*

18th Century

1717 ■ Michael Mercati's *Metallotheca* is published, an inventory of ancient artifacts in the Vatican's collections.
1738 ■ Systematic explorations at Herculaneum and Pompeii begin.
1750 ■ J.G. Eccard's *De Origine Germanorum* awakens interest in the origins of the German people.
1764 ■ Johann Joachim Winkelmann's *History of Ancient Art* prompts modern interest in the classical world.
1784 ■ Thomas Jefferson's systematic excavation of a burial mound on his estate establishes him as the "Father of American Archaeology."
1788 ■ First excavations in Australia are conducted by John Hunter on burial mounds at Port Jackson.
1797 ■ John Frere first applies stratigraphic principles to site excavation and interpretation.
1798 ■ Napoleon's invasion of Egypt sets off a craze for Egyptian antiquities.

Stonehenge

19th Century

1811–17 ■ Claudius James Rich's work at Babylon stimulates the study of ancient Mesopotamia.
1817 ■ Giovanni Belzoni discovers the tomb of Seti I in Egypt's Valley of the Kings.
1822 ■ Jean-François Champollion deciphers Egyptian hieroglyphics on the Rosetta Stone.
1830–33 ■ Charles Lyell's *Principles of Geology* helps establish a long antiquity for the earth.
1836 ■ Christian Thomsen develops the Three Age System, still the basic temporal framework of European archaeology.
1841–43 ■ John Lloyd Stephens and Frederick Catherwood publish accounts of their visits to the ruins of Mexico and Central America.
1845–51 ■ Henry Layard's Nineveh and Nimrud excavations establish Mesopotamian archaeology as a legitimate scientific study.
1847–64 ■ Jacques Boucher de Perthes' *Celtic and Antediluvian Antiquities* provides indisputable proof of human antiquity.
1848 ■ Ephraim Squier and Edwin Davis publish *Ancient Monuments of the Mississippi Valley,* a pioneering work in U.S. archaeology.

Egyptian pectoral ornament

1851 ▪ Daniel Wilson introduces the term *prehistoric* into the English language.
1851 ▪ First chair of archaeology is established at Cambridge University.
1854 ▪ Underwater archaeology is established when Adolphe von Morlot excavates the Swiss lake dwellings.
1856 ▪ Neanderthal remains are recovered at Feldhofer, near Dusseldorf.
1856 ▪ Samuel Haven's scholarly *Archaeology of the United States* is published.
1859 ▪ Charles Darwin's *On the Origin of Species* sees humans as the product of natural evolution.
1863 ▪ Charles Lyell publishes *The Antiquity of Man*, leading to the discipline of prehistoric archaeology.
1866 ▪ Peabody Museum, Harvard, is established.
1870–73 ▪ Heinrich Schliemann excavates Troy.
1879 ▪ Upper Paleolithic cave paintings are discovered at Altamira.
1880 ▪ W.M. Flinders Petrie begins a distinguished career as a Near Eastern archaeologist.
1888 ▪ Well-preserved ruins at Cliff Palace, Mesa Verde, USA, are discovered.
1894 ▪ Cyrus Thomas archaeologically confirms that the mounds of the American Midwest were built by the ancestors of contemporary Native Americans.
1894 ▪ Eugène Dubois discovers Java Man.

20th Century

1900–35 ▪ Arthur Evans excavates Knossos.
1902 ▪ John H. Marshall is appointed India's Director-General of Antiquities.
1911 ▪ Hiram Bingham discovers the Inca city of Machu Picchu.
1912 ▪ Gustav Kossina's nationalistic *German Prehistory* is published.
1922 ▪ Howard Carter discovers the tomb of Tutankhamen in Egypt.
1925 ▪ Raymond Dart announces the discovery of the Taung child, the earliest recognized australopithecine.
1925 ▪ Gordon Childe's *The Dawn of European Civilization* is published.
1927 ▪ Pecos Classification is devised by Alfred Kidder as the organizing temporal framework for American Southwestern archaeology.
1928 ▪ O.G.S. Crawford's *Wessex from the Air* shows the potential for aerial photography.
1929 ▪ Gertrude Caton-Thompson establishes that Great Zimbabwe was built by black Africans.
1939 ▪ Dorothy Garrod is appointed as archaeology's first female professor at either Oxford or Cambridge.
1949 ▪ Willard Libby invents the technique of radiocarbon dating, the first universal absolute dating method.
1952 ▪ Michael Ventris deciphers Linear B.
1959 ▪ *Zinjanthropus boisei* is discovered by Mary Leakey at Olduvai Gorge, Tanzania.
1962 ▪ Lewis Binford introduces the "New Archaeology" in an attempt to make the discipline a hard science.
1974 ▪ Lucy (*Australopithecus afarensis*) is discovered by Donald Johanson in Hadar, Ethiopia.
1982 ▪ Ian Hodder introduces "Postprocessual Archaeology," an attempt to incorporate postmodernism into archaeological interpretation.

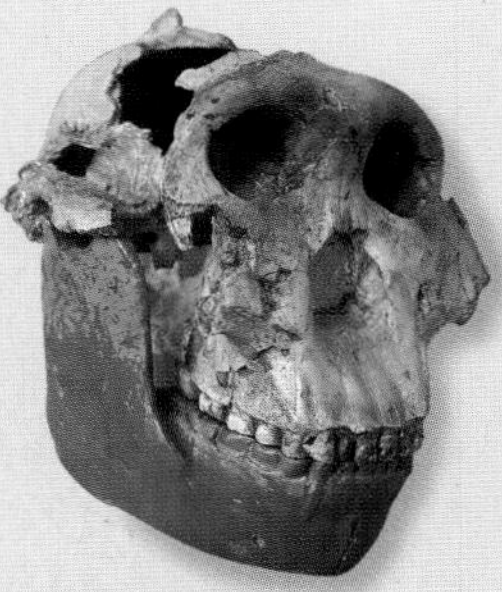

Zinjanthropus boisei

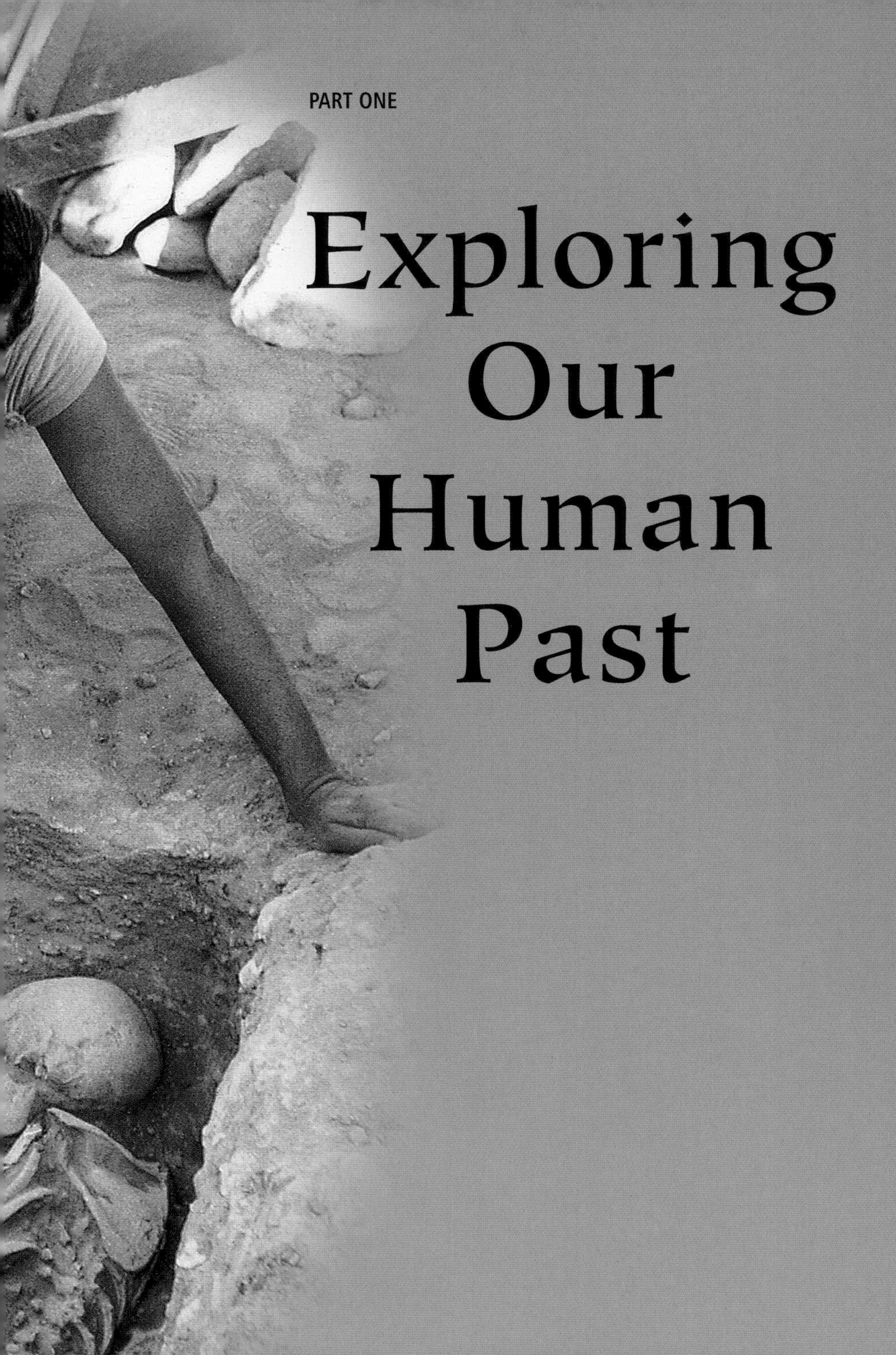

PART ONE

Exploring Our Human Past

Toward a Science

Archaeology's Past

The records left by the earliest civilizations show that human interest in the past can be traced back thousands of years. The craze for collecting antiquities that began in the 16th century eventually matured into a scientific approach to investigating the buildings, artifacts, and bones of our ancestors.

"Since so little is known of the oldest times of this country, at all times a few amateurs in antiquity have attempted to deduce from graves the ways of life and customs of the pagans, and, after satisfying their curiosity to a certain degree, have filled thus the collections of antiquities with urns, shields, weapons and all kinds of utensils."

Martin Mushard (1669–1770),
German pastor and antiquarian

What Is Archaeology?

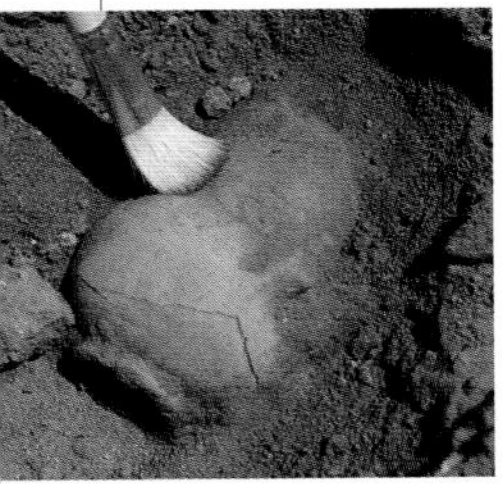

A Brush with the Past
Archaeologists must use delicate, painstaking techniques to uncover the traces of the past without causing damage.

Archaeology is the study of the human past through the recovery and analysis of material remains. As people search for their origins, archaeology provides insights into our shared heritage.

In 1850, Charles Newton of the British Museum observed that "Man's history has been graven on the rock of Egypt, stamped on the brick of Assyria, enshrined in the marble of the Parthenon—it rises before us a majestic Presence in the piled-up arches of the Coliseum." Today, archaeology is no longer confined to Newton's examples from the Mediterranean and Near East, but has become a truly global discipline.

Digging Deep
During an excavation at Nippur, Iraq, archaeologists uncovered a city dating to the 20th century BC. With a depth of 60 feet (20 m), the site contains 20 successive city levels spanning a period of 1,900 years.

ASPECTS OF ARCHAEOLOGY

Archaeology has human developments as its focus, so its starting point is the emergence of humans. The hominid remains discovered in Olduvai Gorge in Tanzania, Africa, can be dated by scientific techniques to almost 2 million years ago (see p. 236). Further fossilized human remains recovered at East Turkana in Kenya have been dated to roughly 1.5 million years ago (see p. 238). For subsequent millennia, especially in the absence of written records, archaeology provides a prime channel for the understanding of human societies and cultures. At the other end of the timescale, archaeology can complement written or historical sources. These may relate, for example, to early colonial settlements in North America, or even to defensive systems in Britain during the Second World War.

Another aspect of archaeology is the recovery of the classical civilizations that have had so great an influence on modern

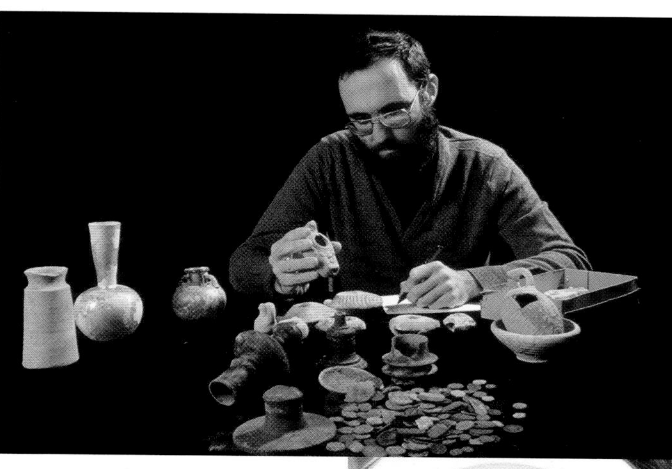

Analyzing Findings
A vital part of archaeology is the accurate cataloging of excavated finds. Here an archaeologist at the Rockefeller Museum catalogs and records objects found in a Jerusalem grave.

western European culture. Investigations of the setting for Athenian democracy or the heart of ancient Rome have helped to explain the political structures and institutions described in written records. Excavations in the Near East have revealed ancient sites and recovered new cuneiform texts, which many hoped would help to illuminate the Old Testament and the historical accuracy of the Bible.

Repairing a Treasure
A conservator at the British Museum reassembles the fragments of the Portland Vase, a celebrated piece of Roman glass that had been shattered in 1845.

A BROAD DISCIPLINE

The recovery of the past has involved the removal of layers of earth to look back in time. Yet archaeology is now more than digging Iron Age sites in Scotland, uncovering Maya temples in the jungles of Central America, or studying rock art in Australia's Northern Territory. It involves teams of science-based archaeologists who analyze bones, seeds, pottery, and metalwork. At the same time, some archaeologists work on museum collections, perhaps identifying stylistic developments for a region. And then there are those involved in drawing up plans of sites and preparing the finds for publication. The discipline also looks beyond itself. Archaeologists learn from anthropologists, who study living societies, since they can suggest social structures or economic patterns for societies that have not left behind written records.

While archaeology can only be speculative, it can bring together a wide variety of evidence to provide an informed interpretation of our human past.

Paleolithic Tools
Stone tools dating to the Paleolithic Age (2.5 million to 10,000 years ago) are the most abundant evidence of humankind's distant past.

The Origins of Archaeology

Babylonian Law
This 7 foot (2.2 m) basalt stela (carved slab) features the code of law left by Hammurabi, the sixth king of Babylon.

Humans have probably always been curious about the past. This interest can be traced as far back as the first civilizations of Mesopotamia and China, which left records of ancient remains.

The earliest recorded history attests to humans' fascination with the traces left by their predecessors. A cuneiform inscription on a brick from Larsa in Iraq records the search by the 6th century BC king of Babylon, Nabonidus, for the sanctuary of an earlier ruler, Burnaburiash (1359–1333 BC): "the dust was lifted and the mound of earth which covered the town and temple." During the digging, the Babylonians found an even earlier text of the king Hammurabi (1792–1750 BC). Thus Nabonidus was able to establish a temple on a site where cult activity could be traced back into the mists of time.

GREEKS AND ROMANS

Ancient Greek historians mention the discovery of the bones of "heroes" (huge skeletons) in large tombs. In the 6th century BC, the Spartans apparently found the bones of the hero Orestes at Tegea, buried under a blacksmith's shop; in the 470s BC, the Athenian general Kimon, during operations against pirates, recovered the bones of the hero Theseus from the island of Skyros, brought them back in triumph to Athens, and placed them in a specially constructed shrine, the Theseion. Though such stories may be anecdotal, the excavation of Bronze Age Mycenaean tombs in Greece have revealed that later generations placed offerings inside, treating them as holy sites (see p. 296).

When Julius Caesar established a colony at Corinth, a prosperous city in Greece that had been

Roman Curiosity
Based on an account left by the Roman historian Livy, this 1525 painting by Polidoro da Caravaggio depicts 2nd century BC Romans investigating the tomb of the Sabine Numa Pompilius, believed to have ruled Rome in the 7th century BC.

TURNING TO THE PAST
Some consider the Greek poet Homer (c. 9th–8th century BC) to be the father of archaeology. His great works the *Iliad* and the *Odyssey* ignited an enthusiasm for the past and the deeds of ancient heroes. This interest continued through to the 1st century BC, when the Roman emperor Augustus collected ancient weapons.

destroyed by Rome in 146 BC and then abandoned, the veteran Roman soldiers dug in the cemetery and "found numbers of terracotta reliefs, and also many bronze vessels." Romans also collected sculptures and other works of Greek art as the Roman empire expanded south into Sicily and into the Greek mainland. These were then displayed in private houses as well as in the public spaces of their cities.

CHRISTIAN DISCOVERIES

The rise of Christianity provided a new motivation for discovering earlier sites, as Christians sought out the places mentioned in the New Testament texts. For example, in AD 323 Helena, mother of the emperor Constantine, started digging through the remains of the Roman colony at Jerusalem and discovered what was believed to be part of the cross on which Jesus had been crucified.

MEDIEVAL RECORDS

The remains of the past were also noted during the Medieval period. In the Quimper region of France, a monastic document records fallen and standing stones, which were no doubt the remains of the megalithic monuments that are common in the area. In Britain at Glastonbury Abbey in 1191, the monks came across the remains of a man and a woman. The bodies were accompanied by an inscribed cross that identified them with the mythical king Arthur and his wife Guinevere.

It was not until the 16th century, however, that scholars really began to seek out artifacts in order to create a rounded picture of the ancient past.

The True Cross
This 7th century AD manuscript shows the discovery of the True Cross and is one of the few Medieval depictions of men excavating.

Arthurian Tomb
In 1191 monks discovered what they believed to be the remains of King Arthur and his queen, Guinevere, at Glastonbury Abbey (below).

Antiquarians and Travelers

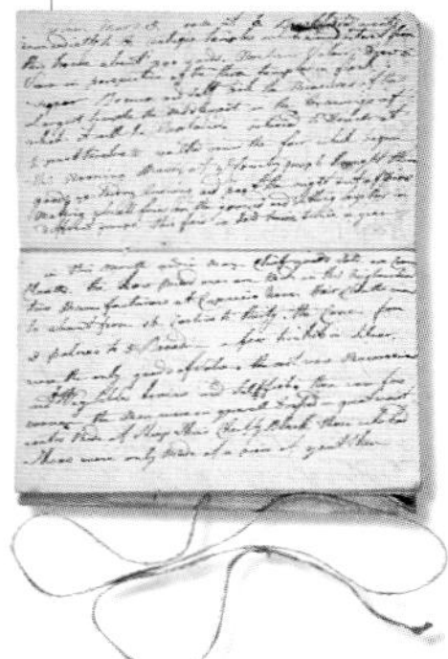

Travel Diary
Charles Townley, a British collector of antiquities, kept a diary of his Grand Tour through Italy and France, recording events such as his 1768 visit to Paestum's Greek temples.

From the 16th century on, Europeans began studying ancient monuments and forming collections of antiquities. Famous sites were visited, painted, and described for those at home.

The Renaissance created a new interest in the classical world of the Greeks and Romans. Ancient remains were pillaged for materials and works of art to be used in building projects in the city of Rome. The attraction of collecting was such that in 1471 Pope Sixtus IV restricted the removal of antiquities from the territory that he controlled. In a late 16th century painting by Hendrik III van Cleve, the gardens of the Palazzo Cesi in Rome are shown dotted with classical sculpture and sarcophagi.

RECORDING THE REMAINS

Across Europe, antiquarians documented the remains of the past and assembled collections of antiquities. While many were little more than treasure-hunters, others took a scholarly approach. Roger de Gaignière's volume, *Antiquité des Gaules* (1666), included a view of the Roman amphitheater at Arles, complete with the houses of the town built into both the arena and the banks of seating. In Britain, William Camden (1551–1623) in his topographical study *Britannia* (1586) drew attention to the wealth of early remains, noting "artificial hills both round and pointed ... called burrowes or barrowes ... bones are found in them." An image of Stonehenge was used as a frontispiece for his work, which established the antiquity of the British Isles.

This interest in Britain's past was extended by antiquarians such as John Aubrey (1626–97), who prepared, but was never able to publish, *Monumenta Britannica,* which attempted to classify Britain's archaeological remains. His work was continued by

ANTIQUARIANS
Antiquarians are individuals who collect or study antiquities. The term usually refers to those scholars and amateurs who investigated artifacts in the 16th–19th centuries, before the development of modern archaeology.

Mysterious Stones
While scholars such as John Aubrey and William Stukeley recognized Stonehenge as a pre-Roman monument, they wrongly associated it with the druids, the priesthood of Britain mentioned by classical writers.

William Stukeley, who studied some of the major prehistoric monuments of Britain, including Stonehenge and the henge monument at Avebury in Wiltshire. In Germany, a similar interest in national origins saw fruition in works such as J.G. Eccard's *De origine Germanorum* (1750).

Modern interest in the classical world can be traced back to the German scholar Johann Joachim Winkelmann (1717–68). His study of Roman sculpture, some of it copying lost Greek bronze masterpieces, was published in 1764 as the *History of Ancient Art.* This work influenced generations of scholars as they viewed and collected the remains of the Roman Empire.

The 1600s and 1700s saw the first accurate explanations of "magic crocks" and "thunderbolts," objects that European farmers had been unearthing for centuries. In 1632 Jan Johnston explained that the mysterious crocks were actually ancient burial urns. Stone tools brought back from the Americas suggested that what had previously been considered thunderbolts or elf-shot were in fact tools made by earlier humans.

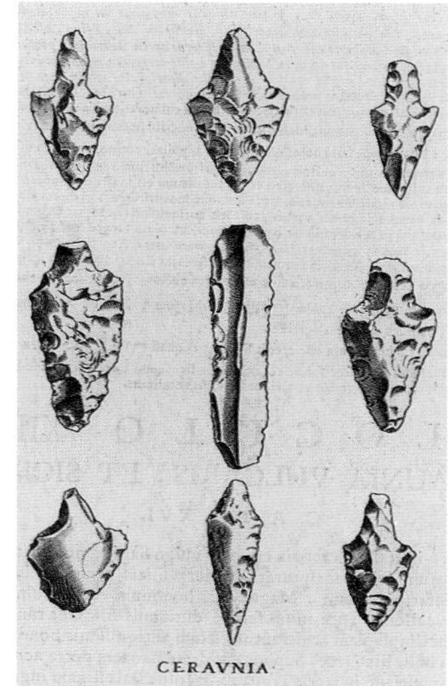

Thunderbolts
The 16th century scholar Michel Mercati recorded the Vatican's collections of early stone tools and arrowheads, which were popularly believed to be "thunderbolts." Mercati concluded that they had been made by humans in a time before iron.

Collector's Item
Ancient Roman sculptures, such as this marble and alabaster bust of Emperor Septimius Severus, have attracted collectors since Renaissance times.

A Desecrated Temple
In 1687 the Parthenon, the classical temple on the Athenian acropolis, was being used to store gunpowder and was badly damaged by an explosion. The damage later encouraged the Turkish authorities to allow Britain's Lord Elgin to remove the marbles from the temple.

TRAVELERS TO THE PAST

In the 18th century, members of the British social elite started making the "Grand Tour" of continental Europe. Many made their way to Rome, where they were captivated by classical remains. This British interest in the classical was fostered by the Society of Dilettanti, which was established in 1733. From about 1740, Grand Tourists heading south to Naples were attracted to the excavations for the ancient Roman cities of Herculaneum and Pompeii, which had been buried by the catastrophic eruption of Mount Vesuvius in AD 79 (see p. 316). These early visitors described how tunnels had been cut through the solidified volcanic mud of Herculaneum to reveal sights such as the theater, complete with its classical statues. One of the favored spots outside Rome was at Tivoli, the site of the emperor Hadrian's extensive villa. During the 18th century,

CURIOSITY CABINET
From the Renaissance on, it became popular among the nobility of Europe to form "cabinets of curiosities," collections that displayed ancient artifacts alongside foreign curios, precious minerals, and exotic animal specimens.

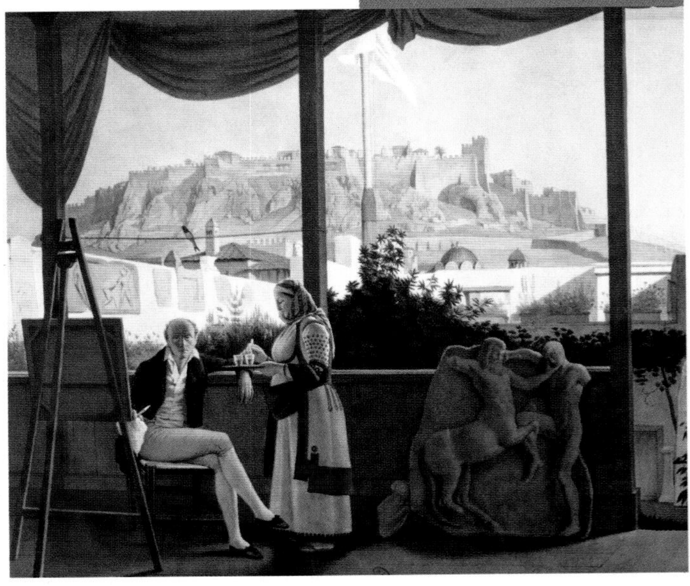

Classical Decor
Classical antiquities were widely used to decorate the homes and gardens of western Europeans, as in this 1819 print, *View of the Acropolis from the house of Monsieur Fauvel, Consul of France*. The relief featuring the centaur was from the Parthenon.

much of the villa's classical sculpture was sent back to Britain to decorate country houses.

EXPLORING GREECE

From the late 18th century on, travelers also started to come across the remains of the Greek world. Thomas Major's 1768 publication of the near-complete Doric temples at the Greek colony of Poseidonia (Paestum) was a major revelation to the British public. On the island of Sicily, the temples from the Greek colony at Agrigento provided inspiration for countless travelers.

Journeys farther east were rare. George Wheeler traveled to Athens in the 1670s, recording his experience in *Journey into Greece.* He was later followed by Nicholas Revett and James Stuart, whose illustrations for their publication *Antiquities of Athens* (1762) remain important since some of the structures have been lost or damaged. Their work encouraged a "Greek Revival" in 18th century England.

FARTHER AFIELD

During the 1600s, a number of travelers explored the Near East. The Italian Pietro della Valle brought back inscribed bricks from Babylon and Ur, the first examples of cuneiform writing displayed in Europe.

Although few antiquarians took a rigorous scientific approach to their explorations, their reports and collections served to raise awareness of the past and prepared the ground for the archaeologists who followed them.

THE ELGIN MARBLES

The growing interest in antiquities led to a collecting frenzy, with ancient artifacts being removed from their context and shipped back to the antiquarian's home. Between 1801 and 1805, the seventh Earl of Elgin (above) removed a series of 5th century BC sculptures from the Athenian acropolis, notably parts of the Parthenon's pediments, its southern metopes (relief sculptures), and much of its continuous frieze (below). Greece was under Turkish rule and Elgin acted with permission from the Turkish authorities. He maintained that he was protecting the sculptures, which had suffered damage from early tourists as well as from lime-burners. The sculptures were eventually acquired by the British Government and are today displayed in the British Museum. Recent efforts to have the marbles returned to Greece have been unsuccessful since a statute prohibits the museum from giving away its collections.

Wonderful Things

In November 1922, English archaeologist Howard Carter and his sponsor Lord Carnarvon made one of the most famous discoveries in archaeology: the spectacular burial of Tutankhamen in Egypt's Valley of the Kings. Tutankhamen had been an insignificant pharaoh buried hastily after an unexpected death, yet he had been provided with a breathtaking array of artifacts, including chariots, furniture, clothing, jewelry, food, and three golden coffins—"everywhere the glint of gold." After opening the tomb's antechamber, Carter wrote: "The day of days, the most wonderful that I have ever lived through, and certainly one whose like I can never hope to see again."

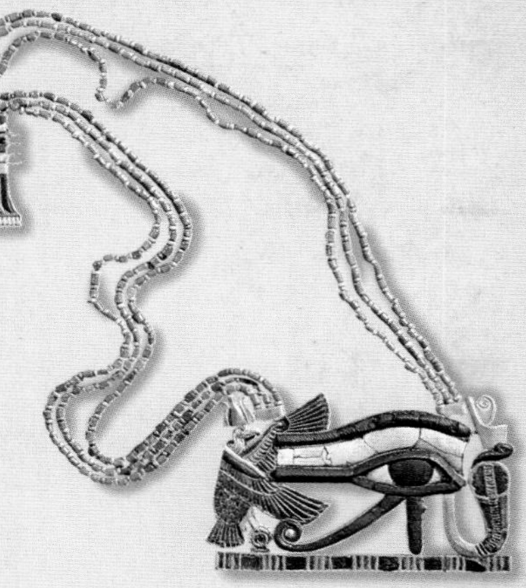

Protective Pendant
Tutankhamen lived during Egypt's golden age of arts and crafts. One of the exquisite pieces discovered in his tomb, this pendant (above) features a *wedjat* eye, symbol of protection, flanked by the vulture goddess Nekhbet and the snake goddess Wadjat, protectors of Upper and Lower Egypt.

The Mummy's Mask
The mummy of Tutankhamen was found inside three nested golden coffins that were enclosed within a quartzite sarcophagus. A magnificent solid gold funerary mask inlaid with semiprecious stones (right) covered the mummy's head and shoulders.

A Persistent Team
Howard Carter (right, explaining his work to visitors) spent five years searching for the tomb of Tutankhamen. When he finally peered into the antechamber, his sponsor Lord Carnarvon (left) asked him if he could see anything. Barely able to speak, Carter replied "Yes, wonderful things."

A Systematic Approach

During the 19th century, a major shift started to occur, as interest moved from antiquarianism, a primarily collecting-based pursuit, to modern archaeology, a systematic, scientific endeavor.

Tools as Clues
Paleolithic stone tools were generally considered the work of Celts or Gauls until the 1800s, when Jacques Boucher de Perthes and others showed that such tools originated in the prehistoric era and had been made by early humans.

The political changes in Europe at the start of the 19th century saw renewed interest in history, particularly concerning the origins of nation states. As curator of the Danish National Museum, Christian Thomsen (1788–1865) developed the Three Age system, arranging antiquities chronologically according to whether they were made during the Stone Age, Bronze Age, or Iron Age. His 1836 guide provided support for the "evolution" of society. With many subsequent refinements, the Three Age system is still widely used today.

AN EXPANDING PAST

In the early 1800s, the accepted view was that the oldest human bones or tools came from Celtic and Gallo-Roman times, so humans could not have coexisted with extinct animals. In France, however, Jacques Boucher de Perthes (1788–1868) noted that handaxes of the Lower Paleolithic period were found in deposits with the remains of long-extinct animals such as mammoths. In Britain, supervised excavations by William Pengelly (1812–94) at Kent's Cavern near Torquay in Devon recovered tools along with fossilized animal remains from a sealed layer of stalagmite. In 1859 a British party went to observe the French finds, concluding that the tools predated 4000 BC, the then-accepted date for the biblical account of creation. Such archaeological and geological findings coincided with the publication of

The Art of Altamira
In 1879 a small girl was playing in the cave of Altamira, Spain, when she suddenly pointed to the ceiling and called out to her father, "Look, Papa, oxen!" The bison images were the first Ice Age paintings ever discovered, but it would be another 20 years before their antiquity was accepted by most archaeologists.

Charles Darwin's controversial study *On the Origin of Species* (1859), which introduced the theory of evolution to the general public. These revolutionary ideas were consolidated in Charles Lyell's *The Antiquity of Man* (1863) and led to the new discipline of prehistoric archaeology.

MILESTONES IN ARCHAEOLOGY

Archaeology began to be popular in North America when settlers observed the antiquity of burial mounds. A pioneer in this field was Thomas Jefferson (1743–1826), who later became the third president of the United States. In 1784 he conducted a systematic excavation of a mound on his Virginia property, concluding that the burials unearthed were of local origin. Similar investigations were later discussed in Samuel Haven's *Archaeology of the United States* (1856).

A milestone in the history of British archaeology was the establishment in 1851 of a chair of archaeology at Cambridge University by Dr John Disney (1779–1857), who was a collector of classical antiquities. The holder of the new chair was expected to give lectures "on the subject of Classical Mediæval and other Antiquities the Fine Arts and all matters and things connected therewith."

A breakthrough in archaeological excavation was made by General Augustus Henry Lane Fox Pitt-Rivers (1827–1900). Although he had conducted some excavations in Ireland during the 1860s, Pitt-Rivers learned much from his short time with Canon William Greenwell excavating Bronze Age barrows in the Yorkshire Wolds in 1867. During a trip to Egypt in 1881, he was greatly struck by the stratigraphy (see box, below) of early stone tools in the gravel silts of the Nile Valley and this influenced his careful recording of the different layers of excavations. After inheriting the Cranborne estate in Dorset in 1880, Pitt-Rivers made a detailed and carefully recorded study of the prehistoric and Roman remains buried on the property.

A Dramatic Conversion
After visiting Boucher de Perthes' excavations in France, Charles Lyell (1797–1875) became convinced of the antiquity of humankind, which he had denied for 30 years. He published *The Antiquity of Man* in 1863.

STRATIGRAPHY

Stratigraphy is the study of layers, or *strata*, in the earth. Borrowed from geology, stratigraphy assumes that older layers are generally found on the bottom. This means that artifacts found in the upper layers of an excavation are likely to be younger than those in the lower layers.

The Mound Detective
In 1784 Thomas Jefferson conducted North America's first recorded excavation, investigating how the burial mounds on his property were constructed.

Death Mask
Heinrich Schliemann found the "Mask of Agamemnon" while excavating a shaft grave at Mycenae in 1876.

The Birth of Egyptology
The study of ancient Egypt can be traced to Napoleon's 1798 invasion, when his team of scholars and artists made detailed records of the country's antiquities.

THE MEDITERRANEAN

Archaeological work in the Mediterranean was focused on the endeavors of Heinrich Schliemann (1822–90), who pursued his dream of excavating the city of Troy, the setting for Homer's poems. During the 1870s, he drove a huge trench into the mound of Troy to discover the history of the site. In 1876 he turned his attention to the Bronze Age citadel of Mycenae in Greece. A series of archaeological schools established at Athens—notably by the French (1846), Germans (1874), Americans (1881), and British (1886)—negotiated for the right to excavate at some of the major classical sites of the Greek world, such as Delphi and Olympia. In 1900 Arthur Evans (1851–1941) started excavating at Knossos on the island of Crete, where he uncovered what became known as "the Palace of Minos," after Crete's mythical ruler.

EXPLORING THE NEAR EAST

In 1798 Napoleon Bonaparte invaded Egypt, bringing with him a team of scholars who attempted to make a systematic record of the antiquities. In 1801 the British confiscated some of the treasures the French had collected, including the Rosetta Stone (see p. 254). Egyptology became prominent through the writings of Sir John

MARVELS OF THE MAYA

In 1839 Frederick Catherwood and John Lloyd Stephens explored Central America, visiting the Maya monuments of Copán, Palenque, and Uxmal. Stephens' accounts of their travels excited a fascination with the Maya that continues to this day.

A Scientific Scholar
Flinders Petrie, shown here inside the bus surrounded by his expedition team, employed a systematic, scientific approach during his long career exploring sites in Egypt and Palestine.

Gardner Wilkinson, in particular his *Manners and Customs of the Ancient Egyptians* (1837), which drew on his extensive travels. The creation of the Egypt Exploration Fund (later Society) led to sponsored excavations, initially in the Nile Delta. Flinders Petrie (1853–1942) developed stratified excavations in Egypt, the Sinai, and what was then termed Palestine.

Interest in the Near East, particularly Mesopotamia, generated a series of archaeological expeditions. Leonard Woolley (1880–1960) excavated at Carchemish, on the Euphrates River, with his assistant T.E. Lawrence (better known as Lawrence of Arabia).

Carchemish Unearthed
Leonard Woolley and his team (which included T.E. Lawrence) gather at the excavations of the Hittite city of Carchemish on the Euphrates River.

FARTHER AFIELD

The British Government of India realized the need to monitor the antiquities of the Indian subcontinent. In 1902 John H. Marshall, who had dug in eastern Crete with the British School at Athens, was summoned to be Director-General of Antiquities. He created the basis of an archaeological service that investigated the early peoples of the Indus Valley.

Developments were also taking place in the New World. From the 1830s on, there were a series of U.S. expeditions to Central America to explore the monumental temples of the Maya. In 1911 the American historian Hiram Bingham (1878–1956) discovered the lost Inca city of Machu Picchu high in the Andes, one of the world's most breathtaking archaeological sites.

Skara Brae
The Neolithic village of Skara Brae, Orkney, was the best known excavation by Gordon Childe, whose theories about the origins of agriculture and the rise of cities greatly influenced 20th century archaeology.

Far Eastern Archaeology
Among Asia's major finds are the magnificent graves unearthed in China and Korea. Discovered in 1974, the Terracotta Army is made up of 7,000 life-size clay figures guarding the tomb of China's First Emperor.

NEW PRACTICES

As the First World War was breaking out across Europe, a young Australian, V. Gordon Childe (see p. 125), was starting his studies in Oxford. He was to become one of the most influential archaeological thinkers of the 20th century, promoting prehistory as a specialized area. His excavation and interpretation of Skara Brae in Scotland's Orkney Islands showed that archaeology could be used to reconstruct social structures without the need for textual sources.

During the 1920s, Mortimer Wheeler (see box, p. 77) applied Pitt-Rivers' techniques from Cranborne Chase to a series of excavations in Wales and at the Roman town of Verulamium to the north of London. He developed the notion of digging sites in a grid so that finds could be accurately recorded.

As European cities that had been bombed during the Second World War were reconstructed, the field of urban archaeology developed. The discovery by William F. Grimes of a Roman temple of Mithras in the post-war excavation of London generated great public interest. Such investigations prepared the way for the rescue archaeology that now commonly forms part of major building projects.

MAKING A DATE

Radiocarbon dating was invented by the American chemist Willard F. Libby (1908–80) while conducting atom bomb research. Today the method can provide a reliable date using a single grain of wheat.

SCIENTIFIC LEAPS

Since the Second World War, archaeology has seized on new technologies and techniques to interpret data. The development of radiocarbon dating revolutionized the chronologies of many societies and cultures. In Tuscany in the 1950s, Carlo Lerici located Etruscan tombs by testing soil resistivity with a probe and camera, which eliminated the need for laborious excavation. The technique was taken up with enthusiasm by American and German excavators at the remote classical site of Nemrud Dagi in eastern Turkey, where attempts were being made to identify a possible burial.

Plant and animal remains can now be recovered from excavations and used to reconstruct the changing environment of the site. Modern technology can also help archaeologists determine how and where ceramics and metalwork were made.

Today, archaeology has become a multidisciplinary field, with archaeologists borrowing from a range of disciplines in order to build up a more accurate picture of the past. Although the history of archaeology is dominated by European developments, the study now extends to every corner of the globe, with many "home-grown" archaeologists exploring their own region's past.

THE LEAKEY FAMILY

Perhaps no single family has influenced the course of a modern scientific discipline to the extent that the Leakey family of Kenya has become entwined with the study of human origins.

Louis Leakey (1903–72) was a charismatic, if maverick, Kenyan "white African," born to British missionary parents. Contrary to prevailing scientific opinion, he became convinced that humans originated in Africa millions of years ago. He survived a shameful divorce, serious mistakes, and decades of back-breaking fieldwork until vindication in 1959. On July 17 that year, his second wife Mary (1913–96) (shown with Louis below) discovered the 1.8-million-year-old skull of a human ancestor named *Zinjanthropus* at Olduvai Gorge in Tanzania (see p. 236). This fossil confirmed Africa as the "cradle of humankind" and ignited a "gold rush" for remains of human ancestors in eastern Africa.

One of Louis and Mary's sons, Richard Leakey (below right), also made spectacular fossil discoveries, wrote popular books on human origins, and became involved in wildlife management and Kenyan politics. He was also head of the Kenyan civil service. Richard's wife, Meave, directs human origins research at the National Museums of Kenya, while their eldest daughter, Louise, is undertaking her own fieldwork and carrying the family tradition into the third generation.

Archaeology Today

Archaeology has become a multi-faceted science, with its practitioners employing a variety of approaches. It will continue to evolve as scientific techniques open up new possibilities, traditional interpretations of the past are contested, and the need to conserve remains competes with the desire to investigate them.

"Whilst geology was to carry us back to periods that had not before been thought of in the history of man, anthropology was to teach us how to estimate the stature and physical peculiarities of the skeletons found in the graves, and ethnology was to enable us to appreciate the social and material condition of the aborigines of our country ... All these branches have now become indispensable to the prehistorian."

General Pitt-Rivers (1827–1900),
English archaeologist

A Fragmented Science

Recording Finds
Archaeologists generally spend much more time documenting their finds than actually digging. Here, a student writes up information cards on arrowheads found at the Hell Gap excavation site in eastern Wyoming.

Today, archaeologists the world over share ideas and techniques and are all devoted to the proper study and preservation of the past, yet archaeology remains a remarkably diverse discipline.

Archaeology can be considered a fragmented science because of the very diversity of interests that has always characterized the study of the past. Throughout its history, archaeologists have drawn from other disciplines. As a result, archaeologists tend to show greater variation than other scientists in the questions they raise, and in the techniques and methods they use to answer those questions. Moreover, archaeology has always been influenced by the interests and ideologies of the different societies in which it is practiced. A good example is what happened to United States archaeology during the 1960s. As the country at large became concerned with population growth and its impact on the environment, so archaeologists began to research this topic. Consequently, the period saw a heavy emphasis on explaining the past through ecological and environmental models. Similarly, a trend in the 1960s toward the scientific method in archaeology was undoubtedly a reflection of the United States' increasing interest in science, the space race, and the development of ever more sophisticated technologies.

OTHER DISCIPLINES

Contemporary archaeology probably owes its greatest intellectual debt to anthropology; indeed, in the United States and Canada, archaeology is taught as a subdiscipline of anthropology, along with cultural anthropology (the study of contemporary peoples), biological anthropology (human evolution and variation), and linguistic anthropology (the

Digging In
Once human remains or artifacts are discovered, excavation becomes a very slow process. Here, an archaeologist cleans a skeleton in an oak coffin at an Augustinian friary site in Hull, England.

Surveying Ruins
Before any digging begins, archaeologists will carry out an extensive survey of the area, which may lead to a decision not to dig at all. Here, archaeologists are surveying ancient ruins at Aphrodisias, Turkey.

study of the social and cultural roles of language). All of these sub-disciplines have as their central concept the study of culture—broadly defined as human behavior that has been learned rather than genetically determined—and their ultimate goal is understanding cultural variation, in the past and present.

Archaeology also relies heavily on history, and in Europe the study of the prehistoric past glides seamlessly into the study of the historic past. Of course, history relies primarily on documentary sources and archaeology on objects, but both are still primarily concerned with describing and understanding the events of the past. A good example of the two disciplines working together is how archaeology has given us masses of information on the prehistoric Celts. These same people can then be studied through the discipline of history after the Romans came into contact with them and began to describe their way of life in texts and documents.

Coin from the Celts
Archaeological finds can be used to supplement historical accounts. This Celtic coin dates to the time of Cunobelinus, who ruled a large area of southeastern Britain from AD 10 to 42, a period when Celts were just starting to appear in Roman histories.

A third important influence on archaeology is that of the hard sciences, such as biology and chemistry. Most archaeologists search for some method of validating their statements about the past, so they use the scientific method to varying degrees. The most extreme use of the scientific method was practiced by processual archaeologists in North America during the 1960s. These archaeologists believed that with explicit hypothesis formulation and rigorous testing of hypotheses, archaeology could actually aspire to discovering universal laws that would explain human behavior.

Revealing Fragments
Through the use of specialist techniques, a single potsherd (below right) can reveal a wealth of information. This fragment comes from the Hohokam culture of North America (c. 300 BC–AD 1400).

Defining a Nation
The remains of the past can help to cement national identity. The African nation of Zimbabwe takes its name from the ruins known as Great Zimbabwe.

SPECIALIZATION

Archaeology can also be seen as fragmented because of the very diversity of the human past that it seeks to understand. No single archaeologist can master all the data and intricacies of the past, so sub-disciplines appeared early in archaeology's history. Thus, for example, we have Egyptology, which concentrates on ancient Egypt, and classical archaeology, which studies ancient Greece and Rome.

Some archaeologists have specialized even further. Today, archaeologists can concentrate on studying just the animal bones of an archaeological site in order to learn about past diets, or they may become pottery or lithic (stone) experts to find out about ancient technologies. The technical expertise of these specialist archaeologists is invaluable in creating an overall picture of the human past.

THE PURPOSES OF ARCHAEOLOGY

Because archaeology is itself such a wide-ranging discipline, it is not surprising that the lessons it teaches us about the past are applied in many different arenas.

Posing in the Past
Archaeological tourism is a growth industry in modern China. Here, visitors ride a horse statue on the Spirit Path that leads to the 15th–16th century Ming Tombs.

Archaeology can help cement a people's heritage, as occurred in Zimbabwe in Africa. When this country finally became independent from Britain, it was important for the new state to affirm its own identity. The site of Great Zimbabwe, a large stone-built settlement (see p. 258), reached its zenith in the 15th century and, contrary to earlier speculation that the site must have been built by non-Africans, archaeological excavations have clearly shown that the site was built by the ancestors of modern-day Africans. This site is an important symbol of Zimbabwean national identity and pride.

Elsewhere in the world, many countries advertise their archaeological sites as a means of attracting tourists. We immediately think of Greece, Rome, or Egypt, but many other countries, particularly in Asia, are beginning to understand the lure of exotic archaeological sites. Despite the foreign currency that these tourist sites bring, it is still important to remember that tourists often get their only lesson about a country's past from these ancient monuments, and how we treat the archaeological past can influence contemporary political relationships, too. For example, there is an ongoing battle between Greece and Britain over the return of the Elgin Marbles, which have resided in the British Museum since they were removed from the Parthenon on the Athenian acropolis at the beginning of the 19th century (see box, p. 27).

TERRORIST TARGET
Egypt's economy relies on the foreign currency that tourism brings. In 1997 Islamic fundamentalists murdered 58 tourists visiting the Egyptian pyramids at Luxor. Not only was the loss of life a terrible tragedy, but it also cost the country millions of dollars in lost revenue.

APPLIED ARCHAEOLOGY

Archaeologists who study ancient agricultural systems have helped contemporary farmers improve their crop yields. In Peru, for example, archaeologists have discovered ancient "raised" fields, platforms made of soil dug from the canals that water them. Raised fields are much better at coping with severe drought or flooding than modern agricultural techniques. The local government has now produced pamphlets to teach local farmers how to create raised-field systems. Such "applied archaeology" shows the practical usefulness of studying the past.

ARCHAEOLOGY'S FUTURE

As we celebrate the very diversity of archaeology, we must never forget that archaeology is a constantly evolving discipline. Although it is always hazardous to predict the future, we can at least look at what has been happening recently in the discipline as a guide to where it might go in the next few years.

The excavation of sites as a primary means of obtaining archaeological data is becoming almost prohibitively expensive. Consequently, archaeologists

WATERING THE DESERT

When the Nabataeans lived in Israel's inhospitable Negev Desert 2,000 years ago, they grew grapes, wheat, and olives. Archaeology has shown that they used a system of ditches to collect rainwater from the area's rare storms.

THE LESSONS OF CHACO CANYON

Archaeologists can reveal how human activity has led to ecological catastrophe in the past. In the American Southwest, the impressive ruins of Chaco Canyon (below) long invited the question of why they were abandoned. Occupied by the Anasazi from AD 950 to 1300, the settlements contained America's tallest buildings until the skyscraper, structures that used up the timber from more than 200,000 trees. By examining ancient packrat middens, which contain plant remains cemented by crystallized urine, archaeologists have determined that the local vegetation gradually changed, as the woodcutting continued over the centuries. The extensive environmental damage contributed to failing crops and was one of the main reasons that the Anasazi were forced to abandon the site.

are developing a whole battery of techniques that will enable them to "look under" the surface of a site without actually digging. Techniques such as resistivity surveying, magnetometry, and ground-penetrating radar allow the archaeologist to detect anomalies as large as buried walls or as small as a campfire without ever having to put a shovel in the ground.

ADAPTING TO TRENDS

We can also predict that archaeology will continue to borrow from other disciplines in its endless quest to discover and interpret the past. As a social science, archaeology is always going to be at the mercy of wider social and political trends, and this will be reflected in the types of questions archaeologists ask about the past and therefore the tools, techniques, and concepts they draw on to answer those questions.

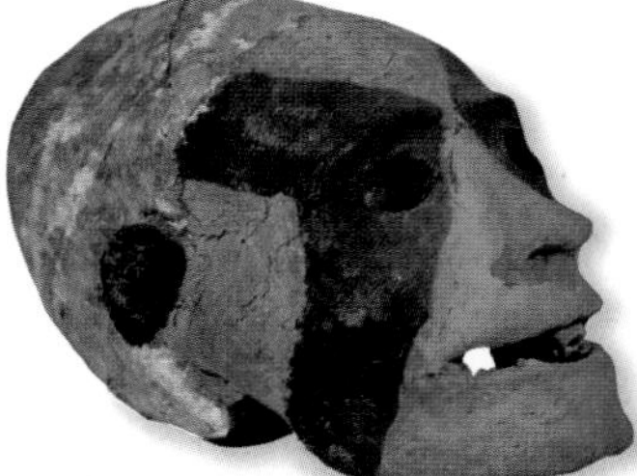

Finally, archaeology will continue to become more sensitive to the cultures whose past it studies. The appearance of indigenous archaeology recognizes that the discipline has a sublime responsibility to ask questions and provide answers that are respectful of the descendants of the archaeological past. For instance, archaeologists throughout the world now realize that human remains cannot just be treated as one more set of scientific data (see p. 49). These human remains are often held in great reverence by their descendants, so archaeology must show them a similar respect.

Productive Planting
Aerial photography helped archaeologists rediscover the raised-field method of agriculture (above). The method is well suited to the poor soils and irregular rainfall of Peru's altiplano (high plain).

Human Remains
Today's archaeologists must work with local communities and respect traditional beliefs when investigating human remains. This painted skull (above left) comes from the Sepik region of Papua New Guinea.

Fantastic Nonsense

The Lost Continent
In the writings of Plato, Atlantis is described as an enormous island destroyed by the gods in a terrible earthquake. Among the many locations that have been proposed for the lost continent is the Greek island of Santorini (above), where a devastating eruption of the volcano Thera occurred in about 1630 BC.

Archaeology has always attracted bizarre theories that titillate the public. One example was the widespread belief that contact with material from Tutankhamen's tomb brought on illness or even death. The prehistoric burial and platform mounds of the American Midwest were believed to have been built by a lost tribe of Israel or survivors from Atlantis. A colonial site in New Hampshire is claimed to have been built by prehistoric Europeans. One bestseller in the 1960s even declared that extra-terrestrials had been responsible for the major advances made by the human species.

Angry Mummies
Countless movies have embraced the theme of mummies coming back to life to torment the archaeologists who disturb them (left). Another popular idea has been that a "mummy's curse" will lead to death or misfortune for anyone who violates an Egyptian tomb.

Moundbuilders

The Etowah Indian Mounds, in Georgia, USA (above), were built between AD 1000 and 1500 by a native society rich in culture and ritual. In the 19th century, such burial and platform mounds were explained as the work of a lost tribe from Israel or survivors from Atlantis.

Alien Skull

In the Paracas culture of Peru (c. 900 BC–AD 400), the heads of infants were bound, leading to an elongated skull (right). Some have claimed such deformities as evidence of extraterrestrial visitors.

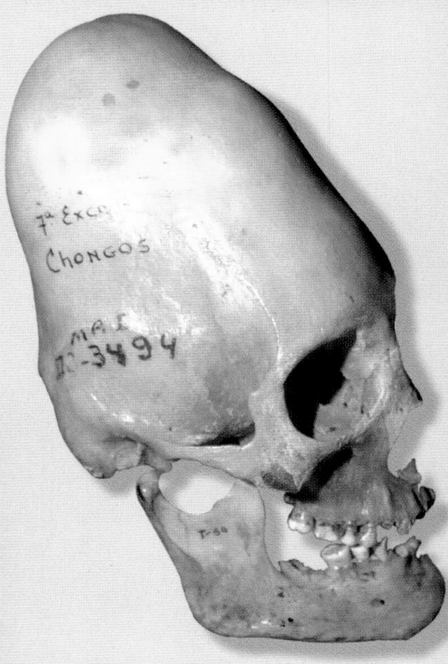

Runways for Aliens

The mysterious lines and figures in Peru (left) are best seen from the air. Archaeologists have determined that they were made by the Nasca culture between AD 100 and 700, but other theories, including the idea that they were alien landing strips, continue to circulate.

Who Owns the Past?

The issue of who owns the past is a complex one, with some countries demanding the return of treasures, and indigenous groups objecting to their ancestors' remains being disturbed.

Returned Treasure
This gold signet ring is one of the many exquisite artifacts in the Aidonia treasure, a collection of Mycenaean antiquities looted from tombs and illegally exported to the United States. The treasure was advertised for sale by a New York dealer in 1993, but was returned to Greece following court action.

In the pursuit of knowledge, archaeologists have traveled throughout the world, unearthing artifacts and human remains in an attempt to construct a more complete picture of the past. Museums have been established to conserve the finds and share the discoveries with the general public. Recently, however, particular countries and indigenous groups have objected to what they see as the plundering of their heritage, demanding the return of treasures and remains.

The Jewel of the Louvre
The Greek government has asked France to return the "Venus de Milo," one of the great treasures displayed in the Louvre museum in Paris. Dating to about 150 BC, the ancient sculpture was found on the Aegean island of Melos in 1820 and removed to France with the permission of the Turkish authorities.

THE RISE OF MUSEUMS

The 19th century saw the rise of national museums, especially in Europe. Britain's Royal Navy regularly assisted antiquarians in the removal of sculptures from sites. For example, in 1856 Charles Newton arrived at Bodrum in western Turkey with the crew of the warship *Gorgon* at his disposal for the excavation of the Mausoleum of Halikarnassos. This followed the pattern established by Elgin's removal of sculptures from the Athenian acropolis (see box, p. 27), and the collection of classical sculptures and inscriptions by Captain Spratt of the Royal Navy during his survey of Crete and other Aegean areas.

The British were not alone in the acquisition of classical sculptures. The French acquired the "Venus de Milo," the statue of the naked Aphrodite from the island of Melos, which is still displayed in the Louvre in Paris. The Germans acquired the pedimental sculptures from the temple of Aphaia on the island of Aegina, and they are now displayed in the Munich Museum. The monumental altar of Zeus from the acropolis at Pergamon was removed and reconstructed in Berlin. Such historic acquisitions were sometimes made with the approval of the host country's authorities, but have since been challenged. In the case of Greece,

it has been argued that Turkey was an occupying power when permission was given for the removal of Greek cultural objects.

NEW INSTITUTIONS

In many of these early cases, archaeologists at least know which buildings and monuments the treasures came from. During the 20th century, however, a rise in demand from the newer museums, especially those in North America, saw some antiquities lose their context. For example, the upper part of a muscular Herakles, now on loan to the Museum of Fine Arts in Boston from private collectors, appears to complete the fragmentary statue from Perge in southern Turkey.

LOOTED TREASURE

In recent years, there have been a number of highly publicized court cases involving illegally exported antiquities. The Metropolitan Museum of Art in New York was forced to return a major hoard of 6th century BC silver from Lydia in Turkey. The silver had almost certainly been looted from tombs. Turkey has also successfully reclaimed the coins from the Dekadrachm Hoard, which had been acquired by a syndicate of collectors and investors. The Greek government has obtained the return of Late Bronze Age treasure that probably

VIKING REMAINS

The question of ownership can become tangled. L'Anse aux Meadows is a Viking settlement in Newfoundland that has been dated to AD 1000. It is controlled by the Canadian government since it stands on Canadian soil, but modern Scandinavians could argue that it belongs to them, since it was created by their ancestors.

Turkey to Germany

The highly sculpted monumental altar of Zeus from the acropolis at Pergamon is one of the many treasures removed from Turkey. The frieze was reconstructed for display in the Berlin Museum.

Retrieved Treasures
Looting is an all too common byproduct of war, and the fate of stolen artworks often remains unknown. Here, however, Odolfo Siviero stands among retrieved artworks stolen from Italy during the Nazi occupation.

Ancestor Mask
Large quantities of Native American artifacts, such as this Bella Coola ancestor mask from the Northwest region, were collected for display in museums. Many Native Americans are now demanding the return of both artifacts and human remains.

came from Mycenaean tombs at Aidonia in the Peloponnese.

In Britain, a number of Romano-British bronzes were looted from private land in Icklingham in Suffolk and soon left the country illegally. Eventually they were purchased by two New York private collectors who have indicated that they will consider presenting the objects to the British Museum at some point in the future.

A COMPLEX QUESTION

The complicated picture surrounding ownership is illustrated by the treasures discovered by Heinrich Schliemann during his excavations at Troy. Although Schliemann made great efforts to cover his tracks, it is clear that the material was removed from Turkey without permission and taken to Athens. It was eventually

acquired by the Berlin Museum, but in the aftermath of the Second World War, the treasure was taken to Russia. The current debate centers on whether the Trojan treasures should now be returned to Germany or should go back to Turkey.

LOSS OF CONTEXT

Looting deprives scholars of information about the looted

objects. The hoard of late antique Roman silver known as the Sevso treasure surfaced on the antiquities market in the 1980s. While the documentation seemed to indicate that the silver had been exported from Lebanon, persistent rumors suggest that it had in fact been dug up in part of the former republic of Yugoslavia. Thus different countries could attempt to lay claim to the hoard, but with little prospect of success. Meanwhile, archaeologists have no way of knowing where the treasure actually came from.

NEW WORLD ISSUES

Looting in the New World has had a major impact on archaeological sites. Maya antiquities, mostly from Belize in Central America, have become highly collectible in North America, and objects are being removed without any adequate record of their findspot. In 1986 wall paintings from Teotihuacán in Mexico were returned from North America to the Instituto Nacional de Antropología e Historia in Mexico City after lengthy negotiations.

THE RETURN OF HUMAN REMAINS

During the 19th and 20th centuries, collections were also made of human remains. To many indigenous people, this amounted to the desecration of sacred burial sites and utter disrespect for their beliefs. In North America and Australia, many human remains that were once displayed in museums have now been returned to indigenous groups for reburial.

In the early 19th century, George Augustus Robinson collected the skulls of Tasmania's Aborigines, and collections of Tasmanian human remains are still held in at least 16 international museums or institutions. Some Australian museums returned their Tasmanian remains to the descendants during the 1980s, and in the 1990s some British collections followed suit.

More controversial is the issue of ancient remains, which some archaeologists see as belonging to a common human heritage. Despite their great age, however, such remains are still considered sacred by many indigenous peoples. Consequently, a unique series of remains from Kow Swamp, dated between 9,000 and 13,000 years old, were returned to the Aboriginal community in 1990. Similarly, "Mungo Lady," the world's oldest known cremation, was returned to the Aborigines of the Mungo area in 1992 (below). Such measures were important steps in the process of reconciliation between the indigenous people and archaeologists.

The return of ancient human remains can become complicated. In North America, bones found on federal land must be returned to native populations for reburial. When an 8,000-year-old human skeleton was found on federal land near Kennewick, Washington, several tribes filed claims. Archaeologists argued that the skeleton was unlikely to be related to any living group and that, as one of the oldest human skeletons found in the New World, it warranted serious analysis. In this case, the courts eventually sided with the scientists.

Reclaiming Women's Past

Archaeology has been criticized for presenting a male-dominated view of prehistory and history, but female archaeologists are now questioning traditional ideas about women in the past.

Trojan Records
The role of women in the early days of archaeology has often been overlooked. For example, Heinrich Schliemann's Greek wife, Sophie, kept most of the records of the excavation of Troy. Here, she wears Early Bronze Age jewelry that was found at Troy in 1873.

Archaeology, of course, reflects the social standards of its time, so traditionally most archaeologists have been men. Some early excavators even opposed women's participation in the field because, rather quaintly, the presence of ladies inhibited frank expression. Nevertheless, some of the pioneers of archaeology were women. A few, such as Dorothy Garrod and Kathleen Kenyon, were well known in their time and their achievements are recognized today. Many others, however, worked as assistants to famous husbands or fathers, or as patrons, and have never had the credit that they deserve. While Heinrich Schliemann, for example, is hailed for finding the site of ancient Troy, it is in fact to his wife, Sophie, that we owe most of the records of the great discovery.

WOMEN IN ARCHAEOLOGY

Although more and more women have entered archaeology since the 1960s, the popular stereotype of an archaeologist remains masculine. Fewer women make their careers in field work: female archaeologists still tend to be concentrated in the laboratory and the museum—doing what Joan Gero has described as "archaeological housework"—while their male counterparts are more likely to be out excavating.

NEW INTERPRETATIONS

With larger numbers of women in the profession have come changes in the way archaeological evidence is interpreted. Women were commonly invisible in many traditional accounts of past societies, where "early man" took center stage. Now a new generation of female archaeologists have started drawing attention to past biases and focusing on the role of women in the past.

A critical study of the roles of men and women in traditional societies shows that many generalizations about gender

Bronze Age Dress
Well-preserved woollen clothes have been recovered from Early Bronze Age mounds in Denmark. The outfit worn by a woman buried in Egtved featured a short skirt and a belt with a large bronze disk. It has been suggested that this represents the costume of married women.

A Meticulous Excavator
During her outstanding career, Mary Leakey (1913–96) oversaw the excavation of various prehistoric sites in Kenya and made a number of key discoveries, including the 1.8-million-year-old fossil of *Zinjanthropus boisei* (see p. 236) and the 3.6-million-year-old footprints at Laetoli (see p. 230).

A PALEOLITHIC PIONEER
Dorothy Garrod (1892–1968) was the first woman to investigate early humans. After studying Paleolithic archaeology in France, she did extensive fieldwork in England, Gibraltar, Palestine, Kurdistan, Bulgaria, and Lebanon, leading the excavations at Mount Carmel (see p. 328) that uncovered the first evidence of Paleolithic and Mesolithic cultures in Palestine.

differences reflect the cultural biases of our own society. Activities that archaeologists have traditionally assumed were exclusively male, such as making stone tools and hunting, in fact vary from culture to culture, and may be done by men or women.

EVOLUTION OF THE SPECIES

Human evolution is one area where feminist criticism has had an important impact. Traditional accounts emphasized the role of "man the hunter," and his key skills of hunting and toolmaking, in the evolution of our species. Studies of contemporary hunter-gatherer societies, however, show that gathered plant foods, which are collected mainly by women, are usually much more significant in the diet than meat from hunted animals. Meanwhile, evidence from the social lives of other primates has drawn attention to the likely significance of the mother-child bond among our early human ancestors. Reconsidering gender roles in this way has greatly contributed to our understanding of the development of distinctively human behavior.

Women's Work
By studying artworks such as this Egyptian figurine of a female brewer (dated to c. 2325 BC), archaeologists can learn about women's work in ancient times.

Conserving the Past

Polluted Marble
Like much of the marble on the Athenian acropolis, this 5th century BC caryatid has been damaged by a black fungus, which is caused partly by the pollution from the modern city that surrounds it.

While many archaeological sites are being destroyed by the development of tourist resorts, the main threat continues to come from the antiquities trade and the looting it promotes.

Archaeological sites are threatened in a number of ways. The weather and pollution are eroding some of the most famous sites—a black fungus, encouraged by climate change and pollution, grows inside the marble of the acropolis in Athens; Mohenjo Daro, in Pakistan, is being worn away by weather and salt corrosion; and floods have cracked and damaged the tomb of Tutankhamen in Egypt. Tourists can also have an immense impact, as their footsteps and moist breath slowly but surely damage the

Safe Removal
In the 1960s, the construction of the Aswan High Dam threatened to drown the temples of Ramesses and Nefertari at Abu Simbel. A UNESCO rescue effort moved them block by block to higher ground.

Neglected Monuments
The ruins of Angkor Wat, encroached by the surrounding jungle, suffered years of neglect during Cambodia's Pol Pot regime. To survive, the temples will need substantial maintenance and restoration.

Looking for Loot
A grave robber excavates an old grave in Colombia, no doubt looking for treasures to feed the ever-hungry international antiquities market.

treasures they have come to see. Conservation groups such as the World Monuments Fund have been able to rescue some important sites, but many more are in need of help. Some archaeologists are even suggesting that the only way to effectively preserve most ancient sites is to rebury them.

The development of areas for mass tourism, along with the expansion of urban areas into the countryside, encroaches on both long-known and previously unrecognized sites. Although any loss of sites is regrettable, such encroachment normally gives archaeologists the opportunity to excavate and record before development begins. For example, the development of Heathrow airport allowed William Grimes to excavate an Iron Age temple.

The most severe threat is the deliberate prospecting for items to be sold on the antiquities market. Although such unscientific digging has taken place for centuries, the development of both private and large museum collections, particularly in Europe and North America, has caused a major demand for antiquities. This has led to organized looting and the targeting of cemeteries, sanctuaries, and urban sites.

TREASURE-HUNTER
One of the most colorful early antiquities-grabbers in Egypt was Giovanni Belzoni (1778–1823), an Italian circus performer who became the first excavator of the Valley of the Kings. His reckless methods, such as using a battering ram to open a tomb, were quite typical behavior for the times.

Greek Collector
Over 37 years as British Ambassador in Naples, William Hamilton amassed huge quantities of ancient Greek pottery, which he sold to the British Museum and private collectors.

THE LOOTING OF TUSCANY

In Tuscany, Italy, the cemeteries of the ancient Etruscans contained large quantities of Athenian figure-decorated pottery. One 19th century writer talked about Greek vases emerging from the soil "like truffles." Certainly the area around Vulci, from the estates of the Prince of Canino, yielded significant numbers—many found their way into collections such as that in the Berlin Museum. The tombs continue to attract looting by *tombaroli,* who sell the contents to a middle man. The pottery is then smuggled illegally into Switzerland, from where it can be despatched without recrimination to the main antiquities sales, such as those in London. A police raid on several warehouses in Geneva in 1997 found some thousands of antiquities, almost certainly from cemeteries in Italy, which is where their owner was arrested.

The Berlin Painter
This Athenian amphora featuring a horse-drawn chariot is attributed to the Berlin painter. Because of looting, few of the Berlin painter's works can be traced to their findspots.

Many of the Athenian pots from Etruria have been attributed to particular anonymous painters, which has elevated their artistic status and thus added to their value. To one of these painters, identified by the classical art historian John Beazley as "the Berlin painter" (after an example in the collection at the Berlin Museum), has been attributed almost 300 pots and fragments. It appears that only some 15 percent of these come from reliably documented findspots, thus preventing a proper study of the distribution of the painter's work.

FURTHER SOUTH

Tuscany is not the only part of Italy to be affected. The highly decorated pottery of the Greek colonies of southern Italy is also seen as highly collectible. Indeed, many of the pots in the Hamilton collection that are now in the British Museum were found in the cemeteries of Campania when William Hamilton was British Ambassador in Naples in the late 18th century. More recently, heavy earth-moving equipment has been used to remove the top layers of a cemetery in Puglia so that artifacts could be collected. A recent study of Apulian pottery from this area showed that a clear majority of the pots have completely lost their context.

OTHER PARTS OF THE WORLD

Looting of archaeological sites is a major problem throughout the world. During Pol Pot's regime in Cambodia, the treasures of Angkor Wat were ransacked and sold into the international antiquities market. In China, looters disturbed 40,000 ancient tombs in 1989 and 1990 alone, with the treasures being smuggled to Hong Kong for trading—despite the fact that the penalty for such crimes is death.

CYCLADIC FIGURES

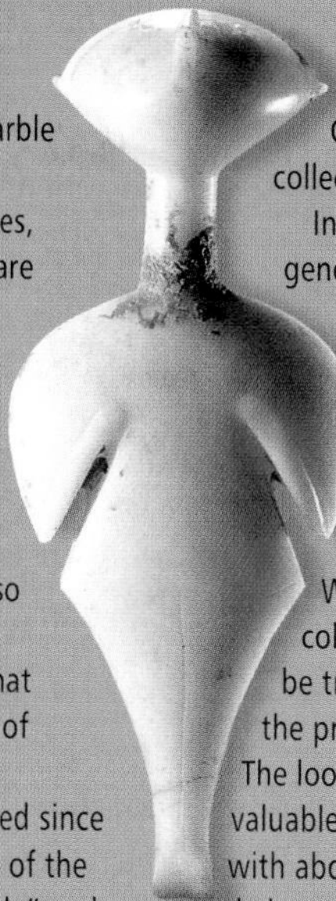

One of the most detailed studies of the impact of looting on a group of archaeological artifacts concerns marble figures from the Cycladic islands of the southern Aegean. These figures, dating from the 3rd millennium BC, are mostly female, and their simple appearance, enhanced by the white marble from which they were made, has given them an aesthetic appeal that has attracted modern painters such as Brancusi and Picasso. Unfortunately, it has also attracted international art dealers and collectors, creating a demand that has led to the wholesale plundering of Cycladic cemeteries.

Cycladic figures have been collected since the early 19th century, though some of the earliest descriptions called them "rude" and "barbaric." Excavations in the Cyclades—for example, on the island of Melos by the British School at Athens—encouraged an academic interest in the prehistoric Aegean, and British university museums, such as the Fitzwilliam Museum in Cambridge, started to develop collections of representative objects.

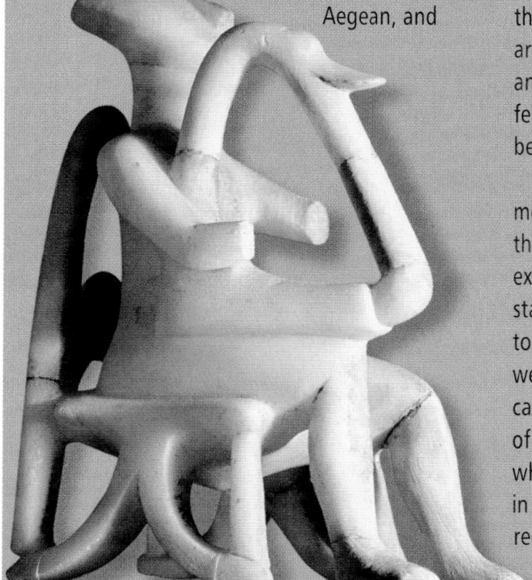

In the 1960s, however, a growing general interest in Cycladic figures led to the looting of thousands of prehistoric graves. One of the most notorious cases was on the island of Keros, a site still not properly understood, where hundreds of fragmentary figures were removed. While most ended up in Swiss private collections, the figures continue to be traded by major auction houses despite the protests of the Greek government. The looting has deprived archaeologists of valuable scientific knowledge. For example, with about 85 percent of the figures losing their context, it has been hard to determine whether such figures were normally placed in male or female graves. Most of the unusual figures, such as harpists (left) and male figures, have been deprived of their context, and, given the high prices fetched in the art market, some are most certainly modern forgeries. The 1970s and 1980s saw the wide distribution of counterfeit figures, leading to some private collections being made up entirely of fakes.

A study of Cycladic figures has shown how modern aesthetic interpretation can obscure the ancient use and appearance of artifacts. For example, museums tend to show the figures standing vertically, as we might expect a statue to be (above). Most of these figures, however, were probably laid in the grave, or at least carried horizontally in the hands. The simplicity of their appearance, enhanced by the plain white marble, appeals to modern viewers, but in fact they were originally brightly painted in red, blue, and black, which might seem garish to the modern eye.

Loving Egypt to Death

In 1798 Napoleon's Egyptian campaign sparked Western interest in Egyptology. Intrepid collectors traveled along the Nile, returning with sculptures torn from the ancient sites. By 1840 Thomas Cook had developed the Nile cruise. Since then, increasing numbers of visitors have brought undoubted financial benefits, along with some serious problems. Strict laws have seen the end of the trade in antiquities, but the need to build hotels, the pollution and vibration of tourist buses, and even the condensation caused by visitors to the confined tombs, are all contributing to the deterioration of the monuments.

Tourist Destination
Firmly established as a holiday destination since the 19th century, Egypt now attracts hundreds of thousands of tourists each year. The Egyptian government has started taking measures to protect its irreplaceable monuments, such as drastically restricting the number of tours inside the pyramids.

Out of Context
The demand of foreign museums for Egyptian antiquities led to many key artifacts being spirited out of the country during the 19th century. While such exports are now severely restricted, museum displays of Egyptian monuments, such as this statue in the British Museum, deprive them of context and can give a misleading idea of their use.

Climbing the Pyramids
Here, Egyptian guides help tourists climb the massive stone blocks of the Great Pyramid of Khufu (Cheops) at Giza in 1900. The 20th century saw massive numbers of visitors, who have incrementally damaged the pyramids.

Visiting the Great Sites

Crowd Control
The most famous sites inevitably attract the largest crowds. While ancient monuments such as the Great Temple of Ramesses at Abu Simbel, Egypt, remain thrilling, visitors must be prepared to share the experience with thousands of others.

Nothing can replace the thrill of walking among the ruins of ancient civilizations, but as visitor numbers increase, authorities need to find new ways of allowing the public access to the past.

The custom of visiting archaeological sites arose in the 18th century with the Grand Tour, as English and German aristocrats traveled to Rome and Greece to collect antiquities for their mansions and gardens. Eventually, other areas—notably Egypt and the Levant—also attracted attention, and a wider range of people, including explorers, soldiers, and scholars, were able to visit ancient sites.

MASS TOURISM

From these select beginnings, archaeological tourism began, gradually becoming available to increasing numbers of people. But it was only in the latter part of the 20th century that mass tourism really got underway, through a combination of cheaper long-distance flights and cruises, a higher standard of living in the Western world, and greater exposure to potential destinations through magazines and television programs. Partly motivated by their quest for sunshine holidays, European tourists went to the Mediterranean lands—Spain, Italy, Greece, and Turkey—and then to more exotic destinations, such as Egypt, Peru, Mexico, and China.

Some tourists cherish their independence and travel privately, making their own arrangements or taking local tours after they arrive, but enormous numbers of Americans, Europeans, Japanese, and other nationalities now travel on pre-packaged archaeological tours, which organize visits to the great sites and museums and are usually accompanied by a specialist lecturer.

EXCESSIVE NUMBERS

The inevitable result of such mass tourism is that huge crowds swamp all the major sites and

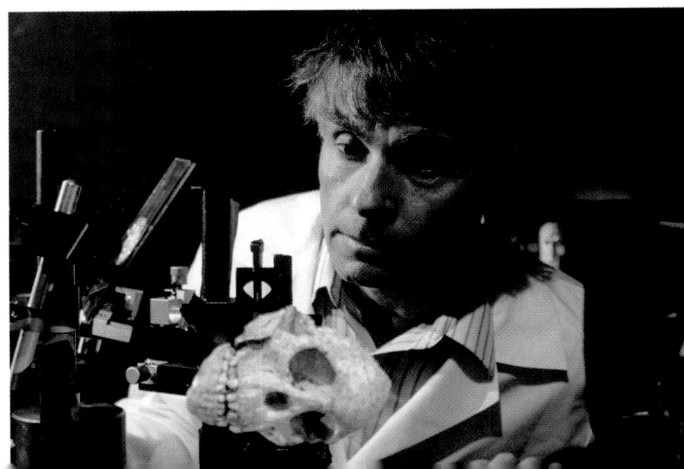

Virtual Fossil
Most prehistoric skeletal remains are too precious to be put on public display, but technology is providing an alternative. Here a scientist uses fluorescence and lasers to create a holographic image of the 2.4-million-year-old Taung child's skull (see p. 234).

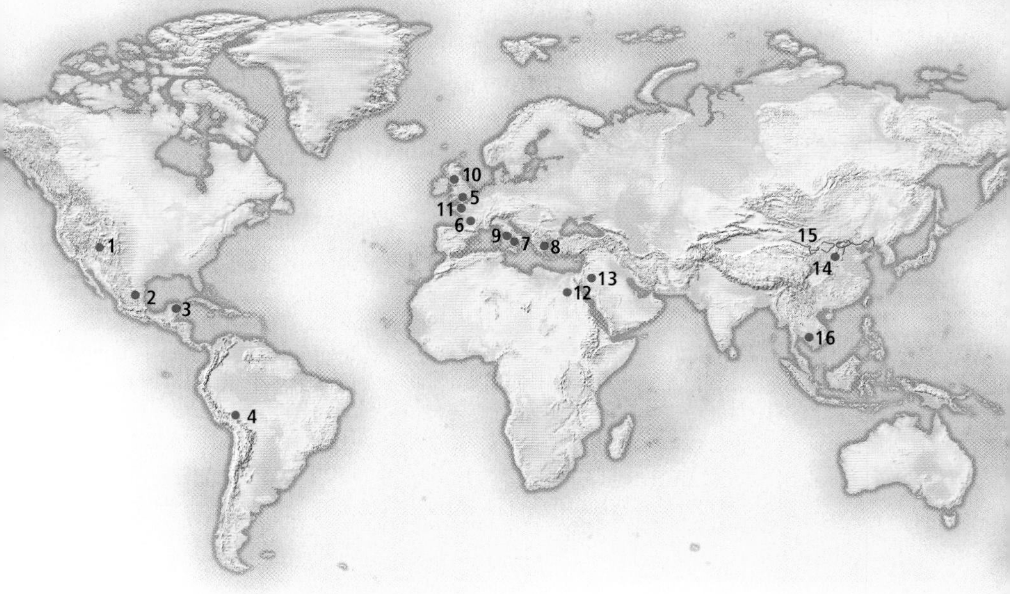

museums. Most authorities at the popular destinations are reluctant to cut back on visitor numbers, for fear of killing the goose that lays the golden eggs. This is particularly the case in countries such as Egypt, Peru, and China, which are heavily dependent on the enormous revenue that archaeological tourism brings. The current dilemma is how to balance the paramount need to preserve and protect the great sites for future generations, against the economic needs of the countries and communities that possess them, and the basic right of humankind to visit its common patrimony (see also p. 56).

NEW SOLUTIONS

One response to the problem of mass tourism is to commercialize the "heritage industry." The main aim is to present the past to the public in instructive but entertaining ways (see p. 60). Modern technology is being increasingly brought into play. For example, some displays feature holograms of artifacts, while others use computer applications that conjure up "virtual" versions of long-vanished buildings or streets through which visitors can take "electronic walks."

Other sites that tourists simply cannot visit because of physical difficulties, fragility, or pollution dangers are being recreated in actual-size facsimile. France's Lascaux II, an impressive copy of the original painted cave (see p. 268), attracts hundreds of thousands of visitors each year, and the same will no doubt be true of the new facsimile of Spain's Altamira Cave, opened in 2001. Other cave facsimiles are already underway, and these, together with virtual technology, indicate the direction that future archaeological tourism will be forced to take as an ever-increasing number of feet wish to tread the world's venerable sites.

KEY TO THE MOST POPULAR SITES

1 Mesa Verde
2 Teotihuacán
3 Chichén Itzá
4 Machu Picchu
5 Stonehenge
6 Lascaux II
7 Pompeii
8 Parthenon
9 Colosseum
10 Hadrian's Wall
11 Carnac
12 Giza Pyramids
13 Petra
14 Terracotta Army
15 Great Wall of China
16 Angkor Wat

Bringing the Past Alive

A Convincing Scene
Viking life is re-created with fiberglass figures of people in period costume, such as this woman carrying water from a well. A soundtrack provides the noises of a busy street, with adults and children speaking Old Norse. Even appropriate smells have been included, especially around the pigsties and latrine.

Personal Finds
At the end of the tour, visitors can examine a display of the main finds from the site, which include these personal items of bone, amber, copper alloy, and glass.

The Jorvik Viking Centre, in York, England, was a groundbreaking innovation that opened in 1984 beneath a shopping complex. Excavations on this site from 1976 onward had uncovered much of Coppergate, one of the main streets of Viking York (9th–10th centuries AD). The immense popularity of the dig led to a decision to preserve the timbers, reconstruct some of the buildings, and re-create part of the Viking neighborhood. Today, visitors can descend from the modern street to the Viking street-level, where a fleet of electronic "time-cars" take them back in time past thatched houses, workshops, ships at the wharf, and a simulation of the excavation.

Viking Excavation
The excavations of the Coppergate site (right) revealed the best preserved timber buildings from the Viking world. The area was laid out as a closely packed set of tenement plots with houses, workshops, and warehouses by the Fosse River.

DIG
VIKING BOAT

Getting Involved

Research in Egypt
Every year thousands of people flock to the great sites of Egypt. Here, a researcher copies the wall reliefs from the tomb of Queen Nefertari at Luxor.

There are a number of ways to pursue an interest in archaeology. You can join a local archaeological society, volunteer on a dig, or even train to become a professional archaeologist.

Amateurs are indispensable to archaeology. Most local and regional societies are run for and by amateurs; many journals could not be published without their subscriptions; and few large-scale excavations could now take place without their input. Amateurs also constitute the main audience for archaeology programs and publications.

VOLUNTEERING

One of the best ways of starting in archaeology is as a volunteer. Wherever digs are run during the summer or at holiday time, there are usually opportunities for volunteers to gain practical experience and to meet people from all sorts of backgrounds and of all ages. Even in countries such as Great Britain where most digs are now carried out by professional archaeologists, there are still a number of training excavations that use volunteers. These usually coincide with university vacations and may be run by universities or by local societies or trusts. Some even offer free or subsidized accommodation and keep. Details can often be found on websites or may be published as an occasional directory. There are also openings for volunteers in museums and local record offices.

In addition to working in your own country, there are opportunities to volunteer abroad. These digs may be organized by foreign universities or summer schools or, alternatively, by local agencies. You should be able to find details on websites, or through an agency such as the British Archaeology Abroad Service or the U.S. organization Earthwatch.

A VOLUNTARY CAREER

Experienced volunteers can become highly sought after. Gary Lindstrom is an American amateur archaeologist known as "Termite." His regular job is as a termite exterminator in California, but for the past 25 years, he has offered his services on summer digs.

KEEP LEARNING

To learn more about the subject of archaeology, consider taking an evening class. These range from general interest courses to certificate, diploma, or even degree level courses.

A local archaeology society is a great way to meet people who share your interest. Most archaeology societies organize a lecture program, while many also offer excursions and run fieldwork. Some groups offer activities specifically for younger members. Britain's Young Archaeologists Club, for example, caters for 9 to 18 year olds.

EMPLOYMENT OPPORTUNITIES

The organization of archaeology tends to vary from country to country, but most full-time posts fall into one of five main categories: heritage management, field archaeology, museum work, teaching, and archaeological science. Archaeologists in heritage management often work as local or national government officers, looking after collections of archaeological records and databases or offering advice to developers on archaeological aspects of planning and development. In some cases, they may be responsible for a particular area or a national park. Field archaeology covers excavators, surveyors, photographers, planners, illustrators, and finds specialists. Archaeologists can work in museums as keepers, curators, or researchers, and can teach at all levels, from schools to universities and in adult further education. For those with a scientific bent, archaeological science employs conservators, environmental scientists, and specialists in dating and analytical techniques.

Archaeologists may be based in government departments or agencies, museums, universities, contracting organizations, or private consultancies. Alternatively, they may be self-employed. There can also be openings in journalism and tourism.

Student Volunteers
The majority of volunteers are archaeology students, such as these American college students working on a springtime dig at Masada, Israel.

Conserving the Finds
Much of the important work in archaeology occurs not in the field, but behind the scenes. This conservator is cleaning clay jars from the *Conde de Tolosa* shipwreck in the field workshop of the Casas Reales Museum in the Dominican Republic.

Publicizing Archaeology

Since much of their work is publicly funded, archaeologists need to find ways to present their discoveries to the public. Television and the Internet provide excellent opportunities to do so.

On Location
In the 1960s, television programs started to feature location work. Here, Louis Leakey is filmed leading a discussion at a dig site.

Being an intensely visual subject, archaeology lends itself naturally to television coverage, with some programs attracting millions of viewers. Whereas Hollywood has traditionally portrayed archaeology as exciting, romantic, and even dangerous, with swashbuckling archaeologists such as Indiana Jones, television has generally treated the subject in a more realistic manner.

The earliest programs were studio-bound and stiffly formal, but as budgets increased, so producers became more adventurous.

Lights and Action
Major tourist attractions explore new ways to bring the past alive. At Giza, a light show illuminates the pyramids and sphinx for visitors (top right).

A Living Monument
Reenactments of historical events, such as this battle staged at Helmsley Castle, Yorkshire, re-create the atmosphere of the past.

By the late 1960s, location work was regularly featured and the first attempts to follow an excavation were being made. Younger and more charismatic presenters and the use of more sophisticated techniques, such as computer graphics and aerial coverage, were to follow.

TYPES OF TELEVISION

A variety of formats are chosen for television programs. Some follow the progress of a discovery or excavation, such as the lifting of the *Mary Rose* wreck (see p. 82). Others set a challenge or problem to solve in a fixed time. Many take the form of thematic documentaries—on the Vikings or the Iceman, for example. Yet others feature experimental archaeology, replicating a feat of ancient technology, such as sailing replica boats. Perennial favorites are shows that examine skeletons or mummies to answer specific problems—and to gratify our obsession with bodies and death! Historical overviews of a particular ancient civilization or a type of monument also appeal to a wide audience. Then there are magazine programs featuring a roundup of recent work, and, finally, programs intended specifically for students that are shown on education channels.

NICHE VIDEOS

A wide range of videos have been produced specifically for schools. Museums and heritage sites have also identified videos as a niche market. Many local or specialist groups have compiled videos that feature early photographic or film coverage of the history of their area or field of interest.

ARCHAEOLOGY ON THE WEB

The Internet has made it possible for archaeologists to reach a new, wider audience. Because websites have been developed only during the last decade, there is still wide variation in their form and content—some are highly sophisticated, others quite basic. Three main types of site have emerged. The first is the "virtual tour" (below), favored by museums and visitor attractions. The second comprises databases or online collections—for example, the Oxford Ashmolean Museum's PotWeb, or English Heritage's National Monuments Record. The third type are information sites featuring the work of an organization, which are regularly updated. The best of these have interactive "noticeboards," where users can make requests or suggestions; they may also feature links to other sites. Another development, used extensively by researchers, is the e-mail discussion group.

PUBLIC EXCAVATIONS

Digging has always attracted visitors, and larger projects now routinely arrange open days or guided tours, and provide site noticeboards and information leaflets. More ambitious projects may erect viewing platforms. In Japan, archaeologists even give well-publicized on-the-spot presentations of the results of a dig as soon as it is completed: these are so successful that they attract huge crowds.

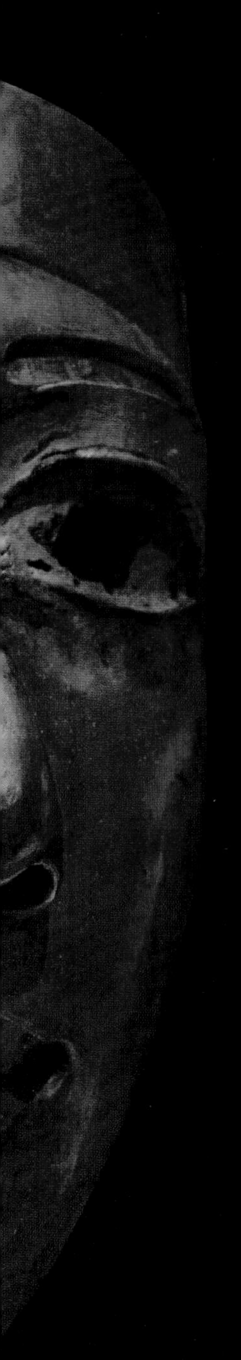

Reading the Past

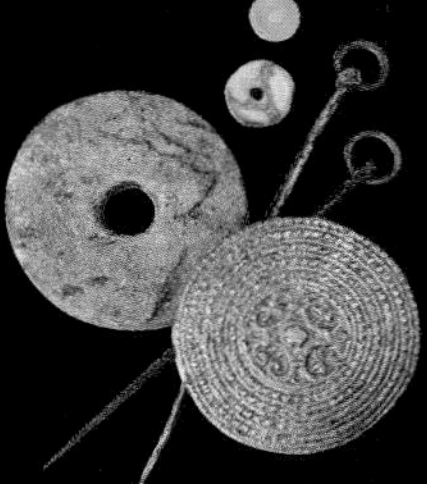

Finding and Exploring Sites

While some excavations are still the result of deliberate searches, other finds are entirely accidental and many more come to light during modern construction work. After the painstaking work of digging a site, both traditional and high-tech dating techniques help to establish the chronology of the finds, the first step in understanding their message.

"Recording is the absolute dividing line between plundering and scientific work ... The unpardonable crime in archaeology is destroying evidence which can never be recovered; and every discovery does destroy evidence unless it is intelligently recorded."

Flinders Petrie (1853–1942),
English Egyptologist

Discovering a Site

The vast majority of archaeological sites lie buried beneath the soil. Finding these can be like a detective puzzle, with clues scattered in all sorts of places—along with a few red herrings!

Early Discoveries
During the 19th century, the search for remnants of past civilizations became more systematic. This print, *Discovery of the Gigantic Head*, shows Austen Henry Layard's excavation of the Temple of Nimrud in the Assyrian city of Nineveh.

Archaeology covers everything from humankind's earliest beginnings up to the present day. An archaeological site can be anything from a Stone Age campsite through to such recent monuments as the Berlin Wall; it can encompass every type of settlement, along with agricultural, industrial, commercial, religious, and military sites, on land or at sea. Even the remains of relatively recent industries—for example, derelict coal mines, quarries, and railways—are studied in the sub-discipline of industrial archaeology.

CHANCE FINDS

Some sites come to light as a result of natural processes, such as coastal erosion or changes in sand-dune formation. Others, particularly in what are now remote locations, may be accidentally discovered by hikers, climbers, shepherds, or tourists—or, in the case of underwater sites, by divers or fishermen. Many sites are disturbed by farmers or

BEGINNER'S LUCK

Archaeology abounds with romantic tales of chance discoveries. Among the most famous are the boys and their dog who stumbled upon Lascaux (see p. 268); the hikers who came across the Iceman in the Alps (see p. 280); and the shepherd boy looking for gold who found the Dead Sea Scrolls instead (see p. 358).

Modern Techniques
Ground-penetrating radar can be used to explore deeply stratified sites (see p. 73). Here, an archaeologist uses the technique to search a bunker complex believed to contain the remains of a U.S. soldier near Chu Chi, Vietnam.

by commercial foresters during plowing. Sometimes the plow hits solid obstacles, such as walls; more often it simply pulls up objects onto the surface, which are then recognized by farmers or by archaeologists field-walking on their land. Yet other sites are found by metal-detector users.

Construction work often reveals archaeological sites. Large developments, such as oil pipelines, motorways, quarries, and reservoirs, can affect hundreds or thousands of previously unknown sites, but the majority of new finds are discovered on building sites—either by archaeologists evaluating the site before development, or during the course of the actual building.

Construction Find
In 1965 workers laying a gas main in a new housing estate in Hertfordshire, England, discovered a large Iron Age grave. Among the finds were these glass gaming counters, which date to about 40–20 BC.

DISCOVERIES BY ARCHAEOLOGISTS

Patient research through old records and the study of early maps, photographs, and engravings can provide a rich trawl of information. References to unusual features or discoveries in antiquarian works or old newspapers have prompted archaeologists to look for specific sites. For example, villas have been relocated from descriptions of earlier discoveries of mosaics. Similarly, the sites of forgotten Medieval settlements have been relocated using early maps.

Systematic field-walking in freshly plowed fields has led to the identification of many thousands of sites. Any finds on the surface are carefully plotted and collected for identification, since concentrations of finds may indicate the presence of earlier settlements.

A similar approach involves plotting all the finds of one period that have been recovered from building sites and excavations within a town, which may help to identify where early settlement was concentrated. Moreover, by examining data collected from commercial boreholes, archaeologists can determine the depths of old land surfaces in different parts of a town and then reconstruct entire buried landscapes through three-dimensional modeling.

AERIAL PHOTOGRAPHY

Pioneered in the early 1920s, aerial photography is now routinely used all over the world, and has led to the recognition of millions of sites. The view from above, even of previously known sites, is usually much clearer than can ever be gained from the ground. Both color and black-and-white aerial photography have been used to great effect, and infrared film and thermal-imaging equipment have also produced some spectacular results. Three main types of site have benefited from aerial photography: cropmarks, soilmarks, and earthworks.

Seeing Through Sand
These divers are using a magnetometer to search for artifacts buried in the sandy floor of the ocean.

Cropmarks are variations in the height and color of a crop that are caused by buried features. Crops growing over a stone wall are likely to be stunted, while deep features cut into the subsoil, such as old ditches, retain water and so produce vegetation that is lusher or ripens more quickly.

Soilmarks—discolorations in freshly plowed fields—betray the presence of sites that have been leveled. For instance, the ditches around a prehistoric barrow may show as darker (soil-filled) rings around a pale (chalk) mound.

Sites that have not been plowed often survive as earthworks—prominent banks and ditches. Walls or house platforms may be represented by low banks or mounds, and ditches may appear as depressions. Earthworks can range from variations of an inch or so in height to the impressive mounds of Norman castles or prehistoric hillforts.

Sizable collections of aerial photographs are now held in national and local archives and by commercial firms. Archaeologists sometimes use such archival photographs to map sites.

NON-DESTRUCTIVE SURVEYS

Comprehensive plans of earthworks can be produced by making a detailed survey of the variations in height over a site. Many different techniques have been employed in the past, but most modern surveys now use either EDM (Electronic Distance Measuring) or GPS (Global Positioning by Satellite) equipment, as these are both quick and extremely accurate.

Geophysical surveys are widely used on rural sites, but they identify geological anomalies as well as archaeological features, so they require real skill to filter and interpret the data. When they work, such surveys can produce spectacular results, but on certain types of subsoil, their results can be misleading. The two major types of geophysical survey that are routinely used are resistivity and magnetometer surveys.

In a resistivity survey, an electrical current is passed through the soil, and the variations in the resistance to that current over a given area are carefully measured and recorded. The resistance levels within the subsoil are closely related to its moisture content, so dry rocky features such as wall foundations will give a high resistance reading, while moist clay-filled pits and ditches will give a low response.

Magnetometer surveys rely on the presence of weakly magnetized iron oxides in the soil. They can be used to detect anomalies such as fired clay structures (pottery kilns and clay hearths, for example) and ditches that have silted up.

Ground-penetrating radar has been used with mixed success in towns, mainly on deeply stratified sites or inside standing buildings. A short pulse of energy is sent through the soil, and the time that the echoes take to come back is recorded and then converted into depth measurements. This method allows archaeologists to build up a three-dimensional picture of a buried site.

Earthworks
The banks and ditches at this earthworks site in Ellerby, East Yorkshire (far left), indicate the presence of a monastic farmstead.

HOW A SITE BECOMES BURIED

While a handful of sites were inundated by calamities such as lava flows (for example, Pompeii, see p. 316) or changes in sea-level (for example, Port Royal, see p. 82), most disappear in far less dramatic circumstances. Once a site is abandoned, natural processes take effect: ditches begin to silt up, timbers and organic roofing materials (such as thatch) begin to rot, and frost and erosion soon accelerate decay. The abandoned premises are a ready source of cheap building materials, so these are often plundered. Left unsupported, the walls may begin to collapse, with even the most prestigious buildings eventually reduced to rubble.

The remains of the site may then be covered with a thin layer of wind-blown or water-laid silts, which allow vegetation to take root; the vegetation, in turn, promotes the development of soil (as has occurred on the Inca ruin, right). Once established, the soil is rapidly augmented by rotting leaf litter (with help from beetles and other insects) and the action of earthworms, which leave their casts on the surface—it has been estimated that a healthy colony of earthworms can raise the soil level by up to 2 inches (5 cm) every 10 years!

If the site is reoccupied, any rubble is usually leveled to form a flat construction platform on which to found the next building. Thus, the ground levels could be raised quite dramatically in just a few centuries. Many historic towns have 6 feet (2 m) or more of stratified archaeology within their centers, while large, long-lived cities, such as London or some of the older Japanese cities, boast up to 30 feet (10 m) of deposits.

The Dig

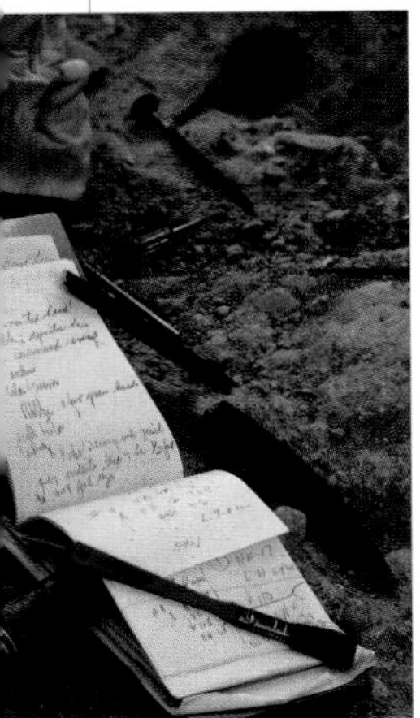

Tools of the Trade
Archaeologists' field tools include a notebook to record measurements and comments about findings and excavation implements such as brushes and picks.

Contrary to popular ideas about archaeologists, they spend far more time on planning digs and publishing their results than on any on-site excavation work.

A site consists of a series of deposits, features, and structures. These represent the end-products of various natural and artificial processes, and the recording and analysis of their interrelationships help archaeologists understand how the site evolved. Where a site has been used over several centuries, there may be a complex sequence of layers from different periods (see p. 85). By applying methodical techniques to the investigation and recording of this stratigraphic sequence, archaeologists can begin to understand the history of the site.

THE STAGES OF A DIG

The first stage of an excavation is to establish an accurate planning grid over the site and to mark out the excavated area. Modern layers are then removed, usually by machine, down to the first obvious change in subsoil, and the surface is cleaned. The cleaning and most of the subsequent digging are still performed meticulously by hand.

Excavation is an interrogation process: which features came first, and what was their extent and nature? Relationships between the features are revealed by cutting vertical sections through a series of deposits in carefully selected places. This determines the order in which deposits will be removed (beginning with the latest, and working back in sequence to the earliest). Detailed written, drawn, and photographic records are made of all features and sections, with relative survey levels taken throughout. All finds are recorded by context—where, in what, and with what the object was found (see box, below).

EXCAVATION FUNDING

Who foots the bill for an excavation depends on whether it is a research dig or a salvage (rescue) dig. Research digs are carried out by universities, museums, or research trusts, and investigate sites that are usually not threatened. These excavations are often limited in scale, and may be carried out over several seasons.

Salvage digs record sites that are going to be damaged or destroyed by development, such

CONTEXT

To understand a find's significance, archaeologists must know its context. This involves three pieces of information:
1. Precisely where the object was found—its "provenience."
2. What the object was found in—the soil, peat, or other material that surrounded it.
3. What the object was found with—any other artifacts that were found near the object.

as building, quarrying, or forestry. The costs may be met either by the government or, increasingly, by the developer (who may be required to pay part or all of the costs). In some countries, developers can now take out insurance against archaeological deposits being present on a site.

Total excavation of a site is both expensive and destructive. Modern salvage practice is to start with an evaluation of the site that determines the extent, nature, depth, date, condition, and significance of its deposits. With this information, archaeologists can decide how best to preserve what survives—for example, by resisting a proposed building to avoid damage, or by suggesting a different and less damaging form of building foundations. Only in the last resort would they dig the whole site.

Patient Excavation
Using brushes, hammers, and fine dental tools, archaeologist Ruth Dee Simpson begins to excavate a possible early human tool from a pit in the Calico Hills, California.

Salvage Mission
A rescue dig at the old Post Office site near St Paul's Cathedral, London, has retrieved about 250 skeletons, mostly dated to between 1186 and 1554.

Using a Grid
Archaeologists work with a grid system to excavate the site of the first Russian–American fort (founded in 1784) at Three Saints Bay, Kodiak Island, Alaska.

DECIDING WHERE TO DIG

With research excavations, research interests determine which sites to investigate and where to place the trenches. Salvage digs, on the other hand, are driven entirely by development. In the early days, archaeologists relied on builders recognizing and reporting discoveries. This was a reactive system that sometimes led to construction delays, bad feelings and publicity, and difficulty allocating archaeology budgets. Many countries have now introduced routine archaeological monitoring into their planning processes. By identifying the threats to known or suspected sites, evaluations can take place before construction begins.

THE TEAM

Besides the diggers, an excavation team can include draftsmen, surveyors, photographers, finds specialists, conservators, environmental and analytical scientists, and documentary historians. A large excavation may involve more than 70 specialists working behind the scenes. Traditionally, these specialists might have been variously employed by the state, museums, or universities, but it is becoming increasingly common for them to be self-employed contractors or to work for private archaeological companies or trusts.

EXCAVATION METHODS

Approaches to excavation have changed considerably over time and varied according to the type of site being investigated.

The quadrant method has often been used by prehistorians to excavate round barrows. The site is divided into quarters, leaving a major section across the two main axes. The final stage is to remove the balks (the dividing ridges) one at a time.

The grid method was much favored by Mortimer Wheeler (see box, below) and is ideal for working with unskilled labor. A grid of square excavation trenches is established over the site, leaving large balks in between. The grid provides sections at regular intervals, a finite area from which finds can be recovered, and a series of routes along which the soil can be easily removed. The last stage is to remove the balks.

Open area excavation developed from the grid method, but, because it requires a much higher level of recording and confidence, is best used by professional teams. The entire area is opened up, and no permanent balks are left. Instead, temporary divisions are placed where they are most useful and are removed in stages as the excavation proceeds. This method provides an overall picture of the site's development—and it avoids the problem of that key change in stratigraphy lying just below where the balk has been positioned!

A FLAMBOYANT EXCAVATOR

An irascible and charming rogue, Mortimer Wheeler (1890–1976) was a consummate showman and assured self-publicist. Quick to spot a good idea, he adopted the best excavation techniques of his day, claimed them as his own, and promoted them with all the zeal of an evangelist. The so-called Wheeler grid divides sites into square blocks that are then excavated, with balks left between the blocks.

A fastidious excavator (below left and right), Wheeler advised: "An ill-considered excavation is liable to develop into a chaos of pits and trenches...It is an axiom that an untidy excavation is a bad one." During his distinguished career, he standardized excavation procedures, introduced methodical, professional discipline into what had often been a gentlemanly pursuit, and influenced several key generations of excavators.

An excellent organizer, Wheeler set up several national museum and archaeology services, both in Britain and India. One of the first people to get press sponsorship for excavations, he went on to pioneer TV presentations of archaeology, and, using his journalistic background, he carved out another career writing popular archaeology books. With his flamboyant personality, Wheeler could have stepped out of the pages of a Hollywood screenplay.

Tools of the Trade

Sifting Screen
An archaeologist sifts dirt in a screen on site, searching for remnants of tools used by early humans. Many excavations now take bulk soil samples to be processed in the laboratory, where there is greater control.

Although topsoil is now usually removed by earth-moving machinery, most excavation work is still done with spades, shovels, mattocks, picks, hoes, wheelbarrows, and buckets. Similarly, most planning continues to be done by hand, using measuring tapes, plumb bobs, planning frames, and drawing materials. Archaeologists are very good at adapting the tools of other trades—by far the most common hand tool for removing soil is the pointing trowel, and brushes of all shapes and sizes are used on dry surfaces, particularly on stone or brickwork.

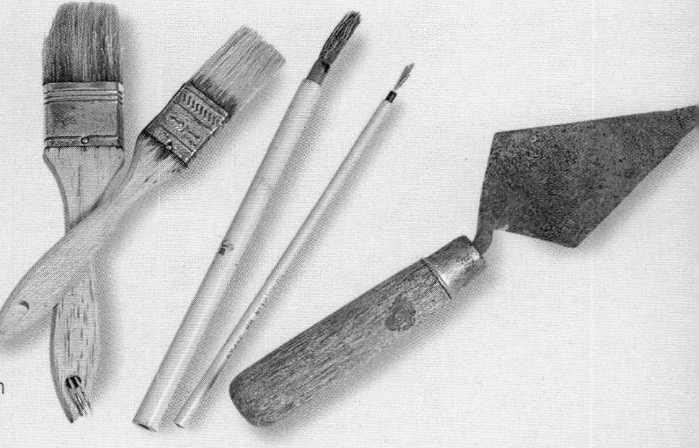

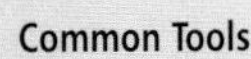

Common Tools
Most tools used in archaeology are available from hardware stores. The most common digging implement is the hand trowel, but in the right hands almost any tool with a clean sharp blade can produce a clean surface.

Digging Team

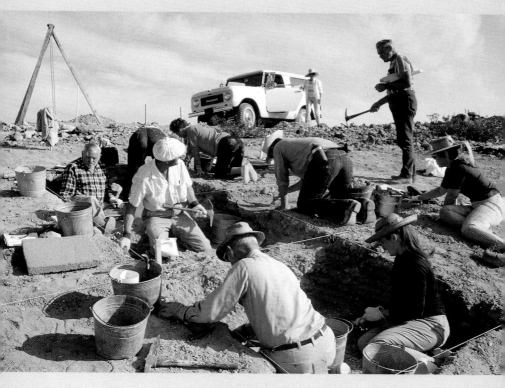

In parts of the world archaeological digs still rely on large teams of volunteers or local laborers. Here, hand-picks and trowels are used for digging, with buckets lined up to remove the debris. Increasingly, however, small professional teams and modern machinery are replacing the large workforce of the past.

Surveying the Scene

A survey at a multi-period site of Kom el-Dik, near el-Minia, Middle Egypt, using Global Positioning System (GPS). This involves the high-accuracy, high-resolution recording of points across the landscape; three-dimensional digital landscape surfaces can then be constructed by interpolation between these positions.

Underwater Archaeology

Helmet Divers
Early investigations of underwater sites relied on cumbersome helmet-diving equipment, with air pumped to the diver from the ship above.

Archaeology underwater presents exciting challenges. The marine archaeologist must develop new techniques to overcome the problems of working in an alien environment.

A common misconception is that underwater archaeology is solely concerned with shipwrecks at sea, but wrecks can occur just as easily in lakes and rivers. Moreover, the discipline entails much more than just the study of shipwrecks, as underwater sites can take many other forms. These can include: sites that are deliberately built into or onto the water, such as quays, harbors, waterfronts, or lake villages; sites that have been submerged by such forces of nature as earthquakes and sea-level changes; and sites that have ritual associations with water, such as votive offerings or bog bodies.

A waterlogged environment helps to preserve materials that would normally decay on land, including organic remains such as wood, leather, and textiles. This special quality means that submerged sites (particularly wrecks) can form a "snapshot" of a historical event and shed great light upon it.

THE UNDERWATER SITE

It can be difficult to draw the boundary between land-based and underwater archaeology—particularly in the intertidal zone. Should a wreck that is accessible at low water be dealt with by land-based archaeologists? Conversely, should a ship that is buried inland be investigated by marine archaeologists, as they are used to dealing with ships? The answer is simply that the site should be recorded by the best and most appropriate means available.

WORKING IN THE WATER

For the marine archaeologist, the most obvious difference from land-based excavation concerns the need to work underwater. This can be met by one of three

Viking Boat Burials
Maritime archaeologists are sometimes involved in the excavation of boats buried inland. The Oseberg ship is a Viking boat burial discovered in a clay and peat deposit in Norway. It contained the bodies of two women, as well as sacrificed animals and many artifacts.

approaches: using divers with an air supply; controlling remote-operated vehicles and remote-sensing equipment from the surface; and using manned submersibles.

Most underwater archaeology is carried out on the continental shelf (the slope between the continent and the ocean floor), well within the range of divers. Much of the diving archaeologist's equipment would be instantly recognizable to any land-based archaeologist—it includes measuring tapes, planning frames, site grids, cameras, and even trowels and paintbrushes! However, a suction dredge is used instead of wheelbarrows, with any overlying silts being gently sucked away into the water above and then removed by the current. When the diver's buoyancy is properly controlled, only the tools being used touch what is being cleaned and a bird's-eye view of the archaeology can be gained by "hovering" over the site.

The drawbacks of underwater archaeology are that the diver's working time is limited, since decompression sickness sets in after relatively short periods in deep water; suspended sediment can create very poor visibility; the cold and currents can affect the diver's ability to work; and occasionally the marine wildlife can pose a threat.

A Watery Dig
Diving archaeologists work in much the same way as their land-based counterparts, employing a grid system and carefully tagging all artifacts before their removal.

Bronze from the Sea
On land, most ancient Greek bronze statues were looted and melted down, but those recovered from the sea have been preserved. This life-size bronze from the 5th century BC was recovered off the coast of Riace in Italy.

SOME MAJOR UNDERWATER DISCOVERIES

ALEXANDRIA (c. AD 1300)
The city of Alexandria was established on the Egyptian coast in 332 BC by Alexander the Great. A series of earthquakes sank much of its ancient harbor, which is now being investigated by archaeologists. So far, they have recovered massive stone sculptures and located Cleopatra's palace on a submerged island.

THE *ANTIKYTHERA* WRECK (4TH CENTURY BC)
The remains of a Roman cargo vessel were discovered by sponge-divers in 1900. The importance of this wreck lies in its preserved cargo of original Greek bronzes, since many others had been melted down in antiquity.

THE *BATAVIA* (1629)
The excavation of this "Dutch East Indiaman" wreck off the Australian coast was a classic example of underwater methodology.

THE *HAMILTON–SCOURGE* WRECKS (1813)
These two schooners, lost on North America's Lake Ontario in a sudden squall, were not only incredibly well preserved in the cold waters, but were also the site of some of the first archaeological remote-sensing investigations.

THE *MARY ROSE* (1545)
The excavation of Henry VIII's warship is the largest single underwater archaeology project to date. Not only was one-third of the hull raised from the Solent (the channel between the Isle of Wight and the English mainland), but thousands of artifacts and environmental remains were recovered, detailing the daily and fighting life on board a Tudor warship. The finds range from massive bronze cannons and silver coins (above) to the corns from an officer's peppermill.

PORT ROYAL (1692)
In 1692 a massive earthquake sent most of the town of Port Royal, Jamaica, into the sea. This major trade port was one of the richest English towns in the New World. Underwater archaeologists began exploring the site in 1956, excavating complete structures with their contents intact.

SEA HENGE, EASTERN ENGLAND (2049 BC)
Excavated in 1999, a unique structure on the North Norfolk coast consisted of an upturned tree stump, surrounded by a "wall" of posts, forming an enigmatic, probably ritual, site.

SWISS LAKE VILLAGES (c. 3000 BC)
The investigations of drowned prehistoric villages in the Alps began in the 19th century, and showed that not only was early human activity more complex than previously thought, but that non-coastal areas could experience significant water-level changes. (See also p. 278.)

***ULU BURUN* (1306 BC)**
Discovered in the waters of Turkey by a sponge-diver in 1982, the *Ulu Burun* is one of the greatest ancient shipwrecks ever found. It appears to have been a trading vessel, possibly from Cyprus or Palestine, with a cargo that included copper, tin, and glass ingots, jars of resin and olive oil, ivory, plant seeds, and jewelry. (See also p. 300.)

THE *VASA* (1627)
The recovery of the *Vasa* in the 1960s marked the beginning of modern underwater archaeology. Built for the King of Sweden, the ship had an extra gundeck added before completion. This modification made the vessel unstable, causing it to capsize on its maiden voyage.

ADVANCED TECHNIQUES

Remote sensing is an excellent method for locating and surveying sites in deep or dangerous waters, but can be prohibitively expensive. Methods available include sonar (bouncing sound-waves off seabed features to create a map); sub-bottom profiling (looking through sediments to locate buried features); magnetometry (detecting anomalies in the magnetic field, which may indicate a buried object); and aerial photography and video-recording.

The cutting edge of marine archaeology and deep-water exploration is epitomized by the use of manned submersibles—a spin-off from the investigation of the *Titanic*. During the exploration of this famous modern wreck, a submersible carried two or three scientists to the deep-water site. An unmanned vehicle carrying cameras was attached to the submersible and could be used to explore the great ship's interior.

Exploring the *Titanic*
The great *Titanic* sank in the North Atlantic in 1912, but its specific location was not verified until 1985. At a depth of 12,500 feet (3,875 m), its exploration required the use of manned and remote submersibles (left). Their cameras captured eerie images, such as this one of the bow (below).

Relative Dating

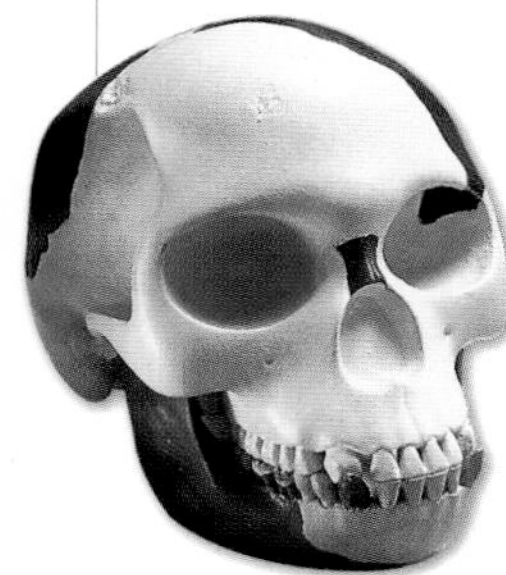

Dating a Fraud
The levels of particular chemicals in bones change over time, so measuring these chemicals will indicate if a group of bones are the same age. This relative dating method helped expose the Piltdown hoax (above) in the 1950s. The 1912 "find" was claimed as the missing link between humans and apes, but the tests showed that the skull was recent and the jaw came from an orangutan.

The traditional ways of dating a site are by studying the type of structures or finds (typology and association) or the interrelationships of the various contexts (stratigraphy).

Relative dating involves placing finds into a chronological sequence. It doesn't specify how much older or younger the finds are from one another, but until recently, it was the only way of establishing a chronology when there was no written evidence. Most excavations are still dated by a combination of typology, association, and stratigraphy.

TYPOLOGY

Coins and gravestones are among the few finds that are conveniently inscribed with a precise date, but many others have characteristics that suggest an approximate date range. Archaeologists classify sites, structures, and objects into hierarchical systems so as to find patterns and order the material into a chronology.

A type is a group of individual structures or objects that share distinctive traits. The shared traits can include aspects of their size and shape, the composition of their materials, how they were made, the layout and arrangement of any components (within a building, for example), and how they were finished or decorated.

By arranging types into an assumed order of development, we can create a model chronology that can then be tested either stratigraphically (see below) or by absolute dating (see p. 88). A typological sequence might assume either a progressive improvement or degeneration within a particular series.

When a series of types in the same material—such as flint—are recurrently found together, they are classed as an industry. A combination of types of different artifacts or structures may be classified as a culture.

Types of Pots
During his excavations in Egypt, Flinders Petrie (1853–1942) noticed that the styles of pots changed among various graves. By charting the style changes, he was able to work out the graves' relative dates.

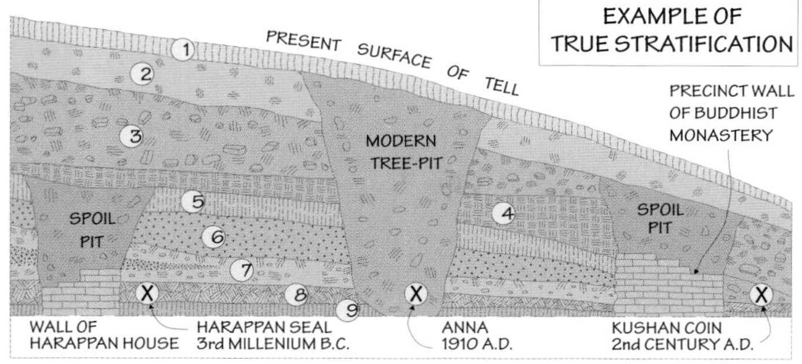

Charting the Layers
This stratigraphic diagram, based on one by Mortimer Wheeler, shows a section across a mound in the Indus Valley. The age of the Harappan seal, known from other similar finds, can be used to date Layer 8.

ASSOCIATION

Dating by association is based on the principle that when two or more types of objects are found together in a sealed context, they were probably deposited at the same time. From this, we may infer that they may have been in use at the same time, and they may even have been manufactured at the same time. This form of dating is most commonly used for objects found in graves and hoards. There is a danger, however, that such contexts can sometimes contain archaic or residual material—for example, a body may have been buried with artifacts from an earlier time.

STRATIGRAPHY

In general, providing later disturbance can be ruled out, the farther we go down into the earth, the older the layers, or strata. Few sites, however, consist of neat, ordered successions of unbroken layers. Instead, contexts are intercut by pits and cellars; overlying layers slump into features beneath them; stone walls may be robbed for their materials; and deposits may be badly weathered. In interpreting a site, the archaeologist must ask how and why each context came to look the way it does.

Stratigraphic dating works on the principle of first arranging the contexts into a relative sequence. Then, by dating any one of the contexts, a relative chronology can be established for the rest. Where a context is found firmly sealed beneath a known dated horizon—for example, the construction levels of a dated building or a layer of volcanic ash that can be linked to a dated eruption—the archaeologist is provided with a latest possible date. Conversely, where a context lies above a firmly dated horizon, the archaeologist can establish an earliest possible date. On most sites, however, no such firmly dated horizons are available for any part of the sequence. In these cases, the latest object found provides the earliest possible date for its context.

By ordering the contexts found in a particular site, archaeologists can build up a series of relative dates for the finds. By extending stratigraphic dating to review a whole series of sites, they can then arrange the sites into an evolutionary sequence.

Making a Date

The pottery of the ancient Greeks falls into distinct types that can broadly indicate the date of origin. Pottery decorated with silhouette figures, often showing scenes of mourning, began to appear during the 8th century BC. Greek contact with the Near East led to the use of oriental motifs, with Corinthian pots featuring lions and other monsters from the 7th to 6th centuries BC. During the 6th century BC, Athenian black-figured pottery became widely exported, replacing the dominance of Corinthian work in the archaeological record. This was replaced in turn by Athenian red-figured pottery at the end of the 6th century BC.

Geometric Style

People of the early states of Greece decorated their pottery with simple geometric patterns. This masterpiece of the geometric style dates to *c.* 750 BC. Found in the Kerameikos Cemetery, Athens, the amphora (storage jar) features a scene of mourning for the dead.

Protocorinthian Style

Dating to about 640 BC, this Corinthian aryballos (perfume bottle) employs the oriental motif of a lion's head. In the 7th century BC, Corinth specialized in the production of small perfume vessels covered with an intricate network of silhouetted figures, a style known as Protocorinthian.

Black-figured Painting

Depicting Achilles killing the Amazon Queen Penthesilea, this black-figured amphora (below) was made in Athens and dates to about 540–530 BC. The amphora is signed, just behind Achilles' right arm, by Exekias as potter. Exekias, who also signs as a painter, was one of the finest decorators of Athenian black-figured pottery

The Brygos Painter

This Athenian cup (below), dated to 490–480 BC, has been attributed to the Brygos painter, one of the leading practitioners of the red-figured style that replaced the black-figured style. The painting shows a young man being entertained by a dancing girl at a symposium (drinking party).

The Kleophrades Painter

This black-figured amphora (above) held oil which was awarded as a prize at the Panathenaic games. It is attributed to the Kleophrades painter who usually decorated red-figured pottery. He worked in Athens from 505 to 475 BC.

Red-figured Painting

Dated to about 460–450 BC, this red-figured calyx-krater (wine mixing bowl) shows the gods creating Pandora above a frieze of dancing and playing satyrs. It is believed to be the work of the Athenian Niobid painter, who is admired for his elegant compositions and harmonious balance of light and dark. The Athenian red-figured style dominated Greek pottery during the 5th century BC. From the end of that century, Corinth, as well as Greek colonies in southern Italy, also produced red-figured pottery.

Absolute Dating

Recorded Dates
Early calendars, such as this Aztec calendar stone, provide a framework for the dating of finds.

Most dating in archaeology is relative, but the use of absolute dates allows typological and stratigraphic sequences not only to be verified, but also to be fixed with greater precision.

A number of absolute dating techniques are available to the archaeologist, but their suitability depends upon the particular circumstances of the site in question. Some techniques are widely used, while others have a more limited application. Similarly, the level of accuracy varies considerably.

ANCIENT CALENDARS

The records of many early literate societies supply archaeologists with some form of chronology, often calculating events from the rule of a leader or the founding of a city. If such chronologies can be equated with modern calendar years, they provide a framework into which buildings or sites can be fitted with much greater precision than could be achieved by relative dating alone.

ICE SHEETS AND VARVES

When an ice sheet retreated, a lake was often formed behind it, and annual layers of sediment were deposited into the lake—a thick coarse layer in summer, and a finer one in winter. These two layers are called a varve. Since varve formation is governed by broad climatic factors, the same thicknesses of layers in a particular year will be observed across a whole region. By counting the varves, a continuous relative dating sequence is produced; if either its start or end point can be fixed, this relative sequence becomes an absolute dating system.

In Sweden, the end point of a varve sequence in one lake could be fixed because the lake was known to have burst during the 18th century. Consequently, a dated sequence for the whole of Scandinavia has been established, extending as far back as 10,000–12,000 BC. A similar relative sequence has been constructed for North America, but has yet to be fixed. In archaeology, varves are used mainly for dating episodes of climatic change.

TREE RINGS

Trees lay down annual growth rings, the thickness of which reflects minor changes in climate, such as fluctuations in solar radiation or the availability of water to the root system. Good summers will produce thick

Rings of Growth
A cross-section of a tree trunk clearly shows the growth rings. Thick rings indicate good summers. Dendrochronology has been most successful in regions with an abundance of preserved wood, such as the boggy regions of northwest Europe and the arid American Southwest.

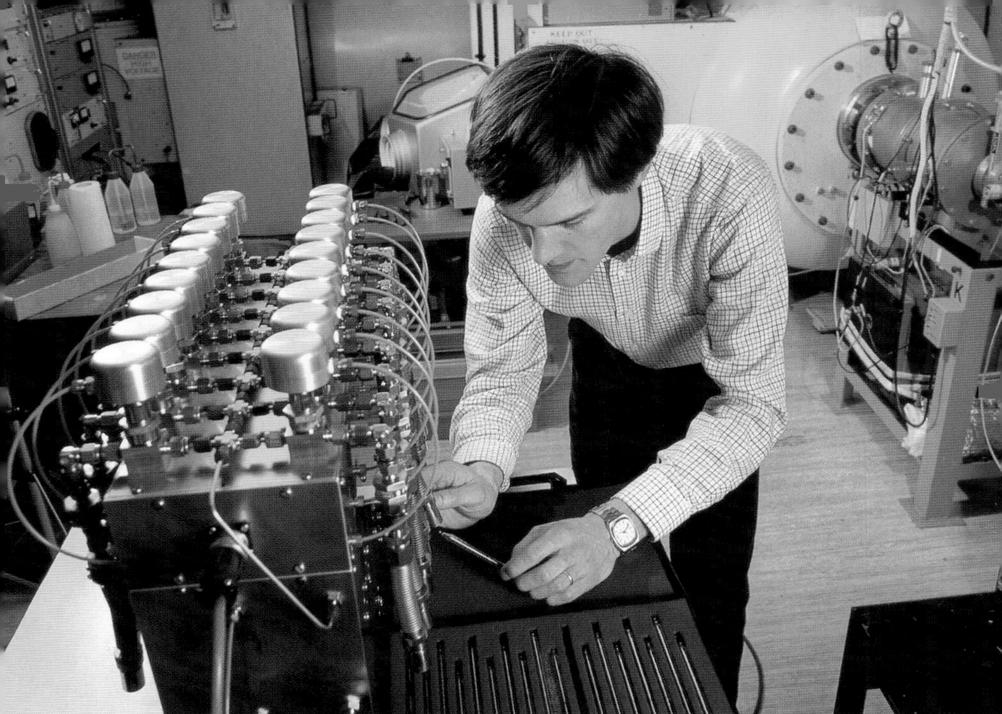

rings, while bad summers will produce thinner ones. The difference is particularly marked in regions with strongly seasonal climates. Trees from the same species, growing under the same conditions across a region, will exhibit very similar growth patterns. By measuring the widths of the rings, and plotting them on graphs, these patterns can be cross-matched. Chronologies can be established by overlapping series of matching tree rings, and comparing these with trees of known date.

The tree-ring method, known as dendrochronology, has been used to establish chronologies for much of Europe back to around 4000 BC. This dating method has proven to be most successful in areas abundant in preserved wood.

RADIOCARBON DATING

Radiocarbon, or carbon-14, is a radioactive variety—an isotope—of carbon, produced by cosmic rays bombarding the earth's upper atmosphere. Since all living matter contains carbon, this isotope becomes absorbed in the same proportions by anything organic throughout the world. Once that matter dies, the radioactive isotope starts to decay and reverts into the more stable form of carbon. The stability of any radioactive substance is expressed scientifically as a half-life—the time it takes for that radioactivity to fall to half of its original value. As the half-life of carbon-14 is relatively long (5,730 years), this process is quite gradual, which makes it ideal as a dating tool. By measuring the amount of carbon-14 left in an organic

Organic Dates
Radiocarbon dating can be used to date samples of organic materials, such as bone, wood, charcoal, and seeds. The amounts of radiocarbon used to establish dates are so tiny that they must be very precisely measured.

Kiln Dates
Fired clay artifacts and structures, such as this kiln excavated at Sawankhalok, Thailand, can be dated back as far as 10,000 years ago using the archaeomagnetic dating technique.

object, and comparing this to the amount now present in the earth's atmosphere, the object's age at death can be calculated.

To establish a radiocarbon date, carbon is extracted from the samples in a laboratory and converted into benzene. Then the amount of surviving radiocarbon is precisely measured; because the amounts involved are quite tiny, various safeguards need to be taken to rule out any contamination, which can lead to false readings. All dates are expressed as statistical ranges before the present (BP, which is always calculated from 1950)—for example, 4,075 +/– 38 BP.

Radiocarbon measurement is normally effective back to 30,000 or 40,000 BP, but it is increasingly possible to date samples back to 60,000 BP. The size of the samples required is also changing. The introduction of Accelerator Mass Spectrometry (AMS) dating has sped up the process and made it possible to obtain dates from tiny quantities of material.

ARCHAEOMAGNETIC DATING

There are periodic fluctuations in both the direction and intensity of the earth's magnetic field. When any fired clay object begins to cool, the iron particles in the clay align themselves with the direction of the earth's magnetic field. By measuring their orientation, archaeologists can calculate the date of the object's last firing. This technique is most often used to date kilns, hearths, or ovens, but it can also be applied to river silts or marine deposits dating back to about 10,000 years ago.

INTO THE DISTANT PAST

A number of advanced techniques allow archaeologists to date objects to hundreds of thousands of years ago.

THERMOLUMINESCENCE DATING

This technique measures the energy stored in a buried sample and can be used to date any fired clay, such as pottery and brick, or burnt stone objects, including flint. All such objects contain certain amounts of radioactive impurities, and the original heating of these objects causes energy from these impurities to be trapped. If the object is heated in the laboratory to at least 550°F (300°C), this energy is released as light. The amount of light will be in proportion to the object's age—the longer that it has been buried, the greater the thermoluminescence. This technique is routinely used to date samples up to 30,000 years old, though the limits for flint extend back to 300,000 BP.

URANIUM-THORIUM DATING

This method has been used for cave deposits up to 350,000 years old. The salts of uranium and thorium can be absorbed into calcite deposits, either in solution as groundwater or by leaching. Both elements have a very long half-life, and by measuring the proportions of each element present, the date of the deposit can be calculated.

OPTICAL DATING

Sometimes referred to as optically stimulated luminescence, this technique works on a similar principle to thermoluminescence dating, except that a laser light (rather than direct heat) is used to release the trapped energy in quartz grains. Though still in an experimental stage, it is hoped that this method can be used to date sediments up to several hundred thousand years or more in age.

ELECTRON-SPIN RESONANCE

Another technique that avoids the heating used in thermoluminescence dating, electron-spin resonance relies on precisely measuring the trapped electrons within tooth enamel, bone, and shell. The number of surviving electrons indicates the age of the specimen.

POTASSIUM-ARGON DATING

Potassium-argon dating involves two measurements—the rate of decay of a radioactive isotope of potassium, and the amount of argon trapped in the crystal lattice of a mineral. This technique can establish very early dates and was used at Olduvai Gorge, Tanzania (below), helping to construct its 2-million-year chronology. It has now been largely replaced by a more sensitive variant, argon-argon dating.

Interpreting the Remains

The remains of the human past encompass microscopic pollen grains, preserved human corpses, stone and metal tools, sherds of pottery, precious jewelry, intriguing paintings, giant monuments, and spectacular temples. In recent decades, a bevy of scientific specialists and theoreticians have emerged to interpret this body of evidence.

"I am not creating a cabinet—vanity not being my objective; I care not at all for showy things, but for the bits and pieces of agate, stone, bronze, pottery, glass, which may serve in whatever way to discover some practice or the hand of the maker."

Comte de Caylus (1692–1765),
French archaeologist

The Archaeological Record

Enduring Stone
The archaeological record is dominated by artifacts fashioned from inorganic materials, such as this jadeite axhead, which was found in England and dates to about 4000–2000 BC.

The archaeological record includes constructions built to last, such as temples, but most of it is more humdrum—the discarded refuse from daily activities, such as food scraps and broken pots.

Practically any archaeological material can survive in exceptional circumstances, but in most sites inorganic materials survive far better than organic ones, which normally decay and disappear. This substantial distortion of reality needs to be kept in mind when constructing an image of the past.

INORGANIC MATERIALS

The most common inorganic materials found are stone, clay, and metals. Stone tools and clay potsherds have long been the mainstay of archaeology, being almost indestructible. These are the dominant artifacts in most assemblages of recovered material, even though wooden and bone tools, and vessels of organic materials, may well have been more important in various periods.

A BIAS IN THE RECORD
The archaeological record can be misleading. In Egypt, most domestic remains have vanished, but the enclosed tombs have survived intact, giving the impression that the Egyptians were obsessed with death.

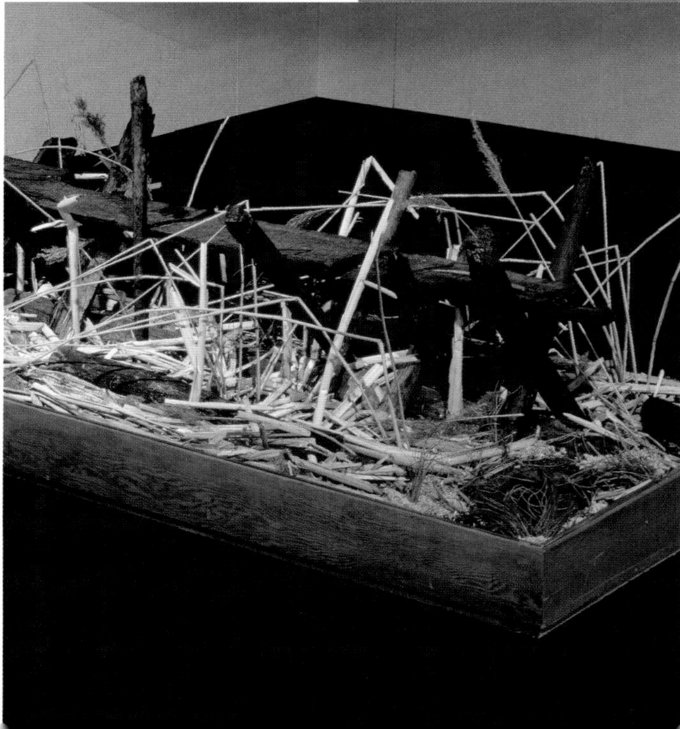

Wet Preservation
Constructed nearly 6,000 years ago by early farmers in Somerset, the Sweet Track runs for more than a mile (2 km) and is the oldest prehistoric trackway in Britain. The marshy lands that the track was built to cover have preserved the wood of its planks, rails, and pegs. The model of the track in the photograph shows its sophisticated workmanship.

Dry Preservation
The dry environment of the American Southwest has preserved woven artifacts such as this decoy duck, retrieved from Lovelock Cave, Nevada.

Metals such as gold, silver, and lead generally survive well, while copper and bronze are attacked by acid soils and can become heavily oxidized, and iron rusts in most soils.

ORGANIC MATERIALS

The survival of organic materials depends primarily on the surrounding sediment—for example, chalk preserves bone well, while acid soils can destroy bone and wood within a few years. Natural disasters can sometimes help to preserve remains. Storms covered the Scottish Neolithic village of Skara Brae with sand (see p. 282); mudslides engulfed the prehistoric site of Ozette on America's northwest coast; and volcanic eruptions buried Herculaneum and Pompeii (see p. 316).

Apart from such exceptional circumstances, the survival of organic materials usually involves extremes of moisture—arid, frozen, or waterlogged conditions. Great dryness prevents decay because most microorganisms cannot flourish without water. Through a process of natural desiccation, the driest regions of the world, such as the American Southwest or Egypt, have preserved many examples of organic materials, including human bodies, plant remains, clothing, tools, and basketry.

Natural refrigeration can also impede decay for millennia, as in the case of the frozen mammoth carcasses of Siberia, the burial mounds of the Scythians (see p. 352), and Italy's famous Iceman (see p. 280). Finally, wetland sites—marshes, peat bogs, lakes, and rivers, as well as shipwrecks on the seabed (see p. 80)—seal organic materials in wet and airless environments, helping to preserve them until they are excavated. On a wet site, up to 90 percent of the finds may be organic, whereas little or none of this material would survive on most dry-land sites. The conservation of such finds can be costly and difficult, but the rewards in fuller information about the past are incalculable.

Frozen Preservation
The permanently frozen ground of Siberia has perfectly preserved the carcasses of woolly mammoths, such as this baby, allowing scientists to learn much about mammoth structure and behavior. Mammoths became extinct on the mainland of Eurasia toward the end of the Pleistocene epoch, 10,000 years ago.

Soils, Plants, and Animals

Ancient Olives

Usually archaeologists must sift through soil samples to identify any plants that may have been eaten, but on rare occasions whole meals survive. This bowl of olives was excavated from the volcanic deposits that buried and preserved Pompeii (see p. 316).

The soils, plants, and animals associated with archaeological sites provide invaluable clues to past environments, the types of food ancient people ate, and other aspects of past behavior.

Geoarchaeology looks at the geological processes that helped create an archaeological site, allowing the archaeologist to reconstruct ancient environments and identify how the site has changed since it was abandoned by the original inhabitants. Studying the site formation processes also helps identify which aspects of the archaeological record were the result of human activity and which were caused by nature. Soil analysis can indicate whether the past climate was wet or dry, hot or cold—heavy clay soils, for example, suggest that the environment was wet and boggy.

ANIMAL REMAINS

The remains of animals also offer clues to the type of environment that existed when the site was occupied—particular types of mollusk, for example, are known to be extremely sensitive to environmental conditions. Faunal analysis, as the study of animal remains is called, can also tell the archaeologist what types of animals were hunted, their relative importance in the overall diet, the season the site was occupied (the eruption sequences of animals' teeth are good indicators of this), whether any of the animals were domesticated, and even how the carcasses were butchered for meat and other products such as hide and sinews. Animal carcasses are obviously attractive to scavengers, so archaeologists use taphonomy (the study of what happens to living things after death) to factor out the effects of scavengers on animal bones.

Buffalo Jump

In North America, collections of bones identify the locations of buffalo jumps, where Indians herded and killed hundreds of animals. These bones were found at the Wahpka Chug'n Buffalo Jump in Montana.

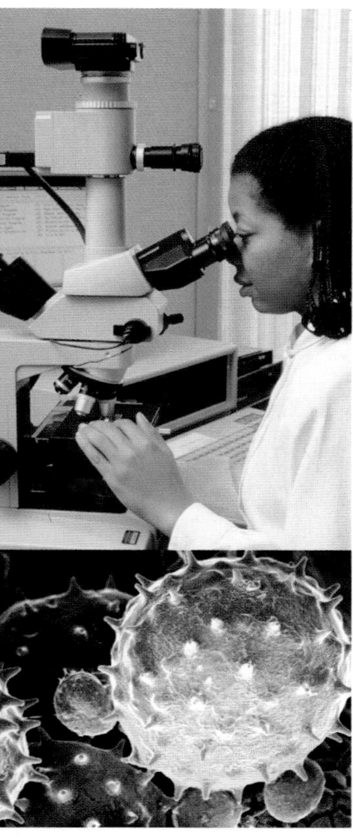

Microscopic Detail
Palynologists (left) study microscopic plant remains, such as pollen (below left), that have been extracted from the soil of archaeological sites or removed from stone tools.

ANCIENT PLANTS

Paleobotanists examine the soil from a site for plant remains, such as wood, leaves, and seeds. Since different kinds of plants grow in particular environments, these plant pieces can suggest what the ancient environment was like.

Palynology, the study of pollen and other microscopic plant organisms such as phytoliths (minute particles of silica found in plant cells), can offer a similar picture. Different plants have different-shaped pollen grains, and although the grains are hard to see with the naked eye, they are readily identifiable under a microscope. Pollen is an extremely durable object, and grains can be extracted using specialized laboratory techniques not only from the soil itself, but also from the surface of stone tools such as grinding stones. By identifying the different plants that grew at a site, the archaeologist can determine environment, diet, seasonality, and whether plants had been domesticated.

SPECIALIST TECHNIQUES

New techniques can identify food residues on tools and inside vessels. These have shown, for example, that Roman amphoras (large storage jars) were used not only for wine and olive oils, but also for wheat flour.

Both faunal analysis and palynology are highly specialized, requiring a very detailed knowledge of biology and botany. Consequently, many archaeologists devote their careers to just these aspects of studying the past and are often called on by other archaeologists for their specialized knowledge in interpreting an archaeological site.

THE DOGS OF ASHKELON
Animal remains do not always relate to diet. A 5th century BC cemetery containing the remains of more than 800 dogs was uncovered at Ashkelon in Israel. The cemetery might have been related to Persian religious practices—the careful positioning of each animal suggests that the dogs were considered sacred.

Human Remains

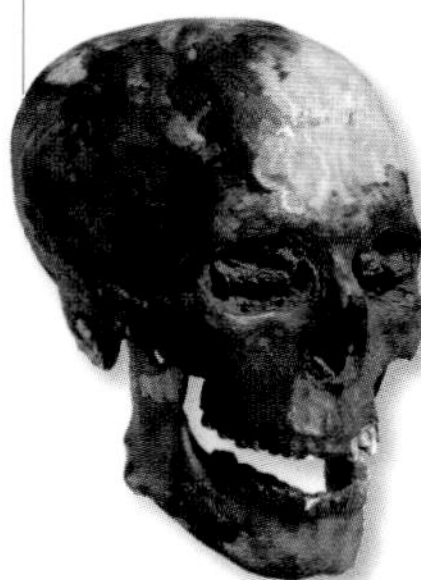

Fractured Skull
This skull of an ancient Egyptian overseer exhibits an extensive unhealed fracture, suggesting that he received a blow to the head that led to his death.

Ancient Footprint
Human remains can include traces such as footprints. This print (above right) was found in the floor of Choga Zanbil, an ancient religious site in Iran dating from the 13th century BC. At Laetoli, Tanzania, a set of footprints provides the earliest evidence of hominids walking on two legs (see p. 230).

Human remains can tell us not merely about the origins of our species, but also about the age and sex of the deceased, their health and how they died, and even their family connections.

The vast majority of human remains that survive do so in the form of whole skeletons, skulls, bone fragments, or teeth. Cremations are also quite abundant in some cultures, though far harder to study. Intact bodies are rare, and only survive in exceptional conditions, such as arid, frozen, or waterlogged sites (see p. 94), or where they have been purposely preserved as mummies (see p. 102).

SEX AND AGE

With intact bodies, the sex can usually be determined from genitalia or secondary characteristics such as breasts or beards. But with remains bereft of soft tissue—that is, where nothing but bones have survived—the best indicator of sex lies in the shape of the pelvis. Male bones

also tend to be bigger and more robust than female bones. The remains of children are notoriously difficult to sex, but DNA analysis can be a great help here.

Archaeologists usually assess age at death in terms of biological age—young, adult, old—rather than in years and months. The best indicators of age are the eruption and wear of teeth, as well as the fusion of limb bones and of the sutures of the skull. For small fragments, the bone's microstructure can also provide clues, since its inner architecture changes with age.

APPEARANCE AND KINSHIP

The height of a person is easy to calculate from an intact body, allowing for shrinkage, but can also be roughly assessed from the lengths of leg and arm bones. Weight is likewise straightforward to calculate for intact bodies, allowing for dry weight as opposed to live weight. Facial features are, of course, clearest on preserved bodies, but can also be reconstructed to a large extent from skulls through the methodical "replacement" of muscle and skin, whose thickness at different points is known from modern specimens.

Relationships between individuals can sometimes be assessed from blood groups, which can be determined from soft tissue, bone, and teeth. Family relationships can also be worked out through

DNA

DNA stands for deoxyribonucleic acid. It exists inside every one of our cells and contains the genetic code that determines everything from facial structure and height to inherited diseases. Mitochondrial DNA, or mtDNA, contains genetic material inherited only from the mother and can be used to trace relatedness over the long term.

Inca Mummy

The mummified body of a 10-year-old Inca child was found in the high Andes, preserved by the frozen environment. Scientists believe the child was sacrificed almost 500 years ago.

Volcanic Victim

The inhabitants of Pompeii and Herculaneum were buried by the eruption of Mount Vesuvius in AD 79. Not only can their skeletons be excavated (left), but when their bodies disintegrated, their shapes were preserved in the volcanic deposits. By pouring plaster into the hollows, archaeologists have been able to create models of the bodies.

analysis of DNA—for example, tissue samples from thousands of Egyptian mummies are being compiled in a databank, which will aid research into kinship patterns, human migrations, and the spread of diseases.

DEATH AND DISEASE

With intact bodies, the precise cause of death can sometimes be established—and in some cases, as at the ash-covered city of Pompeii (see p. 316), it is obvious from the circumstances. But for skeletons, cause of death can be ascertained only rarely, since most fatal afflictions leave no trace on bone. Paleopathology (the study of ancient disease) can shed light on such topics, as can the new field of forensic archaeology, which helps in the recovery and interpretation of murder victims, especially in war zones.

Where soft tissue survives, archaeologists can often learn a great deal about the presence of infectious diseases, viruses, and parasites. Some diseases, such as polio or smallpox, leave traces

A Hard Life
Discovered by hikers in the Alps in 1991, the Iceman (above) has been dated to the Copper Age, about 5,300 years ago. The corpse had blackened lungs, worn teeth, fractured ribs, and frostbitten toes.

Body from a Bog
Bogs have yielded many well-preserved bodies. Neu Versen Man, also known as "Red Franz" for his striking red hair, was found in 1900 in a bog on the border of Holland and Germany. He lived between AD 220 and 430, during the Iron Age.

in DNA. Scientists can also look inside bodies using endoscopes, X-rays, and CAT scans. Where only bones are present, the available evidence may be either traumatic damage (caused by violence, accident, or even repetitive strain injury) or the effects of disease or congenital deformity. Certain illnesses can cause erosion, growths, or altered structure in bone—for example, leprosy erodes the bones of the face and extremities in an easily recognizable way.

DIET AND HEALTH

Finally, human remains can also provide direct clues to diet and nutrition. The degree of tooth wear, or the presence of dental cavities, reflects what was eaten, while bone thickness and growth patterns may be affected by ill health or malnutrition. But the clearest evidence comes from the relatively new field of bone chemistry, since some chemical elements present in our bones are diet related, and their presence or ratios can indicate, for example, whether a diet was heavily dependent on maize, animal protein, or seafood.

TREPANATION

Trepanation, or trepanning, is the surgical removal of a piece of bone from the cranium. The practice appears in the archaeological record as healed holes in skulls. It seems to have occurred throughout the world, with examples dating back to at least the Neolithic Age.

INUIT MUMMIES

In 1972 a stunning discovery was made near the abandoned settlement of Qilakitsoq in Greenland. Two graves contained eight mummified Inuit clothed in animal skins. Buried in AD 1475, they are the oldest find of people and garments from the Thule culture, the ancestors of today's Inuit population in the eastern Arctic. The arid, cold climate kept the bodies dry and well preserved.

There were six women, aged from about 18 to 50 years, and two children—a baby of about 6 months (right) and a boy of about 4 years. All wore two layers of clothes, with an outer layer of sealskin and a warm inner layer of bird and caribou skins. Most seem to have been healthy, although there was evidence of some diseases, including an extensive cancer of the throat, a kidney stone, parasites, a hip disorder, a few fractures, and probably Down's syndrome. Tissue typing indicated that the group was closely related and consisted of three generations.

All Wrapped Up

Well Preserved

Egyptians probably began to intentionally mummify their dead about 3000 BC. The best prepared mummies date from the Late New Kingdom and the Third Intermediate Period (1200–800 BC), and include that of Seti (above).

Although the term "mummy" can refer to any well-preserved body, most people immediately think of the embalmed and bandaged corpses of the ancient Egyptians. For more than 3,000 years, the Egyptians believed that the preservation of the corpse would allow the soul to achieve eternal life. In its classical form, mummification involved the extraction of the soft tissue from the head and the abdomen, with only the heart being left in place. The corpse was then covered in natron salt, and left for a ritual period of 40 days. Finally the dried body, now much lighter, was washed, anointed, and wrapped with tight linen bandages.

Mummified Feline

In later periods of Egyptian history, animals associated with deities were regularly mummified.

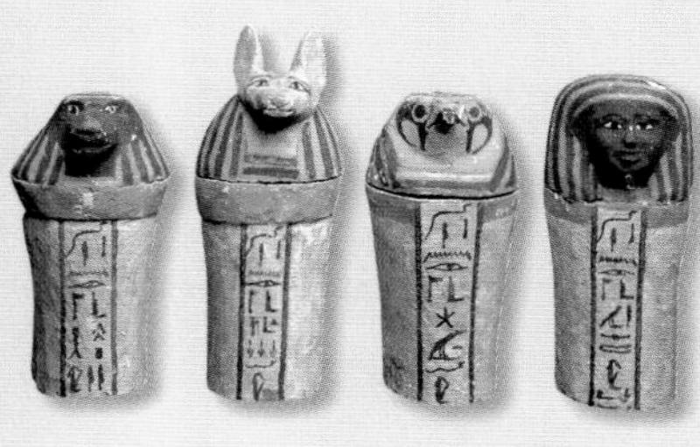

Painted Coffin

This mummy case of a boy named Pemsais dates to around the late 1st century BC. The iconography is mainly classical and shows the child wearing a Hellenistic Greek costume.

Canopic Jars

A mummy's internal organs were removed and embalmed, then wrapped and placed in wooden canopic jars. The organs were protected by the Sons of Horus, four minor deities: the baboon-headed Hapy, the jackal-headed Duamutef, the falcon-headed Qebhsenuef, and the human headed Imsety.

Entombed Wreath

Wreaths and bouquets were often placed on top of the outer coffin before the tomb was closed. This unusual wreath (below) is made of linen and was found in the tomb of a woman named Cleopatra (2nd century AD).

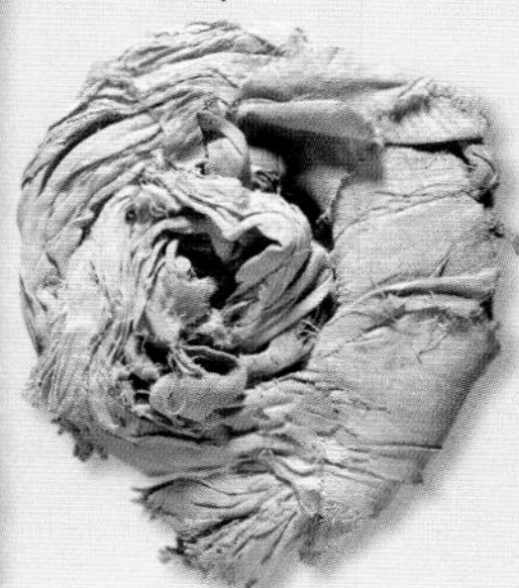

Seeing Through the Bandages

Modern technology, such as X-rays and CAT scans (below), allows scientists to study mummies without destroying the elaborate outer wrappings. Such study can reveal diseases, average height and lifespan, the age at death, and ties of kinship.

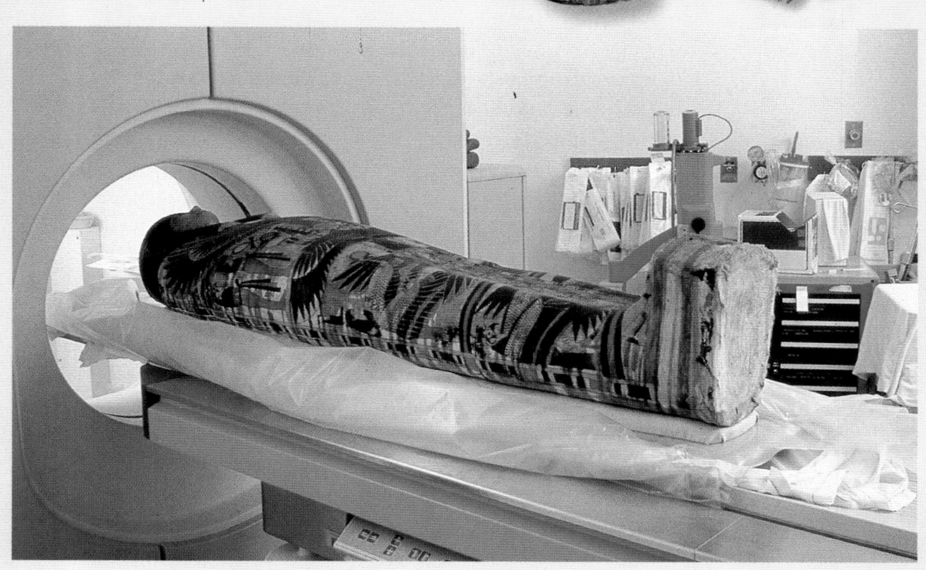

Artifacts

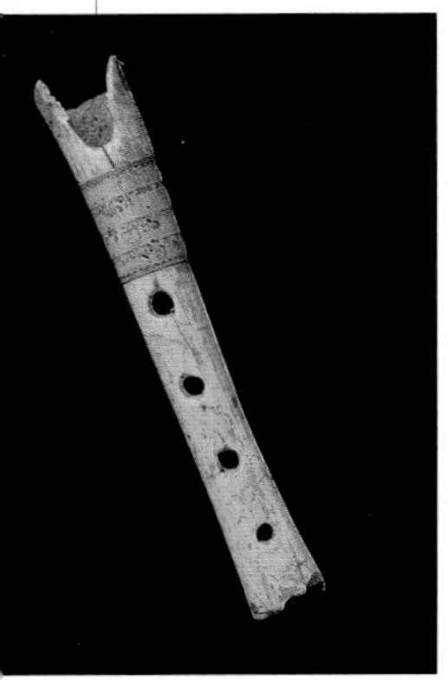

Early Music
The oldest recognizable musical instruments are flutes carved from bone. This example was found in the Dordogne region of France. Flutes of this kind date from the last Ice Age (30,000–10,000 years ago).

Living Material
Waterlogged soils or deposits can favor the survival of organic material such as this Medieval leather boot from Hull, England. Thick wet clays or peat deposits make it difficult for air to get in, which would otherwise accelerate the decay of wood, leather, textiles, and plant and insect remains.

There are two main classes of archaeological evidence: structural evidence concerns buildings and the form and layout of sites, while finds, or artifacts, are objects made or used by past societies.

An artifact is any tool or object made or finished by humans. In very early contexts, the term *ecofact* is used to describe objects that appear to have been used by humans, but that may not have been deliberately fashioned.

The great majority of artifacts fall into one of the following categories: tools, crafts, and industry; weapons and armor; dress and personal possessions; horse and riding gear; furnishings and household equipment; structural fittings related to buildings (such as doors, windows, locks, and ceramic building materials); and games, recreational, and leisure pursuits.

CONSERVING FINDS

Many objects begin to deteriorate once they are buried, particularly in adverse soil conditions. To determine whether or not a find needs some sort of conservation treatment—either while it is still in the ground or shortly after its excavation—archaeologists make an initial distinction between finds made of organic materials and those made of inorganic materials. Organic materials are prone to rapid decay and will survive only if soil conditions are favorable (see p. 95). They include bone, horn, antler, wood, leather, skins, textiles, and vegetable and animal fibers (such as hemp,

ropes, and paper). Inorganic materials are usually more stable and so are much more prevalent in the archaeological record. They constitute anything made of stone (including flint, obsidian, jet, amber, and coal), fired clay (pottery, bricks, tiles, clay pipes, and terracotta), glass (including faience), and metals (principally gold, silver, iron, copper, and lead, and their various alloys).

READING ARTIFACTS

Since certain types of object are characteristic of specific cultures (see p. 84), their identification is crucial to understanding a site, so archaeologists must try to identify what each object is and exactly what its purpose was. Unfortunately, few objects are complete when discarded, and their organic parts (such as wooden handles, or the textiles of a garment) may have rotted in the soil. Even when there seems to be clear evidence for an object's use, it may have been used for something completely different from the function that its maker had in mind.

By dating the objects within each layer or context, archaeologists can provide a relative dating sequence for the site (see p. 84). While this is certainly an important element of finds studies, artifacts can offer a great deal more information than just a date.

The careful analysis of residues and wear-marks on an object can sometimes reveal what it was used for and and how it was used. Residues can be both internal (such as the remains of food or drink in containers) and external (such as sooting marks). To identify the residues on artifacts, archaeologists often turn to scientific techniques, such as chemical analysis or amino-acid residue analysis.

The position of an object within its excavated context can offer clues not only about how it functioned, but also about accompanying items that no longer survive. A buckle or brooch found in position on a skeleton may indicate the former presence of a belt or cloak. Moreover, corrosion on a bronze or iron object may help to preserve small pieces of organic material (such as leather or cloth), which can provide a better idea of the type of costume that was worn.

DISTRIBUTION OF FINDS

Finds distributions across a site can be informative. For example, by plotting all the sherds of the same pot, archaeologists can demonstrate what happened to the vessel after it was broken. This helps them not only to reconstruct the patterns of rubbish disposal, but also to show which parts of the site may have been used at the same time.

Food for the Afterlife
The dry, airless conditions of Egyptian tombs have superbly preserved their grave goods. The tomb of the priestess Henutmehyt (c. 1290 BC) contained this sycamore box full of food—four whole ducks and several joints of meat, all mummified and wrapped.

Metalwork Hoard
The Ribchester Hoard, a collection of Roman military metalwork, was found in 1796 by a clogmaker's son playing behind his father's house. Dating to about AD 120, the pieces may have belonged to a single soldier.

Porcelain for Export
This Ming porcelain flask (right) is decorated with the arms of Spain. Made in Jingdezhen, China, around AD 1573–1620, it is an example of "export" porcelain, manufactured specifically for European markets.

TECHNOLOGY AND ECONOMY

Archaeologists study the technological aspects of artifacts, looking at how and from what raw materials they were made. Detailed examination of both the objects themselves and their production sites (if they can be located) can distinguish the products of different manufacturing centers. A wide range of scientific techniques—from X-rays and investigative work under a microscope, to detailed chemical or physical analyses of the composition of objects—has revolutionized our understanding of past societies. Such techniques have also been used to distinguish forgeries in museum collections.

Study of the economy of a society addresses how raw materials were obtained and exploited, and how finished commodities were traded. Some objects are so distinctive that their source can be relatively easily identified (foreign coins, for example), so if they are found outside of that area, they clearly represent trade. Others may be traced to their source using scientific techniques.

By examining a thin section of a stone object, scientists can identify the particular type of stone used and then trace the object to outcrops of that stone. Similarly, samples of timber can be traced to their source. This technique

COMMON TERMS
An *artifact* is anything used, made, or modified by humans. A *structure* is any sort of building. A *feature* is the remains of a structure. A group of artifacts that are found together is referred to as an *assemblage*. A *findspot* is the location in which an object was discovered.

has also been used to identify the stone grits in the clay from which pots have been made, and thus to distinguish similar-looking pots made in a number of centers throughout a large region and (ideally) to tell exactly where a pot was made.

Other artifacts are sometimes sourced using advanced techniques such as optical emission spectrometry. This method identifies the proportions of different elements in an object, which can indicate where the artifact was made. Such techniques can be used for sourcing such different materials as metallic alloys and glasses, as well as natural materials such as amber or jet.

SOCIAL STATUS AND RELIGION

Finds occasionally offer clues to the social status of their owners. Particularly rich goods in a grave or building may reflect the high social standing of its occupier; conversely, a very plain and simple assemblage might denote a less important person or family, particularly if associated with smaller and plainer buildings or graves. Certain objects, such as those made from precious materials, are generally considered to be prestige items, which, even as casual finds, reflect the status of their owners (see p. 118).

Yet other objects are likely to be religious or magical. For finds from historic societies, the connections may be quite clear (depictions of Roman or Greek gods, for example), whereas the identification of prehistoric objects as religious items tends to be more conjectural.

Intricate Jewelry
These Byzantine gold and enamel earrings would have belonged to a powerful woman. Archaeologists dated them to the early 10th century AD after similar earrings were found buried with coins.

Bronze Deposits
A Buddhist shrine found at Wardak, Afghanistan, contained a bronze vase and bronze coins, both dated to the 2nd century AD. The inscription on the vase helped archaeologists reconstruct the chronology of the Kushan kings.

Experimenting with the Past

Understanding Microwear
To learn about what kinds of activities produce particular patterns of wear on prehistoric tools, archaeologists copy the tools and use them for specific tasks. Here, an archaeologist uses a stone cutting tool to slice a branch.

Iron Age Farmhouse
The experimental farm of Little Butser in Hampshire, England, features an exact replica of an Iron Age thatched-roof farmhouse (below). Such replicas provide information about the strength and the construction techniques of early dwellings.

Archaeologists have always been interested in how the objects and features of the past were made, used, and destroyed, and experimental archaeology is one way in which these processes can be studied. The manufacture, use, and destruction of replicas can provide valuable insights—for example, into how long it takes to make an implement, or how many people are required to build a monument. At the same time, experimental archaeology helps to bring the past to life for the public in an extremely vivid way, with permanent reconstructed prehistoric "villages," whose buildings are experiments in themselves.

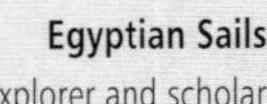

Egyptian Sails
The Norwegian explorer and scholar Thor Heyerdahl built *Ra II,* a replica of an ancient Egyptian papyrus boat, to prove that such vessels were seaworthy enough to have sailed along Atlantic Ocean currents from Africa to the east coast of Mexico.

Remains of Religion

Neolithic Grave Good
At Vinca near Belgrade, Serbia, a Neolithic burial mound (c. 4500–3000 BC) contained this figurine in the form of a cross. Presumably it is some sort of votive figure.

Humans have practiced some kind of religion for thousands of years. Archaeology can uncover the traces of these practices, providing an insight into what people of the past believed.

Religion and ritual have been prevalent in human society for at least 50,000 years, as shown by the deliberate and sometimes elaborate burials of Neanderthals (see p. 137) and modern humans. Ice Age cave art (see p. 144) also provides evidence of religious feeling. Some of it was hidden away in dark depths or inaccessible niches, and often the artists simply made the images and never returned, which suggests that the art was produced for, and perhaps offered to, some kind of deity or spirit. Archaeologists have even found decorated caves containing special objects that are thought to be votive offerings.

ICONOGRAPHY

Where no written records exist, it is very hard to understand the art of early cultures—for instance, how much ancient Greek art could we understand without our written knowledge of Greek mythology? But in many cases—such as statues in what seem to be shrines, or images of fantastic beings—the content and context of ancient art indicate that some kind of deity or mythology is involved.

MONUMENTS

In later periods, the recognizable remains of religion can be divided into three categories: surviving religious buildings, such as temples and churches; tombs and iconography; and the traces of what seem to be ritual activities, such as offerings, sacrifices, and cult objects. With the rise of

Temple Complex
Where written records exist, the religious purpose of monuments can be more easily ascertained. At Baalbek, a massive Roman temple complex in the Biqa'a Valley of Lebanon, temples are devoted to the cult of a triad of divinities—Jupiter, Venus, and Mercury—as well as Bacchus, as shown here.

agriculture and the growth of larger, more sedentary settlements, evidence for an institutionalized priesthood emerges and the first monumental temples, including ziggurats, pyramids, and stone circles, appear. The scale of these constructions and the labor they required reflect the power of the religious beliefs and institutions that lay behind them.

BURIALS

The very act of burial often denotes some kind of belief in an afterlife, and this is enhanced when objects, particularly valuables, and foods are placed with the dead for use in the next world. In extreme cases—such as the lavish royal burials of Egypt, China, Ur, and Peru—servants or retainers, sometimes hundreds of them, have also been sacrificed so they could continue to serve their employers in the afterlife.

NATURAL SITES

Many ritual sites were natural features that people found awe inspiring or mysterious. Examples include rock-shelters with echoes; sacred pools or lakes, such as the Maya's Cenote (Well of Sacrifice) at Chichén Itzá, into which all kinds of objects, together with human sacrifices, were thrown as offerings; Lake Guatavita in Colombia, into which numerous gold objects were tossed; and the high Andean peaks where children were taken and killed, to be left as sacrifices to the gods.

Some of the bog bodies discovered in northern Europe are considered to be human sacrifices, since they seem to have been ritually killed before being deposited in the bogs. Many other finds from the waters of Iron Age Europe—shields, armor, weapons, boats—are probably also offerings to the gods.

Carved Buddha
The Colossal Buddha in the Yungang Caves, Datong, China, has been dated to c. AD 460–494, making it the oldest known example of Buddhist rock carving.

The Art of the Past

Status Symbol
Art can be an indication of wealth and power: opulent mosaics decorate the huge villa built by the emperor Hadrian in AD 125–34 at Tivoli near Rome.

Ancient Tradition
Aboriginal cave paintings at Kakadu National Park, Australia, belong to the world's oldest continuous art tradition, which dates back at least 40,000 years. These examples were painted in the 1950s.

Art is something that exists in every present-day human society and that seems to have existed in every ancient one, too, back to at least 40,000 years ago, and probably beyond.

Because it encompasses such a vast variety of activities and products, art is notoriously difficult to define. Furthermore, in many cultures it is not seen as a distinct entity, but simply as an inherent aspect of normal social or religious life, with no clear boundaries between the aesthetic and the practical. For example, in most Australian Aboriginal cultures, there is no word for "art" as such, and all their aesthetic manifestations—paintings, carvings, musical instruments, song, dance—are simply considered extensions of the cultural and natural environment. For archaeological purposes, however, the best approach is probably to see "art" as a deliberate visual communication, a message expressed in durable form.

ART ON THE ROCKS

Rock art—paintings and engravings on rocks, shelters, and cave walls—exists in virtually every country in the world, and extends back to at least 40,000 years ago in some areas. One of those

THE EARLIEST ART
Dated to at least 230,000 years ago, a pebble of volcanic rock found at Berekhat Ram in Israel may be the earliest known art object. The pebble's natural shape resembles a woman, but grooves have been added to create the neck and arms.

areas is Australia, where some Aboriginal groups still produce rock art today, making it the world's longest continuous art tradition. Rock images probably have innumerable functions, serving as narratives, territorial boundaries, memory triggers, myths, rites of passage, and tribal secrets and laws, and fulfilling many other religious and secular roles. Portable art also extends far back. In Australia, for example, the Mandu Mandu Creek necklace of perforated shells is about 32,000 years old.

DECORATION

Art has had a huge role in archaeology. Ceramics and metalwork, which dominate the archaeological record of many cultures, have been classified according to their shapes and decorative motifs. The concept of style helps to differentiate the products of periods and areas, since artifacts and decoration are often produced in distinctive ways that are shared by a community or culture. Lapita pottery, for example, helped to reveal the colonization pattern of the Pacific islands.

Religion and Art

Art was often used to glorify the gods of the ancient world. This statue of the Greek god of the sea, Poseidon, is dated c. 450 BC and was possibly created by Kalamis.

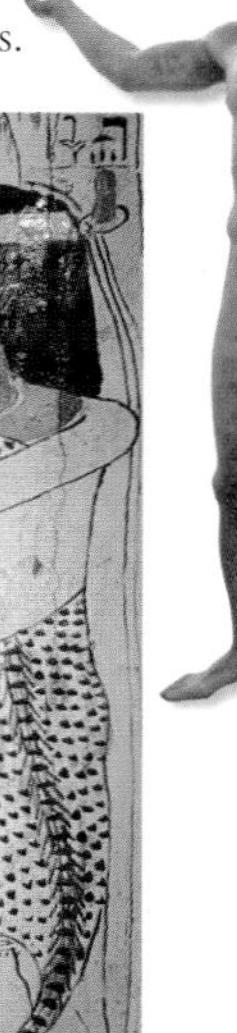

CONVENTIONS OF REPRESENTATION

All art styles employ conventions, especially regarding depiction—the representation of beings or objects in the real world. For example, the ancient Egyptians (above) drew humans with the head in profile, but the eye seen full-face; the shoulders were shown full-width from the front, but the rest of the body was in profile. The major personage—usually the pharaoh or tomb-owner—was drawn bigger than the other figures, which were often arranged in horizontal rows, set one above the next. Similar sets of conventions are known in every corpus of ancient art, from Ice Age art, which shows mostly adult animals drawn in profile with no ground lines and few scenes, to recent art in every part of the world.

The Earliest Astronomers

Intricate Calendar

The most complex and accurate of the world's ancient calendars is that devised by the Maya and later adopted by the Aztecs, which combines a ritual cycle of 260 days with the solar year of 365 days. This reconstruction of an Aztec calendar stone (below) features the face of the sun god, Tonatiuh, in its center.

Ways of reckoning the passing of time and observation of the heavenly bodies have always been of paramount importance to humankind. A whole sub-discipline of archaeology, known as archaeoastronomy, has arisen to focus on studies of this phenomenon, encompassing artistic representations and early written accounts, as well as the purposeful orientation or alignment of a range of archaeological features. There are many potential pitfalls, with some specialists exaggerating the sophistication of early peoples or the accuracy of their measurements, so it is safest to concentrate on examples where an archaeoastronomical interpretation is definite or highly probable.

Astronomical Alignment
Some have speculated that the megalithic monument of Stonehenge, on England's Salisbury Plain (above), may have served as an early calendar. During the summer solstice, the sun rises directly over the prominent Heel Stone, shining down the axis of the site.

Maya Skywatchers
Maya astronomer-priests traced the complex motions of the sun, the stars, and the planets, recording their observations in pictorial manuscripts known as codices. Many Maya temples are aligned with the sun or stars and may have served as observatories.

Scripts and Texts

Cuneiform Tablet
The Mesopotamians usually wrote with a stylus on clay tablets. Their cuneiform ("wedge-shaped") script was invented by the Sumerians, but was later used for many of the languages of the region.

Egyptian Hieroglyphs
The hieroglyphs used in Egyptian texts, such as the *Book of the Dead* (below), are a form of pictorial writing. The symbols sometimes represent the objects they depict, but more often stand for particular sounds.

Texts may seem to explain literate past cultures, but they tend to reflect the history of the powerful. Archaeology remains indispensable to understanding the broader society.

Many writings of some ancient civilizations, such as those of the Greeks and Romans, have long been available to historians, but for other cultures, key texts continue to be discovered during archaeological digs. In some cases, a particular archaeological find has allowed the decipherment of a script—the Rosetta Stone, for example, allowed scholars finally to understand the Egyptian hieroglyphic script (see p. 254).

THE DEVELOPMENT OF WRITING

The first writing systems developed in different places at different times—in Mesopotamia and Egypt around 3400 BC, in China around 1600 BC, in Mesoamerica around 500 BC—and writing subsequently spread to other regions of the world at an uneven pace.

Ancient civilizations used writing to record many different things: the glorious deeds of kings; the proper rituals for gods; myths and stories; transactions of government institutions and private individuals; provisions and procedures of legal systems; technicalities of sciences and medicine; and so forth.

Writing opens windows to many aspects of ancient societies that archaeology is simply incapable of tackling, and the history recorded in texts would seem to make much archaeological research redundant. Appearances can, however, be deceiving.

THE STORY OF LINEAR B

Michael Ventris's decipherment of Linear B in 1952 demonstrated that the Mycenaean inhabitants of Bronze Age Greece spoke an early form of ancient Greek. These archives give us an insight into the social, economic, and religious organization of Late Bronze Age Greece.

Linear B was discovered by Arthur Evans during his excavations at Knossos (see p. 292). It was one of three scripts used in the Aegean during the 2nd millennium BC. The other two scripts—Hieroglyphics and Linear A—involved a non-Indo-European language and continue to defy attempts at decryption. Linear B was developed later, probably at some time in the 14th or 13th century BC.

The main Linear B archives are from Pylos and Knossos, but Linear B documents have also been found at other important Mycenaean centers. The archives were written on tablets of unbaked clay (left), which survive only because they were burned in the massive conflagrations that destroyed the centers of Bronze Age Greece. These were temporary archives and were probably transferred onto a perishable medium. The script is syllabic, with individual signs representing the value of a syllable, and has a number of pictograms, such as a sign for wheat. Linear B inscriptions are also found on pottery and seal impressions. Most of the tablets are economic documents, but there are also a number of religious texts—some of which mention gods that in later periods were numbered among the Olympian deities.

Maya Hieroglyphs
Maya writing contains about 800 known hieroglyphs. The earliest examples were carved into stone, such as this stela from Tikal, Guatemala, but Maya writing is also found on murals, pottery, and bark-paper books.

ARCHAEOLOGY AND TEXTS

Until the advent of widespread literacy—a comparatively recent and incomplete development—scribes wrote for the elites in society. Consequently, texts reflect the activities and attitudes of the socially powerful, and archaeology remains the only means of understanding the lives of the silent majority.

Moreover, ancient texts require interpretation. Even with hypothetically perfect command of grammar and vocabulary, scholars may still not understand the meaning and intent of a text. Ancient authors composed within alien cultural and institutional contexts, and modern readers must struggle to conjecture those contexts in order to understand the texts. Even a pragmatic bureaucratic report often leaves unclear the practices it reports, and historical annals often follow a theological framework (as in the Bible's Old Testament). So while texts do expand the questions that scholars can profitably ask, they cannot replace archaeology and they give their answers no more easily than archaeology does.

Symbols of Power

Aztec Mask
A mosaic of turquoise and shell decorates this Aztec mask, which represents the god Quetzalcoatl. On the death of a king, the Aztecs placed masks over effigies of the gods and on the deceased for burial.

Power and prestige have been expressed in many different ways, with lavish graves, the use of precious materials, and the creation of giant statues being among the most obvious signs.

The last Ice Age is generally reckoned to have been a fairly egalitarian period of simple hunter-gatherers, yet they not only produced some fantastic stone tools and portable carvings, many of which were probably prestige objects for display, but also sometimes buried their dead with huge amounts of finery.

Two children buried at Sungir, Russia, 23,000 years ago were each accompanied by thousands of beads of mammoth ivory, which were probably sewn on their clothing and represented thousands of hours of work. In view of the young age of the deceased, such "wealth" cannot have been acquired and therefore must have been inherited.

PRECIOUS MATERIALS

From the earliest times, humans have devoted a great deal of effort to acquiring and working scarce or striking materials that were of little practical use, but that were prized for their aesthetic or other qualities. Such precious materials have included colored flints; hard stones; hard woods; colorful feathers, fossils, and shells; amber, ivory, jade, and turquoise; and, of

Scythian Gold
The Scythian chiefs who ruled the Russian steppes during the 5th to 3rd centuries BC were buried with finely worked gold artifacts. This gold plaque, found in a 4th century BC barrow at Kul-Oba, shows a Scythian horseman brandishing a spear.

course, the precious metals, especially gold and silver, as well as copper, bronze, and iron. All of these materials have been found in the archaeological record, often as splendidly worked artifacts preserved in burials or in caches, and clearly represent examples of ornaments, ritual objects, or prestige items of different kinds. Such "valuables" constitute an important feature of past societies as indicators of wealth and status. Little has changed, and our own modern culture still attaches astonishing importance to essentially pointless items such as diamonds or designer labels.

LAVISH BURIALS

The ultimate—in every sense—expression of power, status, and wealth lay in the lavishness of the burial. Many of the most famous finds in the history of archaeology are the incredibly rich burials of the rulers of Egypt, Ur, China, Peru, and elsewhere. It boggles the mind that Tutankhamen, for example, was a young and relatively insignificant pharaoh. In view of the array of treasures buried with him, one wonders what the grave goods accompanying the really great pharaohs must have been like. Unfortunately, they were all plundered long ago, because even the most powerful despots become vulnerable in death, and the knowledge of the great wealth being "uselessly" buried with the powerful has always acted as a magnet to unscrupulous thieves. Power and prestige count for little after death.

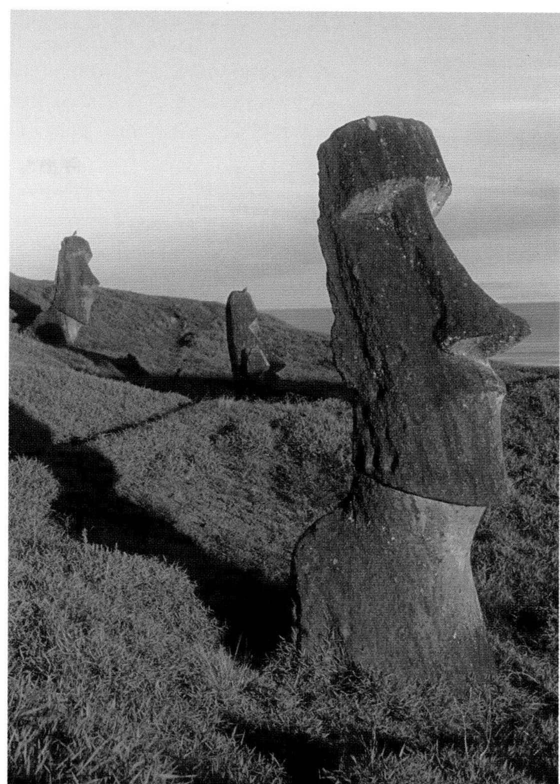

GIANT STATUES

A practice that goes at least as far back as the Egyptians and Assyrians, the production of greater-than-life-size images of rulers and other notables served to impress their importance and power upon their subjects and political rivals. The sheer effort and labor force that were needed to quarry, carve, transport, and erect such monuments to egomania were as colossal as the statues themselves, and again underlined the power wielded by these individuals. In some cases, power was likewise expressed by the construction of great buildings or nonfigurative monuments, such as the obelisks of Egypt. On Easter Island, however, the giant statues (above) seem to have depicted not rulers, but rather ancestor figures who watched over the islanders, so they probably represented the power and status of a village community rather than of an individual ruler (see p. 378).

Settlement Patterns

A Recorded Pattern
Complex states often leave behind written bureaucratic records, making it much easier to assess their social organization. The cuneiform inscriptions of the Sumerians (above) detail fields and crops, major projects, and craftspeople.

To understand the economic and social organization of prehistoric societies, archaeologists study the distribution of settlements and how they relate to their environment.

In the past 50 years, settlement pattern studies have provided some of the most important analytical discoveries in archaeology. They have also played a key role in moving the discipline of archaeology from one preoccupied largely with antiquities and their classification to one concerned with the reconstruction of earlier societies.

CHOOSING A LOCATION

The decision about where to locate its settlements is one of the most fundamental choices that a society can make. It represents the relationships among consumers, producers, resources, and capital, and it governs the competitive and cooperative relationships among communities. The patterning of settlements reflects the degree to which communities were—or were not—in contact with one another. It may be the product of people choosing optimal locations with a specific feature, such as proximity to resources or security, or it may result from a compromise among various factors. In a mobile society with short-term settlements, how the settlements are arranged often reflects seasonal behavior or specific tasks. In sedentary societies, permanent settlements involve considerable investment of time and energy in a particular location, so the locations of settlements can reflect longer-term characteristics of the society.

THE STUDY OF SETTLEMENT PATTERNS

Settlement pattern studies grew from the ethnographic research of Julian Steward during the 1930s on groups such as the Owens Valley Paiute in the southwestern United States and from the work of geographers such as Cyril Fox in England. After the Second World War, the first substantial application of settlement pattern analysis in archaeology occurred with the work of Gordon R. Willey and his collaborators in the Viru Valley in Peru. Over the following two decades, an increasing number of archaeologists pursued settlement studies in many parts of the world. By the 1970s, this analytical technique

Zooming In
Chaco Canyon (top right), located in New Mexico, contains the ruins of several major pre-Columbian Indian settlements and many smaller archeaological sites. Pueblo Bonito (center right) is the most thoroughly excavated site in the canyon. The settlement dates from the 10th century and features detailed masonry such as this Kiva (bottom right).

EGALITARIAN BURIALS

Even when little evidence of a society's settlements survives, monuments can provide some insights. The communal burial mounds of Neolithic Britain seem to have served egalitarian societies. The landscape is divided into roughly equal territories by imaginary lines halfway between the mounds, suggesting that each mound was used by the surrounding farming community.

was familiar to almost every archaeologist and had begun to produce important insights into prehistoric society. At the same time, it required archaeologists to examine the regions they studied very systematically to obtain a representative sample of settlements. This led to a general improvement in survey methods and sampling techniques.

UNDERSTANDING SUBSISTENCE

Archaeologists often analyze settlement patterns to help them understand subsistence. They map a settlement's natural setting and the resources it would have provided. Seeds and bones from the settlement can indicate diet and seasonality, while evidence of permanent dwellings may provide clues to how long the settlement was occupied. When these data are combined, it may be possible to reconstruct the annual movements of a group of prehistoric foragers or to trace changes in an agricultural system.

For example, almost all the earliest farming sites in central Europe around 5500 BC are clustered in the valleys of small streams. Most are found on the floodplain but set back from the stream. This pattern occurs consistently in many regions, suggesting the practice of relatively intensive horticulture in small plots close to the settlements. About 1,500 years later, the pattern shifted to one of dispersed settlement on the higher ground, which probably represents a change in the agricultural system, with more extensive land clearance for larger fields and pastures.

CLASSIFYING SOCIETIES

Another important contribution of settlement pattern analysis has been in the study of prehistoric social and political organization. Archaeologists have many ways to classify prehistoric societies, but their categories are only approximate. One common scheme is that proposed by Elman Service, who divided societies into four groups: bands, tribes, chiefdoms, and states (see box, below). Some have argued that the term "tribe" is too imprecise and instead use the term "segmentary society." Service's scheme takes into account the relative scale of the various social groupings and also the degree of political centralization and hierarchy they exhibit. Bands and segmentary societies are relatively egalitarian and non-hierarchical, while chiefdoms and states exhibit different levels of status, power, and wealth.

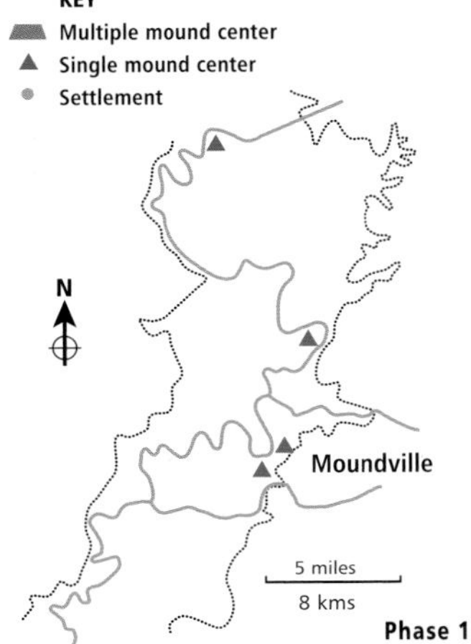

Changing Patterns
Moundville developed from being a simple site with a single mound in Phase 1 (AD 1050–1250), through its growth as a regional center in Phase 2, to its peak as a great ceremonial center in Phase 3 (14th–15th centuries AD). It then declined, and was no longer a significant site in Phase 4 (after 1550).

PREHISTORIC CHIEFDOMS

Our understanding of prehistoric chiefdoms has particularly benefited from the study of their settlement patterns. A fundamental assumption is that variation in size reflects the relative importance of settlements, with the large settlements being the seats

TYPES OF SETTLEMENT

Archaeologists often classify settlements into four broad categories: bands, segmentary societies, chiefdoms, and states.

BANDS

Bands are small societies of hunter-gatherers, usually with fewer than 100 people. Their sites tend to be seasonal camps or areas associated with particular activities, such as butchery or toolmaking.

SEGMENTARY SOCIETIES

Also known as tribes, these tend to be settled farming or mobile pastoralist societies, with up to a few thousand people. Their sites usually comprise villages that are of similar size and fairly evenly spaced, so that no single settlement appears to dominate.

CHIEFDOMS

Chiefdoms generally involve between 5,000 and 20,000 people, with prestige determined by the relationship to the chief. Chiefs are usually buried with rich grave goods. The settlement pattern tends to exhibit a center of power with temples, wealthy houses, and craft specialists.

STATES

States, such as that of the Maya (right), feature a ruler who can make laws and enforce them with an army; the division of society into classes; and a bureaucracy to collect and redistribute taxes.

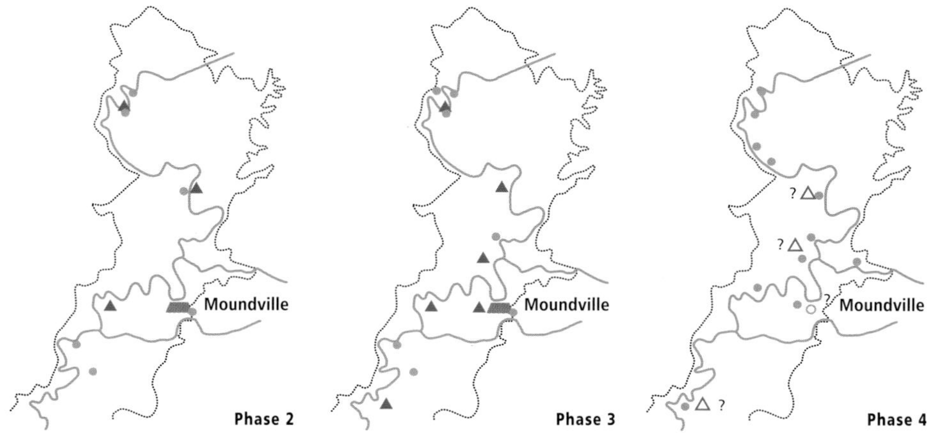

of power and status. Thus archaeologists will conclude that a society in which one settlement is decidedly larger than all the others was a simple chiefdom, while one with a large central settlement, several smaller but still substantial settlements, and many outlying small settlements may have had multiple levels of administration and hierarchy. If large settlements have different or more elaborate architecture and fortifications, or are divided into specific precincts, then archaeologists can be more certain that they represent centers of economic and political power.

Along the Black Warrior River in Alabama, for example, the site of Moundville is substantially larger than neighboring sites, has many large mounds and plazas, and was surrounded by a palisade with bastions. While some nearby sites also have mounds, they are smaller and less elaborate than at Moundville. On the basis of this pattern, archaeologists have interpreted the society that occupied the Black Warrior Valley between AD 1000 and 1500 as a complex chiefdom, in which Moundville was the seat of the paramount chief, while lower-level chiefs occupied the smaller mound sites. Most of the common population, however, lived in dispersed farmsteads and hamlets.

Understanding Change

Changing Tools
Change is marked in the archaeological record by the appearance of new technologies, such as this Neolithic hammerhead.

The Shift to Farming
One of the major changes throughout most of the world was the shift from hunting-gathering to agriculture (right). Today, only isolated groups of hunter-gatherers exist.

Archaeology seeks to understand why ancient cultures changed through time, whether the shift is from hunting and gathering to agriculture or simply involves the adoption of a new technology.

In the 19th century, Lewis Henry Morgan and other anthropologists adapted Darwin's theory of evolution. Morgan's unilinear model of human evolution posited a universal trend from savagery (hunting and gathering) to barbarism (agriculture) to civilization (cities and states). His model was fodder for those who believed that Western civilization, as the apex of human culture, had a "natural" right to "convert" inferior societies. By the early 20th century, such models had been replaced by a more tolerant attitude to "the other."

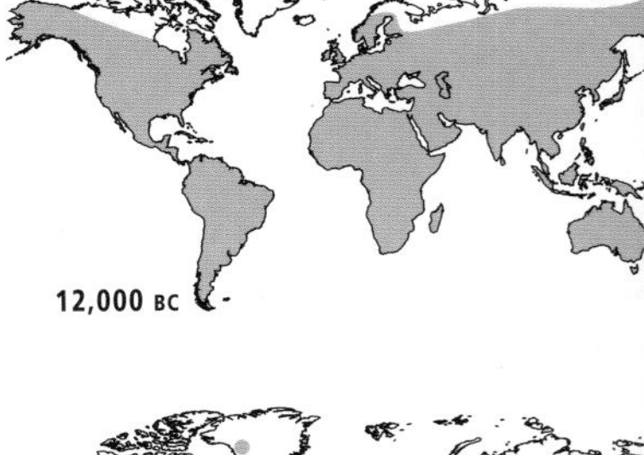

REVOLUTIONS

In the first years of the 20th century, archaeology was concerned with organizing the events of the archaeological past into a chronological order. Change was seen as the result of such factors as diffusion (the transmission of ideas from one society to another) or actual migrations of people. The studies of the Australian archaeologist, V. Gordon Childe, are excellent examples of this type of explanation (see box, above right). Childe proposed the term "revolutions" for some of the major changes in human evolution, such as the rise of agriculture and the appearance of cities. These revolutions initiated a more efficient technology and a huge increase in population levels.

The hydraulic theory, proposed by Karl Wittfogel and others, saw

A REVOLUTIONARY ARCHAEOLOGIST

One of the 20th century's most influential archaeologists, Vere Gordon Childe (1892–1957) concerned himself with big questions. He proposed that a "Neolithic revolution" led to agriculture, and an "urban revolution" led to the rise of cities and states. He also believed that diffusion—contacts with other cultures—was the engine of prehistoric social change. Childe is well known for his excavation of Skara Brae in Orkney (see p.282), though his scholarly and popular writing was in fact much more prolific than his fieldwork.

Born in Sydney, Australia, Childe lived in Britain throughout his long career, becoming professor of prehistoric archaeology at the University of Edinburgh, a position he held from 1927 to 1946, and then director of London University's Institute of Archaeology until 1956. He returned to Australia on retirement, but soon after threw himself off a cliff. His suicide note explained that he did not want to become a burden on society in old age.

the control of water and its distribution as the primary agent for the development of centralized and bureaucratic ancient states, such as Egypt.

THE ROLE OF THE ENVIRONMENT

After the Second World War, archaeologists increasingly saw the environment as a prime mover in cultural change. In the United States, Julian Steward promoted cultural ecology—the study of the interaction of human societies with their surrounding environment. Grahame Clark's excavations at the Mesolithic site of Star Carr in Yorkshire, England, were the culmination of a long tradition of viewing the natural environment as the necessary backdrop to understanding cultural change.

PROCESSES OF CHANGE

The development of processual archaeology in the 1960s and 1970s saw human societies as systems of energy transfer. Studying the processes of change would allow archaeologists to develop scientifically valid models for why cultures changed through time.

Recent developments—such as the rise of a postprocessual archaeology—see a changing environment only as a precondition to cultural change. Post-processualists argue that specific cultural changes are the result of internal social dynamics, such as power politics or shifting gender and class relationships.

Sudden Change
A cataclysmic change is sometimes evident in the archaeological past. This concrete cast (far left) represents a body buried at Pompeii by the eruption of Mount Vesuvius in AD 79.

The Ages of Humankind

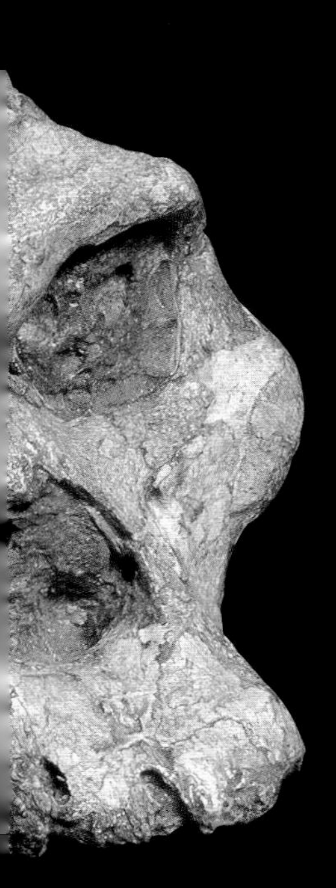

128 Prehistoric Times

Before the invention of writing, the past is revealed to us only through the archaeological evidence. The careful analysis of bones, soil, artifacts, and early dwellings has allowed archaeologists to piece together the first several million years of human existence.

156 The Historical Past

Even when a society has left behind historical records, archaeology can help with their interpretation and fill in the gaps, often providing the only glimpse into the lives of ordinary people.

Prehistoric Times

The story of humankind begins several million years ago, with the appearance of the first upright-walking hominids. Over time, modern humans evolved and gradually spread throughout the world. With the adoption of agriculture, settled communities developed and prepared the way for the emergence of the great civilizations.

"In this study these beings who are no more, their superimposed traces, a sort of scale of passing days, will be our historical tablets, because the dust of ages can hardly be improvised and the colour of the centuries is inimitable."

Jacques Boucher de Perthes (1788–1868),
French amateur archaeologist

Human Evolution

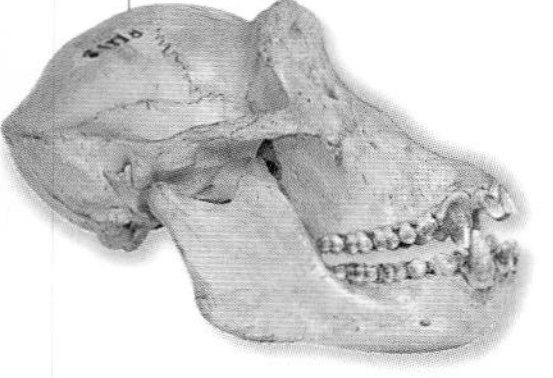

Changing Jawbone
The evolution of the human jawbone is shown in this comparison of the jawbones from a chimpanzee (top), an australopithecine, *Australopithecus afarensis* (middle), and a modern human, *Homo sapiens* (bottom).

After evolving from an African apelike ancestor several million years ago, humans spread throughout the world to become the dominant creature on the planet today.

Humans are closely related genetically to African apes, with whom we share an ancestor, and are grouped with apes and monkeys in the biological order known as primates. The first primates appeared about 65 million years ago, following the extinction of the dinosaurs.

THE HOMINID FAMILY

Sometime between 8 million and 6 million years ago, early members of a family of upright-walking creatures referred to as Hominidae, or hominids—to which the immediate ancestors of humans as well as modern humans belong—branched off from the ape line. This happened in Africa, the only place where fossils of early hominids have been found. Part of the hominid family comprises a biological tribe known as the Hominini, or hominins, of which there is only one species surviving today—modern humans, or *Homo sapiens* (Latin for "wise man"). All other hominids are extinct.

Unlike our primate relatives, modern humans have little body hair. We walk on two limbs and have evolved a specialized skeleton and muscles to accommodate this rather inefficient way of getting about. Our brains are large and complex, while our hands allow a precision grip as well as finely controlled movements. Like other primates, we live in social groups, but we can communicate more effectively

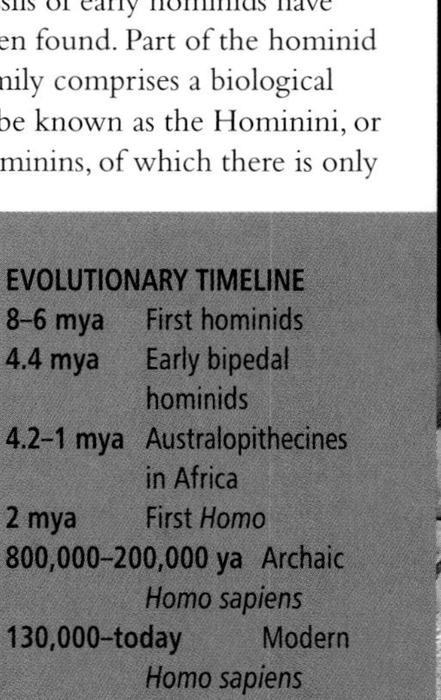

EVOLUTIONARY TIMELINE

8–6 mya	First hominids
4.4 mya	Early bipedal hominids
4.2–1 mya	Australopithecines in Africa
2 mya	First *Homo*
800,000–200,000 ya	Archaic *Homo sapiens*
130,000–today	Modern *Homo sapiens*

through the use of spoken and written language as well as symbolism and abstract ideas. We not only use but make tools habitually—our technology allows us to exist in a wide variety of habitats and even provides us with the means to destroy our own world.

Qafzeh
Skhul
Bahr El Ghazal
Hadar
Aramis
Gona
Nariokotome
Olduvai Gorge
Laetoli
Sterkfontein
Kromdraai
Swartkrans
Makapansgat
Taung
Klasies River Mouth

IN THE BEGINNING

Early hominids were probably quite rare creatures compared to other African animals. As they did not deliberately bury their dead, the chances are slim that their remains would be covered over quickly enough to become fossils before being destroyed by other animals or by nature. The consequent rarity and fragmentary nature of early hominid remains sometimes fuels passionate scientific debates, but enough pieces of the puzzle have been assembled for the broad outlines of the story of human evolution to be told.

The first steps on the journey toward humanity are thought to have been taken when hominids began walking on two legs (a theory supported by the fossil footprints at Laetoli, left). In addition to providing a better view of potential predators and meals, this would have freed their forelimbs to carry young and food and to use tools.

The oldest known remains of bipedal hominids may be the bones of a 4.4-million-year-old apelike creature from Aramis in Ethiopia, named *Ardipithecus ramidus* (*ardi* means "ground" or "floor" and *ramid* means "root" in the Afar language of Ethiopia, while *pithecus* is Greek for "ape"). Some researchers claim that this ardipithecine may be the founder of the human lineage.

First Footprints
In 1978–79 Mary Leakey and her team excavated the fossils of footprints made by at least two australopithecines at Laetoli, Tanzania (see p. 230). Dated to 3.6 million years ago, the trail confirmed that walking upright on two legs was the key development in human evolution.

Mrs Ples

This fossil skull belonged to *Australopithecus africanus,* a gracile australopithecine. It was found by Robert Broom in a limestone cave at Sterkfontein, South Africa, in 1947. Broom named it *Plesianthropus transvaalensis,* which led to its nickname of "Mrs Ples."

THE AUSTRALOPITHECINES

In the period between 4.2 million and 1 million years ago, several different kinds of African apelike creatures, all probably dark-skinned and hairy, strode on two limbs, only slightly differently from a modern bipedal gait. Their tongue-twisting name, australopithecines, was coined by Raymond Dart in 1925, when he called the first early African hominid to be discovered, a young child's fossil from Taung in South Africa, *Australopithecus africanus,* which is Latin/Greek for "southern ape of Africa" (see p. 234).

Apart from a few discoveries made in Chad in northeastern Africa, australopithecines have been found only in southern and eastern Africa, and became extinct some 1 million years ago. It is thought that some of the lightly built, or gracile, species of these creatures were human ancestors, while their more robust relatives became evolutionary dead-ends on the human family tree. Australopithecines probably used leaves and twigs as tools, like modern chimpanzees in the wild do. The oldest known stone tools date to the time when

RECENT DISCOVERIES

A 3.5 million-year-old partial skull of *Kenyanthropus platyops* (meaning "flat face"), found at Lomekwi in northern Kenya in 1999, indicates that australopithecines were not the only hominids present in Africa at this time. Also, six-million-year-old fossil bones discovered in 2000 in Kenya, named *Orrorin tugenensis,* are claimed to represent the oldest known hominid.

Upright Lucy

In 1974 the partial skeleton of a new early hominid species was found at Hadar, Ethiopia (see p. 232). Nicknamed "Lucy" and assigned the scientific name of *Australopithecus afarensis,* the skeleton has been dated to 3.18 million years ago. There is no doubt that "Lucy" walked upright, but she did not have the long legs of modern humans.

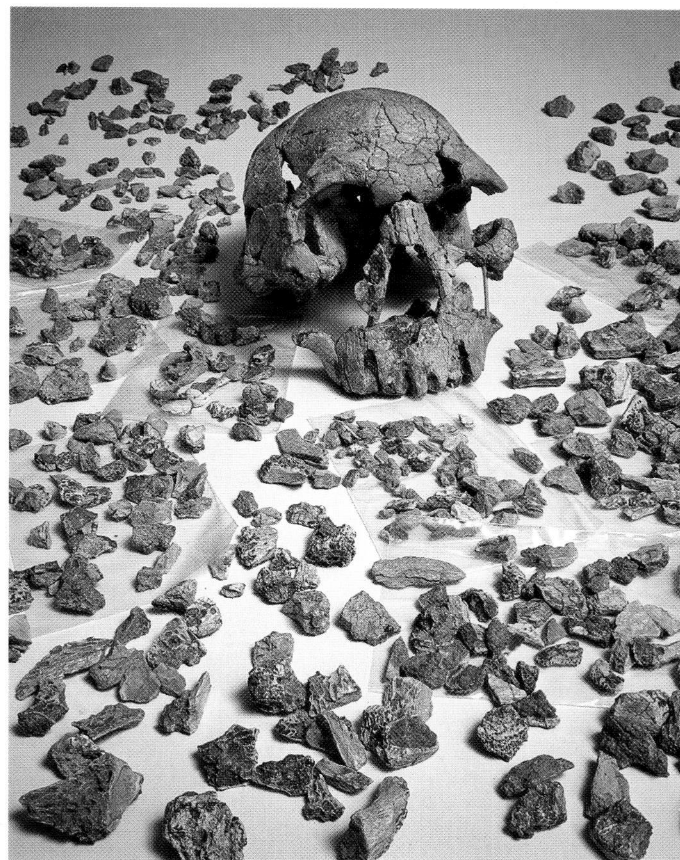

The Handyman
This hominid fossil skull and fragments probably belonged to *Homo habilis*. Despite its general resemblance to an australopithecine skull, its features are more "advanced" in the human direction.

australopithecines existed, and their hands were equal to the task of chipping simple stone implements, but it is not known whether they made such tools regularly or at all.

THE FIRST OF OUR KIND

Scientists think that hominins belonging to our genus, *Homo,* evolved in Africa shortly before 2 million years ago, at a time when australopithecines still roamed about. In comparison with australopithecines, early *Homo* had a larger brain, a skeleton designed for more efficient two-legged walking, smaller jaws and teeth, and an increasing reliance on technology and culture.

Several different kinds of early *Homo* have been named, famously including *Homo habilis* ("the handyman"), who is credited with making simple stone tools at Olduvai Gorge in Tanzania between 1.9 million and 1.6 million years ago (see p. 236). However, the guidelines for identifying particular fossils as belonging to *Homo* are the

THE BIRTH OF TECHNOLOGY

The earliest known stone tools are simple sharp cutting flakes chipped off a cobble (also known as a core or chopper) dated to between 2.6 million and 2.5 million years ago at Gona in Ethiopia. They belong to the Oldowan industry, named after Olduvai Gorge in Tanzania, where many such tools were first found.

About 1.6 million years ago, early humans began producing more complex tools by shaping both sides of a cobble or large flake to produce a double-sided tool, or biface, which was handheld and seems to have been used for a wide variety of tasks. Pointed bifaces are called handaxes (left), while those with a broad cutting edge are known as cleavers. They are characteristic of the Acheulian industry, which persisted until some 200,000 years ago and which is one of the longest-lasting technologies known.

Although tantalizing claims have been made for the mastery of fire by early hominids more than a million years ago, unquestionable hearths—for example, at shoreline campsites at Terra Amata, France—appear only after some 400,000–200,000 years ago.

subject of ongoing debate. Some claim that the oldest known *Homo* remains are a 2.3-million-year-old upper jaw and teeth from Hadar in Ethiopia, while others argue that the earliest species to satisfy the criteria is 1.9-million-year-old *Homo ergaster* ("the workman") from eastern Africa, also known as early African *Homo erectus* ("the upright man"), a name originally given to "Java Man" and "Peking Man"—the first early hominin fossils discovered in Asia. Early *Homo* fossils dating to 1.7 million years ago or earlier have been found in Asia, indicating that the larger brain and toolmaking know-how of the first humans enabled them to extend their range and make their first move out of their African homeland at this time.

SPECIES OR SUBSPECIES?
Some experts refer to modern humans as *Homo sapiens sapiens.* This implies that we are a subspecies of *Homo sapiens* and that there are other subspecies, such as the Neanderthals. Most believe, however, that the Neanderthals are a separate species.

THE EMERGENCE OF MODERN HUMANS

Hominid fossils dating to between some 800,000 and 200,000 years ago have been assigned to various species of "archaic" *Homo sapiens,* including *Homo antecessor,* which some view as the ancestor of both extinct Neanderthals and modern *Homo sapiens.*

The oldest known modern *Homo sapiens* remains date to between about 130,000 and 80,000 years ago and include fossils from Klasies River Mouth in South Africa (see p. 240), as well as Skhul and Qafzeh in

Israel. Some researchers argue that the existence of the oldest known modern human fossils in Africa and the Near East, as well as genetic studies, indicate that modern humans originated in an African "Garden of Eden" and then dispersed "Out of Africa." Others consider that modern humans evolved "multiregionally" in the many parts of Europe and Asia, which they colonized after hominids left Africa for the first time nearly 2 million years ago.

Although early modern *Homo sapiens* may have had modern-looking bones, it seems that fully modern behavior did not appear until about 40,000 years ago, when abundant evidence for art, ritual, and symbolism "explodes" into the archaeological record for the first time. Even then, humans continued to be the wandering hunter-gatherers that they had been for almost all of their history. Settled farming and urban communities, as well as metal and ceramic technologies, developed only during the last 10,000 years.

Qafzeh Skull
Among the earliest representatives of modern humans are the fossils found in Qafzeh, Israel (above). Originally thought to be Neanderthal remains, they have been dated to 91,000 years ago and are now definitely considered *Homo sapiens.*

Asian Findings
The famous Zhoukoudian Cave, outside Beijing, China, has yielded the remains of some 40 *Homo erectus* individuals (including "Peking Man") and more than 100,000 stone tools, making it one of the most important sites in the world.

The Neanderthal Enigma

Skull Comparison
A Neanderthal skull from La Ferrassie (left) is shown here beside the skull of a modern human found at Cro-Magnon. Neanderthal skulls are characterized by a receding forehead, a long, low braincase, and heavy brow ridges.

Since they were first recognized as a primitive form of human almost a century and a half ago, the Neanderthals have been a focus of debate and controversy.

Many paleoanthropologists view Neanderthals as a specialized evolutionary offshoot of the human genus (*Homo neanderthalensis*) who were eventually replaced by modern humans (*Homo sapiens*). Others argue that they were similar to modern humans and contributed to their genetic heritage.

A GRADUAL DEVELOPMENT

The trail of Neanderthal fossils reveals that they began evolving in western Europe roughly half a million years ago. Their characteristic skeletal features appeared gradually over a period of several hundred thousand years. Eventually, the distribution of Neanderthal remains extended across all of Europe and into the Near East and central Asia, perhaps reflecting an ability of the Neanderthals to adapt to a wider range of environments than their predecessors.

The Neanderthals were powerfully built people with thick bones and deep muscle attachments. They possessed a low flat skull with heavy brow ridges and a large brain, and their jaws and teeth were placed forward beneath a prominent nose. Their stocky physique and short limbs seem to have been especially well suited to cold climates. In recent studies, DNA extracted from Neanderthal fossils was shown to be significantly different from the DNA of living humans, which probably reflects their evolutionary history as a specialized northern offshoot of the genus *Homo*.

NEANDERTHAL TECHNOLOGY

The Neanderthals were skilled technicians in the making of stone tools, and in this respect were probably not far behind their modern successors. Pieces of rock were carefully shaped and hammered to produce flakes of predetermined size and form. The flakes were then retouched into various types of scrapers, knives, points, and other tools, and some of them were attached to wooden handles for added leverage and power. Wooden implements were also made, but few have been preserved.

In other respects, Neanderthal technology seems to have lagged behind that of modern humans. Neanderthal sites lack any evidence of the artificial shelters, small-mammal traps, throwing sticks, insulated clothing, and other technological innovations that are linked to the appearance of modern humans in Europe. On the other hand, the study of animal remains from their sites indicates that they were effective hunters of large mammals such as bison and red deer. The heavy meat diet may well have been a critical factor in their adaptation to cold environments, as it is among recent foraging peoples of the circumpolar regions.

THOUGHTS AND BELIEFS

The social and mental life of the Neanderthals remains an enigma. Although they certainly buried their dead, the motive for such behavior is unknown. A few Neanderthal sites have yielded simple ornaments and even possible art objects, but their interpretation is disputed. The almost complete absence of convincing evidence for the use of symbols may represent the greatest gulf between the Neanderthals and ourselves.

THE DISAPPEARANCE

Roughly 40,000 years ago, modern humans invaded Europe, and within 10 millennia, the Neanderthals had disappeared—probably out-competed for resources by the technologically superior people from Africa.

A Deliberate Burial

A skeleton discovered at Kebara Cave, Israel, provided definite evidence of a Neanderthal burial, since the grave pit must have been deliberately excavated. Speculation continues, however, as to whether such burials indicate a Neanderthal religion or belief in an afterlife.

Around the Campfire

In this artist's reconstruction, a Neanderthal hunter brings food to his family group. Originally seen as ancestors of modern humans, Neanderthals are now considered by many to be our cousins.

The Spread of Humans

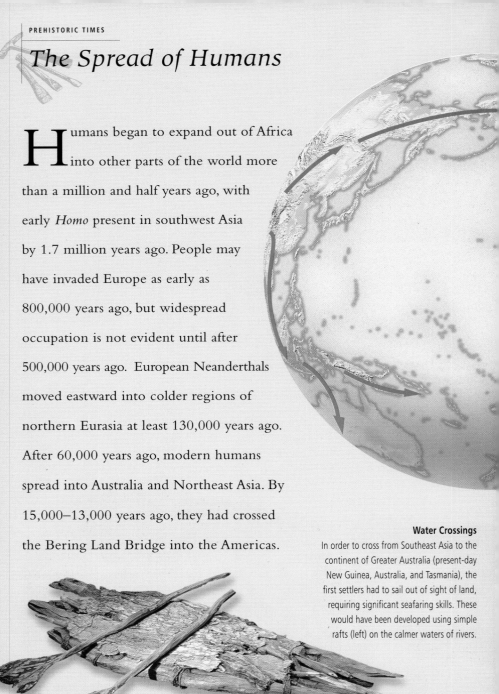

Humans began to expand out of Africa into other parts of the world more than a million and half years ago, with early *Homo* present in southwest Asia by 1.7 million years ago. People may have invaded Europe as early as 800,000 years ago, but widespread occupation is not evident until after 500,000 years ago. European Neanderthals moved eastward into colder regions of northern Eurasia at least 130,000 years ago. After 60,000 years ago, modern humans spread into Australia and Northeast Asia. By 15,000–13,000 years ago, they had crossed the Bering Land Bridge into the Americas.

Water Crossings
In order to cross from Southeast Asia to the continent of Greater Australia (present-day New Guinea, Australia, and Tasmania), the first settlers had to sail out of sight of land, requiring significant seafaring skills. These would have been developed using simple rafts (left) on the calmer waters of rivers.

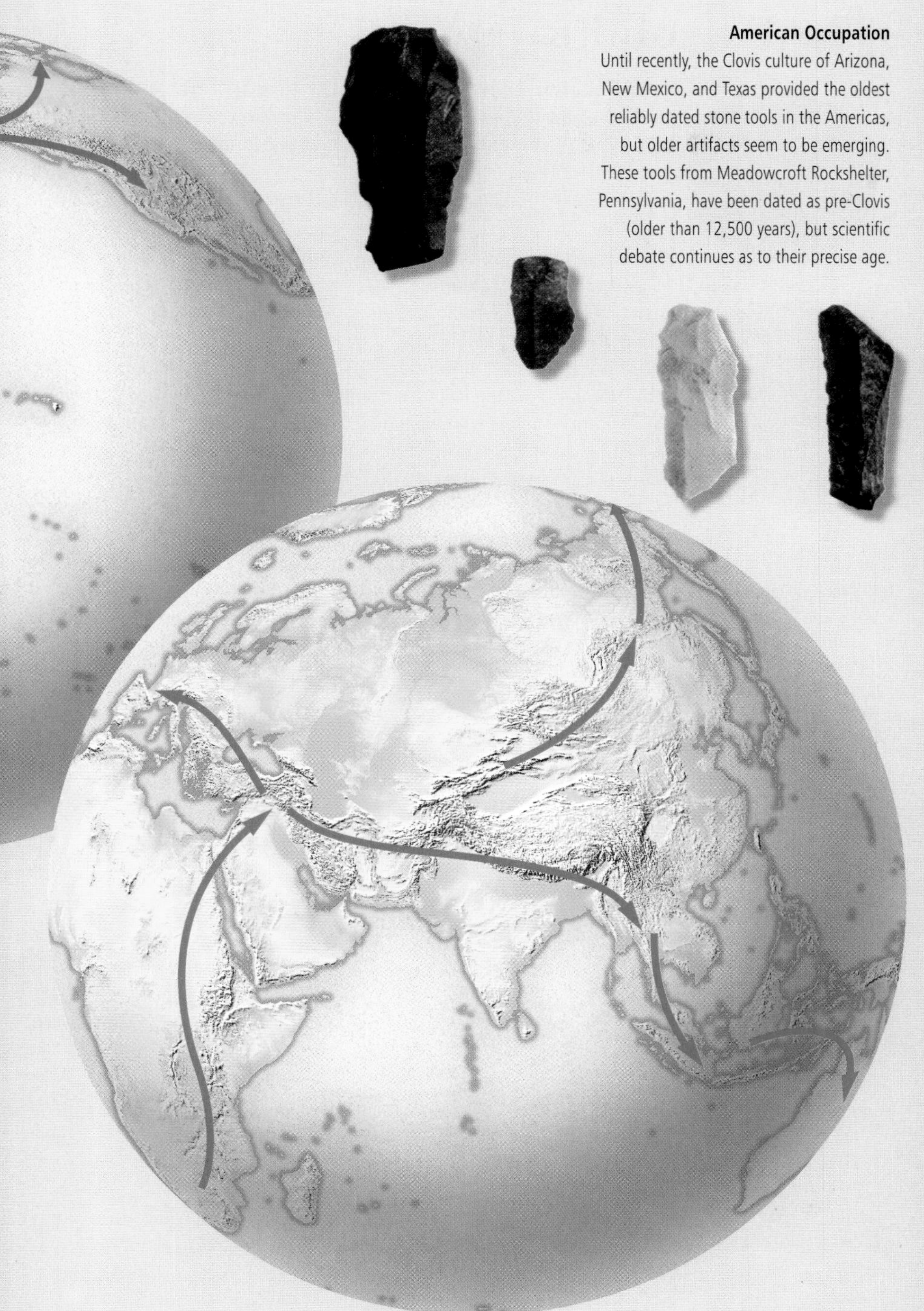

American Occupation

Until recently, the Clovis culture of Arizona, New Mexico, and Texas provided the oldest reliably dated stone tools in the Americas, but older artifacts seem to be emerging. These tools from Meadowcroft Rockshelter, Pennsylvania, have been dated as pre-Clovis (older than 12,500 years), but scientific debate continues as to their precise age.

The Paleolithic Age

The Paleolithic Age spans most of the time that humans have walked upon the earth, beginning 2.5 million years ago and lasting until the end of the Ice Age, roughly 10,000 years ago.

Oldowan Chopper
As well as small flakes of stone, Oldowan tools include large cores, or choppers (above).

The term *Paleolithic* was introduced by the British prehistorian John Lubbock in 1865, and is derived from the ancient Greek for "Old Stone." Generally characterized by the use of stone tools and a hunting-gathering lifestyle, the Paleolithic, or Old Stone, Age was subsequently divided into lower, middle, and upper stages that correspond broadly with major phases in human evolution.

The First Toolmakers
More than 2 million years ago, early *Homo* began making stone tools from pebbles collected from riverbeds. Their chopping-tool technique is known as the Oldowan industry.

THE OLDOWAN INDUSTRY

The oldest widely recognized Lower Paleolithic remains are found at African sites occupied approximately 2.5 million to 1.6 million years ago by the earliest representatives of the genus *Homo*. These remains belong to the Oldowan industry—named for Olduvai Gorge in Tanzania, where they were first discovered by Louis and Mary Leakey (see p. 236). Artifacts of the Oldowan include crude pebble chopping tools and simple scrapers made from stone flakes. The Oldowan sites are located along the margins of ancient lakes and streams, and sometimes contain animal bones with traces of tool marks. However, the occupants of these sites probably subsisted primarily on a diet of collected plant foods, and the animal bones may simply represent occasional scavenging of carcasses. It remains unclear whether the Oldowan toolmakers had mastered the control of fire. Despite the simplicity of their technology, they had expanded out of Africa into southern Eurasia by 1.7 million years ago.

ACHEULEAN TIMES

After 1.6 million years ago, artifacts of the Lower Paleolithic Acheulean industry appear in Africa and parts of Eurasia. The Acheulean marked a significant advance in stone-tool technology, reflected in the widespread production of handaxes. These are large, symmetrically shaped implements, flaked on both sides, that require a sequence of stages for manufacture. Handaxes may have performed a variety of functions, which probably included dismembering large animal carcasses. They are found in Africa and Eurasia, although they are rare in eastern Asia and central Europe, where pebble tools were more common throughout the Lower Paleolithic.

Human settlement expanded further during Acheulean times, as later forms of *Homo* moved northward into cooler Europe, which suggests early evidence for the controlled use of fire. On the other hand, evidence for the hunting of large animals is limited, and the diet may not have differed fundamentally from that of the early Lower Paleolithic.

PALEOLITHIC TIMELINE

2.5 mya–250,000 ya Lower Paleolithic

2.5 mya Appearance of Oldowan industry

1.6 mya Appearance of Acheulean industry

500,000 ya Appearance of Levallois technique

250,000–30,000 ya Middle Paleolithic

45,000–10,000 ya Upper Paleolithic

Olduvai Gorge

One of the world's richest fossil sites, the spectacular Olduvai Gorge in northern Tanzania has preserved traces of human occupation for most of the last 2 million years (see p. 236). The finds include many early hominid fossils as well as large collections of stone tools. The Oldowan stone-tool industry was named after Olduvai.

Bone Prongs
Dated to approximately 12,500 years ago, during the Upper Paleolithic, these sophisticated bone points were used for line fishing. They were discovered in the cave of Courbet by the Aveyron River, France.

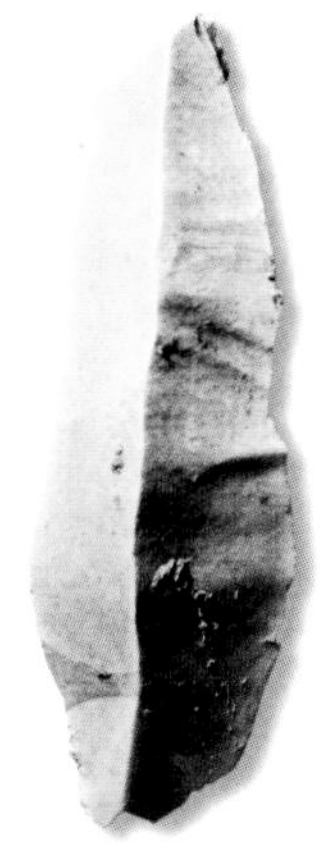

Stone-blade Knife
Fashioned toward the end of the Upper Paleolithic, this knife is characteristic of the stone-blade technology that emerged during the period.

INTO THE MIDDLE PALEOLITHIC

After 500,000 years ago, another major advance in stone-tool technology began to spread across Africa and western Eurasia. The Levallois technique of tool production entails careful preparation of the stone from which smaller flakes or blanks are struck. It allows improved control over the size and shape of the blanks used for various types of tools, and may be linked to the practice of attaching tools to wooden handles. Although the Levallois technique first appeared in the late Acheulean, it did not become widespread until the Middle Paleolithic period, which is dated from approximately 250,000 to 30,000 years ago and is associated with the Neanderthals in western Eurasia (see p.136) and ancestral modern or near-modern humans in Africa.

Middle Paleolithic industries lack large handaxes but contain a variety of standardized scrapers and other tools made from stone flakes. Traces of wear on the stone tools indicate that many were used to shape wooden implements (although few of the latter have been preserved), and that some were attached to wooden handles. Middle Paleolithic sites contain abundant evidence for the controlled use of fire, but few examples of structured hearths or artificial shelters. It is clear, however, that in Eurasia Middle Paleolithic people were hunting large animals and that meat had become an important part of the human diet, especially in newly inhabited colder regions where fewer edible plant foods were available.

SPREAD OF MODERN HUMANS

Major changes in behavior are evident from approximately 50,000 years ago, which is when many researchers believe that modern humans began to disperse from Africa (see p. 138). Some archaeologists believe that these changes reflect the development of language. The spread of modern humans is associated with industries of the Upper Paleolithic, which date from at least 45,000 to 10,000 years ago. These Upper Paleolithic industries are generally characterized by increased production of stone blade (as opposed to flake) tools, and an array of non-stone implements such as bone points and needles. They contain the first indisputable evidence for art and ritual in the form of engravings, sculptures, cave paintings, and grave goods. Upper Paleolithic people probably used a greater ability for technological innovation to expand into new environments. They apparently constructed watercraft to reach Australia at least 40,000 years ago, and occupied subarctic landscapes in northeastern Asia and Alaska to reach the New World at least 13,000 years ago.

PALEOLITHIC SOCIETY

Throughout the Paleolithic Age, humans lived in small mobile groups similar to the Bushmen and other foraging peoples who have survived into the present era. However, the organization of Paleolithic societies prior to the appearance and spread of modern humans may have been quite different from that of recent foraging peoples. Some archaeologists believe that changes in social behavior also may have played a role in the global dispersal of modern humans after 50,000 years ago, although older sites offer few clues as to how Lower and Middle Paleolithic groups were organized.

The First Art
The Upper Paleolithic saw the rise of art. This ivory carving from Brassempouy, France, dates to about 29,000–22,000 years ago, making it one of the earliest depictions of the human face.

THE LAST ICE AGE

North polar cap during last Ice Age

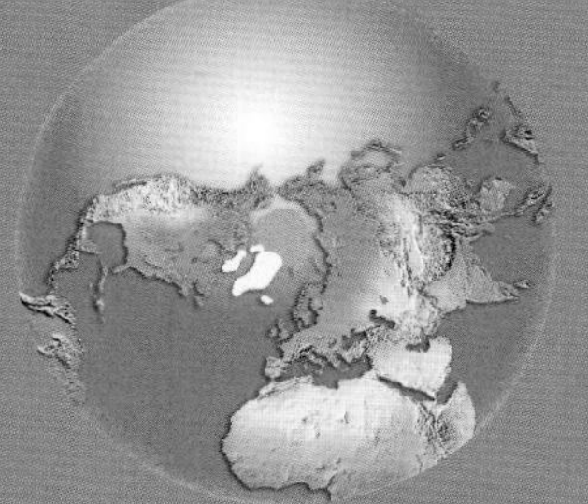

North polar cap today

The Paleolithic Age roughly coincides with the Pleistocene epoch, which experienced a fluctuating pattern of cold periods, known as glacials or ice ages, interrupted by warm periods, known as interglacials. The most recent Ice Age began about 115,000 years ago and ended about 10,000 years ago. It was in this period that modern humans developed.

During the Ice Age's peak, about 20,000 years ago, much of northwest Europe and North America and parts of central Asia disappeared under huge sheets of ice (top left). These glaciated regions were surrounded by windswept tundras, and all the vegetation and climate zones were much farther south than they now are. The sea-level was 400 feet (120 m) lower than it is today, with land bridges across the English Channel, Bering Strait, and some of the sounds between Southeast Asia and Australia. Woolly mammoths, woolly rhinoceroses, cave bears, and many other large mammals that roamed the tundra during this time became extinct once the climate started to warm up toward the end of the Ice Age.

Ice Age Galleries

The art of the last Ice Age, dating from about 35,000 to 10,000 years ago, is known on every continent, but is best known and currently most abundant in Eurasia. It comprises: a wide variety of portable objects, from engraved stones to carvings in antler or ivory; art on the walls of caves and rock-shelters, from finger-markings and engravings to bas-relief sculpture and painting; and similar art on rocks in the open air, both deeply pecked figures and engravings. The art features many animal figures, rare anthropomorphs (stylized humans), and abundant non-figurative motifs and "signs." Some is "public," on open view, but much is hidden, which points to a religious motivation. Much appears linked to a complex mythology, and no single explanation can possibly suffice for the phenomenon.

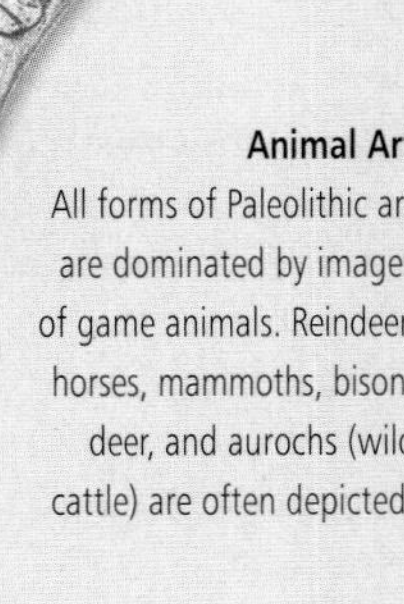

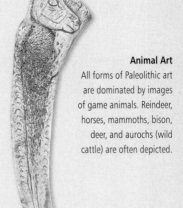

Animal Art
All forms of Paleolithic art are dominated by images of game animals. Reindeer, horses, mammoths, bison, deer, and aurochs (wild cattle) are often depicted.

Ancient Altamira
The painted bison in the cave of Altamira, in Spain, were painted some 14,000 years ago. Discovered in 1879, few believed they could have been made by Stone Age people, and it was years before the scientific world was convinced of their great age.

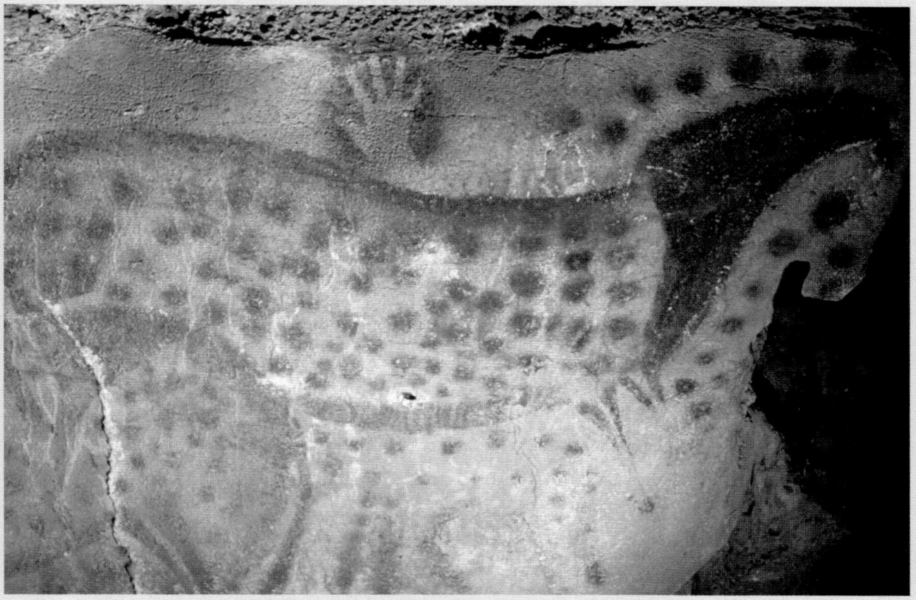

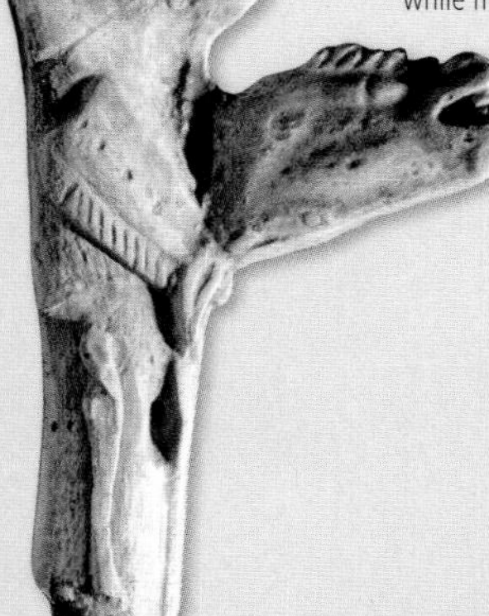

Working with Nature

One of the characteristics of Paleolithic art is the use of preexisting natural forms as an integral part of the work. This antler (left) has been carved to represent two horses, while many cave paintings use the natural shapes of the walls.

Dotted Horse

The cave of Pech-Merle, near Cahors in southwestern France, is famous for its dotted horses (above). The horse's tiny stylized head was carefully placed within this rock's natural horse-head shape. Note the hand stencil above the horse.

Open-Air Engraving

This isolated open-air image of a horse (right), deeply hammered into a rock high on a hill at Piedras Blancas, southeast Spain, can be dated only by style, but is unquestionably of Paleolithic type.

The Transition to Settled Life

Fertility Figurine
This small statue of a couple making love comes from the Natufian culture of about 10,000 years ago. It may reflect a new understanding of the part played by men in reproduction.

Mesolithic Dwellings
At the Early Mesolithic settlement of Mount Sandel in Northern Ireland, people may have used skins to cover their huts.

One of the most momentous transitions in human behavior and diet occurred toward the end of the most recent Ice Age, as people began to adopt a settled way of life.

Around 18,000 years ago, the ice sheets of the Northern Hemisphere began to retreat, and the warmer climate in Europe and the Near East opened new possibilities for human settlement. People broke out of the limited areas of southern Europe into which they had been pushed during the glacial maximum, and recolonized northern Europe, where they hunted immense herds of reindeer. In the Near East, increasing populations gathered and hunted a variety of plants and animals in a mosaic of steppe and woodland. By about 10,000 years ago, the ice sheets had more or less reached their current dimensions, and forests began to cover parts of Europe that had previously been tundra or steppe.

SETTLED LIFE TIMELINE
18,000 ya Ice sheets retreat
13,000 ya Sedentary Natufian culture appears
Just before 10,000 ya First farmers appear in Near East
Just after 10,000 ya Mesolithic period begins in Europe

During this period, people ceased to move continually from campsite to campsite and began to settle in one place for longer periods, even year-round. Such settled life is known as sedentism. Sedentary people build sturdier houses, accumulate more belongings, and have a clearer sense of place, territory, and property

than their mobile predecessors. This behavioral change appears in the archaeological record of the Near East and Europe following the retreat of the ice sheets.

NATUFIAN CULTURE

Of particular significance is a group of sedentary communities that occupied the region between the Sinai Desert and the upper Euphrates Valley around 13,000 years ago. Known as the Natufian culture, their settlements contained semisubterranean houses, storage pits, grinding stones, and burials. Key evidence for Natufian sedentism is the marked increase in the bones of house mice, indicating that fresh rubbish was available for most of the year. This area also contained extensive stands of wild wheat and barley, which the Natufians collected as a major part of their diet. They also hunted gazelle and other game species, including migratory waterfowl.

THE FIRST FARMERS

Just before 10,000 years ago, descendants of the Natufians and their neighbors became the first farmers. They had come to depend so heavily on the wild cereals that they began to cultivate them intentionally. The motivation for this change is still unclear, but it is possible that it was in reaction to a brief cold period that reduced options for using other resources. Intensive harvesting of wild cereals would have selected for plants in which the small stem holding the grain was tough rather than brittle. Although this would have made wheat and barley easier to harvest, it also made them dependent on humans for their propagation.

Animal domestication occurred slightly later. Goats were first domesticated nearly 10,000 years ago in the Zagros Mountains, while sheep were first herded at sites in the upper Tigris and Euphrates valleys a few centuries later. Cattle and pigs were domesticated about a thousand years later, probably in Anatolia.

THE MESOLITHIC PERIOD

In Europe, the period just after 10,000 years ago is called the Mesolithic. People responded to the warmer climate and the new forests by developing new devices for hunting and fishing, including the leister, a clever tool for impaling fish. Dugout canoes came into use, enabling communities to live in one place yet hunt, fish, and gather across a much larger territory. Traps made from hazel and willow branches permitted the harvesting of fish on a massive scale, and shellfish provided a steady diet for coastal communities. In the inland mountains, sedentary communities such as the one at Lepenski Vir (see p. 272) took advantage of abundant resources in lakes and rivers.

Antler Head-dress
This head-dress fashioned from red deer antlers was found at the Mesolithic site of Star Carr, in Yorkshire, England. It may have been worn by hunters as a disguise, but it is more likely to have been part of a ceremonial costume.

Early Settlements of Western Asia

Samarran Statuette
This alabaster statuette of a woman with crossed arms was found in a grave at the Samarran site of Tell es-Sawwan. It dates to about 5800 BC.

With the adoption of agriculture, the first permanent villages were established in the Levant, Syria, Turkey, and Mesopotamia. These prepared the ground for the leap to civilization.

The first hamlets in western Asia started appearing around 10,000 BC, when people could rely on rich stands of wild cereals as a dietary staple (see p. 146). This step eventually led to agriculture. The new economy promoted village life and by about 6000–5500 BC villages had appeared even in environments where agriculture required irrigation. These villages, especially in southern Mesopotamia, nourished the roots from which civilization would grow.

THE LEVANT AND ANATOLIA

Communities of western Asia were the first in the world to develop agriculture—the deliberate planting of stored seed harvested the previous year. The practice was definitely in place by 8000 BC, at least in the southern Levant, where farming villages appeared. At Jericho, a place of perhaps 500 residents, enterprising farmers constructed a wall around their village and erected a massive tower—the oldest examples of civil engineering yet found. By 7000–6000 BC, sizable villages, some with several thousand inhabitants, had developed in northern Syria and in Anatolia (Asian Turkey), as well as in the Levant. Communities such as Çatal Höyük contained densely packed houses and were similar to traditional Near Eastern villages of today. Although effective pottery had not yet been developed, lime plaster was used for containers and flooring. Some

EARLY POTTERY STYLES OF MESOPOTAMIA

The first appearance of painted pottery occurred in the Hassuna culture of northern Mesopotamia. The paintings on the pottery of the Samarran culture in southern Mesopotamia were more dynamic, featuring dancing girls and animals such as goats, deer, and scorpions. The Samarrans also made sophisticated female figurines, decorated with tattoos.

The finest pottery ever produced in prehistoric Mesopotamia was created by the Halaf culture of northern Mesopotamia. Handmade from very fine clay, it had thin walls and was decorated with skillfully applied paintings of geometric motifs (left) and, occasionally, figures of animals, birds, and flowers.

The delicate pottery work of the Samarrans and Halafians later gave way to the efficiently produced but often plainly decorated wares of the 'Ubaid culture in southern Mesopotamia.

Tower of Jericho
Archaeological workers stand on top of the massive circular stone tower built against the inside town wall of Jericho. The tower is 30 feet (9 m) high and dates back to 7000 BC.

people, especially in Anatolia, worked native copper (a naturally occurring pure form), which was a big step toward metallurgy. Religious and aesthetic feelings found expression in shrines, wall paintings, figurines and statues, carved stone stelae, and elaborate burial rituals.

VILLAGES OF MESOPOTAMIA

Sometime around 6000 BC, the focus of development shifted to Mesopotamia. Rain-fed agriculture can flourish in northern Mesopotamia, and villages—first of the Hassuna and then of the Halaf cultures—dotted the landscape. Judging by the size of the houses they built, these people lived in nuclear families, but also organized group storage facilities. The elegantly painted Halaf pottery was the pinnacle of the potter's art in ancient western Asia.

The first settlements to appear in southern Mesopotamia, where farming requires mastery of irrigation, belonged to villagers of the Samarra and 'Ubaid cultures. These peoples built larger, more elaborate houses than did their contemporaries to the north, and probably lived in extended families better suited to the exigencies of irrigation farming. The 'Ubaid culture contained the seeds of Mesopotamian civilization. Small towns—local centers of political authority, economic services, and religious devotion—slowly grew in the midst of the village landscape. The 'Ubaid culture came to dominate even northern Mesopotamia, presaging the impact of the south on surrounding regions in later times.

Neolithic Europe

Agricultural Art
The adoption of agriculture in Europe is reflected in this baked clay figure, which is holding a sickle. The figure was made in the 5th millennium BC.

After its emergence in the Near East, agriculture spread rapidly to Europe, appearing first in Greece around 6500 BC. Within 3,000 years, it had taken root in most parts of the continent.

Agriculture spread throughout Europe along two major pathways and through two main processes. The first route ran from Greece along the Mediterranean coastline west to the Iberian Peninsula, while the second followed the rivers of interior Europe to the north and northwest. In some cases, the spread of agriculture occurred through the movement of farming peoples who colonized habitats that had been sparsely occupied by indigenous hunter-gatherers. Elsewhere, it is clear that domesticated plants and animals were adopted by foragers who settled down and replaced hunting with farming. Moreover, farming did not expand at a steady rate. After spreading quickly through certain regions, its dispersal would be arrested for several centuries before the next advance occurred.

MEDITERRANEAN FARMING

Along the Mediterranean coastlines of Italy, France, and Spain, as well as those of islands such as Corsica, agriculture appears to have been spread through seaborne contacts among settlements of hunter-gatherers, whose watercraft enabled them to travel long distances. Existing trade routes may have provided the pathways along which domestic sheep and grain moved from one settlement to another, beginning just before 6000 BC. Many of the cave settlements of the Mediterranean coast show continuity from hunter-gatherers to agriculturalists with no break in occupation.

The Spread of Farming
European agriculture began when farming arrived in Greece from southwestern Asia. It then spread via two major currents of movement: one through the Mediterranean along the coast and across the sea to the major islands (red arrows), and the other through the river valleys of the Balkans and into central, northern, and western Europe (blue arrows).

COLONIZATION IN CENTRAL EUROPE

In central Europe, colonization by farmers appears to have been the method by which agriculture spread between about 5500 and 4500 BC. Along small streams among the rolling hills of Austria, the Czech Republic, Germany, Poland, the Low Countries, and eastern France, small clusters of timber longhouses were inhabited by farmers who tilled the fertile soils. These farmers favored areas that were covered with windblown sediment called loess, but in time they also established settlements in areas not covered by loess.

IN THE WEST

After a pause of several centuries, the hunter-gatherers who lived along the Atlantic seaboard and in southern Scandinavia adopted agriculture around 4000 BC. Again, the use of watercraft permitted the movement of livestock and grain to the British Isles and around the Baltic coastline from one native community to another. Around the same time, hunter-gatherers who lived in the foothills of the Alps also adopted agriculture and settled on the shores of lakes in Switzerland and neighboring areas. By 3000 BC farming settlements such as Skara Brae had appeared in the Orkney Islands in the far northwest of Europe, at the environmental limit of prehistoric agriculture.

Orkney Occupation
Covered passageways link the stone-built houses of Skara Brae, in the Orkney Islands off Scotland (see p. 282). This farming village was occupied from about 3100 to 2500 BC.

MEGALITHIC TOMBS

The centuries following the establishment of farming saw the construction of remarkable burial monuments from Spain to Sweden called megalithic tombs. The name comes from the use of megaliths—very large, flat stones that were set upright to form chambers, which were then roofed over with additional large stones. Megalithic tombs take a variety of forms, but the most common are passage graves and dolmens (such as the Poulnabrone Dolmen of Ireland, right). Most were communal crypts used over many generations by farming communities, possibly to perpetuate ancestral ties to particular territories. Famous examples include West Kennet in England, Newgrange in Ireland (see p. 286), and Gavrinis in France.

Other Farming Communities

Maize Gods
This Moche effigy jar, from the north coast of Peru, depicts three anthropomorphized maize cobs. The fanged mouths and staring eyes suggest that they are gods associated with fertility and food.

While some hunter-gatherer communities continued to prosper for millennia, in many parts of the world farming gradually took hold, with both plants and animals being domesticated.

After its beginnings in western Asia, agriculture gradually spread to Africa and the Indian subcontinent. In other parts of the world, such as South America, China, and New Guinea, farming appears to have developed independently.

AGRICULTURE IN AFRICA

In both the Nile Valley and Sahara Desert, the transition from forager to food producer was heralded by the appearance of semi-permanent settlements near water sources where people intensively exploited a broad range of plant and animal resources. Such increasingly sedentary lifestyles both enabled and required changes in values and social organization that paved the way for the adoption of agriculture. At first, herding and planting probably occurred on a small scale alongside hunting and gathering as an insurance against lean times, but they then became more important when populations grew.

Agriculture began in western Asia around 8000 BC (see p. 148), and the first North African farmers appeared at least 3,000 years later. Although Africans probably experimented with domesticating native plants and animals, remains from their first farming villages suggest they relied on crops and livestock that were originally domesticated in western Asia.

The earliest evidence of farming in North Africa comes from Egypt, with sites along an ancient lakeshore in the Fayum Depression in the desert of western Egypt and in the Nile Delta dating to

Herding Scene
The Sahara Desert was occupied by Stone Age hunter-pastoralists from about 8000 to 3000 BC. Some of the rock art they left behind depicts herders and cattle.

shortly before 7,000 years ago. In the Sahara Desert, nomadic herding societies based mainly on domestic cattle flourished during and after a wet period between about 6,500 and 4,000 years ago, and are depicted in many scenes of pastoralist life in rock art.

As farming spread westward and southward across North Africa from Egypt, exotic domestic animals were introduced to the continent, while indigenous African plants suited to the local conditions, such as millet and sorghum, began to be cultivated.

SOUTH AMERICAN FARMERS

In Andean South America, the origins of settled farming villages are somewhat more diverse than those seen in other parts of the world. The domestication of plants and animals, along with an intensification of fishing on the coast, took place over a period of several thousand years and appears to have its origins in the management of wild resources.

In the highlands of Peru, the remains of the wild ancestors of plants that were later domesticated are found in archaeological sites as old as 10,000 years. Over the next several thousand years, these and many other plants were used by the hunter-gatherers who lived throughout the Andes. From around 5,000 years ago, as populations increased, wild crops, animals, and marine resources were managed and harvested increasingly intensively. Some plant species, including peppers, beans, and maize, were domesticated by 5500 BC. They were followed by Andean grains such as quinoa, tubers such as potatoes and manioc, and many other native plants. On the coast, economically important but nonedible plants, including cotton and gourds, were among the earliest intensively used crops.

By around 2500 BC, agricultural communities were found throughout the Andes. On the coast and into the middle highlands, irrigation agriculture along the river valleys was the rule, while in the higher elevations rainfall agriculture could also be maintained in some areas. In the highest elevations, where agriculture is limited by climate, herding of domesticated camelids (llamas and alpacas) was the primary economic activity. The patterns established by this time—including coastal fishing, agriculture at most elevations, and highland herding—formed the economic foundation for all later Andean civilizations.

New World Staple
Maize became the most important indigenous grain in the New World, helping to build the civilizations of the Maya, Aztec, and Inca empires. In return, these peoples worshiped corn gods.

Indian Farmers
The ruins of a mud-brick village dating back to 7000 BC stand in Mehrgarh, Pakistan. The settlement's early farmers domesticated some local plants and animals, but imported others from western Asia.

TIMELINE OF FIRST FARMERS

8000 BC	Western Asia
7000 BC	Papua New Guinea
7000 BC	India
6500 BC	China
5500 BC	Andean South America
5000 BC	Egypt
4500 BC	Sahara Desert
1500 BC	Pacific

AGRICULTURE IN ASIA

Although the evidence is often difficult to pin down, agriculture probably developed independently in many parts of Asia. Some regions, such as Japan, were home to prosperous hunter-gatherer groups for many millennia after farming had begun elsewhere in Asia.

Mehrgarh, in Pakistan, provides the solitary clue to the origins of farming in the Indian subcontinent. Occupied from around 7000 BC, this village of small mud-brick houses was home to people who combined the activities of herding, hunting, cultivating, and gathering. Some of the herded animals, particularly cattle, were locally domesticated, but others, notably goats, were probably imported from western Asia, either through trade or by incoming settlers. Barley and wheat also probably came from western Asia. With the passing of time, farming gradually became more important than the exploitation of wild resources. By 5000 BC, many agricultural settlements had been established in the region.

FROM CHINA TO SOUTHEAST ASIA

Farming began in China around 6500 BC. Villagers on the Yellow River cultivated millet, along with various pulses and vegetables, and raised pigs, dogs, and chickens, while further south on the Yangtze River, rice was grown and pigs and water buffalo were herded. From around 3000 BC, rice farming began to spread southward from the Yangtze Valley, perhaps moving with immigrant settlers, and farming gradually became established throughout southern China and mainland Southeast Asia, eventually reaching the islands of the region. From here, farming was also carried into the Pacific by the intrepid seafaring settlers who began their major expansion around 1500 BC.

Although rice became the staple basis for Southeast Asian agriculture, the early evidence of agriculture in Papua New Guinea (see box, below) demonstrates the potential importance of plants whose cultivation is difficult to trace. Fruits, root crops, and tubers were among the staples of the Pacific island colonists and may have been cultivated in Southeast Asia long before the development of wet-rice agriculture.

Chinese Pottery
This pottery model of a human head from Neolithic China dates to roughly 2500 BC, when rice farming was becoming established in southern China.

EARLY EVIDENCE IN NEW GUINEA

The Wahgi Valley in the remote highlands of Papua New Guinea contains some of the oldest evidence for agriculture in the world, with plants apparently domesticated independently of other farming communities. Archaeologists working at Kuk Swamp in the 1970s documented 9,000 years of agricultural development. As the last Ice Age ended and the climate improved, people began to clear land, drain swamps, and plant crops.

The oldest evidence from Kuk includes a distinctive gray clay deposited about 7000 BC. This clay is the result of soil eroding from land cleared for gardens and washing into the swamp. A ditch, stakeholes, pits, and hollows at the same date show that water-loving crops were also grown. No plant remains have been preserved, so we do not know exactly what these crops were. Sugarcane and local species of banana and yams are the most likely possibilities. Later on, new crops were introduced. Taro and Asian yams were in use by about 5,000 years ago. Finally, sweet potato was introduced from South America about 400 years ago. These changes are reflected in the types of features discovered—altogether, archaeologists have traced six distinct phases of increasingly complex agricultural systems at Kuk (below).

The Historical Past

Around the globe, great civilizations have come and gone, leaving behind a wealth of distinctive artifacts, new technologies, elaborate burials, stupendous monuments, and sophisticated cities. From the Babylonians, Egyptians, and Greeks, to the Indus, Chinese, and Maya, ancient cultures continue to enthrall archaeologists and the public alike.

"Why wonder we that men doe die?
Since monuments decay,
And towers fall, and founders names
Doe perish cleane away."

from *The Preacher's Travels* (1611),
by John Cartwright, English merchant and cleric

Civilizations of Western Asia

Scenic Cylinder Seal
First appearing during the Uruk Period (3800–3100 BC), the cylinder seal was used by many Mesopotamian cultures. This Akkadian example dates to 2300–2100 BC.

Encompassing much of modern-day Iraq and stretching to the Persian Gulf, Mesopotamia was the birthplace of the first cities and saw the rise of a succession of great civilizations.

The civilizations that arose in Mesopotamia and adjoining regions of western Asia created a "stream of tradition" that flowed for more than three millennia. This stream was fundamentally written, based on the cuneiform script (wedge-shaped writing)—a seemingly ethereal foundation for a surprisingly resilient tradition that weathered the long sweep of ancient Near Eastern history.

URUK PERIOD

The 'Ubaid culture (*c.* 5500–3800 BC) was well advanced at its culmination, but not noticeably poised for a leap to civilization. Nevertheless, the next five centuries witnessed the birth of the Mesopotamian tradition. Research at Uruk, for which this period (3800–3100 BC) is named, shows that by 3300 BC it was a large city centered on two great temples, where administrators developed cuneiform writing to keep their accounts, specialized craftsmen turned out pottery and other goods, and artisans created works of art. The Mesopotamian form of seal—a cylinder with a scene carved around its circumference, intended to roll out its image on moist clay—also appeared.

AKKADIANS AND SUMERIANS

The transformation continued into the Early Dynastic Period (2900–2300 BC), when 80 percent of the population resided in cities or large towns. Palaces of kings

Uruk Ruins
The ruins of the ancient southern Mesopotamian city of Uruk in present-day Iraq feature two great temples. Uruk was over 10 times larger than any of the settlements of the earlier 'Ubaid culture.

now appeared, suggesting that civil authority may have shifted from a religious to a secular setting. Scribes started recording the deeds of kings as well as the administration of public institutions. Their texts reveal a political landscape of cities struggling for strategic advantage, and highlight the political and economic power of kingly families. The astonishing wealth of the Royal Cemetery at Ur (see p. 330) is but one material reflection of this power. Some rulers, such as Gilgamesh of Uruk, passed into legend.

The cuneiform texts also show that the southern Mesopotamia of 2500 BC contained Sumerians and Akkadians, two peoples differing in language (Akkadian being Semitic, Sumerian of uncertain affiliation) but sharing most cultural features. As the first cuneiform inscriptions are Sumerian, these people are credited with the development of civilization.

The Akkadians rose to political power when Sargon the Great (*c.* 2330–2274 BC) managed to conquer the cities of southern Mesopotamia and then expand into the north. The loosely knit Akkadian empire endured for 150 years, after which followed a Sumerian revival under the kings of Ur (the Ur III Period, *c.* 2112–2004 BC), who formed a smaller, tighter empire with an even shorter duration. These episodes of empire, particularly Sargon, set the model for later imperial aspirations. Moreover, the religious literature of Mesopotamia took written shape, while a typically Mesopotamian architectural concept, the ziggurat (a tall multi-stepped platform), emerged.

KEY DATES IN WESTERN ASIA

3500 BC	First cities in Sumer
3300 BC	First cuneiform writing in Sumer
3100 BC	Bronze Age towns in Levant
2700 BC	Tell Asmar cultic statues
2600 BC	Royal Cemetery of Ur
2600 BC	Cities in northern Mesopotamia
2400 BC	Ebla archive
2300 BC	Sargon of Akkad
2300–2000 BC	Widespread collapse of town life in Levant
2100 BC	Ziggurats in Ur and other Sumerian cities
1750 BC	Old Babylonian empire, Hammurabi law code
2000–1800 BC	Reappearance of town life in southern Levant
1800/1500 BC	Alphabet in southern Levant (Canaan)
1550 BC	Egyptians begin conquering southern Levant
1350 BC	Hittites form empire
1250 BC	Assyrians form first (Middle Assyrian) empire
1200–1150 BC	Collapse of Hittite and Egyptian empires; appearance of Israelites, Philistines, Aramaeans
900 BC	Assyrians form second (Neo-Assyrian) empire
610 BC	Assyrian empire collapses, rise of Neo-Babylonian empire
539 BC	Persians conquer Mesopotamia and Levant
330 BC	Macedonian Greeks take over Persian empire
AD **75**	Last dated cuneiform inscription

Hittite Capital
The Hittites made their capital at Hattusas, near the present-day village of Bogazkoy in central Turkey. The main temple had a central courtyard and contained shrines dedicated to the sun-goddess Arinna and the weather-god Hatti.

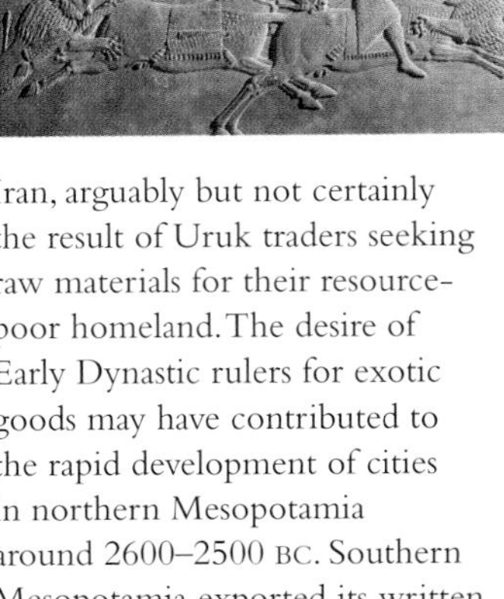

Assyrian King
Under King Assurnasirpal (883–859 BC), Assyria experienced its first wave of empire-building. This stone relief (top right) from his capital at Nineveh shows various scenes of the king killing lions.

AMORITES AND THE CITY OF BABYLON

When the Ur III state collapsed, the gates to Mesopotamia opened to the Amorites, tribal groups who spoke a western Semitic tongue. Rather than replace the existing population, the Amorites were "Mesopotamianized," but Amorite tribal leaders did establish themselves as the kings of numerous Mesopotamian cities, the hitherto unimportant Babylon among them. When Hammurabi (1792–1750 BC), the Amorite ruler of Babylon, created an empire that extended to northern Syria, his capital become the preeminent southern city, a position it would maintain for nearly 2,000 years.

A NEIGHBORLY INFLUENCE

The southern Mesopotamian civilization exerted a strong, if intermittent, influence on its neighbors during the long stretch between 3500 and 1600 BC. During the Uruk Period, southern culture had already appeared in northern Syria and western Iran, arguably but not certainly the result of Uruk traders seeking raw materials for their resource-poor homeland. The desire of Early Dynastic rulers for exotic goods may have contributed to the rapid development of cities in northern Mesopotamia around 2600–2500 BC. Southern Mesopotamia exported its written culture when foreign students at scribal schools returned with their learning to places such as Ebla (see p. 336). Trade relations introduced various aspects of Mesopotamian culture as far afield as Turkmenistan and Afghanistan, where small cities were also emerging.

Other regions of western Asia remained longer outside

the Mesopotamian ambit. The Levant, and especially the southern Levant (modern Israel, Palestine, and Jordan), followed its own path toward city life and then witnessed a temporary abandonment of towns, all during the Early Bronze Age (3500–2000 BC). Egypt provided the Levant's closest contact with civilization for this region, and elements of Egyptian art and practices embedded themselves in the Levantine milieu. And much of Anatolia maintained its own course during the same period. By 1800 BC, however, trade and diplomacy had created links that connected, at least indirectly, places as distant as Cyprus and Afghanistan. The venturesome Assyrians established trading colonies in Anatolia, caravans from Syrian cities reached the southern Levant, and ships from Ur sailed the Gulf.

AGE OF INTERNATIONALISM

The next two centuries are sometimes called a "dark age" simply for lack of evidence. When the curtain again rose, after 1500 BC, the stage had been transformed. The Kassite Dynasty, of eastern mountain origins, ruled a reinvigorated Babylonia as a regional state, but stood largely on the sidelines of the multisided struggle for empire that lasted until 1200 BC. Egypt conquered much of the Levant (Canaan) during the 15th century BC, and then contested control of northern Syria in turn with Mitanni and Hittites. The Assyrians entered the field late in the game.

This period was an age of internationalism—Akkadian was the diplomatic lingua franca; kings exchanged sumptuous gifts, daughters in marriage, and craftsmen on loan; trade flourished by both caravan and sea, connecting Greece and the Aegean with western Asia; and new technologies (such as glass-making) and artistic concepts circulated widely. Nevertheless each of the contestants retained its own character.

Mitanni, a network of vassal states in northern Mesopotamia and Syria, was the political creation of Hurrians, speakers of a language with roots in the Caucasus Mountains. Although the artists of Mitanni produced some distinctive objects—notably graceful painted pottery and elegant cylinder seals—Hurrian culture remains little known. The Hittites ruled most of Anatolia, a land of diverse cultures, and their ongoing contacts with the Mesopotamian world further opened them to external influences. They used seven different languages (including Akkadian and Sumerian) and two scripts—cuneiform and Hittite hieroglyphics, the latter an indigenous invention. Their art incorporated Egyptian concepts while remaining thoroughly Anatolian in character. The large figures of lions and sphinxes that framed the ceremonial gates to the Hittite capital, Hattusaas, near Bogazkoy belonged to this indigenous tradition, as did the sanctuary at nearby Yazilkaya, cut into rock, and decorated with reliefs of the Hittite pantheon.

Goddess Pendant
This Hittite pendant, dated to about 1400–1200 BC, probably represents the sun-goddess Arinna.

THE RISE OF THE ASSYRIANS

This world of internationalism fell apart around 1200 BC, in a convulsion of population movements and new beginnings. The Hittites disappeared except for princelings ruling some cities in northern Syria and eastern Anatolia, and the Egyptians withdrew to the Nile Valley. Assyria retained control over its possessions for a time, but then also retrenched. The Aramaeans emerged as a significant political force in Syria, imposing kings on some Syrian cities and displacing Neo-Hittite dynasties in others. In the Levant, the Phoenicians perpetuated Canaanite culture, but elsewhere the Philistines, newly arrived from the Aegean, took possession of the southern coast while small villages in the hills marked the beginning of the Israelites.

The notorious Assyrian empire (see box, below) arose in this politically fragmented and culturally divided world of the Iron Age. Assyrian empire-building came in two spurts, one in the 9th century BC and the second between 745 and 650 BC, separated by an episode of internal problems. The kings familiar from the Old Testament belonged to the second surge of conquest, when Pul (Sargon II, 721–705 BC) defeated Samaria, and Sennacherib (704–681 bc) besieged Hezekiah in Jerusalem. At its maximum extent, the Assyrian empire controlled all the lands of the Fertile Crescent and, briefly, Egypt.

NEBUCHADNEZZAR'S BABYLON

Despite its seeming strengths, the Assyrian empire collapsed with stunning swiftness—at its peak around 650 BC, the empire was in

THE ASSYRIAN EMPIRE

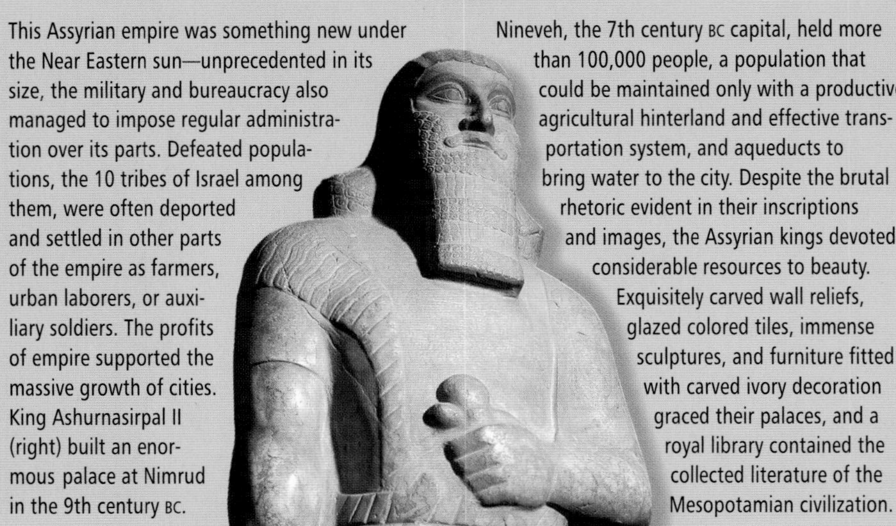

This Assyrian empire was something new under the Near Eastern sun—unprecedented in its size, the military and bureaucracy also managed to impose regular administration over its parts. Defeated populations, the 10 tribes of Israel among them, were often deported and settled in other parts of the empire as farmers, urban laborers, or auxiliary soldiers. The profits of empire supported the massive growth of cities. King Ashurnasirpal II (right) built an enormous palace at Nimrud in the 9th century BC.

Nineveh, the 7th century BC capital, held more than 100,000 people, a population that could be maintained only with a productive agricultural hinterland and effective transportation system, and aqueducts to bring water to the city. Despite the brutal rhetoric evident in their inscriptions and images, the Assyrian kings devoted considerable resources to beauty. Exquisitely carved wall reliefs, glazed colored tiles, immense sculptures, and furniture fitted with carved ivory decoration graced their palaces, and a royal library contained the collected literature of the Mesopotamian civilization.

its death throes when the army of a rebellious Babylonia and its allies sacked Nineveh in 612 BC. Babylon inherited the imperial mantle when Nebuchadnezzar (604–562 BC)—another name familiar to readers of the Old Testament—acquired by force a large portion of the former Assyrian possessions; his destruction of Jerusalem in 586 BC began the Babylonian exile of the Jews. Like the Assyrian kings before him, Nebuchadnezzar invested the proceeds of empire in the magnificence of his capital, Babylon (see p. 340), but he failed to establish a comparably durable dominion—in 539 BC the last independent Babylonian ruler fell to the Persians.

THE PERSIAN EMPIRE

The Achaemenid Persians descended from an Indo-European-speaking group that had moved into Iran from central Asia a millennium earlier, ultimately settling in the district of modern Shiraz. Their empire was the creation of Cyrus the Great (559–530 BC), who conquered a vast territory from central Asia to Anatolia in addition to Babylonia. Cyrus's immediate successors added northwestern India, Egypt, and Thrace, but failed to absorb Greece. Empire on such an unprecedented scale required new methods of organization, which Darius the Great (522–486 BC), the builder of glorious Persepolis (see p. 350), implemented with an effectively flexible system of provincial governments known as satrapies. The Persians adopted many features from the culture of their Mesopotamian predecessors, including the use of cuneiform, but melded these with their own heritage and with traits from other civilizations such as Greece.

Mesopotamia was now part of a truly vast world, and it began to lose its ability to assimilate newcomers. When Alexander the Great (336–323 BC) in turn conquered the Achaemenids and forcefully introduced Greek patterns to western Asia, the Mesopotamian civilization sputtered on, slowly yielding to new ways of life, before finally flickering out. Cuneiform writing, that emblem of ancient tradition, found its last expression around AD 75.

Persian Tomb
The tomb of Cyrus the Great (above) commemorates the founder of the extensive Achaemenid empire. In legend, Cyrus is depicted as a tolerant and just monarch, the father of his people.

Plaque of Darius
The trilingual inscription on this silver plaque defines the limits of the empire of the Persian king Darius the Great, who founded the magnificent capital of Persepolis.

Ancient Egypt

The Narmer Palette
Credited with the initial unification of Egypt, King Narmer is shown on this palette wearing the crowns of Upper and Lower Egypt and smiting an enemy.

The sands of Egypt have preserved some 3,000 years of dynastic history, yielding a rich variety of evidence, including architecture, literature, and the mummified bodies of the Egyptians themselves.

The Nile River was crucial to Egypt's development. Flowing north from Ethiopia to the Mediterranean Sea, the Nile brought water to an otherwise dry land. The fertile soil deposited along its banks not only allowed the development of agriculture, but provided the thick mud used to make sun-dried mud bricks. In addition, the Nile acted as a roadway, a sewer, and a valuable source of fish.

TOWARD UNIFICATION

Egypt's prehistoric age saw the development of independent communities—villages, towns, and eventually city-states—along the Nile. The people worshiped local gods, hunted, fished, and farmed the fertile soil, or "Black Land," that fringed the river, while the sterile desert, or "Red Land," was reserved as the home of the dead. Gradually these separate communities united and Egypt emerged a long, thin country extending from Aswan in the south to the Mediterranean in the north. There was now one king, or pharaoh, and a collection of recognized state gods. Alongside unification came the development of writing.

THE OLD KINGDOM

By convention, the kings of Egypt are divided into dynasties of connected monarchs. The dynasties are further grouped into periods and kingdoms (see box, right).

The kings of the Old Kingdom (Dynasties 3–6, 2649–2150 BC) were recognized as semidivine beings. Pharaoh had become the indispensable link between the people and their gods, and life without a king on the throne was unthinkable. This was the age of the pyramids, when the followers of the sun god Re built royal tombs to link Egypt to the sky.

The Old Kingdom eventually collapsed, and was succeeded by the First Intermediate Period (Dynasties 7–11, 2150–2040 BC), which saw the independent city-states jostling for power. Two centers eventually emerged—a Theban dynasty ruled the south, while a Herakleopolitan dynasty controlled the north. Gradually, however, the Theban kings proved the stronger. Having reunited the country, they established a new capital at Ij-Tawy, close to the Old Kingdom capital of Memphis. The Middle Kingdom (Dynasties 11–13, 2040–1690 BC), a time of prosperity and tranquillity, had begun.

PERIODS AND KINGDOMS OF ANCIENT EGYPT

3000–2649 BC	Archaic Period, Dynasties 1–2: *Unification of Egypt*
2649–2150 BC	Old Kingdom, Dynasties 3–6: *The pyramid age*
2150–2040 BC	First Intermediate Period, Dynasties 7–11: *Political chaos*
2040–1690 BC	Middle Kingdom, Dynasties 11–13: *Political stability*
1690–1550 BC	Second Intermediate Period, Dynasties 14–17: *Foreign invasion*
1550–1070 BC	New Kingdom, Dynasties 18–20: *Creation of the Egyptian empire*
1070–664 BC	Third Intermediate Period, Dynasties 21–25: *Political chaos*
664–332 BC	Late Period, Dynasties 26–31: *End of dynastic age*

The River Nile
Before the construction of the Aswan Dam in modern times, an annual flood of the Nile would deposit rich alluvial soil onto its banks, allowing agriculture to flourish in the region.

The Great Pyramid
Ancient Egypt is famous for its pyramids, the largest of which is the Great Pyramid at Giza. Housing the burial chamber of the 4th Dynasty pharaoh Khufu (Cheops), this massive structure used about 2 million blocks of limestone and took 23 years to build. (See also p. 244.)

Heretic King
The 18th Dynasty king Akhenaten is shown here in a limestone carving dated to c. 1350 BC. His attempt to replace Egypt's traditional gods with a single deity ultimately failed.

EGYPT AS SUPERPOWER

A combination of uncontrollable factors—mass migration across the Near East plus a series of high Nile floods—led to political and economic instability and the collapse of the Middle Kingdom. The Egypt of the Second Intermediate Period (Dynasties 14–17, 1690–1550 BC) was again fragmented, with Thebes ruled by local kings while the north was controlled by Palestinian invaders known as the Hyksos. This foreign rule was a deep humiliation—Egyptian propaganda had taught that foreigners were to be despised, not obeyed. After a series of battles, the Theban Ahmose expelled the Hyksos to found the unified New Kingdom (Dynasties 18–20, 1550–1070 BC). He was followed by a succession of competent warrior-kings, and Egypt acquired an empire stretching from Nubia to Syria. Egypt had become the acknowledged world superpower. Tribute poured into the royal coffers, financing a series of lavish building projects. The refurbished temples, including the Karnak temple of Amen at Thebes, were built in stone, although mud brick remained the material of choice for all domestic architecture.

GODS AND KINGS

By this time, the sun god Re had been demoted from his role as head of the state pantheon in favor of the Theban Amen. This change in allegiance allowed the abandonment of the highly conspicuous pyramid, and the royal workmen now began to excavate rock-cut tombs deep within the Valley of the Kings. Only one king challenged the supremacy of Amen. The "heretic king" Akhenaten attempted to impose a single god, the Aten, on his people. His unique religious experiment failed, and the so-called Amarna Period ended after 17 years with the death of Akhenaten and the reintroduction of the traditional gods.

ROYAL NAMES

Many of the Egyptian pharaohs are known by two names—Khufu, for example, is also known as Cheops. Before hieroglyphs were deciphered, scholars used the Greek names for the pharaohs. On reading the hieroglyphs, however, they adopted the Egyptian names.

Tutankhamen, today the most famous New Kingdom monarch, succeeded Akhenaten on the throne and ruled Egypt for nine years. More famous in his own lifetime was Ramesses II, a king whose reign of almost 70 years allowed him time to develop his own personal cult.

INSTABILITY AND INVASION

Internal problems—inefficiency and corruption, high inflation, and low Nile levels—were compounded by international instability. Slowly the seemingly invincible New Kingdom began to crumble. First the eastern territories, then Nubia, were lost; eventually the south was controlled by the High Priests of Amen, with pharaoh confined to the north. The dawn of Egypt's Third Intermediate Period (Dynasties 21–25, 1070–664 BC) saw a local dynasty ruling the north from Tanis, and the High Priests of Amen ruling the south from Thebes. Eventually the kings of Nubia were able to march northward and reunite Egypt. A century of stability followed this move, but in 671 BC the Assyrian army invaded. The Nubians were forced to flee southward and the Assyrians installed the puppet Saite kings on the vacant throne.

At the beginning of the Late Period (Dynasties 26–31, 664–332 BC), Egypt was reunited under the now autonomous Saite rulers. In 525 BC, however, the Persian army conquered Egypt, installing their own dynasties. Finally, in 332 BC, Alexander the Great arrived and incorporated Egypt into his Greek empire. The dynastic age was over.

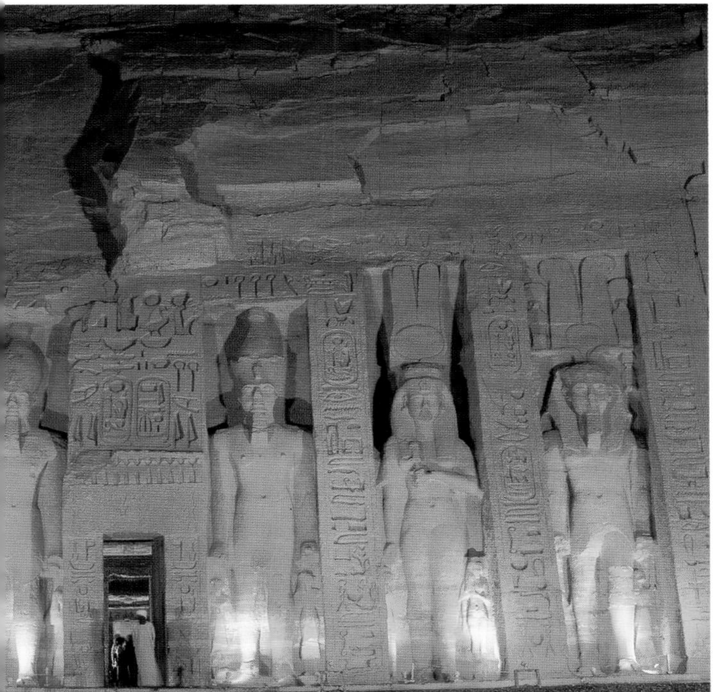

Colossal Statues
Egypt is filled with great monuments built by Ramesses II (1279–1213 BC). Colossal statues of Ramesses and his queen, Nefertari, flank the entrance to the Temple of Hathor at Abu Simbel in Nubia. Carved out of a sandstone cliff on the west bank of the Nile, Abu Simbel served as both a religious and an economic center.

Minoans and Mycenaeans

During the Bronze Age, two civilizations flourished in Greece—the Minoans on the island of Crete, and the Mycenaeans on the mainland. They left behind palaces, burials, and writing systems.

Buried Painting
A volcanic eruption buried the Late Bronze Age town of Akrotiri on the island of Thera around 1630 BC, preserving its splendid wall paintings, such as this fresco of two young boxers.

Palace of Knossos
Minoan palaces such as that at Knossos (above right) were large structures built around a central court, with an explicit economic and religious function.

The Bronze Age civilization of Crete is named Minoan after the legendary ruler of Knossos, King Minos. Bronze technology was introduced to the island during the 3rd millennium BC, but throughout much of the Early Minoan Period, the island was characterized by a simple farming-based economy centered on small villages, such as Vasiliki and Myrtos-Fournou Korifi. Burial customs—in particular the large circular communal tombs (tholoi) of the Mesara plain—indicate that society was organized around kinship groups or clans. The increasing wealth concentrated in a small proportion of the burials implies the emergence of an elite group toward the end of the period.

MINOAN PALACES

Major social changes occurred at the beginning of the 2nd millennium BC. Their clearest architectural expression is in the palaces at Knossos (see p. 292), Phaistos, Zakros, and Mallia. The palaces dominated large urban centers (the earliest towns in Europe), and elegant villas dotted the landscape. Many buildings were richly decorated with wall paintings featuring naturalistic scenes, acrobatic bull-sports, and richly dressed ladies. Although Minoan Crete remained essentially prehistoric, the palaces supported a scribal class, chiefly to administer the unwieldy palace bureaucracy. The undeciphered Linear A script is found beyond Crete, at possible Minoan colonies or trading partners in the Cycladic islands. In the Late Bronze Age, the palaces, town houses, and villas were destroyed in violent fires. Certainly by the 14th–13th century BC, Crete appears to have come under Mycenaean control, and was ruled from Khania and Knossos.

KEY EVENTS IN BRONZE AGE GREECE

c. 3000 BC	Beginning of the Bronze Age
c. 1900 BC	First Minoan palaces built in Crete
c. 1630 BC	Volcano of Thera erupts
16th century BC	Mycenaean shaft graves constructed; Destruction of Minoan palaces
14th–13th century BC	Mycenaean palaces built; Mycenaeans control Crete
13th century BC	Mycenaean fortifications built
1200 BC	Destruction of Mycenaean palaces

A NEW CIVILIZATION

The Mycenaean civilization dominated central and southern Greece from 1600 to 1100 BC. Preeminent sites include Thebes, Athens, Pylos, Tiryns, and above all Mycenae (see p. 296). Rich textual data from the Linear B archives (see p. 117) illuminate the archaeological evidence. Mycenaean Greece was ruled by a hereditary warrior class, with a king (*wanax*) at its head. The focal point of the kingdom was the palace, usually within the impressive stone walls of an impregnable citadel, as at Mycenae, Tiryns, and Athens. The best preserved of the palaces is at Pylos and dates to the 13th century BC. The palaces featured wall paintings, often with scenes of warfare and charioteers.

Most Mycenaean graves are multiple burials in chamber tombs, but the elite class had more elaborate graves. The earliest are the shaft graves, but the stone-built beehive tombs (tholoi) were more typical, the best known being the Treasury of Atreus at Mycenae (see p. 296). These burials were furnished with a rich array of grave goods, including ceramics, jewelry of gold and semiprecious stones, and weapons. Religious practices are more enigmatic, although the Linear B archives refer to gods and goddesses that later appear in the pantheon of classical Greece. A number of cult centers have been excavated within the citadel walls at Mycenae, Tiryns, and most recently at Midea.

The Mycenaeans were active participants in long-distance trade and exchange, with Italy, Cyprus, the Levant, and even northern Europe. Their prime export was pottery, such as drinking sets and perfume containers. In return, they imported raw minerals, such as copper, and luxury materials, such as ivory and ostrich eggs.

Around 1200 BC, the palaces disappear, destroyed in massive conflagrations. The Mycenaean civilization persisted for about a century, albeit with the disappearance of the upper echelons of society. During the 12th century, there was a revival in the minor arts, primarily in pictorial pottery, and a shift of sites toward the coast. After that, there was an apparent Dark Age until the emergence of classical Greek civilization around 700 BC.

Vaphio Cup
The lavish graves of the Mycenaean elite were accompanied by a wealth of grave goods. This ornate golden cup is one of a pair that were discovered in a beehive tomb at Vaphio.

The Greeks

Early Pottery
These Greek funerary vessels date from the 7th to 6th centuries BC. The globular container or aryballos was for perfumed oil, which was exported throughout the Mediterranean during this period.

Classical Greek culture has had a profound effect on the architecture and learning of western Europe, and sites such as the Parthenon and Delphi continue to attract visitors.

After the collapse of the palaces of Mycenae, there is a significant gap in the Greek archaeological record that is generally referred to as the Dark Ages. Greece emerges from this obscurity in what archaeologists describe as the Early Iron Age. One of the most important sites from this period, dating to the 9th century BC, is a long covered building at Lefkandi on the island of Euboea. Possibly an early religious building, it contained the buried remains of a hero.

COLONIES AND TRADE

A major colonizing movement took place from the 8th century BC, reflected by the ancient Greek cities that are found round the shores of the Mediterranean in Italy and of the Black Sea in the Levant. The Greeks were engaged in trade across the Mediterranean. The settlement at Naukratis in the Nile Delta was established by Greeks to facilitate trade with Egypt. Athenian pottery has been found on the Atlantic coast of Africa, most likely carried there

ITALY
Rome
Carthage
Gela
Mediterranean Sea

by Phoenician rather than Greek merchants. A major Greek bronze krater (wine-mixing vessel) has been found in a burial at Vix in central France, suggesting not only contact between the Greek colony at Marseilles and central Europe, but also the acquisition of the taste for wine (and banqueting) by the local communities.

Some Greek colonies show the introduction of town-planning. The settlement of Euesperides in Cyrenaica (near today's Benghazi in Libya) probably dates from the late 7th century BC. The earliest city was laid out in nearly square blocks, each containing four houses, whereas later blocks were more linear. Excavated finds from the sanctuary of the goddesses Demeter and Persephone just outside the city of Cyrene have shown the close links between the Greek mainland and its colonies.

KEY DATES IN ANCIENT GREECE

776 BC	Traditional establishment of the Olympic Games
c. 750 BC	Greek cities begin establishing colonies around the shores of the Mediterranean and the Black Sea
late 8th century BC	Greek alphabet appears; oldest Greek literature, by Homer and Hesiod, written
490 BC	Battle of Marathon and defeat of Persian expedition
480–479 BC	Persian invasions of Greece; battles of Thermopylae, Salamis, and Plataia
447–432 BC	Construction of the Parthenon
431–404 BC	Peloponnesian War between Athens and Sparta
333–323 BC	Alexander the Great's campaigns against Persia
323–31 BC	Hellenistic Age
146 BC	Destruction of Corinth by Rome

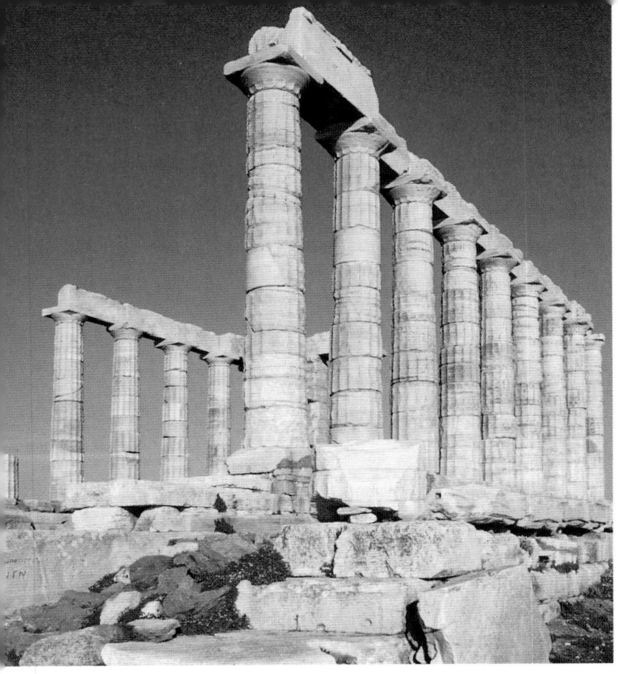

Doric Temple
The Temple of Poseidon at Cape Sounion in Attica was built at the same time as the Parthenon, about 440 BC. The elegant symmetry of the original temple is suggested by the 16 Doric columns that remain standing.

Delphi Charioteer
After victories in the Panhellenic games, statues of athletes would be dedicated to the gods. While most of these are known only from copies, the bronze charioteer from Delphi survives. Colored stones mark out the figure's striking eyes.

THE RISE OF CITY-STATES

Back in Greece itself, events led to the development of city-states—independent, self-governing cities such as Athens, Sparta, Corinth, and Thessaly. Despite their autonomy, the city-states united to defeat the Persians at the battles of Marathon, Plataia, and Salamis in the early 5th century BC.

Greek culture and identity were reinforced by Panhellenic sanctuaries, such as Olympia and Delphi, where Greeks could compete in competitive games. The life-size bronze figure of a charioteer found at Delphi (see p. 308) formed part of a chariot group dedicated by the tyrant Polyzalos of Gela in Sicily after his team won chariot events in the 470s BC. Remains of a stadium or running track have been discovered adjacent to the sanctuary of Zeus at Olympia. Inside the sacred site there were numerous bases that had once supported bronze statues of some of the victors in the games. The Temple of Zeus—originally featuring a massive gold and ivory statue, one of the wonders of the ancient world—was decorated in a series of sculptures that showed the myth surrounding the establishment of the games.

FLOURISHING ATHENS

One of the most splendid cities of the classical world was Athens. The home of classical Greek philosophy and drama and the birthplace of democracy, Athens boasted a magnificent navy and a flourishing trade network. In contrast to cities such as Sparta, it was decorated with numerous monumental buildings, notably on the acropolis, which featured the Parthenon (see p. 312), and in the agora, the main public space (see p. 306). The countryside of Attica, which surrounded the city, also benefited from the wealth of Athens, with the refurbishment of sanctuaries at Eleusis (where the mysteries of Demeter were held) and Sounion (with its Temple of Poseidon).

Although Athens and Sparta had formed a united front to defeat the Persians, they later fought against each other. The protracted Peloponnesian War (431–404 BC) was eventually won by Sparta, but the fighting weakened both cities, leaving them vulnerable to attacks from the kingdom of Macedon in the north. Eventually, Macedon's ruler Philip II (who ruled 359–336 BC) incorporated all of the Greek city-states into his empire.

ALEXANDER THE GREAT

Under the rule of Alexander the Great, Greek culture was spread far to the east, as he campaigned against the Persian empire. Greek settlements were even established in India at places such as Taxila. In each of the conquered lands, Greek colonists introduced the Greek language and culture, leading to what is known as the Hellenistic Age.

Alexandria in Egypt became a focus for Greek sculpture, in part because of its remarkable library. The library of Alexandria held more than half a million papyrus documents containing many of the written works of the Greek world, but was eventually torched during fighting. Underwater surveys of Alexandria's harbor have found remains of the famous Pharos Lighthouse, another wonder of the ancient world.

THE SEVEN WONDERS OF THE ANCIENT WORLD

Callimachus of Cyrene, a librarian in the harbor city of Alexandria in Egypt, wrote a treatise on "Wonders of the Ancient World," though the following definitive list of seven was not created until the Medieval period.

- The Great Pyramid of Giza in Egypt, built by pharaoh Khufu about 2550 BC, still stands today.
- The Pharos Lighthouse at Alexandria in Egypt was built around 280 BC and destroyed by an earthquake in AD 796. Sculptures that may have been displayed around the lighthouse have recently been identified by underwater archaeologists.
- The Hanging Gardens of Babylon were built by Nebuchadnezzar in about 600 BC. Excavations at Babylon have revealed terraced platforms that give the impression of hanging gardens.
- The Mausoleum at Halikarnassos in western Turkey was built in about 360 BC as a tomb for the Persian governor Mausolos. Major excavations during the 19th century recovered parts of the monument, which were taken to the British Museum in London.
- The Colossus of Rhodes was a massive bronze statue of the god Helios, built around 290 BC, but later toppled by an earthquake. No trace of the statue has been found.
- The Temple of Artemis at Ephesus in western Turkey was built by King Croesus around 560 BC, but was eventually destroyed by the Goths in AD 262. Parts of it (such as the marble column, above) are now on display in the British Museum.
- The Statue of Zeus at Olympia was a gold and ivory work created by the Greek sculptor Pheidias in about 430 BC. Although the spectacular statue is long vanished, German excavators have found the workshop where it was made.

The Romans

The Second Emperor
Tiberius, shown here on a Roman coin, was the adopted son of Augustus and became the second emperor of Rome in AD 14 until his death in AD 37. He maintained Augustus's empire, but became a reclusive tyrant in later life.

The Roman Empire established its military forts and classical cities from the Middle East to the Atlantic, and from the fringes of the Sahara Desert to Scotland.

Before the unifying force of Rome, a number of cultural groups were scattered across Italy. One of the most important and sophisticated was the Etruscans, who occupied an area bordered to the south and east by the Tiber River. The most prominent remains left by the Etruscans are the cemeteries cut into the tufa (solidified volcanic mud) of Tuscany. Some of the tombs, such as those at Tarquinia (see p. 310), were decorated with wall paintings. The Tomb of the Reliefs at Cerveteri was carved like a banqueting chamber, complete with couches round the sides and "cups" hanging on the walls. Many tombs contained imported objects from the Greek world and the eastern Mediterranean, including carved ostrich eggs and silverware from Phoenicia. One faience pail found at Tarquinia was decorated with Egyptian hieroglyphs.

One of the best explored Etruscan sanctuaries is at Pyrgi, the harbor-town of Cerveteri. During the excavations of the temple, archaeologists found gold plaques with parallel Etruscan and Punic texts, which have helped with the decipherment of Etruscan. The sanctuary at Gravisca has also yielded a stone anchor inscribed in Greek and dedicated to Apollo. Excavations at sanctuaries at the town of Veii, just north of Rome, have demonstrated that the temples of the Etruscans were decorated with elaborate multicolored terracotta reliefs.

KEY DATES IN ANCIENT ROME

753 BC	Traditional foundation of Rome
700–100 BC	Etruscan civilization
509 BC	Expulsion of the Etruscan kings of Rome; start of the Republic
264–241 BC	First Punic War
218–202 BC	Second Punic War
44 BC	Assassination of Julius Caesar
27 BC–AD 14	Augustus, the first emperor
AD 70	Destruction of Jerusalem by Rome
AD 79	Eruption of Vesuvius and the destruction of Pompeii and Herculaneum (see p. 316)
AD 212	Roman citizenship extended to all free-born members of the empire
AD 324–337	Emperor Constantine moves capital to Byzantium (renamed Constantinople)
AD 395	Roman empire divided
AD 476	Fall of Rome

THE RISE OF ROME

Etruscan culture formed the foundation of Roman civilization, and its influence can be detected in some of Rome's early monumental buildings.

Etruscan kings ruled Rome until 509 BC, when they were overthrown and replaced by the Republic, which adopted a system of representative government. The Romans started to expand their borders, conquering much of Italy before subduing north Africa's Carthaginians in the bloody Punic Wars (264–146 BC). With this expansion, the system of representative government faltered. Julius Caesar (100–44 BC) led the Romans against Gallic and German tribes and amassed enormous power, but was assassinated when he attempted to take greater control. His heir, however, eventually became the first Roman emperor, Augustus, in 27 BC.

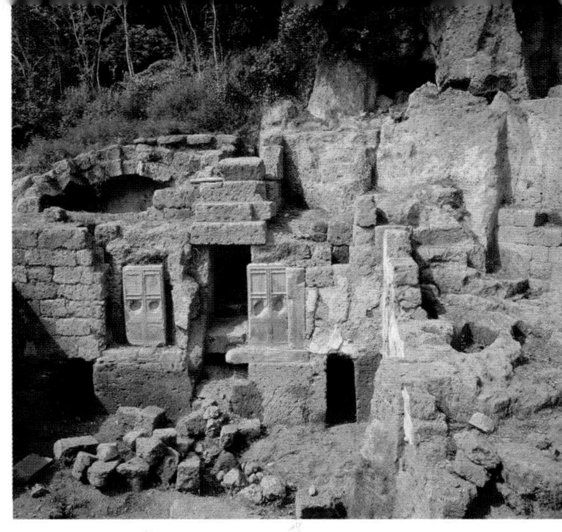

Tombs in Etruria
More than a hundred Etruscan tombs have been excavated at the necropolis of Cerveteri.

Rome had remained a relatively humble city until this time. One of Augustus's claims was that he turned Rome from a city of brick to one of marble. His contributions to the city included a new forum, development of the Palatine Hill (from which the word "palace" is derived), and the creation of the Altar of Peace, which was decorated with a series of relief friezes showing members of the imperial family and household. Subsequent emperors continued to beautify Rome with temples, victory monuments (such as the Arch of Septimius Severus in the Roman Forum), and places of entertainment (such as the multitiered Colosseum, which served as a stadium for animal fights).

KEY
Extent of the Roman Empire

Hadrian's Wall
BRITANNIA
Colchester
Rhine River
GERMANY
GAUL
Nîmes
IBERIA
Atlantic Ocean
Tarquinia
Veii
Cerveteri
Rome
Ostia
Pompeii
Black Sea
Constantinople
ANATOLIA
Carthage
Corinth
Miletus
Mediterranean Sea
Jerusalem
Jericho
Masada
AFRICA
EGYPT

Frontier Defense
Built by the emperor Hadrian (AD 117–38), Hadrian's Wall extends 72 miles (118 km) across northern England. Its 17 forts were manned by some 8,400 soldiers.

FORTS, ROADS, AND HARBORS

As different parts of central Europe and the Mediterranean came under Roman influence, so Roman architecture and culture spread. An extensive network of roads assisted with the movement of troops. In frontier provinces such as Germany and Britain, a network of forts and roads was used to secure the empire's boundaries. The stone frontier of Hadrian's Wall between the Tyne River and the Solway Firth in northern England was a complex network of walls, ditches, forts, fortlets, and watchtowers. Hadrian's successor, Antoninus Pius, established a turf wall in Scotland between the Firth of Forth and the Clyde River.

The population of a major city like Rome depended on imported foodstuffs, especially corn. Following the loss of the grain fleet in storms, the Romans established a major sheltered harbor facility at Ostia, at the mouth of the Tiber River. They also created major harbor facilities elsewhere in the Mediterranean, for example, at Corinth in Greece. In Rome itself, the reliance on imported wine and olive oil is reflected by the Monte Testaccio, a massive mound of fragments of amphoras (clay containers) from Spain.

ROMULUS AND REMUS

According to legend, Rome was founded in 753 BC by Romulus. With his twin brother, Remus, the young Romulus was thrown into a river by an evil uncle and then rescued by a she-wolf. As an adult, Romulus fought and killed his brother and went on to establish Rome.

THE EMBRACE OF ROMAN CULTURE

Roman culture spread throughout the empire as retired Roman soldiers established colonies. One of the finest complete Roman temples can be found at Nîmes in the south of France. At Colchester in southeast England, the foundations of a temple of the deified emperor Claudius can still be seen in a later Norman castle. British villas began to be decorated with mosaic floors illustrating scenes from classical mythology. For example, at Lullingstone villa, the dining room contained an image of the rape of Europa (by Zeus in the form of a bull), along with a verse in Latin.

The well-established cities of the Greek east also embraced Roman culture. By the 1st century AD, Roman-style bathhouses were introduced in cities such as Miletos in western Asia Minor. Roman taste even penetrated Judea. The palace created by King Herod at Masada incorporated the latest in Roman wall paintings, and his winter palace at Jericho was served by a long aqueduct, no doubt constructed with the help of Roman engineers using hydraulic cement. In Jerusalem, archaeologists have found Jewish houses, destroyed when the Romans sacked the city in AD 70, that were decorated with Roman-style paintings and even contained imported Roman glassware.

THE FALL OF THE EMPIRE

For four centuries, a succession of emperors provided Rome with an erratic rule. By the 4th century AD, the enormous Roman empire had become so difficult for one ruler to manage that it was divided into western and eastern halves. The western half collapsed in AD 476, when a German warlord conquered the city of Rome. The eastern half survived for another thousand years as the Byzantine empire.

Buried Town
The eruption of Mount Vesuvius in AD 79 buried the Roman town of Herculaneum in ash and mud, preserving features such as this wall painting (below left) of a banqueting couple and their slave.

Roman Aqueduct
The Pont du Gard (below) is an 885 feet (270 m) long Roman aqueduct near Nîmes in southern France. It was constructed about 20 BC to carry water across the river valley.

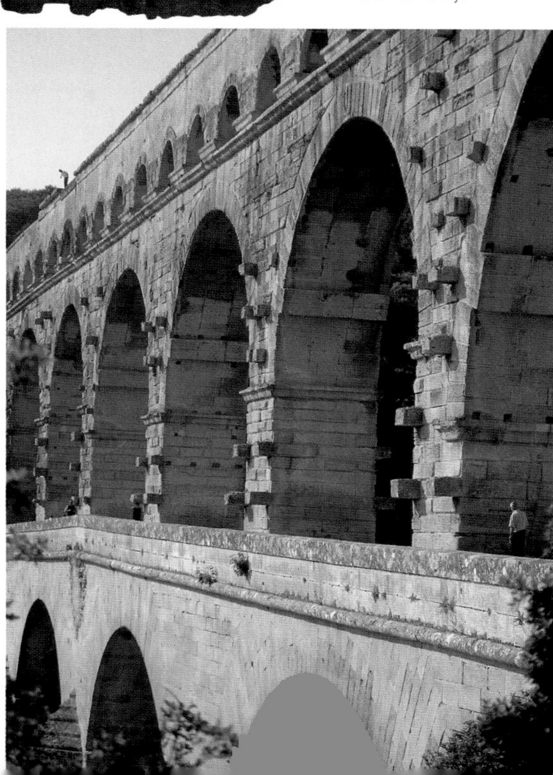

The Sculpture of Greece and Rome

Monumental Greek sculptures from the 7th century BC onward tended to be used as dedications in sanctuaries and as grave markers. Some of the earliest types were the naked youths (kouroi) and draped women (korai). Roman taste for Greek sculpture has meant that some of the lost Greek bronze sculptures of the 5th and 4th centuries BC are known from Roman marble copies, such as that of the Doryphoros ("Spear Carrier") by the Argive sculptor Polykleitos, which was found at the buried town of Pompeii.

Spear Carrier

The 5th century BC sculptor Polykleitos was famed for his bronze sculptures of young athletes, now known only from Roman copies. Departing from the tradition of rigid frontal poses, he depicted the body twisted on the vertical axis. This is a Roman marble copy of one of his greatest statues, the Doryphoros, a bronze he made about 450–400 BC.

Discus Thrower

This Discobolos (below) is a Roman marble copy of the bronze original by the Athenian sculptor Myron, c. 450 BC. The form of the discus thrower displays the mastery of anatomy developed in Greek sculpture.

Draped Figure

Inspired by Egyptian art, early Greek sculptors created korai, statues of draped maidens. Appearing from about 660 to 500 BC, the form gradually became more naturalistic. This terracotta kore dates to the 6th century BC.

The Farnese Herakles

The Farnese Herakles (below) was created by the 3rd century AD Athenian sculptor and copyist Glycon. It is a copy of a colossal bronze work by Lysippos, a 4th century BC Greek sculptor renowned for the naturalism and slender proportions of his figures.

The Metal Ages of Europe

The use of copper, bronze, and iron transformed Europe and encouraged the emergence of new groups such as Scythians, Celts, Vikings, Goths, and Huns.

Copper Idol
Until people learned to strengthen copper by casting it, the metal was mostly used for ornaments such as this idol from Bulgaria.

A Stronger Metal
To create a stronger metal, copper was mixed with tin to produce bronze. This bronze ax dates from the 10th–9th century BC.

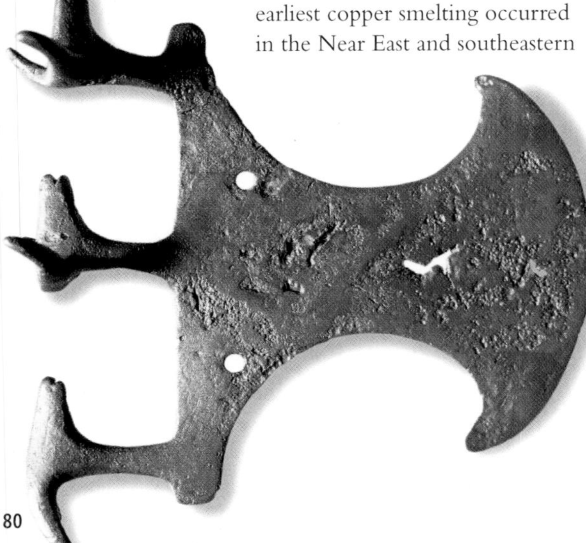

For more than 2 million years, people had been able to alter materials such as stone, wood, and bone by chipping or cutting, but not until relatively recently did they learn how to create temperatures high enough to alter materials chemically. Pyrotechnology, as the mastery of heat is called, was first used to fire clay to make pottery. Later, ores were smelted to release metals that could be hammered and cast into tools and ornaments. In prehistory, the most important metals in Europe and Asia were copper, bronze, and iron, although gold and silver are also encountered in rich burials and hoards.

THE FIRST METAL
The first type of copper used was probably native copper—a rare, pure form—since copper ores such as malachite needed to be smelted. Copper's melting point is 1981°F (1083°C), so it could not be separated from an ore until this temperature was achieved in pottery kilns.

THE SPREAD OF COPPER

Copper was the first metal to be regularly used in Eurasia. The earliest copper smelting occurred in the Near East and southeastern Europe during the 6th millennium BC. Between about 4500 and 3000 BC, its use became widespread, especially in eastern and southern Europe and the Levant. Copper mines dating to this period have been found at Rudna Glava in Yugoslavia and Aibunar in Bulgaria, while copper artifacts have turned up far from sources at sites such as Brzesč-Kujawski, and Oslonki in northern Poland. Since copper is a relatively soft material, its first uses were for ornaments such as beads and pendants. Later, the ability to cast copper enabled the production of large tools such as axes. The Iceman found in the Alps in 1991 was carrying such an ax when he died around 3300 BC (see p. 280).

THE PRODUCTION OF BRONZE

Prehistoric metalworkers would have recognized that some copper contains natural impurities, such as arsenic, that produce a stronger metal. They then tried alloying copper with other metals. The most successful of these experiments, in the 3rd millennium BC in the Near East, was the combination of copper and tin, which produces bronze. Since copper and tin sources do not occur naturally in the same places, this development required not only metallurgical skill but also the ability to procure the two metals from separate locations. Bronze is much harder than copper, making it suitable for a range of tools such as axes, spears, swords, and buckets, as well as more complicated forms of ornaments. The use of bronze spread quickly throughout Eurasia during the 2nd millennium BC.

UTILITARIAN IRON

Iron has a much higher melting point than copper and tin, so it was not smelted until people had learned to produce and maintain the necessary temperatures. This occurred about 1200 BC in the Near East and about 500 years later in Europe. Since iron is such a widespread metal, however, the ability to smelt it permitted the manufacture of very cheap and plentiful tools and weapons. Centers of iron production, such as Stična in Slovenia, emerged as hubs in a commercial system that promoted the extraction of other materials, such as salt at Hallstatt in Austria. Whereas bronze was the metal of the elite that controlled exchange, iron was a utilitarian metal that was available throughout society.

THE STEPPE TRIBES

The Scythians were a nomadic people of the steppes near the Black Sea in the 7th to 4th centuries BC. They are well known from texts by classical authors, especially a detailed description of their customs, history, and myths written by Herodotus. Archaeological investigation of Scythian culture began in the 18th century, and since then hundreds of burial mounds (see p. 352) and settlements have been excavated over a huge territory. The culture of the Scythians proper was found to be just one part of the so-called "Scythian-Siberian World," a group of related cultures that arose and converged in the Early Iron Age (8th to 3rd centuries BC) over the vast territory of the Great Steppes of Eurasia, from the Danube in the west to the Great Wall of China in the east.

All these cultures have three things in common: their weaponry, the use of horse harnesses, and an "animal style" in their art (below). The similarity of their geographic setting and hence of their way of life (nomadic pastoralism) plus the ease of communication (through horse-riding) accounts for these shared characteristics, while their mobile lifestyle led to the spread of new ideas.

La Tène Mirror
This decorated bronze mirror is one of the finest examples of the La Tène style in Celtic art. It features a complex symmetrical clover-leaf pattern. Dated to 50 BC–AD 50, the mirror was found in Desborough, England.

THE RISE OF THE CELTS

During the final millennium BC, Europe was inhabited by peoples who are known to us both from the archaeological record and from their contact with literate peoples such as the Greeks and Romans. The Greeks called them *Keltoi,* and they have become known to us as the Celts. Although they did share many common linguistic traits, decorative styles, and settlement types, there is no evidence to suggest that the Celts ever thought of themselves as having such a shared identity. Rather, they were divided into many communities and tribes that had enough in common to appear relatively homogeneous to outsiders.

The Celts have their deep roots in the central Europe of the Bronze Age, before 800 BC. This tradition continues through the Hallstatt chiefdoms of west-central Europe between 600 and 450 BC, in which trade with Greek merchants produced remarkable demonstrations of status and wealth. Hillforts such as Mont Lassois and Heuneburg were the seats of powerful individuals who controlled this trade. They amassed imports from the Mediterranean, which appear in burials such as Vix and Hochdorf (see p. 304). The importance of this trade is reflected in lavish displays of foreign contact, such as the construction of a Mediterranean-style mud-brick wall completely inappropriate for the central European climate at Heuneburg.

Although these trading contacts abated around 450 BC, the Celts had now become known to the Mediterranean world. Some groups moved south, into the Balkans and Italy, even as far as Anatolia. From writings of Greek authors such as Polybius and Posidonius, we know something of Celtic society. Although their polities are frequently called "tribes," they were really complex chiefdoms or even nascent kingdoms. Warfare was endemic, and success in battle was a key claim to power and authority. Feasting and drinking cemented relations among the elite. Another important Celtic institution was the practice of clientship. Noble patrons provided clients with protection and prestige while obtaining support and service in return. Their religion involved

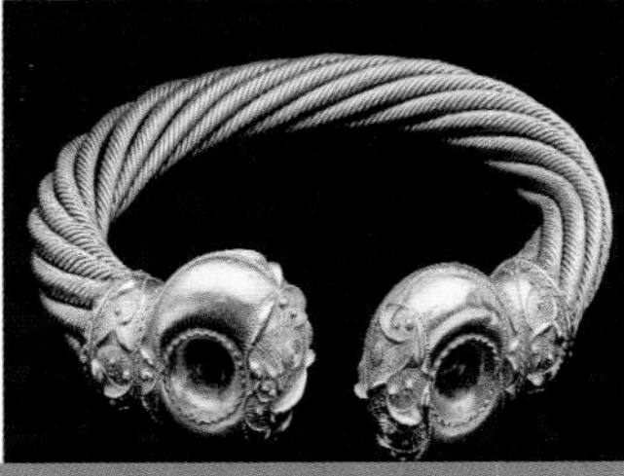

Great Torc
The Snettisham Great Torc, one of Britain's finest antiquities, was fashioned with great skill by Iron Age Celts. Made from gold mixed with silver, the torc was worn as a neckring.

KEY DATES OF THE CELTS

c. 800 BC	Iron working introduced into central Europe
c. 700 BC	Appearance of industrial centers such as Hallstatt and Stiçna
c. 600–450 BC	Trade with Greeks leads to emergence of wealthy chiefdoms in central Europe
c. 400 BC	Appearance of La Tène art style
391 BC	Celtic warriors sack Rome
c. 300 BC	Appearance of Celtic coinage
c. 100 BC	Development of oppida in western and central Europe
58–51 BC	Caesar conquers Gaul
AD 43	Roman invasion of Britain

100BC
500BC
Hochdorf
Heuneburg
Manching
Vix
Mont Lassois
Hallstatt
Bibracte
La Tène
325BC
600BC–250BC
386BC
278BC
279BC

many different deities to whom sacrifices (including human sacrifices) were made. Bogs, lakes, and groves of trees were sacred locations.

CELTIC STYLE

The period between 300 and 100 BC was the zenith of Celtic art, reflected in the La Tène style that spread throughout much of western Europe. Named after a site in western Switzerland, the La Tène style is characterized by swirling vegetal and animal ornament, especially on metal objects. It represents a marked divergence from the rigid geometric designs of earlier periods. Specialist workshops and craftsmen produced their own distinctive patterns.

In the final two centuries BC, the Celtic world saw the emergence of large fortified towns called oppida. These combined residential, manufacturing, market, and administrative functions, and many even minted their own coins. At Manching in Bavaria, the oppidum walls enclosed an area of approximately 940 acres (380 ha) that contained workshops and houses. The oppidum of Bibracte (Mont Beuvray) in France was the capital of the Aedui mentioned by Caesar. Small rectangular enclosures nearby were probably locations of ritual activities.

With the Roman conquest of western Europe, most Celtic tribes were absorbed into a cosmopolitan urban society. Only in Ireland and Scotland did Celts remain free but isolated for several more centuries. Celtic traditions, however, have managed to survive throughout this area into modern times.

KEY

Celtic Heartland

Celtic Expansion

Celtic Expansion
From the 5th century BC, Celtic culture spread from its central European homeland to the British Isles, Iberia, Italy, the Balkans, and Asia Minor.

The Battersea Shield
Too short to be suitable for serious warfare, the Battersea Shield was probably made for flamboyant display. Dating to 350–50 BC, it is made of bronze with glass inlays. Cast-bronze disks decorate the shield in a typical La Tène design.

Frankish Axhead
The francisca, or throwing ax, was a favorite weapon of the Franks. This example, from Neuwied in Germany, dates to the 7th century AD. Its elaborate silver-inlay decoration is a clear sign of the owner's high status.

BARBARIAN EUROPE

The decay of Roman power in the 4th century AD ushered in a period of upheaval. Traditionally known as the Migration Period, it seems to have involved the movements of large barbarian groups over long distances. Yet the evidence for such migrations is equivocal. Ethnohistorical accounts describe large ethnic groups shifting across the landscape, sometimes running into each other and at other times wreaking havoc in what remained of the Roman empire. Archaeologically, however, these movements are not particularly visible. Variability in archaeological remains suggests that in much of Europe migrating peoples mingled with local groups in multicultural societies and were transformed themselves.

The first indications of powerful well-organized groups on the borders of the Roman empire came during the 3rd century AD. The Franks first appeared in written sources in AD 257 and several decades later began raiding Roman territory west of the Rhine. In AD 286 the Saxons appeared to the north of the Franks, while to the south, the Alemanni threatened the Roman frontier. During the next century, the intensity of these attacks increased. In AD 350–351 the Alemanni penetrated deep into Gaul before being forced back.

GOTHS AND HUNS

From the east came Goths to add further to the Romans' worries. The origins of the Goths are shrouded in mystery. Although some scholars believe that they originated in Scandinavia, others trace them archaeologically to the area along the lower Vistula River in the 2nd century AD. From there, war bands ranged to the southeast to gather allies, thus creating an ethnically mixed tribal population north of the Black Sea. Roman writers referred to such tribes as Goths. They appear in the historical record in AD 238, when they sacked the city of Histria at the mouth of the Danube. Several Gothic political units, each with its own king, flourished along the Black Sea. Those groups nearer

KEY DATES OF THE BARBARIAN TRIBES

1st–2nd centuries AD	Turbulent conditions in eastern and northern Europe trigger population movements
AD 238	Goths sack Histria on lower Danube
AD 257	First written mention of Franks
AD 285	Administrative division of Roman empire into eastern and western parts
AD 286	Saxons appear in written sources
AD 370	Huns pressure Goths in eastern Europe; Frankish attacks in Rhineland
AD 376	Goths enter Roman frontiers
AD 395–410	Alaric is king of Visigoths
AD 406	Franks and Alemanni cross the Rhine
AD 410	Visigoths sack Rome; death of Alaric
AD 440–50	Angles, Saxons, and Jutes begin to invade England
AD 453	Attila dies, Huns retreat
AD 455	Vandals sack Rome
AD 476	Final collapse of Roman empire

the Roman frontier maintained close, but often strained, relations with imperial authorities.

Shortly after AD 370, the eastern neighbors of the Goths—the Huns—suddenly pushed west, and a few years later, two large Gothic groups asked for asylum inside the imperial frontiers. The origins of the Huns are as mysterious as those of the Goths. We can say confidently only that they came from east of the Volga River, and some scholars place their origin in the Altai Mountains near China. The Huns continued to filter into southeastern Europe, and by the 420s the center of Hunnic power could be found in the Hungarian Plain. From there, led by Attila, they launched their forays into central Europe and northern Italy. After Attila's death in AD 453, they were defeated and retreated eastward.

As the Roman empire disintegrated during the 5th century AD, more barbarian groups found themselves within its European provinces. In AD 406, a confederation of German tribes penetrated southeast across the Rhine and eventually reached Spain several years later. The Goths were also on the move, and in AD 410, one Gothic group, the Visigoths, sacked Rome, before moving on to Spain and western France. In the second half of the 5th century, groups of Franks settled in northern France and were eventually unified into a kingdom late in the century by Clovis. After the final collapse of the Roman empire in AD 476, another Gothic group, known as the Ostrogoths, established its kingdom in northeastern Italy.

Germanic Migration
The collapse of the Roman empire triggered a series of large-scale migrations by Germanic peoples.

Visigoth Coin
This coin depicts Recared (AD 586–601), the Visigoth monarch whose conversion to Catholicism helped secure the allegiance of the Spanish people.

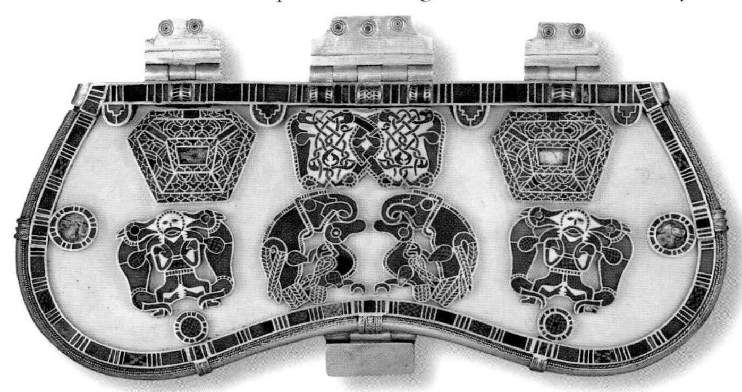

Anglo-Saxon Purse
The Anglo-Saxon ship-burial at Sutton Hoo contained this fine purse lid, adorned with gold and cloisonné enamel.

THE VIKING AGE

The Vikings are notorious as warriors who made terrifying raids on the Christian lands of western and southern Europe. Yet they were also a literate society that engaged in trade, exploration, and colonization. From their homelands in Denmark, Norway, and Sweden, Vikings ranged far afield to control large parts of the British Isles, to colonize Iceland and Greenland, to establish towns in Russia, and to be the first Europeans in North America.

Viking society developed from the Late Iron Age communities of southern Scandinavia. A warrior elite had emerged in this area during the first centuries AD, and the practice of trading complemented by raiding was already common. Trading centers appeared at many locations, such as at Gudme on the Danish island of Fyn. The accumulation of valuables by the elite and competitive gift-giving may have been important in establishing this highly stratified social order. Craft production under elite patronage produced remarkable jewelry and decorated weapons. Examples of these are found in the Vendel and Valsgärde burials near Uppsala in Sweden.

Gotland Stone
This Viking funerary stone from the 8th century AD was found in Gotland, Sweden. The top panel depicts the war god Odin on his magical horse Sleipnir. The middle panel shows a Viking ship, while the bottom panel features the trickster Loki and his wife Sigya.

TRADERS AND RAIDERS

There was no dramatic transformation when this Late Iron Age society became what we know as the Vikings. To some degree, the term "Viking Age" refers more to the foreign adventures of the inhabitants of southern Scandinavia than to any significant internal transformation. A rough indicator of the start of the Viking period might be their first recorded raid on Britain, an attack on the island monastery at Lindisfarne, in AD 793. Around this time, several of the trading emporia that dominated the Viking economic world, such as Hedeby on Jutland and Birka near Stockholm, emerged.

Most inhabitants of southern Scandinavia were farmers, who grew rye, barley, and oats and kept cattle on small family farmsteads.

KEY DATES OF THE VIKINGS

AD 600–800	Late Iron Age societies in southern Scandinavia emerge as traders and warriors
AD 793	Vikings sack Lindisfarne on the English coast
C. AD 800	Establishment of trading emporia such as Hedeby and Birka
AD 845	Vikings sack Paris
AD 862	Viking prince Rurik establishes Russian state at Novgorod
AD 870	Vikings begin to settle Iceland
C. AD 900	Gokstad ship built
AD 985	Vikings colonize Greenland
C. AD 1000	Vikings establish settlement at L'Anse aux Meadows in Newfoundland
AD 1000–1100	Scandinavian kingdoms adopt Christianity
AD 1350–1450	Viking settlements in Greenland abandoned

The custom of land being inherited by the firstborn son created a surplus of younger sons who could leave the farm and become craftsmen, traders, and warriors. Before long, some began to look beyond their homeland for new trading and raiding opportunities. Their deeds are documented on runes (stones inscribed with characters).

MIGRATION AND EXPANSION

The sea was hardly a barrier. With their mastery of shipbuilding, Vikings crossed large expanses of water. Viking ships found at Skuldelev, in Roskilde Fjord in Denmark, illustrate the variety of craft. One was a 54 foot (16.5 m) long deep-sea cargo vessel, while another was more than 90 feet (30 m) long and would have carried a party of warriors. The significance of ships in Viking life is reflected in the numerous boat-burials of their elite, as at Gokstad and Oseberg (see p. 322).

Vikings from Sweden penetrated into eastern Europe and established trading centers such as those at Novgorod (see p. 324) and Kiev. Here they mingled with the local population and formed the leadership of the early Russian state. In the west, Vikings from Norway and Denmark overran much of England. They also set out into the North Atlantic to settle Iceland and Greenland. In 1960 a Viking settlement was found at L'Anse aux Meadows in Newfoundland (see p. 408).

During the 11th century, the acceptance of Christianity and the emergence of central royal authority brought an end to Viking expansion and raiding. Many of their settlements, such as Dublin and Kiev, grew into major cities, and their trading centers, such as the island of Gotland, continued to prosper for centuries to come.

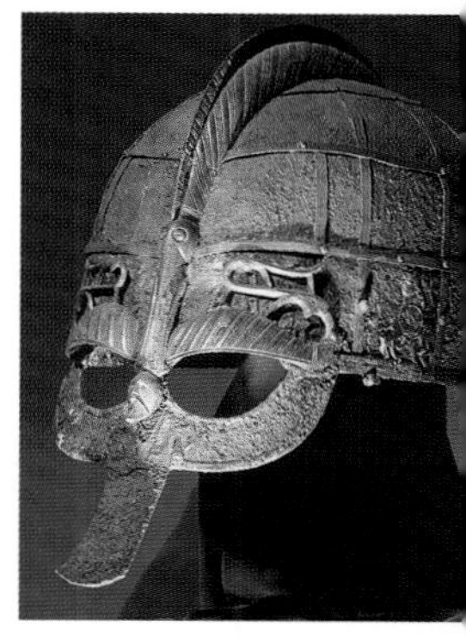

Buried Helmet
This helmet was discovered in a boat burial in Uppland, Sweden. It has been dated to the 7th century AD.

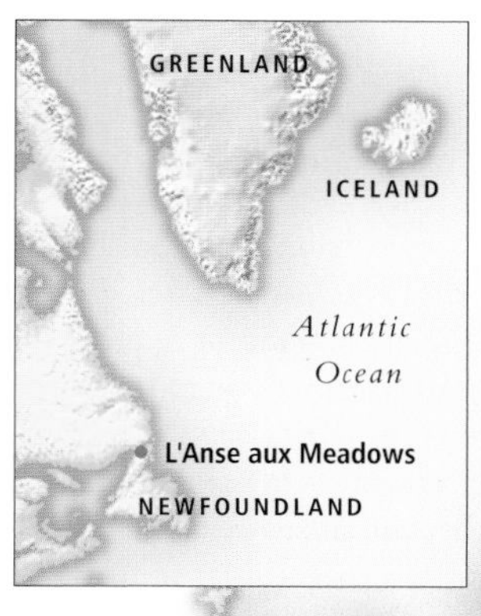

The Viking World
Danish and Norwegian Vikings expanded to the west mainly through raids, while Swedish Vikings built up a trading network in the east.

Bodies from the Bog

Huldremose Woman
Huldremose Woman (above) was found in a bog near Ramten, Denmark, in 1879. Sometime between 160 BC and AD 340, the woman met a gruesome end—her limbs had been repeatedly hacked and her right arm was completely cut off.

Bogs and ponds played a central role in the religion of the Iron Age peoples of northern Europe, and the bodies of human sacrifices from this period are often found preserved in the peat bogs of Denmark, northern Germany, and the British Isles. Most met gruesome deaths. Some were strangled or drowned, others beheaded or hanged. A man found in Lindow Moss in England was first struck violently on the head; then he was garrotted; finally, his throat was slit. The tranquil expression on the face of Tollund Man belies the fact that around his neck was a leather noose.

Tollund Man
Discovered during peat cutting in Denmark in 1950, Tollund Man was in his thirties and stood about 5 feet (1.6 m) tall. Around his waist was only a belt; on his head, a leather cap. The absence of summer fruits in his stomach suggests that he met his violent death in winter or early spring.

Damendorf Man
The bog bodies show a great variation in the degree of preservation. Damendorf Man (right) was discovered in a bog in northern Germany. His bones have completely dissolved, leaving only extremely flattened skin, nails, and hair.

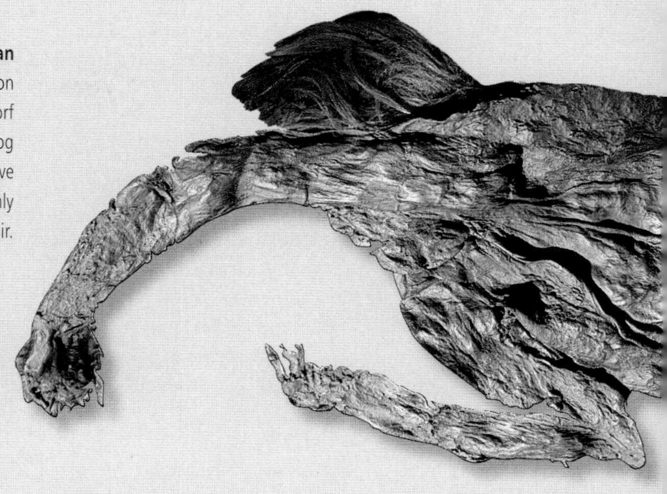

Lindow Man
In 1984 the body of a man (below) was found in Lindow Moss, near Manchester, England. In his twenties when he was so violently killed between AD 20 and 130, Lindow Man was well built with small ears, a full head of dark hair, and a short beard.

Kingdoms of Africa

Ife Terracotta
During the 11th to 15th centuries AD, Ife in southwest Nigeria was a prosperous trading settlement, with a royal palace, shrines, and paved courtyards. While most remains of its mud-brick buildings have disappeared, archaeologists have discovered a series of remarkable naturalistic terracotta figures (above).

Africans south of the Sahara Desert went straight from the Stone Age to the Iron Age, bypassing a Bronze Age. It was during the Iron Age that Africa's first great kingdoms and states arose.

People living in western Asia early in the 2nd millennium BC are thought to have been among the first to discover how to extract workable quantities of iron metal from ore by means of a complex chemical reaction called smelting. Knowledge of this process reached North Africa and Egypt in about the 8th century BC.

IRON IN WEST AFRICA

The earliest known evidence for iron-working in West Africa dates to about the 7th–5th centuries BC in Niger and Nigeria. Some researchers think that iron technology spread southward to West Africa from North Africa, either across the Sahara Desert or from centers such as Meroë in the Nile Valley (see box, p. 193). Others suggest that iron metallurgy could have developed independently in West Africa from local copper-smelting techniques. Still others consider that both importation and local invention were involved. Indeed, there are many examples of locally developed improvements to iron technology during the African Iron Age, which also saw

KEY DATES OF AFRICA'S KINGDOMS

3RD OR 1ST MILLENNIUM BC (?)	Bantu migrations
8TH CENTURY BC	Appearance of iron in North Africa
7TH CENTURY BC	Appearance of iron in West Africa
C. 900–300 BC	Napatan Empire
C. 600 BC–AD 300	Nok early Iron Age culture in north-central Nigeria
C. 800 BC OR 500–300 BC	Appearance of iron in East Africa
C. 300 BC–AD 300	Meroitic empire
1ST–7TH CENTURIES AD	Aksum, capital of an Ethiopian kingdom
AD 400	Bantu-speakers and iron present south of Limpopo River
C. AD 600	Lydenburg heads
AD 300–1400	Jenne-Jeno (or Djenne) one of earliest African towns
8TH–11TH CENTURIES AD (?)	Igbo-Ukwu Nigerian burial of elite ruler
8TH–11TH CENTURIES AD	Kingdom of Ghana
C. AD 1220–1270	Mapungubwe
13TH–15TH CENTURIES AD	Empire of Mali
C. AD 1464–1589	Kingdom of Songhay
AD 1300–1450	Great Zimbabwe capital of Shona state

the working of other metals such as copper and gold.

Iron-smelting sites in Tanzania date to at least the late 1st millennium BC. Iron Age communities were present in Zambia and Zimbabwe by some 2,000 years ago, but there is no clear evidence for their presence south of the Limpopo River before AD 400.

THE SPREAD OF IRON

The spread of iron through most of central, eastern, and southern Africa is generally linked to movements of groups of Negroid Bantu-speaking peoples, who originally came from the border between Nigeria and Cameroon. Some archaeologists, however, now think that the Bantu migrations may have begun before the advent of the Iron Age.

Iron Age Africans were farmers who found iron effective for agricultural tools and weapons. They lived in permanent villages and brought not only knowledge of metal-working, but also domestic animals, cultivated plants, and pottery to much of sub-Saharan Africa. Traditional styles of decorated pottery enable archaeologists to trace the movements of Iron Age Africans and the relationships between various groups over time.

From the 1st millennium AD onward, the rise of trade networks led to the development of towns, the emergence of an elite social class, and the appearance of kingdoms and states.

THE RISE OF WEST AFRICAN KINGDOMS

Shortly after the arrival of iron in West Africa, mud houses replaced dwellings made from wood and grass; farming villages became hubs in local trade networks; and the Nok culture of north-central Nigeria produced eerie baked clay heads, which are the oldest known sculptures in sub-Saharan Africa (see p. 252).

Early Iron Work
Found at Muteshti, Zambia, this iron blade dates from early in the 1st century AD, when iron-working spread throughout much of south-central Africa.

By AD 800 a small settlement at Jenne-Jeno(or Djenne) in Mali had grown into one of the earliest known African walled urban centers and was home to some 27,000 people. Extraordinary collections of bronze and copper artifacts from the burial chamber of an important individual at Igbo-Ukwu in Nigeria indicate that by the 8th–11th centuries AD an elite class vested with wealth, religious authority, and political power had emerged.

In the 8th century AD, the first sub-Saharan African state, the Kingdom of Ghana, was established between the Niger River and the Senegal River (in a different location from its modern African namesake). Its riches were based on trade: gold, slaves, ivory, and animal products moved north across the Sahara Desert in exchange for salt, cloth, pottery, and glass. It was followed by a series of successors, notably the Empire of Mali and the Kingdom of Songhay. The Empire of Mali covered approximately the same area as the modern country of Mali, and its city of Timbuktu became famous as a center of scholarship from early in the 14th century AD. Songhay's kings reigned supreme from Gao on the Niger River during the 16th century AD.

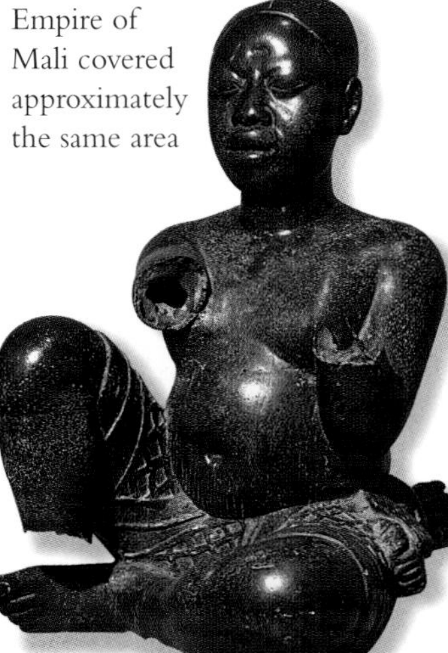

Nigerian Kingdom
The legendary hero Tsoede reputedly brought this sculpture with him when he founded the kingdom of Nupe, near the confluence of the Niger and Kaduna rivers in central Nigeria, in the 16th century AD.

ORIGINS
The histories of many African kingdoms are recorded in oral traditions. These usually start with a male founder who persuaded or forced people to accept his rule. Often he is presented as a stranger with a supernatural power, such as the ability to make rain or to work iron.

KINGS AND COMMONERS IN SOUTHERN AFRICA

Control of trade also initiated the creation of powerful kingdoms in other regions of sub-Saharan Africa. From at least the 9th century AD, communities in the southern African interior exchanged ivory and gold for glass beads and cloth imported from Swahili traders on the East African coast. When Mapungubwe in northern South Africa was laid out in about AD 1220, the leader and his family settled on a hilltop and lived separately from the commoners in the valley below. Separation of social classes was continued at Mapungubwe's successor, Great Zimbabwe (see p. 258), the capital of a huge Shona empire that covered the territory of modern Zimbabwe and beyond at its height during the 14th century AD.

MEROË AND AKSUM

Throughout its dynastic age, Egypt's southern border lay at the first Nile cataract (modern Aswan). To the south of this natural boundary was Nubia, with Southern or Upper Nubia being known as Kush. From the beginning of Egypt's Old Kingdom to the end of its New (2649–1070 BC), Egypt sought to control and colonize Nubia, exploiting its natural resources. Times of Egyptian weakness, however, allowed the independent Nubian culture to flourish.

The first independent Kingdom of Kush, based at the third cataract city of Kerma, developed during Egypt's troubled Second Intermediate Period (c. 1690–1550 BC), but collapsed with Nubia's reabsorption into the Egyptian empire. More than six centuries later, a second independent Kushite kingdom developed. By tradition, this essentially homogeneous culture is divided into two periods: the Napatan empire, the time from c. 900 to 300 BC, when the royal cemetery was situated south of the fourth Nile cataract near Napata; and the Meroitic empire, c. 300 BC–AD 300, when the royal family were buried further south, beyond the fifth cataract at Meroë. During Egypt's troubled 25th Dynasty, the Meroitic kings were able to march northward and conquer Egypt, returning home for burial.

The memory of the ancient city of Meroë was preserved by classical authors and by the Bible, but it was not until 1772 that the city itself was rediscovered. The site was later excavated by John Garstang (1910–12) and George Reisner (1920–23). Their investigations revealed a successful industrial city incorporating a royal capital embellished with temples dedicated to several gods, including the Egyptian Amen and the local lion-headed Apedemak. The royal tombs of Meroë were small, solid, steep-sided pyramids topping rock-cut burial chambers (above). Eventually, following the capture of Meroë by Ezana of Aksum, the city was abandoned.

Aksum (or Axum), the capital of an extensive kingdom whose lands included northern Ethiopia and the Yemen, flourished from the 1st to the 7th centuries AD. This was a society based on international trade—control of the Red Sea coast allowed links with lands as far away as India and the Roman empire. Aksum quickly became a wealthy city decorated with impressive obelisks. Eventually, disruptions to the trade networks brought about Aksum's decline.

The Indus Civilization

The civilization of the Indus Valley was the largest of its time, a thriving state with wide-ranging trading contacts. Our inability to read its texts, however, makes it also the least understood.

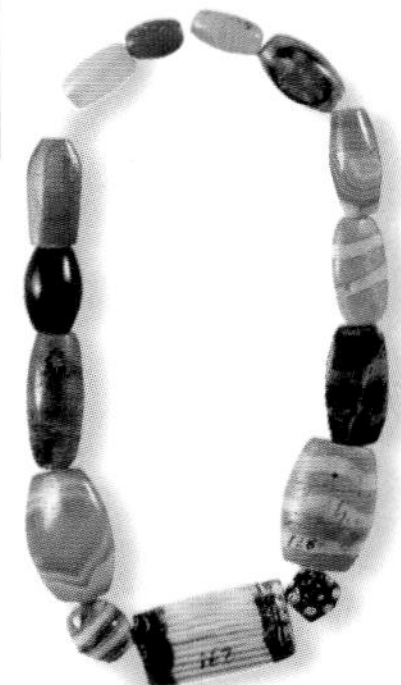

Fine Craft
A necklace of polished gems dating to the 3rd millennium BC shows the skill of Indus craftsmen.

Indus Seal
The undeciphered Indus script appears on this seal (right). Although almost 4,000 inscriptions have now been found, most are very short.

Herders and farmers from Baluchistan in the west spread onto the plains of the Indus and (now-dry) Saraswati rivers during the 4th millennium BC. They gradually established towns, often building walls around them as protection against flooding. Between 2700 and 2600 BC, a transformation took place that saw the cultural diversity of this enormous region being replaced or overlaid by a unified culture referred to as the Indus civilization.

THE RISE OF CITIES

Cities emerged as the center of huge regional domains—Harappa in the Punjab, Rakhigarhi in the east, Ganweriwala in the Saraswati Valley, Dholavira in Gujurat, and Mohenjo Daro in the heartland of the Indus Valley. Baluchistan to the west was also culturally and probably politically integrated into the Indus realm.

Many towns grew up, uniform in their overall conception but each having features related to their individual role within the civilization. Most were divided into two parts: a lower town with houses and workshops, and a raised or separately walled citadel containing public buildings—religious structures, such as the Great Bath at Mohenjo Daro; administrative buildings, including a huge warehouse at Lothal; and perhaps the residences of the unknown rulers, who may have been religious leaders.

ELUSIVE TEXTS

Clues from Indus art and architecture suggest that many aspects of later Hindu religion, such as the worship of Shiva, find their roots here. But our understanding of Indus religion, social structure, and political organization is severely hampered by our inability to read their writing. The brevity and limited nature of the texts, inscribed mainly on steatite seals, make their decipherment virtually impossible.

TRAVEL AND TRADE

Cities and towns were centers of industrial activity, producing high quality pottery, fine jewelry, and flint and metal tools. These distinctive artifacts were distributed throughout the Indus realm, reaching even the rural homes of the farmers, fishers, and pastoralists who produced the food upon which the townsfolk depended. Herders traveling between seasonal pastures acted as carriers for the internal distribution network, while the rivers also acted as major highways. Indus traders had dealings with fishermen and hunter-gatherers in neighboring regions, exchanging Indus foodstuffs and manufactured goods for metal ores and other raw materials. They also traveled as far as Mesopotamia, exporting timber, ivory, gold, and jewelry, particularly carnelian beads.

THE DECLINE OF THE INDUS

By 1800 BC, however, the cities and towns of the Indus were starting to decline. International trade ceased, urban features—such as the sophisticated drainage and sanitation systems, the writing system, and the highly structured distribution network—gradually disappeared, and individual regional communities emerged. While some of these communities were prosperous, they were on a much smaller scale than the great Indus civilization.

Mohenjo Daro

The largest Indus city was Mohenjo Daro (see also p. 338). Its high-walled citadel featured the Great Bath (below). The planned lower town exhibited a high standard of living.

KEY DATES IN INDUS HISTORY

7000 BC	First farmers in region bordering Indus River; trade with Central Asia
5500 BC	Earliest pottery in this region
3800 BC	Settlement on plains of Indus Valley; copperwork develops
3200 BC	Towns emerge in Indus plains and uplands
2700–2600 BC	Transformation of Indus towns and emergence of Indus state
2600–1800 BC	Mature Indus civilization with planned settlements, sophisticated water supply and drainage, high quality crafts
2600 BC	Beginning of Indus script
2300 BC	Sargon of Akkad (Mesopotamia) refers to trade with Indus civilization
2000 BC	Cultivation of rice and millets begins in Indo-Gangetic divide and Gujurat
2000 BC	Saraswati River, central to Indus agriculture, begins to dry up
1800 BC	Indus cities and towns decline and international trade ceases
1800–1500 BC	Farming communities with Indus roots emerge in adjacent areas

States of Southeast Asia

Thai Buddha
The religions of Buddhism and Hinduism gradually spread from India throughout Southeast Asia. This bronze Buddha comes from 12th century Thailand.

The 1st millennium AD saw the rise of states in mainland Southeast Asia and the islands of Indonesia, strongly influenced by the culture of India, with which they had traded for centuries.

Southeast Asia, rich in spices and metal ores, was ideally placed as a major participant in the international trade networks that began in the late 1st millennium BC and reached new heights by the early centuries AD. The Chinese employed Southeast Asian shipping to carry silks and other goods westward by the southern, seaborne route. This arrangement gained greatly in importance when the political situation drove the Chinese court south in the 3rd century AD.

INDIAN INFLUENCE

Of more significance to the peoples of Southeast Asia was their trade with India and thence with the Roman world—lands whose luxury goods have been found in many sites. The rulers of emerging kingdoms in Myanmar (Pyu), Thailand (Dvaravati), Cambodia (Funan), Vietnam (Linyi), and Indonesia adopted many elements of Indian culture. They began recording their deeds in inscriptions using the Sanskrit language and Indian scripts, adapted Indian legal and political institutions, took Indian names, and claimed Indian ancestry. Most important was their espousal of the Hindu and Buddhist religions.

Indian styles of religious art and architecture became widespread, developing local characteristics and new forms. Successive Khmer kings founded temples in which the central object of worship, the lingam (stylized phallus) of the Hindu god Shiva, also represented royal authority. The most splendid of these monuments, however, was the Mahayana Buddhist Bayon temple at Angkor. Later Khmer rulers were adherents of Theravada Buddhism. Similar peaceful changes in religious allegiance characterized other realms of Southeast Asia.

Trade probably remained the main underpinning of the kingdoms that developed in Indonesia, although the great agricultural prosperity of central Java also contributed to the might of the 8th–9th century Sailendra

KEY DATES IN SOUTHEAST ASIAN HISTORY

AD 100	Peak of trade between India and Southeast Asia, established centuries earlier
AD 200	City of Oc Eo in Cambodia established, with sophisticated canals and reservoirs
AD 550	Kingdom of Zhenla in Cambodia expands
670–1320	Srivijaya Empire in Sumatra
775–830	Sailendra Dynasty constructs Buddhist shrine of Borobudur in Java
790	Jayavarman II establishes Khmer kingdom of Kambujadesa in Cambodia
850–1287	Kingdom of Pagan in Myanmar
921	Kingdom of Champa in southern Vietnam
939–1288	Kingdom of Dai Viet in northern Vietnam
1181	Jayavarman VII becomes Khmer king; builds Angkor Thom and Bayon
1250	Thai kingdom of Sukhothai established
1431	Angkor abandoned and Khmer kingdom in decline

kingdom, best known for its creation of the magnificent Buddhist shrine at Borobudur (see p. 362).

KHMER EXPANSION

Rice farming had been spreading and growing in importance in mainland Southeast Asia. The area of the Mekong River and around the great Tonle Sap Lake, heartland of successive Khmer kingdoms, was particularly fertile, its productivity burgeoning as new techniques for conserving and distributing water were developed. Successive kings organized the construction of massive canals and reservoirs, the resulting productivity supporting the expansion of the Khmer kingdom. Around 790 Jayavarman II began the conquest of much of mainland Southeast Asia. The Khmer kingdom reached its greatest extent under Jayavarman VII, who built the great city of Angkor Thom in the 12th century (see p. 364). Thereafter the kingdom declined; much of it fell to the neighboring Thai and Cham kingdoms by the 14th century.

Pagan
MYANMAR (PYU)
Sukhothai
Mekong River
South China Sea
THAILAND (DVARAVATI)
Angkor
VIETNAM (LINYI)
CHAMPA
Andaman Sea
CAMBODIA (FUNAN)
Oc Eo
KHMER
SRI VIJAYA
Sumatra
Borneo
INDONESIA
SAILENDRA
Java
Borobudur

KEY

- Limits of Sailendra
- Limits of Srivijaya
- Limits of Khmer
- Limits of Champa

Indian Script
The Indian Sanskrit language was adopted throughout much of Southeast Asia. This Sanskrit inscription is featured on a column in the east entry tower of the temple mountain Ta Keo, in Cambodia.

Angkor Wat
The 12th century temple of Angkor Wat, in Cambodia, blended Hindu cosmology and architecture with pre-existing Khmer beliefs. The enclosure symbolizes the Hindu cosmos, while the temple itself stood for the five peaks of Mount Meru, the abode of the gods.

Dynasties of China

The Great Wall Repaired and improved over the centuries, the wall extends for roughly 4,500 miles (7,300 km).

Chinese civilization looks back on 3,000 years of dynastic history. Archaeological discoveries and written sources have provided us with a detailed picture of life and death under the emperors.

By 5000 BC six coevolving Neolithic cultures had emerged along the banks of China's Yangtze and Yellow rivers. With these permanent settlements, new forms of social organization arose and ushered China into the dynastic era. Around 2000 BC the Neolithic cultures along the middle reaches of the Yellow River gave rise to the more complex Bronze Age civilizations ruled by the Xia and Shang dynasties (2100–1100 BC). The Shang featured domestication of the horse, bronze casting, and a metropolis with a cult center where religious deeds were performed. The following Zhou Dynasty (1100–256 BC) introduced the pivotal concept of the heavenly mandate, with its rulers mediating between heaven and the realm of humans.

CHINESE HISTORICAL PERIODS AND DYNASTIES

c. 6000–2100 BC	Neolithic
2100–1600 BC	Xia Dynasty
1600–1100 BC	Shang Dynasty
1100–771 BC	Western Zhou Dynasty
770–256 BC	Eastern Zhou Dynasty
722–481 BC	Spring and Autumn Period
481–222 BC	Warring States Period
221–206 BC	Qin Dynasty
206 BC–AD 9	Western Han Dynasty
AD 9–24	Xin Dynasty
24–220	Eastern Han Dynasty
220–265	Three Kingdoms
220–265	Jin Dynasty
420–589	Northern and Southern Dynasties
589–618	Sui Dynasty
618–907	Tang Dynasty
907–60	Five Dynasties
960–1172	Northern Song Dynasty
1172–1276	Southern Song Dynasty
1276–1368	Yuan Dynasty
1368–1644	Ming Dynasty
1644–1911	Qing Dynasty
1911–1949	Republic
1949–	People's Republic

THE FIRST EMPEROR

China's Bronze Age lasted about 2,000 years, reaching its zenith in philosophy and artistry during the Spring and Autumn Period (722–481 BC) and the Warring States Period (481–222 BC). Confucianism, with its emphasis on rites and virtues, and Taoism, with its idea of a new world order, redefined the fundamentals of Chinese culture. This was an era of great upheaval as seven mighty states struggled for control. Finally the leader of the Qin unified the country and appointed himself as the First Emperor of China, Qin Shihuangdi (221–206 BC). A ruthless ruler, he standardized weights, writing systems, administration, and currencies, all of which were largely adopted by the Han rulers (206 BC–AD 220) who

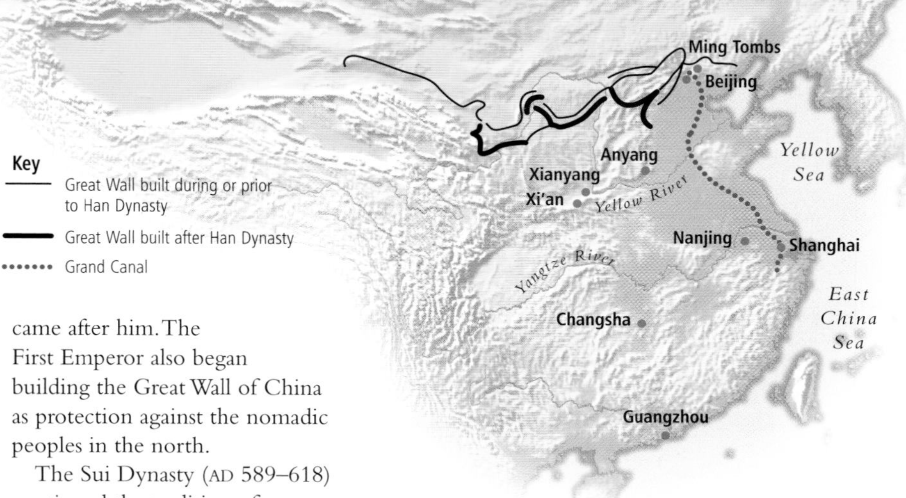

came after him. The First Emperor also began building the Great Wall of China as protection against the nomadic peoples in the north.

The Sui Dynasty (AD 589–618) continued the tradition of great works by building the Grand Canal, a 3,000 mile (5,000 km) structure that connected north and south for the first time and involved more than 5 million forced laborers.

CULTURAL EXCHANGE

Diplomacy and trade opened China to the outside world. Now under the Tang rulers (618–907), China stretched from southern Vietnam to inner Mongolia. The famous Silk Road linked continental China with western Asia, and the introduction of Buddhist culture from India is reflected in the period's mural painting, ceramics, and metalwork. Decentralization and natural disasters led to the short-lived Five Dynasties (907–60) and the Northern Song Dynasty (960–1172) in the north. The country was reunified under the Southern Song Dynasty (1172–1276), which oversaw an age of fine porcelain production and landscape painting.

Over the course of four centuries, progressively greater parts of China were conquered by inner Asian tribal people, culminating in 1276 with the foundation of the Yuan Dynasty by Kublai Khan, who incorporated all of China into his empire. During the Mongol occupation, China was tied into a Eurasian empire, with foreigners such as Marco Polo visiting the court.

THE LAST DYNASTIES

A peasant's revolt finally overthrew the alien rulers in 1368 and the Ming emperors (1368–1644) came to power. They established the great walled city of Beijing in the north as their capital. Here they built the Forbidden City, a closely guarded palace compound.

China's last emperors were the Manchus from Manchuria, who established the Qing Dynasty (1644–1911). They oversaw an age of cultural ascendancy, with great imperial art collections. Internal and external problems finally led to the foundation of the Republic in 1911. The dynastic age was over.

A Tale of Two Rivers

Two great rivers flow east through China, the Yellow River in the north and the Yangtze in the center. The north is colder, with shorter growing seasons, while the regions along the Yangtze are warmer and allow rice cultivation.

A Transforming Leader

Under Qin Shihuangdi, China was transformed from a feudal society into a strong, centralized state. The First Emperor mobilized hordes of workers to carry out massive construction projects, including the Great Wall, extensive roads and canals, and his own elaborate tomb near Xianyang (see p. 354).

Dynasties of Japan

Japan's dynastic age began in 660 BC. The first emperor, Jimmu, was said to be a direct descendant of the sun goddess Amaterasu, and all the emperors who followed ruled with a heavenly mandate.

Haniwa House
Earthenware models known as *haniwa* were deposited in burial mounds during the 3rd–5th centuries AD.

Warrior Wear
Japanese armor is made up of thousands of small plates of lacquered leather or steel. The Do-maru style (below) was worn from the 8th to 12th centuries AD.

The story of Japan can be traced back to at least 30,000 BC, although we do not know when humans first settled on the Japanese archipelago. The Paleolithic and Mesolithic cultures, variously dated from 30,000 BC on, were followed by the Neolithic Jômon culture around 10,000 BC. This hunting and fishing culture remained stable for thousands of years. Around 250 BC, a new tribe known as the Yayoi spread from southern Kyushu slowly to the east. The Yayoi grew rice and had pottery, weaving, and iron, technologies that came from China.

FIRST UNIFICATION

Contact with China and Korea in the early centuries AD brought profound changes to Japan, including the Chinese writing system and Buddhism. From the 3rd century AD, large keyhole-shaped tombs with burial mounds (*kofun*) proliferated throughout the islands. Ceramic figures known as *haniwa* have been excavated from these tombs. The first steps toward political unification of the country occurred during the Kofun Period in the late 4th to early 5th centuries AD under the Yamato court. Prince Shotuku set up the first constitution, following the Chinese model of centralized government. Buddhism gained ground and eventually became the state religion.

The 7th and 8th centuries saw an age of cultural ascendancy. In

JAPANESE HISTORICAL PERIODS	
c. 10,000–2000 BC	Jômon
c. 200 BC–AD 250	Yayoi
c. AD 250–552	Kofun (Tumulus)
552–710	Asuka
710–794	Nara
794–1185	Heian
1185–1392	Kamakura
1392–1573	Muromachi
1573–1603	Momoyama
1603–1868	Edo
1868–1912	Meiji
1912–26	Taishô
1912–	Shôwa

Nagoya Castle
During the Edo Period, Japan was ruled by shoguns (military leaders). The powerful Tokugawa shogunate erected a great castle at Nagoya in 1610. The castle was destroyed by fire during the Second World War, but was reconstructed in 1959.

the new capital of Nara, the Todai temple was built and is now the oldest wooden structure in the world. This was a time of a lively exchange with the Chinese court, with Japan being the end of the Silk Road. The following Heian Period (794–1185), named after the new capital (today's Kyôto), cut off formal relations with China.

WARRIOR GOVERNMENT

When the Japanese empire finally declined in the Kamakura Period, around the end of the 12th century, military governments made up of the samurai warrior class gained political authority. These were headed by a shogun, who was the emperor's military agent and held the real power. Internal revolts and the Mongolian invasion prepared the way for the Muromachi rulers (1392–1573). From 1549 on, early contacts with the Western world started bringing foreign goods and Christianity to Japan. The following period of the Momoyama rulers (1573–1603) was short-lived and ended with a tremendous battle. Japan entered a long period of military rulers, culminating in near isolation from the outside world during the Edo Period (17th–19th centuries). The economy flourished and cultural activities, such as Kabuki theater and Ukio-e painting, were highly praised.

The reopening of the country in the 18th century ushered in contact with the West and a time of unprecedented change. The Meiji era (1868–1912) saw the restoration of the Japanese emperor and established the basis for the modern Japanese state.

Hokkaido
Sea of Japan
Honshu
Pacific Ocean
Mt Fuji
Heian (Kyôto)
Nagoya
Nara
Shikoku
Kyushu

Island Chain
Japan consists of a string of islands in a northeast–southwest arc stretching through the western Pacific Ocean. The land is rugged, with hundreds of volcanic mountains, such as Mt Fuji.

Nomadic States of Central Asia

Kyrgyz Warrior
This metal plaque is the image of a Kyrgyz warrior. These tribal people rose to power in the ninth century AD.

The history of central Asia is characterized by the rapid formation of extensive nomadic empires, with the largest ruled by the Hsiung-nu, the Turks, the Kyrgyzs, and the Mongols.

Success in battle and the borders of each nomadic empire were defined by the size of their military forces, the talent of their leaders, and the power of their opponents. While the Hsiung-nu, the Turks, and the Kyrgyzs merely united nomadic peoples and seized some cultural areas, the Mongol invasion destroyed a number of states all over Asia, amassing more territory than any empire before it.

HSIUNG-NU

At the end of the 3rd century BC, in the steppes of central Mongolia and Trans-Baikal, there arose the Hsiung-nu, an alliance of pastoralist tribes. The use of iron weaponry and the invention of a long-range bow helped them to create a unified state that spread from Hinggan in the east to Tien Shan in the west. The Hsiung-nu suffered defeats at the hands of their neighbors in the 1st century AD. Some of them moved west, incorporating all the tribes on their route into a movement known as The Great Migration of Peoples. Later, they apparently formed another alliance of nomads, known as Huns, who invaded Europe in the late 4th to early 5th centuries (see p. 184).

THE OLD-TURKIC EMPIRE

In AD 552 the political situation in the central Asian steppes radically altered when the Turkic tribes of the Altai, led by a Hsiung-nu tribe, founded the Turkic kaghanate (empire). After a dynamic campaign, its frontiers extended to Manchuria in the east and the Amu-Darya River in the west.

The highest achievement of Old-Turkic culture was the invention of a written language. First discovered in the early 18th century, Old-Turkic inscriptions are found on stelae and gravestones, on rocks, and on metal and wooden objects and ceramics.

The Turks were involved in continuous wars, and were eventually conquered by rival empires in the 740s. The kaghanate helped to consolidate the Turkic population in Eurasia, contributing to the development of ethnic groups that formed the basis of today's Turkish-language peoples.

THE KYRGYZ KAGHANATE

In the 9th century, tribes of the Yenisei Kyrgyzs took power in

KEY DATES IN CENTRAL ASIA

209 BC	Rise of the Hsiung-nu
AD 552–745	Turkic kaghanate
AD 840	Formation of the Kyrgyz kaghanate
AD 1155/1167	Birth of Genghis Khan in Mongolia
AD 1206	Genghis Khan becomes Mongol ruler
AD 1207	Mongols conquer the Kyrgyz kaghanate
C. AD 1211	Mongol hordes invade China, and cross the Great Wall
AD 1395	Tamerlane, descendant of Genghis Khan, invades large parts of southern Russia
AD 1398	Tamerlane takes Delhi

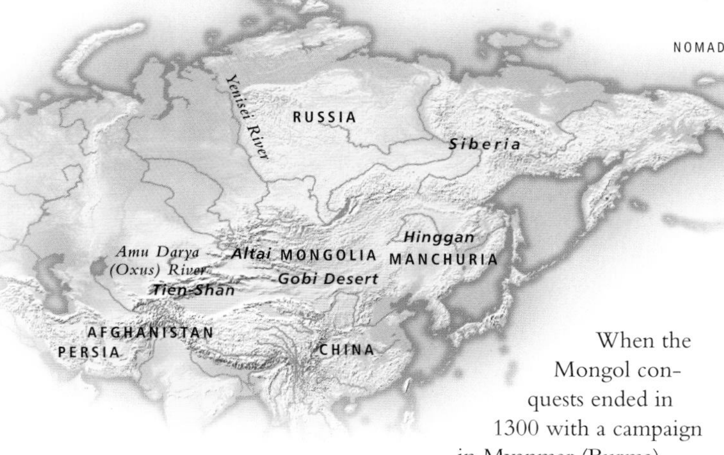

southern Siberia, spreading from the Amur River in the east to the Tien-Shan Mountains in the west. The native territory of the Kyrgyzs—the Minusinsk Basin—still features their *chaa-tas* (rocks of war), cemeteries with stone constructions above the graves. Burned bones, iron objects, and elegant clay vessels have been found inside the graves, while harnesses and gold and silver utensils furnish the nobles' tombs. A devastating conquest by the Mongols in the early 13th century put an end to the Kyrgyz state.

THE MONGOL EMPIRE

The nomadic culture of Eurasia reached its culmination in the 13th century, with central Asia dominated by Mongol tribes. In 1206 their bravest leader was chosen as khan (ruler), and took the name Genghis, or Lord Absolute. He aimed to conquer the world, and in 1211 his armies entered China, capturing Zhongdu (Peking) in 1215. They then overran central Asia, Afghanistan, and much of Persia. Genghis's successors conquered southern Russia and invaded eastern Europe.

When the Mongol conquests ended in 1300 with a campaign in Myanmar (Burma), they turned to the systematic exploitation of the conquered countries, using Chinese administration and experience in management. The formation of the Mongol empire, accompanied by the mass destruction of populations and cities, the devastation of large territories, and the decline of agriculture, held back the development of these countries for a long time.

Mongol Tomb
The Mongol empire was extended into southern Russia and India during the late 14th century AD by Tamerlane, a descendant of Genghis Khan. Tamerlane's mausoleum, known as Gur-e Amir (below), features intricate mosaic work.

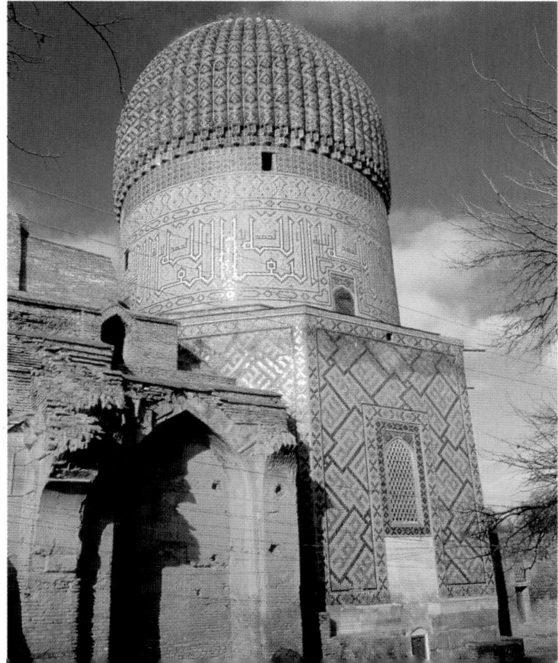

Settlements of Oceania

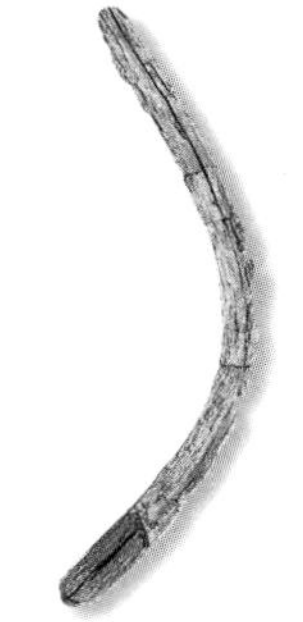

Ancient Boomerang
At roughly 10,000 years old, this is the oldest boomerang yet found in Australia. It may have been used to hunt waterfowl.

The first settlement of Australia and the colonization of the Pacific islands are remarkable stories of voyaging skills and adaptation to new and often challenging environments.

For millions of years, the continent of Greater Australia—made up of present-day New Guinea, Australia, and Tasmania—was separated from Southeast Asia by water barriers. Sometime before 50,000 years ago, fully modern humans spread through island Southeast Asia and settled Greater Australia. This was during the last Ice Age, when the sea-level was lower and many of the crossings would have been shorter, but it was still impossible to travel to Australia without sailing out of sight of land. Clearly, the first settlers had the practical knowledge and skills for successful seafaring; some archaeologists suggest that such journeys also required sophisticated communication skills.

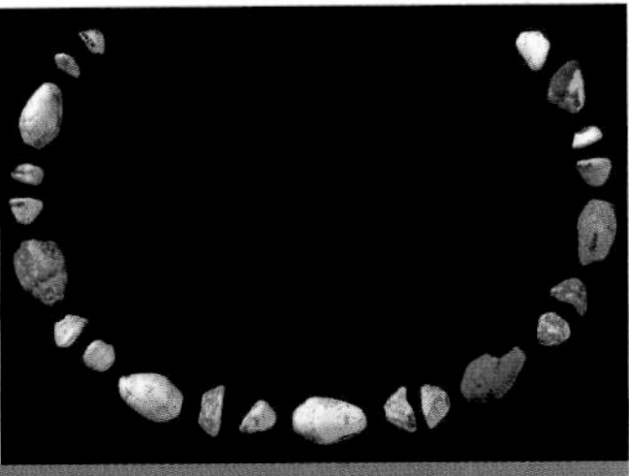

Sea-Shell Necklace
This 30,000-year-old necklace of sea shells was found in a rock-shelter in Western Australia.

The first inhabitants of Australia and Melanesia demonstrated a remarkable ability to adapt to new conditions and quickly spread through the diverse environments. By about 35,000 years ago, or a little later, there is archaeological evidence of human occupation from the tropical north of Australia to the glaciated highlands of Tasmania, and in the desert of the interior, as well as on the islands of the Bismarck Archipelago, which lie off the northeast coast of Papua New Guinea. About 6,000 years later, people had successfully reached the Solomon Islands.

KEY DATES IN THE SETTLEMENT OF OCEANIA

50,000–60,000 YEARS AGO	Humans reach Australia
35,000 YEARS AGO	Humans in Tasmania and Bismarck Archipelago
29,000 YEARS AGO	Humans in Solomon Islands
25,000 YEARS AGO	Cremation at Lake Mungo
9,000 YEARS AGO	Agriculture in New Guinea Highlands
10,000–8,000 YEARS AGO	Rising sea-levels isolate Tasmania and separate Australia and New Guinea
4,000 YEARS AGO	Dingo in Australia
3,500 YEARS AGO	Lapita cultural complex appears
AD **400 (?)**	Humans in Hawaiian Islands and on Easter Island
AD **1200**	Humans in New Zealand
AD **1606**	First European landfall on the Australian continent by Willem Jansz of the Dutch East India Company, at Cape Keerweer, western Cape York
AD **1700**	Macassan fishermen begin regular visits to northern Australia

ICE AGE AUSTRALIA

The glimpses archaeology gives us into the way of life of the Ice Age inhabitants of Australia suggest that it was far from a struggle for existence. They were skilled hunters, often targeting particular species, and they used nets for fishing inland lakes. Skins were made into cloaks in colder regions. There is evidence for art and for personal ornaments at a very early date, and ritual burials suggest that the rich spiritual traditions of contemporary Aboriginal people are very ancient.

Australia is unique in being the only continent that was exclusively occupied by hunter-gatherers at the time of European colonization. Far from being passively dependent on whatever resources were available, Aboriginal people were active land managers. Fire and detailed ecological knowledge were their main tools. Archaeologist Rhys Jones coined the term "firestick farming" to describe the Aboriginal use of fire to clear land and promote the growth of particular plants. In some areas, complex trapping systems were used to manage water flows for fishing. Changes in archaeological remains through time show that these people were also technological innovators, with the boomerang being the best known of their inventions.

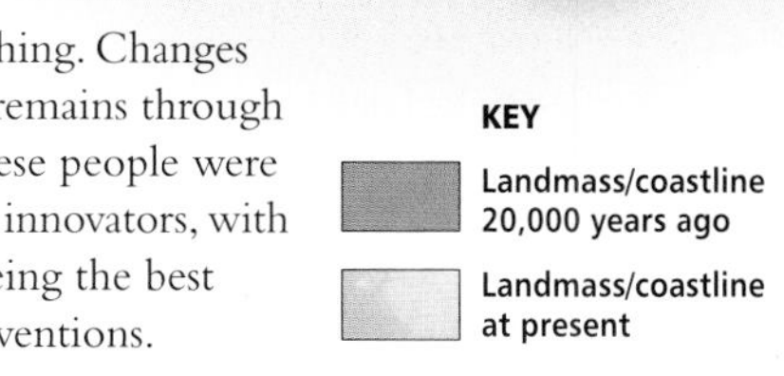

X-ray Fish
On Nourlangie Rock in Arnhem Land, in Australia's Northern Territory, the X-ray style has been used to depict a fish.

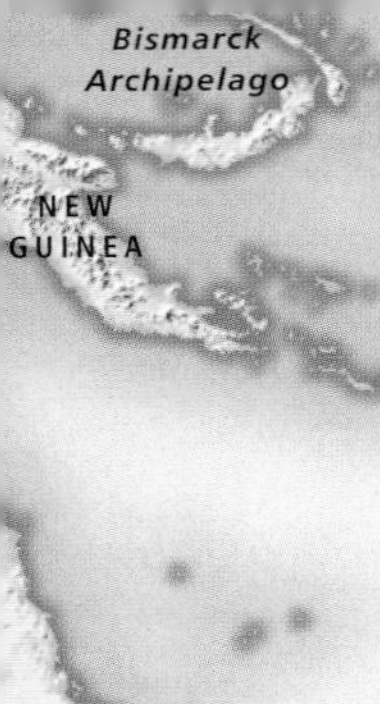

COLONIZING THE PACIFIC

The Pacific Ocean covers a third of the earth's surface and has many tiny islands or island groups separated by vast expanses of sea. Thousands of years before the great European voyages of exploration, the ancestors of the Polynesians had already colonized many of its islands.

About 3,500 years ago, the Lapita cultural complex appeared in the western Pacific. Lasting for roughly a thousand years, it is characterized by distinctive and highly decorated pottery, known as Lapita ware after the site in New Caledonia where it was first discovered (see p. 376). Lapita sites are widely distributed from the Bismarck Archipelago as far as Fiji, Tonga, and Samoa. Lapita colonists were beach dwellers, who voyaged throughout the

Lagoon Ruins
The ruins of Nan Madol are found in a lagoon on Pohnpei, in Micronesia. The stone structures were built on top of artificial islands sometime after 1000 AD.

Great Fleet Petroglyphs
Petroglyphs on the wall of New Zealand's Kaingaroa Cave depict canoes at sea. Estimated to be some 700 years old, the images may represent the "Great Fleet" migrations that brought the Maori to New Zealand. A discarded Maori canoe lies at the base of the wall.

region. They introduced domestic pigs, dogs, and chickens to the areas they settled, and cultivated tuberous plants and tree crops. Marine resources, such as fish, seabirds, turtles, and shellfish, formed an important part of their diet.

There is considerable debate about whether Lapita culture developed in the western Pacific or was introduced by migrants from island Southeast Asia. It is widely agreed, however, that the descendants of the Lapita people were the Polynesians. Their culture seems to have developed from the Lapita culture of the Fiji, Tonga, and Samoa area.

POLYNESIAN SOCIETY

Polynesian society was generally hierarchical. Chiefs wielded considerable centralized power, both spiritual and economic. In some areas, most notably Hawaii, with its large and dense population, extremely stratified forms of social organization emerged, with rigid class barriers between chiefs and commoners. Polynesian economy was based mainly on fishing and the cultivation of a range of tropical tubers and fruits.

The Polynesian colonization of the remote Pacific began some 2,000 years ago with the settlement of the Marquesas Islands. By 1,000 years ago, the Society and Cook islands, Hawaii, and Easter Island were all occupied. New Zealand was first settled in the 13th century AD. These great voyages were deliberate colonizing expeditions.

Lapita Sites
The distribution of Lapita pottery throughout the western Pacific (far left) has helped archaeologists identify the pattern of island colonization.

THE EASTER ISLAND SCRIPT

The unique rongorongo script of Easter Island now survives only as thousands of markings on 25 pieces of wood. These markings comprise engraved parallel lines of characters, many of them bird symbols and hooks, with every alternate line upside down. The outside world discovered Easter Island in 1722, but none of the early European visitors mentioned rongorongo until a missionary in 1864 reported that the tablets were found in every house. This suggests that the script may be a late, post-contact phenomenon.

The island's experts in rongorongo died in a smallpox epidemic in the late 19th century, so the script has remained an undeciphered enigma, but linguistics specialist Steven Fischer recently achieved a breakthrough. The key was the Santiago Staff, a 4 pound (2 kg) wooden scepter, whose large rongorongo text is subdivided by irregularly spaced vertical lines (right). Fischer noticed that each glyph (symbol) starting a subdivision has a phallus-like motif, and in each subdivision almost every third glyph also has this feature. In other words, the text has a basic triad structure, which also seems to occur on some other rongorongo tablets, and it is thought that these inscriptions are cosmogonies (creation chants), a whole succession of copulations (each triad denoting that X copulated with Y and the result was Z) to explain the creation of everything in the world. But the script still retains much of its mystery.

Early New World Cultures

Zapotec Urn
Ceramic funerary urns, often adorned with a figure, are a distinctive feature of the Zapotec culture that was centered on Monte Albán from about 500 BC to AD 750.

Characteristics identifiable as Mesoamerican first appear about 1300 BC, with the Olmec culture. Other complex societies soon emerged in the Valley of Oaxaca and later at Teotihuacán.

The Olmec inhabited the coastal lowlands of what is now Veracruz, a region known for its lush but swampy environment. Lacking many important raw materials (such as stone for tool-making), the Olmec established far-flung trading partners throughout central Mexico and Pacific Guatemala to acquire such valued commodities as obsidian, basalt, jade, and fine kaolin clay. In exchange, the Olmec supplied jaguar skins, precious feathers, and, most importantly, Olmec concepts of religious and political legitimacy. It was this last ideological contribution that continued to influence Mesoamerican cultures throughout the pre-Columbian period, causing some scholars to refer to the Olmec as "Mesoamerica's Mother Culture."

The most prominent of the Olmec's numerous ceremonial centers were San Lorenzo and La Venta. Both featured monumental architecture in the form of earthen mounds and platforms, and monumental sculpture made of massive blocks of basalt, including the famous colossal heads (see p. 388).

THE VALLEY OF OAXACA

Although Olmec traits have been found over a wide region, the Olmec were not the only complex society to emerge in the Formative period. Evidence of similar developments, albeit without the same degree of monumentality, are found in Chalcatzingo, Tlatilco, and other locations. In the Valley of Oaxaca, a long history of cultural evolution has been charted, especially at San José Mogote and Monte Albán.

San José Mogote began as a farming hamlet around 1500 BC, and by 1100 exhibited signs of ritual specialization and social hierarchy. The site continued to grow until by 500 BC it featured prominent mounded architecture, including a ball-court, and was the capital of a multi-tier settlement system.

About 500 BC, the site of Monte Albán was founded and quickly subordinated other sites in the region. Monte Albán is located atop a high ridge from which its inhabitants could look

MESOAMERICAN KEY DATES

1500–1000 BC	Early Formative Period: *San Lorenzo, San José Mogote*
1000–600 BC	Middle Formative Period: *La Venta, San José Mogote, Cholula*
600–200 BC	Late Formative Period: *Monte Albán, Cholula*
200 BC–AD 200	Terminal Formative Period: *Monte Albán, Cholula, Teotihuacán*
AD 200–400	Early Classic Period: *Monte Albán, Cholula, Teotihuacán*
AD 400–700	Late Classic Period: *Monte Albán, Cholula, Teotihuacán*
AD 700–900	Epiclassic Period: *Monte Albán, Cholula*
AD 900–1200	Early Postclassic Period: *Cholula, Tula*
AD 1200–1520	Late Postclassic Period: *Cholula, Tenochtitlán*

out on all parts of the valley and, significantly, occupants of the valley floor and foothills could look up to the pyramids and platforms of the ceremonial center silhouetted on the ridge top. The main plaza of Monte Albán is the result of massive earthmoving, with the top of the ridge leveled off and huge earth and masonry platforms constructed around a rectangular plaza. The slopes of the ridge system were covered by terraces where the non-elite inhabitants lived—the population may have numbered up to 30,000 at Monte Albán's peak between AD 300 and 600.

TEOTIHUACÁN

Most of the public art of Monte Albán represents conquest, with sculptures of captured and sacrificed rulers, defeated towns, and bound captives. One notable exception to this propagandistic style, however, depicts an emissary to Monte Albán wearing the headdress of Teotihuacán and carrying a staff representing his status as a visitor.

Located in the Valley of Mexico, Teotihuacán was founded in the Late Formative Period, around 400 BC, but underwent dramatic urban reorganization in the 1st century AD when the city was laid out on a rigid grid system oriented around the Avenue of the Dead (see p. 396). During the Classic Period (AD 200–700), it was Mesoamerica's largest urban center, with a population of about 150,000. Whereas Monte Albán's empire barely extended outside of the Valley of Oaxaca, Teotihuacán maintained colonial cities outside its immediate region (for example, at Matacapan) and influenced political events in distant Maya cities such as Tikal and Copán.

Gulf of Mexico
MESOAMERICA
Tula
Teotihuacán
Chalcatzingo
Cholula
La Venta
San Lorenzo
San José Mogote
Monte Albán
Tikal
MAYA AREA
Copán
Pacific Ocean

KEY
- Limits of Mesoamerica
- Limits of Maya areas
- Valley of Mexico
- Valley of Oaxaca

Ancient Capital
The majestic site of Monte Albán, set high on a mountaintop, features a massive plaza that served as the center of government activity between about 500 BC and AD 800.

The Maya

Warrior Vessel
This cylindrical vessel, featuring a procession of warriors, dates to about AD 750–800, during the Late Classic Period.

Characterized by monumental architecture, complex settlement, and hieroglyphic writing, Maya city-states flourished during the Classic Period (AD 250–900) in the lowlands of Central America.

The Maya created one of the most sophisticated civilizations in the Americas. By 1500 BC, they had adopted farming and village life, and over the next 1,700 years, their ceremonial centers grew into large cities with great stone pyramid temples, palaces, and plazas. They also developed a written language, a complex calendar, and considerable astronomical knowledge.

During the Classic Period, a total of about 2 million people were living in more than 40 Maya cities. Recent hieroglyphic decipherments and careful settlement studies demonstrate that the southern Maya lowlands were politically fragmented into relatively autonomous, often warring city-states. Tikal and Calakmul were the primary states of the Early Classic Period (AD 250–550), both seemingly inheriting portions

Royal Ritual
This stone lintel carving from Stucture 21 of Yaxchilan (c. AD 753–755) portrays the bloodletting ritual of "Bird Jaguar" III and a junior wife, who draws a thorn-studded rope through her tongue. Interpolity marriage and joint ritual activities cemented ties between kingdoms in the fractious world of Maya politics.

Tikal Temples
The temple complex of Tikal, in the Guatemalan jungle, served as the burial ground for most of the Tikal kings throughout the Classic Period. Buried below the complex are constructions dating back to the city's origins, about 500 BC.

of the trade-routes and catchments of El Mirador, the great Late Preclassic kingdom (400 BC–AD 100). They provided smaller subject-states, such as El Peru and Copán, with protection from enemies, prestigious affiliations, and a share in the spoils of war. In return, they were able to amass political and economic power in the form of tribute collection. Sumptuary items such as jade, chocolate, and quetzal feathers—as well as staples such as maize and salt—were the life-blood of these tribute economies, and endless canoe-loads of these commodities threaded the waterways of the Maya world to feed the demands of Tikal and Calakmul.

A SHARED CULTURE

Diplomatic relations kept subject-states in thrall and eased tension between the large city-states. Interpolity marriage, interdynastic kinship ties, competitive feasting, and a shared elite culture also created common ground, and a shared written language facilitated the development of a common political charter and religious ideology. Though each city-state worshiped different patron gods, a core pantheon and key symbols—the creation of the world, resurrection of the Maize god, origins of humanity—ensured some measure of solidarity.

By about AD 900, however, most of the big lowland cities in the south had been abandoned to the jungle. The reasons for the decline of the lowland Maya are unclear, but most recent work suggests that they involved a combination of drought and invasion by outsiders. During the Postclassic Period (900–1530), northern cities such as Chichén Itzá, Uxmal, and Mayapán battled for supremacy in the north. By the time the Spanish arrived in the early 16th century, the earlier city-states had been replaced by regional hegemonies controlled by a few central cities.

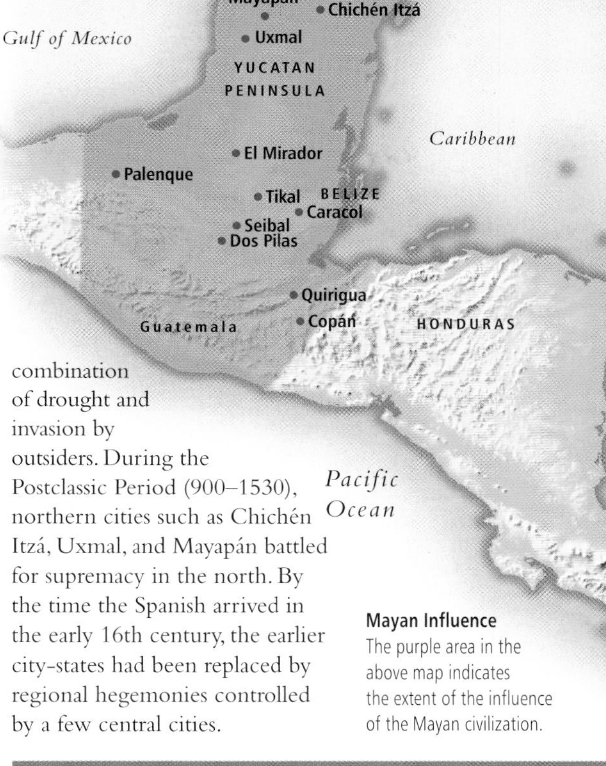

Mayan Influence
The purple area in the above map indicates the extent of the influence of the Mayan civilization.

KEY DATES IN MAYA HISTORY

400 BC	Beginning of Late Preclassic Period; founding of El Mirador
AD 100	Abandonment of El Mirador and other centers
C. AD 219	Founding of Tikal Dynasty under Ya'ax E'hb' Xook I
AD 250	Beginning of Classic Period
AD 378	King of Teotihuacán conquers Tikal and places his own son, Ya'ax-Nu'n-Ahyiin I, on the throne
AD 562	Calakmul conquers Tikal, leading to a long hiatus in monument-erection at the site
AD 599	Calakmul attacks Palenque and burns its temples
AD 615	K'inich Janaahb' Pakal I accedes as King of Palenque
AD 682	Jasaw Chan K'awiil accedes as King of Tikal
AD 683	K'inich Janaahb' Pakal I of Palenque dies
AD 695	Jasaw Chan K'awiil of Tikal conquers the Calakmul king Yich'aak K'ahk'
AD 910	Last date recorded on a Classic Maya monument; beginning of Postclassical Period
AD 1530	Arrival of Spaniards in Yucatan; end of Postclassic Period

The Aztecs

In just 100 years, the Aztecs of central Mexico established an empire stretching from the Pacific to the Atlantic coasts and south into Oaxaca, the largest polity ever known in Mesoamerica.

Imperial Style
With their rise to political power in the 15th century, the Aztecs developed a distinctive style of stone sculpture. This example depicts the seated figure of Xiuhtecuhtli, Lord of Fire.

Centered at their capital city of Tenochtitlán in the Valley of Mexico, the Aztecs conquered their neighbors and negotiated alliances until they could demand tribute from a vast area. Tenochtitlán grew to an unprecedented size, with a population of hundreds of thousands living on artificial islands around a ceremonial center in a natural lake.

Our knowledge of the Aztecs comes from complementary historical and archaeological sources. In the 16th century, Spanish conquistadors and priests recorded insightful accounts of Aztec culture, while pre-Columbian pictorial manuscripts, such as the *Codex Borbonicus,* depict religious rituals relating to the sacred calendar of the Aztecs. Archaeological evidence comes from the Templo Mayor in Tenochtitlán (see p. 410), as well as from sites such as Cihuatecpan and Yautepec in the surrounding hinterland.

KEY DATES OF THE AZTEC EMPIRE

c. 1200	Fall of Tula, creating multiple small city-states
1325	Mythical founding date of Tenochtitlán
1375–95	Reign of Aztec lord Acamapichtli
1417–27	Reign of Chimalpopoca
1427–40	Reign of Itzcoatl
1428	Defeat of Tepaneca; Aztec-led Triple Alliance supreme
1440–69	Reign of Moctezuma Ilhuicamina (Moctezuma I)
1469–81	Reign of Axayacatl
1481–86	Reign of Tizoc
1486–1502	Reign of Ahuitzotl
1502–20	Reign of Moctezuma Xocoyotzin (Moctezuma II)
1519	Arrival of Spaniards in Tenochtitlán
1520–21	Reign of Cuauhtemoc, last Aztec ruler
1521	Defeat of Tenochtitlán; founding of Mexico City

SOCIETY AND RELIGION

The Aztecs lived in a highly stratified society. The ruling elite were comprised of lineages tracing their ancestry back to the semi-mythical Toltecs of the Early Postclassic Period. The ruler, known as a Tlatoani ("First Speaker"), was selected from among these noble lineages. Another important administrator was known as the Cihuacoatl, or "Snake Woman," and may have played a leading role in commanding the army. Lesser nobles held other offices in the administrative hierarchy or worked as merchants or artisans. Commoners were generally limited in their ability for social mobility, but military or mercantile success could be a means of advancement.

The daily life of the Aztecs was clearly divided between male and female activities. The men worked in the fields, went to war, and performed public rituals, while the women tended to household needs: cooking, caring for children, performing domestic rituals, and spinning and weaving.

Aztec religion is best known for its bloody cult of human sacrifice. Blood was believed to have been a requirement for the

Gulf of Mexico

Sierra Madre

Pacific Ocean

MEXICO

Tamuin

Tenochtitlán

Yautepec

Monté Albán

Oaxaca

Chichén Itzá

YUCATAN PENINSULA

Tuxtla Mountains

KEY

Extent of Aztec influence (AD 1520)

nourishment of the sun, and periodic sacrifices were conducted in which victims were spread-eagled over an altar stone and their still-beating hearts removed by a knife-wielding priest. "Flowery Wars" were conducted between the Aztecs and neighboring nations for the explicit purpose of capturing victims for sacrifice. Many other rituals were also practiced, involving song, dance, and feasting corresponding to cycles of the 260-day ritual calendar.

THE DEFEAT OF THE EMPIRE

When the Spanish arrived on the Gulf Coast of Mexico in 1519, the locals told tales of the magnificent city of the Aztecs, rich in golden wealth, perhaps as a ploy to get the barbarian Europeans to move on. Because the Aztec empire was relatively new, and their tribute demands high, the Spanish were able to establish alliances with many of the subjugated tribes and assemble a sizable army of indigenous warriors to supplement the 500 or so Spaniards. Despite an initial defeat, the Spanish were able to overwhelm the Aztecs through technological superiority, a different ideology of conquest, and especially the spread of European diseases. After a brief 100-year reign, the Aztec empire was defeated.

Serpent Ornament
This turquoise pectoral ornament in the form of a double-headed serpent was worn by a high priest.

Aztec Deity
In this page from the *Codex Cospi*, the major Aztec deity Tezcatlipoca is dressed as a warrior. Below the figure is the bar and dot numerical system used by the Aztecs.

Cultures of the Andes

Early Carving
In the Casma Valley, on the north coast of Peru, the temple site of Cerro Sechín features a row of stones with unique carvings of men carrying clubs (above), severed heads, and other designs. The site is certainly an early one, but it is not clear whether it predates the Chavín culture.

Andean civilization developed over several thousand years from small populations of mobile hunter-gatherers to states controlling vast territories and hundreds of thousands of people.

Many regional cultures developed technologies and artistic and cultural traditions that contributed to the overall flavor of ancient Andean society. Trade, colonization, and conquest allowed the major civilizations of each period to use resources and ideas from many areas. The final prehispanic civilization, the Inca state (see p. 218), was built on thousands of years of cultural tradition and achievement.

EARLY SETTLEMENTS

The earliest documented habitation of the region is more than 10,000 years old and consists of the remains of campsites and tools left by groups that hunted wild game and gathered plants. Along the coast, they also began fishing and gathering shellfish. Within a few thousand years, Andean people had begun the process of domesticating local plants and animals, and by around 2500 BC, many groups were living in permanently occupied towns and were building temples and other monumental structures. The origins of the artistic and iconographic traditions of the Andes are seen in some of the temples and portable artifacts (such as carved gourds and textiles) found on the central coast and northern highlands of Peru. Along the coast, the earliest monumental sites are large mounds featuring rooms with plastered walls, friezes, and niches. These date to a time before pottery when agriculture was limited.

FIRST CIVILIZATIONS

The earliest highland civilizations also appear before pottery. The site of Kotosh, located about

KEY DATES IN THE ANDES

10,000 ya	Earliest habitation of the Andean region
2500 BC	Permanent towns appear
1300–200 BC	Chiripa culture in Lake Titicaca Basin
900–200 BC	Chavín culture in central Andes
500 BC–AD 200	Paracas culture on south coast
200–50 BC	Salinar culture on north coast
200 BC–AD 300	Pukara culture in Lake Titicaca Basin
50 BC–AD 300	Gallinazo culture on north coast
AD 0–700	Moche culture on north coast
AD 100–700	Nasca culture on south coast
AD 500–750	Wari empire in central and northern Peru
AD 500–1000	Tiwanaku city-state in Lake Titicaca Basin
AD 900–1400	Chimú civilization in northern Peru

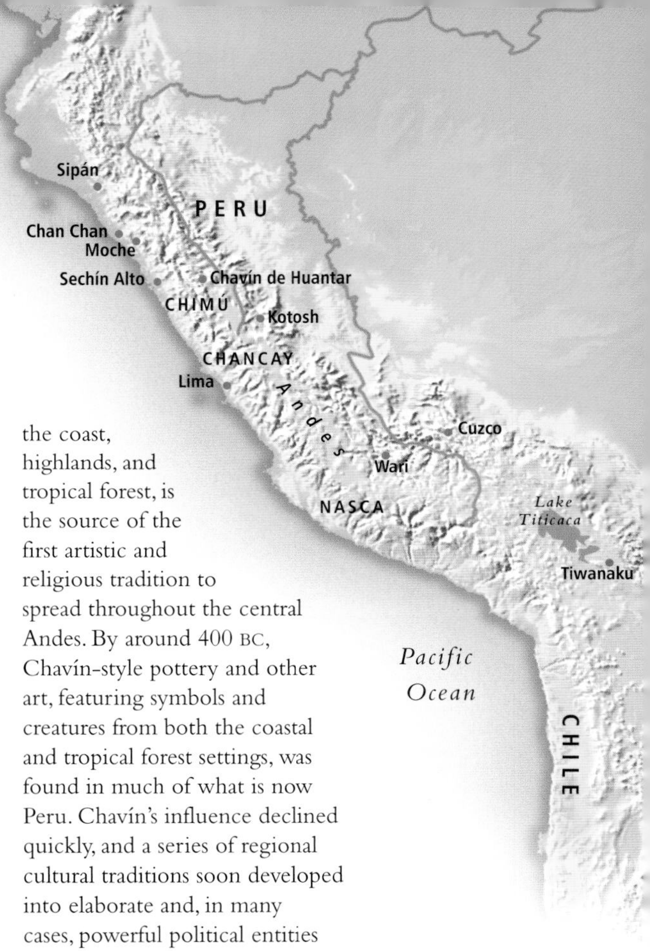

6,500 feet (2,000 m) above sea-level, was built around 2000 BC on the eastern slopes of the Andes, very close to the tropical forest. Here, the excavation of an ancient temple revealed a plastered frieze of two human hands, crossed at the wrists. Other nearby highland sites from this period appear linked to Kotosh, often by religion. Both coastal and highland traditions continued to emerge over the next thousand years, as pottery became important and artistic styles developed. Other areas, including the north coast of Peru and the highland Lake Titicaca Basin, also saw regional cultures develop.

By about 1000 BC, regional civilizations were flourishing around the Andes. Soon afterward, coastal sites went into decline (possibly because of an environmental disaster), even as a new cultural influence spread throughout much of the Andean region. The site of Chavín de Huantar (see p. 390), located along an important trade route between the coast, highlands, and tropical forest, is the source of the first artistic and religious tradition to spread throughout the central Andes. By around 400 BC, Chavín-style pottery and other art, featuring symbols and creatures from both the coastal and tropical forest settings, was found in much of what is now Peru. Chavín's influence declined quickly, and a series of regional cultural traditions soon developed into elaborate and, in many cases, powerful political entities in different areas of the Andes.

Sipán
PERU
Chan Chan
Moche
Sechín Alto
Chavín de Huantar
CHIMÚ
Kotosh
CHANCAY
Lima
Andes
Cuzco
Wari
NASCA
Lake Titicaca
Tiwanaku
Pacific Ocean
CHILE

Chavín Setting
The Chavín Valley in the Andean highlands of northern Peru was the setting for the development of the Chavín de Huantar culture, which had influenced much of the region by around 400 BC.

Moche Ceramics
The Moche civilization had no writing system, but still left a vivid artistic record of their activities, environment, and supernatural beliefs. Their extraordinary ceramics included this vessel depicting a man wearing a bird headdress.

MOCHE CULTURE

On the north coast, the poorly known Salinar (*c.* 200–50 BC) and Gallinazo (*c.* 50 BC–AD 300) cultures led to the powerful Moche civilization that dominated the coastal valleys from roughly AD 0 to 700. The Moche built at least one set of huge mud-brick pyramids in each coastal valley. Used for ceremonies and continually rebuilt, perhaps once a generation, some of the pyramids also contain the elaborate burials of the Moche rulers. During the 1980s and 1990s, research at major Moche sites, including the Moche pyramids (Huaca de la Luna and Huaca del Sol), Sipán (see p. 394), San José de Morro, and El Brujo—all of which may be visited today by tourists—have provided vast amounts of new information on this once enigmatic ancient kingdom.

PARACAS AND NASCA CULTURES

On the coast south of Lima, an entirely different cultural tradition took hold. The Paracas culture (*c.* 500 BC–AD 200) of the Chincha, Pisco, and Ica valleys is known for elaborate burials featuring layer upon layer of some of the most elaborate textiles ever found, as well as incised pottery, the earliest of which was clearly influenced by Chavín designs. The later Nasca civilization (*c.* AD 100–700) left behind some of the most famous archaeological monuments in Peru—the Nasca lines (see p. 392)—although these tend to overshadow other important accomplishments. The agricultural technology of the Nasca people was unique, and featured a network of pits and tunnels excavated to bring underground water to the surface. The major monumental site of the Nasca was Cahuachi, a set of low hills along the Nasca River that were sculpted with adobe temples and other structures. Nasca cemeteries abound, although most have been badly looted. The Nasca maintained links to the highlands, and their influence may be seen in the later Wari culture.

TIWANAKU AND WARI EMPIRES

Another center of Andean civilization was the Lake Titicaca Basin. Here, a cultural tradition that began with Chiripa (1300–200 BC) and Pukara (200 BC–AD 300)

Paracas Cloak
Among the finest examples of textile-making are embroidered cloaks of the Paracas culture, which were used for wrapping mummified corpses and funeral offerings. The striking designs resemble the painted pottery of the Nasca culture.

AN ANDEAN CHRONOLOGY
The German archaeologist Max Uhle (1856–1944) is considered the father of South American archaeology. Over a period of 20 years in Peru, Bolivia, Chile, and Ecuador, Uhle conducted rigorous stratigraphic excavations that allowed him to establish a pre-Inca chronology for the Andean region.

culminated in the great city-state of Tiwanaku (see p. 400), which flourished between roughly AD 500 and 1000. Tiwanaku, a large planned city with massive stone-block architecture, colonized and influenced vast areas of what is now southern Peru, northern Chile, and northern Bolivia. During the height of Tiwanaku influence over this area, a related but quite different state, the Wari empire, emerged from the Ayacucho area of highland Peru to conquer vast territories throughout central and into northern Peru. These two states were to have profound influence on the cultures that came afterward.

CHIMÚ CIVILIZATION

After the fall of Tiwanaku and Wari, local chiefdoms emerged throughout the Andes, and many became quite powerful. One of the most important was the Chimú civilization, which built Chan Chan, the largest adobe city anywhere, and controlled huge areas of what is now northern Peru. This powerful state proved a challenge to the later Inca, who eventually conquered it, incorporating many aspects of Chimú statecraft into their political system. Other groups emerging at this time included the Chancay, Ica, and Collao (Aymara) cultures, as well as the Killke, from whom the Inca eventually developed.

The Inca

Chosen Woman
This gold figurine wrapped in a woven textile represents one of the "Chosen Women," or mamaconas—concubines of the emperor.

Until the Spanish arrived in 1532, the Inca of South America ruled one of the largest areas ever controlled by an ancient state anywhere in the world.

The vast area under Inca control, which was known as Tawantinsuyu, included coastal desert, rugged mountains, forests, and tropical jungles throughout most of western South America. Although the Spanish quickly took over the Inca state, it was many years, in some cases centuries, before they controlled more remote areas with anything like the effectiveness of the Inca.

ORIGINS AND EXPANSION

The Inca state sprang from a series of small warring chiefdoms that inhabited the region surrounding Cuzco, in Peru, after the fall of the Tiwanaku and Wari states around AD 1000 (see p. 216). By sometime before 1400, the Inca had become highly successful, taking over the area, constructing their capital city of Cuzco, and remodeling much of the landscape of surrounding areas, including the Urubamba Valley, which is also known as the Sacred Valley of the Incas.

Even as they took over the Cuzco heartland, the Inca began to expand into other areas, incorporating territory and peoples through whatever combination

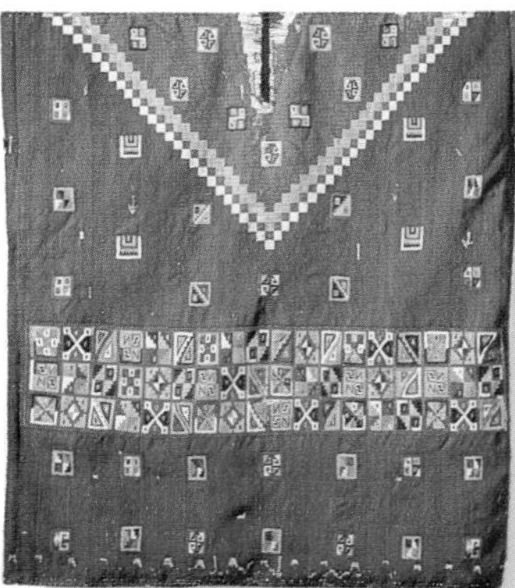

Elite Textile
The Inca inherited one of the world's greatest textile traditions from their Andean predecessors. Tunics made for the elite were woven of extremely fine interlocked tapestry (above right).

Organic Architecture
The Inca shaped their settlements as an organic part of the environment in which they were built. Here, the ruins of the Winay Wayna settlement are integrated into the steep terraced slope.

of diplomacy, threats, conquest, and colonization was required. When feasible, the Inca used local rulers as governors of newly incorporated areas, bestowing riches and privileges on them and bringing their sons to Cuzco for an Inca-style education. Otherwise, they appointed loyal subjects from other areas to rule the new territories. The Inca also used religion to subdue their subjects, relocating major shrines of local groups to Cuzco, which forced the faithful to make their pilgrimages to the center of the empire. Troublesome and rebellious groups were dealt with largely through resettlement.

LABOR AND TECHNOLOGY

Land and labor were strictly controlled under the Inca, divided among the local people, the state, and religious shrines and cults. Labor and political entities were organized in a decimal system of administration, with nested groups of 10 serving for most purposes. Labor taxes and tribute, including such items as animals, crops, and textiles, were levied. People were also appropriated, with young men forced to serve the state as herders, and the most beautiful young girls placed in special compounds where they wove cloth and served religious shrines and cults. The girls from these compounds were often given in marriage or as concubines to cement the political and other alliances of the Inca.

Inca technology, architecture, and engineering are deservedly famous. The Inca moved around their vast territory on a network of roads that covered the entire empire. Along the most important roads, official runners (chaski) were stationed at way stations known as tambos. Chaski carried messages and small packages relay-style in a communication system that was far faster and more efficient than anything the Spanish were able to accomplish, even with horses.

Inca architecture is perhaps the most enduring monument to this great people. The finest of it is made of cut stone blocks, each one shaped individually to fit perfectly with the stones that surrounded it. In Cuzco, buildings made more than 500 years ago by the Inca still stand, even as later Spanish and Peruvian buildings have been destroyed by earthquakes in the years since the Spanish conquest.

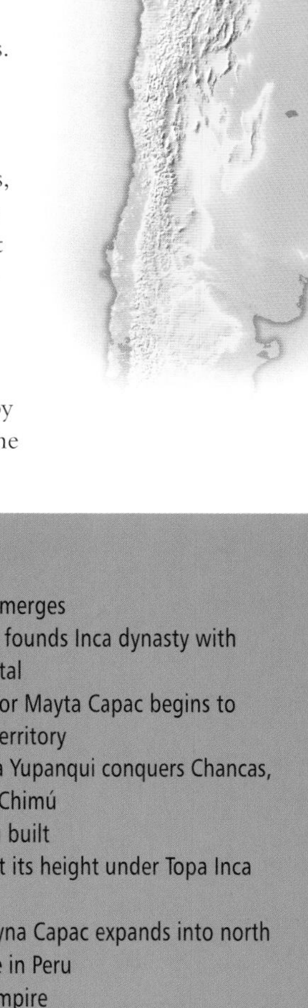

THE INCA EMPIRE

AD 1000	Inca culture emerges
AD 1220	Manco Capac founds Inca dynasty with Cuzco as capital
14TH CENTURY	Fourth emperor Mayta Capac begins to expand Inca territory
1438–71	Pachacuti Inca Yupanqui conquers Chancas, Quechu, and Chimú
MID-15TH CENTURY	Machu Picchu built
1471–93	Inca empire at its height under Topa Inca Yupanqui
1493–1525	Emperor Huayna Capac expands into north
1532	Spanish arrive in Peru
1535	End of Inca empire

New World Pyramids

Carved God
Maya temples are decorated with elaborate stone carvings of deities, such as this bas-relief of the Smoking God from Palenque.

Temple of the Magician
At the major Classic Maya center of Uxmal, the Temple of the Magician was built in honor of the magician Adiviko between the 7th and 10th centuries AD.

The pyramids of Mesoamerica served multiple functions: they were platforms for temples (for example, the Aztec Templo Mayor); some served as as funerary monuments (for example, the Maya Temple of the Inscriptions at Palenque); and they were effigy mountains of a sacred landscape (for example, the Pyramids of the Sun and the Moon at Teotihuacán). The Great Pyramid of Cholula, the largest pyramid in the world by volume, was the epitome of what the Aztecs called an *altepetl,* a water-mountain that served to define the axis of a sacred community.

Sacred Mountain

The Great Pyramid of Cholula, shown above in a lithograph, was known as Tlachihualtepetl ("man-made mountain"). First begun in about 500 BC, the enormous structure was rebuilt four times over a 1,500-year period. Cholula is the longest continuously occupied urban center in the Americas, and has been an important pilgrimage site for the past 2,500 years.

Tikal Temple

The Temple of the Giant Jaguar rises 148 feet (45 m) above the Great Plaza at the Classic Maya temple complex of Tikal, in northern Guatemala. During its heyday from AD 600 to 900, Tikal was the largest urban center in the southern Maya lowlands.

Recovering Our Recent Past

Archaeology can shed light on the recent past, as well as on more distant times. Historical, or text-aided, archaeology combines archaeological techniques with documentary research.

Miners' Camp
Archaeologists have searched the ruins of Ludlow, Colorado, for information about the living conditions of the miners involved in the tragic 1914 strike.

In many instances, archaeology is used to supplement historical knowledge, often giving insights into the lives of the unnamed individuals overlooked by historical research. In other cases, historical archaeology can unearth a texture to the events of the past that otherwise would have been entirely lost. A good example is the excavations of Martin's Hundred, one of the earliest English settlements in Virginia. This tract of land on the banks of the James River is located about 10 miles (16 km) downriver from Jamestown, which had been settled in 1607, the first English settlement in the New World. Just three years after its founding, Martin's Hundred was attacked and its inhabitants massacred by local Indians. Only archaeology has been able to recover the details of this very early English settlement in the New World. The recovery of the settlement, artifacts, and, more gruesomely, the many graves of

TRACING INDUSTRIAL ARTIFACTS
Finds from the Industrial Age can be difficult to identify. All the objects that were manufactured on one type of machine look the same and, unlike hand-crafted objects, mass-produced objects do not bear the style of an individual craftsperson. Consequently, archaeologists tend to rely on documents and plans to trace finds from this period.

Iron Industry
One of the key sites of England's Industrial Age is Coalbrookdale. It was here that cast iron was first produced from a coke-fueled furnace, in 1709, and that the world's first iron bridge was built, in 1779. Using details gathered during archaeological investigations, the era has been re-created at the Ironbridge Museum.

the settlers, some of which show evidence of a violent end, all give a fabric and texture to our understanding of the past that is often not accessible in the historical documents of the period.

RECONSTRUCTING PORT ARTHUR

Historical archaeology can help researchers reconstruct old buildings and settlements with great accuracy and precision. Often such reconstructed sites become important parts of a region's cultural heritage. An excellent example is Port Arthur on the Tasman Peninsula in Tasmania, Australia. Founded in 1830 as a timber station, Port Arthur was quickly converted to a prison settlement as part of Britain's penal colony system. It became nearly self-sufficient—a mini-town—but it also gained a reputation as a "hell on earth." The prison closed in 1877 and the settlement dwindled away, with its buildings gradually falling into disrepair. In 1979, however, a conservation and development program allowed a number of the buildings to be restored. The Port Arthur Historic Site now provides modern-day visitors with a vivid glimpse of what life in a 19th century penal colony would have been like.

UNCOVERING A MINERS' STRIKE

Another good example of how the investigation of the recent past can resonate with the present is the ongoing work at Ludlow, Colorado. Here, in 1914, striking coal miners and their families were killed by the Colorado National Guard. Excavations of the "tent colony" where the families lived, as well as of the towns occupied by the miners and their families before and after the strike, are helping to paint a much more precise picture of living conditions for these strikers. The archaeological investigations also help to raise awareness of this terrible event among visitors to the site.

Penal Settlement
The Penitentiary Guard Tower and Officers' Quarters overlook Port Arthur. Tasmania's largest prison from 1830 to 1877, the site has been restored and is now open to the public, providing an insight into Australia's convict era.

PART TWO

A Guide to

Sites and Treasures

How to Use This Guide

Packed with fascinating glimpses into the lives of our ancestors, this Guide will expand your knowledge of the past and may even inspire the itinerary of your next trip.

CHAPTER BANDING KEY

This *Guide to Sites and Treasures* explores a vast range of the human experience across time and geography. It divides the world's most significant archaeological finds into five chapters according to their geographic region, and arranges them chronologically within each chapter. The entries have been chosen to reflect the diversity of archaeology's discoveries and to highlight often overlooked areas. While some finds are inaccessible or so fragile that they are kept under lock and key, many of the sites can be visited and the world's great museums are full of their unearthed treasures.

At the top of each entry, *key facts* summarise the site's significance, age, discovery and excavation, most important finds, and accessibility.

A handy *locator map* appears in the top left corner of each entry. The location of the site is indicated by the small red square.

***Colored banding* identifies the region in which the site is located. Five different colors relate to the Guide's five chapters (see the key, above left).**

THE AMERICAS

Mesa Verde

- The best preserved set of archaeo
- Dated from AD 400 to 1300
- First recognized by Euroamericans
- Finds include well-preserved orga
- Ruins open to the public; artifacts

Mesa Verde (Spanish for "green table") is located in southwest Colorado where a series of mesas (flat-topped mountains) is dissected by deep canyons. On the mesa tops and in deep overhangs on the canyon walls are hundreds of well-preserved archaeological sites belonging to the Anasazi (ancestral Pueblo) tradition. The most spectacular of the sites, such as Cliff Palace, Spruce Tree House, and Balcony House, date to the 13th century and comprise well-constructed masonry structures, several stories in height. These included houses and storage rooms, as well as circular s known as kivas, which were used for ceremonial activi

The dry environment of the Southwest has preserve organic artifacts, such as pots full of corn, and sandals r from yucca plants. The Anasazi were heavily reliant on farming of corn, beans, and squash, although they also and gathered a wide variety of natural resources. They famous for their beautifully decorated pottery.

Together with the rest of the Four Corners region, Verde was abandoned by the Anasazi toward the end o 13th centu ably becaus drought, alt incursions Indian grou also have p the move. I itants travel the south a and became ancestors o Pueblo Ind

398

aster Island Statues

One of the most spectacular Stone Age cultures in the world
Dated to c. AD 1000–1500
First known discovery by Westerners made on Easter Sunday, 1722
Most statues still in situ, with many re-erected on platforms;
single statues in museums in Chile, London, Brussels, Paris

ern visitors to what was baptised Easter astounded—as were all subsequent stone statues that ringed the volcanic nall, with an area of only 66 square miles prehistoric inhabitants had erected stone d its perimeter, eventually setting up ures (moai) on them. The numbers the biggest such platform, held no less

ly remain undiscovered, buried in the p the sides of the Rano Raraku crater rried, but it is reckoned that between nade. The statues were carved from a own as tuff. They are all variations on e abdomen and featuring elongated ly at the sides, and long fingers meeting . The ears are sometimes lengthened ed. The moai range in height from 6 to to 10 m) and weigh up to 82 tons es). They were carved at the quarry with alt picks, thousands of which have been the site along with hundreds of statues stage of production.

Standing Guard
Many of the statues have now been restored and returned to their ahu. Thought to represent ancestral chiefs, the moai face inland to overlook and protect the villages.

Work in Progress
In and around the quarry of Ranu Raraku, about 400 unfinished statues in every stage of manufacture were mysteriously abandoned by their makers.

AD 2000
AD 1500
AD 1000
AD 500
379

States

s
m

f Dwellers
th century, hifted their es from the the canyon Cliff Palace, esa Verde's , contained 200 rooms.

direct he ker peo- hind such as left).

acts
nic objects the dry Mesa Verde ganic arti- kets. These t) were House.

co Canyon
ajor Anasazi our Corners co Canyon. 13 villages, f which was nito (right).

AD 2000
AD 1500
0
399

Stunning *color photographs* display the site and its finds to full advantage. Informative captions expand on the main text.

A *timeline* is positioned along the right-hand margin of each entry to provide a quick visual reference to the age of the site.

Sites and Treasures of

Africa

The footprints and skeletons of our earliest ancestors; the pyramids, lavish grave goods, and hieroglyphic script of the Egyptians; the mysterious sculptures of Nok and Lydenburg; and the impressive ruins of Great Zimbabwe have all been found on the continent of Africa.

"In that 110-degree heat we began jumping up and down. With nobody to share our feelings, we hugged each other, sweaty and smelly, howling and hugging in the heat-shimmering gravel, the small brown remains of what now seemed almost certain to be parts of a single hominid skeleton lying all around us."

Don Johanson (born 1943),
U.S. anthropologist, discoverer of "Lucy"

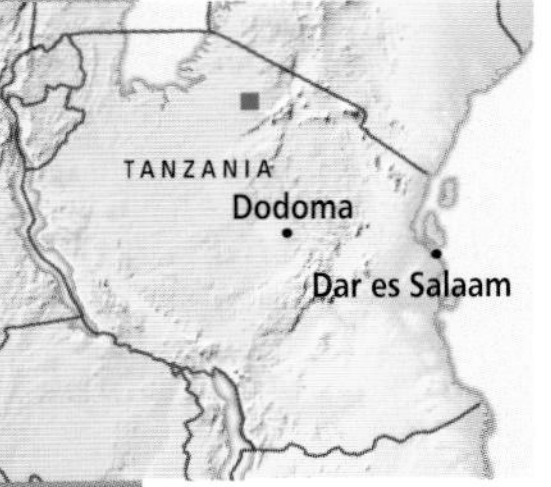

The Laetoli Footprints

- Oldest known footprints of bipedal hominid
- Dated to 3.8–3.6 million years ago
- Uncovered in northern Tanzania 1978–79
- Finds include early hominid footprints and fossils
- Footprints reburied for protection and inaccessible to the public

After brief visits to the northern Tanzanian site of Laetoli—meaning "red lily" in Maasai—by Louis and Mary Leakey in 1935 and Ludwig Kohl-Larsen in 1938–39, intensive work under the direction of Mary Leakey between 1974 and 1981 led to the discovery of some 30 early hominid fossils, as well as hominid and animal tracks. The early hominid fossils are fragments attributed to the australopithecine *Australopithecus afarensis* and dated by the potassium-argon technique to about 3.8–3.6 million years ago. A more recent skull of an archaic *Homo sapiens,* the Ngaloba skull, probably some 150,000 years old, was also found.

A Slow Revelation
Mary Leakey (right) supervised the excavations at Laetoli, remarking that it was "quite a different feeling from the discovery of a major hominid fossil... The Laetoli hominid trails were something that grew in extent, in detail, and in importance over two seasons."

Hints of wonders hidden at Laetoli first came to light in 1976, when Andrew Hill found remarkably preserved animal tracks that had been made some 3.6 million years ago in wet volcanic ash from the nearby volcano Sadiman. The tracks later hardened and became buried, until they were exposed by recent erosion. In 1977 Peter Jones and Philip Leakey found more animal tracks. Then in 1978 Paul Abell discovered unique evidence of fossilized early hominid behavior in the form of a 29 yard (27 m) long trail of more than 69 hominid footprints of two or perhaps three individuals who walked alongside each other. The weight distribution, as well as the size and position of the big toe in the footprints, indicates that the 3.6-million-year-old australopithecines walked upright with a striding gait rather than with the rolling gait seen in apes such as chimpanzees. The australopithecines were small-brained and did not make stone tools, so the Laetoli footprints confirm that bipedalism, rather than bigger brains or stone toolmaking, was the true beginning of the human story.

Upright Prints
In the Laetoli footprints, the big toe lies alongside the other toes and is only slightly longer—almost exactly the same weight-distribution pattern as a modern human makes walking along a beach.

1 million

2 million

3 million

4 million

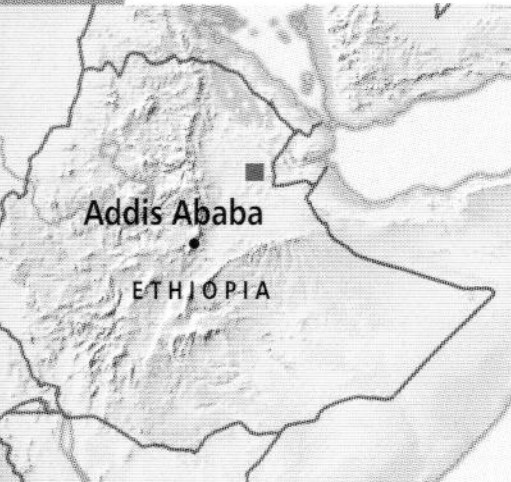

Lucy

- Early hominid fossil celebrity
- Dated to 3.18 million years ago
- Discovered in Ethiopia by Donald Johanson in 1974
- Finds comprise partial skeleton of australopithecine
- Not accessible to the public

On November 30, 1974, at Hadar in the Afar Desert of northeastern Ethiopia, Donald Johanson noticed a fragment of early hominid arm bone sticking out of the side of a gully. Wildly excited, he and his crew carefully collected bone fragments that made up about 40 percent of the skeleton of a female australopithecine, cataloged as number AL 288-1. The first night after the discovery, the camp partied to a tape of the Beatles' song "Lucy in the Sky with Diamonds," and the nickname "Lucy" was given to the partial skeleton. In 1978 she was assigned the scientific name of a new species of early hominid, *Australopithecus afarensis,* an apelike upright-walking human ancestor that roamed eastern Africa between about 4 million and 3 million years ago, the same creature that made the Laetoli footprints (see p. 230).

Our Famous Relative
The partial skeleton of Lucy shows that she was about 3 feet 7 inches (1.1 m) tall. The shape of the hip bone indicates that the skeleton was female, and an erupted wisdom tooth in the jaw places her in her late teens or early twenties.

Lucy probably died from illness or drowning at the edge of a lake or stream. Her corpse became covered by sand or mud, which later hardened into rock. Millions of years later, rains exposed her bones. Remains of early human ancestors usually consist of small bits of bone. At the time of Lucy's discovery, she was the most complete and oldest early hominid skeleton ever found, and also showed that human ancestors were bipedal long before the appearance of stone tools. Even though more complete and older early hominid remains have since come to light, she remains a point of comparison and debate with other early hominid fossils, as well as humankind's most famous early relative.

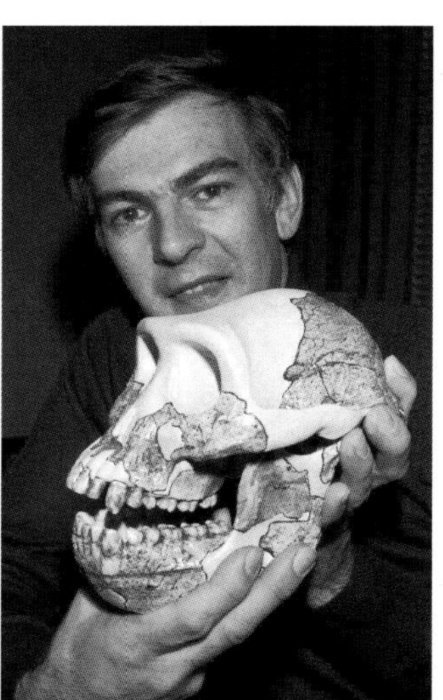

A Reconstructed Skull
The U.S. anthropologist Donald Johanson, who discovered Lucy in 1974, displays a plaster cast of the skeleton's skull.

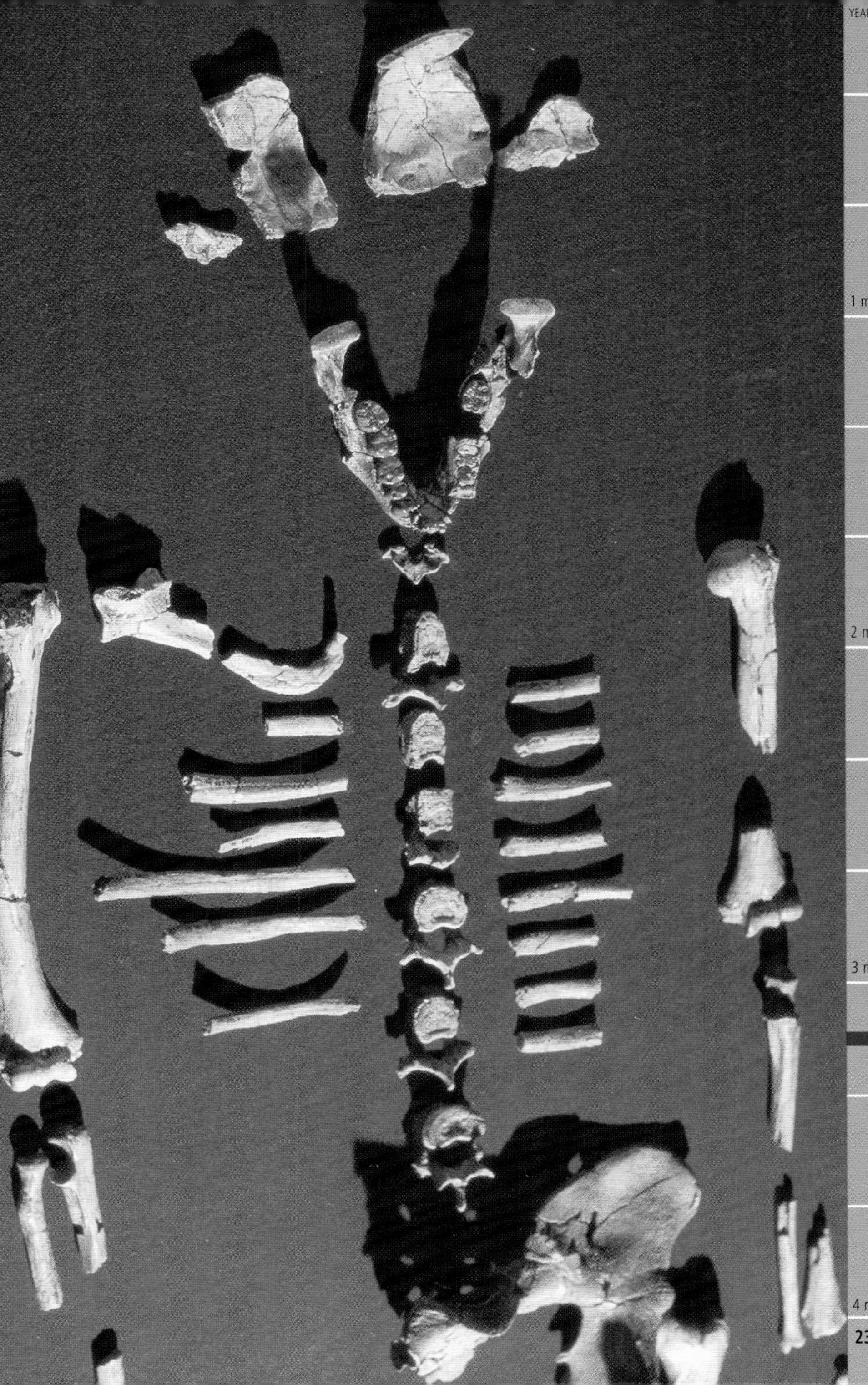

YEARS AGO
1 million
2 million
3 million
4 million

The Taung Child

- The first australopithecine discovered
- At least 2.4 million years old, possibly 2.8 million years old
- Delivered to Raymond Dart in 1924
- Finds comprise fossil of face and cast of brain of young child
- Site destroyed by blasting but marked by plinth accessible to visitors

Early Child
The Taung specimen consisted of a skull and jawbone (bottom) and a mold of the right half of the brain (middle). Raymond Dart, who first described the find in 1925, made the skull reconstruction (top).

In late 1924 Raymond Dart, professor of anatomy at the University of the Witwatersrand, was sent two boxes of material blasted by lime miners from a quarry at Norlim (previously Buxton) in the district of Taung (Tswana for "the place of the lion"), now in the North-West Province of South Africa. In one of them, he found the face of a young child, along with a mold of its brain formed from sand that had filled the inside of the skull after death and then hardened. In 1925 he named the find *Australopithecus africanus* (Latin/Greek for "the southern ape of Africa") and argued that it represented a form intermediate between apes and humans. Dart's claims were dismissed for decades because they did not correspond with then-prevailing views on human evolution, but won overwhelming support after the discovery of many more such fossils from southern and, later, eastern Africa.

Studies of the growth lines in its teeth suggest that the child was between 2.7 and 3.7 years old when it died. Marks on the frontal bone may be from the talons of a large bird of prey. It is thought that the child could have been killed and torn apart by a carnivore before an eagle snatched the head to its nest. Animal bones found at the place where the skull was blasted out are similar to remains found near modern eagle nests.

Vindication
The finds and notes of Robert Broom (left) confirmed that australopithecines were bipedal, erect, with human-like teeth, and relatively small brains, helping to end the ridicule that had greeted Raymond Dart's claim that the Taung child was an early human relative.

The Taung child was the first early African hominid found and gave the name "australopithecine" to the apelike upright-walking creatures now recognized as early human relatives.

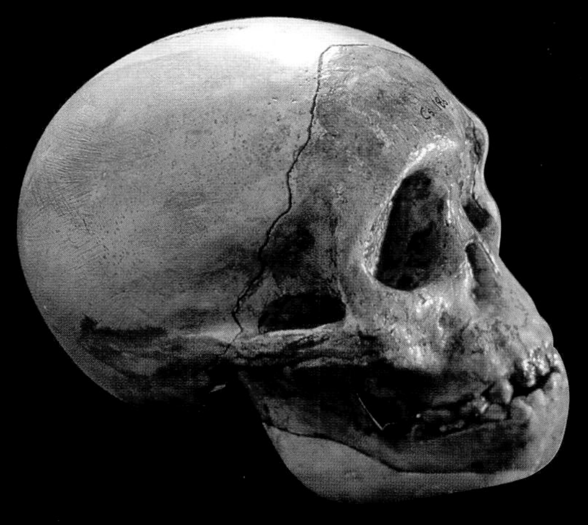

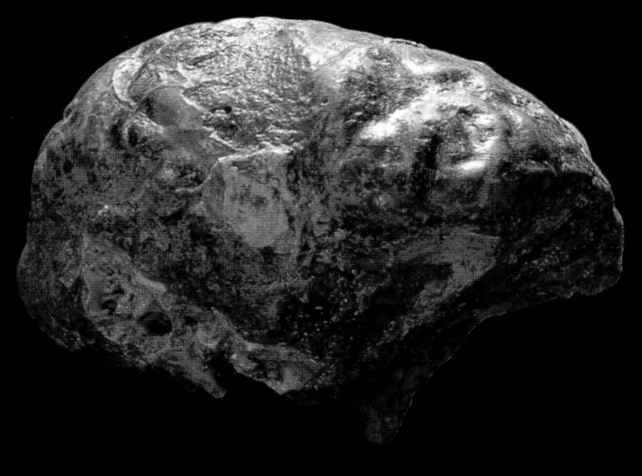

YEARS AGO

1 million

2 million

3 million

4 million

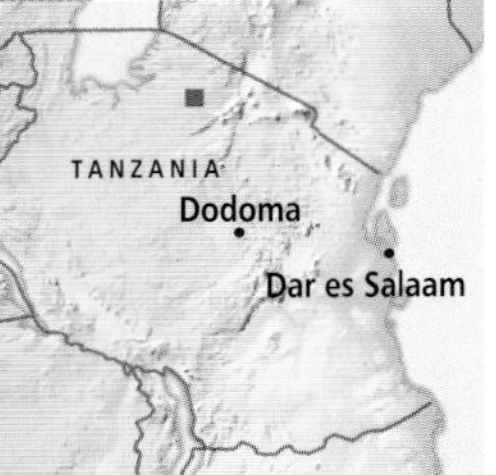

Olduvai Gorge

- Canyon containing one of the world's longest archaeological records
- Dated from about 1.9 million years ago to less than 10,000 years ago
- Discovered in northern Tanzania in 1911
- Finds include early hominid and animal fossils; stone artifacts
- Site and site-museum displays open to the public

Olduvai, meaning "place of the wild sisal" in Maasai, is a spectacular gorge and side gorge some 25 miles (40 km) long and up to 33 yards (100 m) deep in northern Tanzania. About 70,000 years ago, a river began slicing through sediments laid down in an ancient lake basin to expose an archaeological archive of many sites covering most of the last 2 million years.

Following its discovery in 1911 by Wilhelm Kattwinkel, a German entomologist, fossils were collected from the site by a German geologist, Hans Reck, in 1913. These inspired Louis Leakey to lead his first expedition to Olduvai in 1931. The abundance of early stone tools and animal fossils encouraged Louis and Mary Leakey to continue expeditions to Olduvai over the following decades in search of early human fossils, and the name "Oldowan" came to be applied to the earliest known stone tools.

In 1959 Mary Leakey at last struck gold by discovering the skull of a 1.8-million-year-old australopithecine called *Zinjanthropus* (now *Australopithecus* or *Paranthropus*) *boisei*—popularly known as "Zinj." The resultant publicity ignited still-continuing early hominid research in eastern Africa. In 1960 the Leakeys' son Jonathan discovered the 1.75-million-year-old remains of the then oldest known fossil of the human genus and presumed Oldowan toolmaker, later named *Homo habilis,* or "handyman." The Leakeys subsequently found other *Homo habilis* fossils, giving them nicknames such as "George" and "Twiggy."

Ongoing rich discoveries of early hominid fossils, as well as large collections of animal bones and stone tools meticulously recorded by Mary Leakey, provide valuable information on the dating, environment, appearance, and behavior of early and more recent hominids.

Rich Yield
Olduvai Gorge, in the Serengeti Plains of northern Tanzania, has supplied the remains of more than 50 hominids and the longest record of the development of stone tools, making it one of the world's richest archaeological sites.

A Fragmented Skull
While exploring Olduvai with her dalmatians, Mary Leakey spotted parts of a skull eroding from the gorge wall. After excavating more than 400 fragments, she reconstructed the skull of "Zinj" (left).

YEARS AGO
2 million
3 million
4 million

The Turkana Boy

- The most complete early human skeleton ever found
- Dated to between 1.56 and 1.51 million years ago
- Excavated from the Nariokotome III (NK3) site in Kenya 1984–88
- Find comprises well-preserved, almost complete skeleton
- Not accessible to the public

In August 1984, Richard Leakey and Alan Walker were conducting excavations on the western shores of Lake Turkana in northern Kenya. The legendary Kenyan fossil hunter Kamoya Kimeu took a stroll on a rest day and noticed a fragment of the skull of an early hominid lying among pebbles. Subsequent excavations over five field seasons resulted in the recovery of almost the entire skeleton of a boy equivalent in age to a modern 11-year-old. Nicknamed "The Turkana Boy," the remains were cataloged as KNM-WT 15000 and identified by the scientific name of either African *Homo erectus* or *Homo ergaster*—a hominid intermediate between the first upright walkers and modern people.

In One Piece
The Turkana Boy's skeleton was missing only its feet and a few other pieces. It had been covered so quickly with mud that no scavenger had a chance to chew the bones.

Potassium-argon dating of the layers in which the skeleton was found showed that the boy had died some 1.53 million years ago. The only clue to the cause of his death is a lesion on his jawbone, which might indicate gum disease resulting in fatal septicemia. It is thought his body either fell or was washed into a marsh, where it decomposed and then was quickly covered by mud and volcanic ash, until erosion exposed the bones to Kimeu's sharp eyes. Researchers were initially surprised by the Turkana Boy's long limbs, which indicated he would have been about 6 feet 1 inch (1.82 m) tall had he survived to maturity. Reexamination of like-aged early hominid remains confirmed that humans reached their present stature at least 1.5 million years ago, much earlier than originally thought.

Excavation Site
Kamoya Kimeu made his groundbreaking discovery at the Nariokotome III (NK3) site on the western shores of Lake Turkana in northern Kenya.

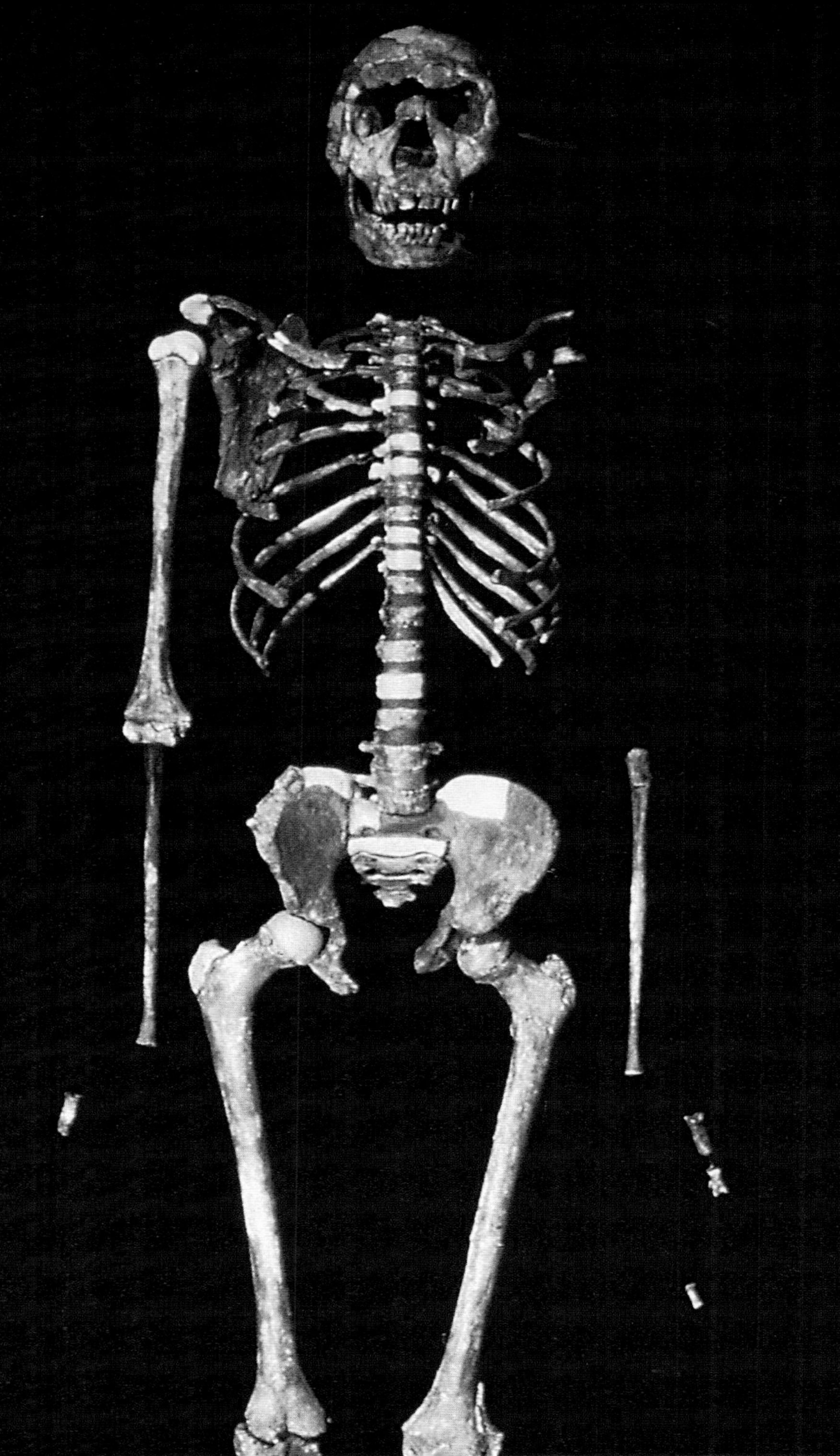

1 million

2 million

3 million

4 million

Klasies River Mouth

- Some of oldest remains of modern or near-modern *Homo sapiens*
- Dated to 125,000–60,000 years ago and last 5,000 years
- Locality's potential identified by mountaineer Ludwig Abel in 1955
- Finds include Middle and Later Stone Age human fossils and artifacts
- Not accessible to the public

Klasies River Mouth is a series of coastal caves located in the Eastern Cape Province of South Africa. Between about 125,000 and 60,000 years ago, artifacts, food remains, and bones of Middle Stone Age campers accumulated until there was a pile of layers up to 22 yards (20 m) high. In the last 5,000 years, one of the caves was used for rich burials of Later Stone Age people.

During excavations by Ronald Singer and John Wymer in 1966–68 and by H.J. Deacon since 1984, fragments of human bone with modern anatomical features were found in Middle Stone Age layers dating from 125,000 years ago. They are among the earliest such remains known and support the hypothesis that modern humans evolved in Africa (see p. 135). Intriguingly, some are charred and exhibit cut marks suggestive of cannibalism.

The Klasies Middle Stone Age folk may have looked modern, but whether they behaved like modern hunter-gatherers is debatable. They left some of the oldest known evidence for systematic shellfish exploitation, but did not fish, and preferred hunting docile rather than dangerous animals. Small blades of the Howieson's Poort Industry in the middle of the Middle Stone Age sequence, as well as the occurrence of hearths and ocher, have been cited as evidence for modern behavior. Unlike most other Middle Stone Age industries, the Howieson's Poort is characterized by small blades, segment-shaped tools, and the use of quantities of fine-grained raw materials, which are reminiscent of Later Stone Age industries. However, there is little if any indisputable evidence for art or bone artifacts during Middle Stone Age times—the dates of apparent Middle Stone Age bone points from Blombos Cave farther west on the South African coast await confirmation.

Klasies River Main Site
Eroded archaeological deposits banked up against the cliff face expose cave-like openings. The deposits include abundant Middle Stone Age artifacts as well as shell and bone food remains of the early modern human occupants.

Students at Work
A group of students excavate and sort the rich deposits from the lower levels in cave 1/1A at Klasies River main site. Some of the finds date to 100,000 years ago .

Modern Mandible
This modern-looking jawbone from the excavations at Klasies River Mouth is dated to about 100,000 years ago, suggesting that modern humans evolved in Africa.

YEARS AGO
50,000
150,000
200,000

Abydos

- Long-lived Egyptian cemetery plus associated settlement
- Used from predynastic times to Roman period, 3500–100 BC
- Known since ancient times; excavated from 19th century onward
- Finds include funerary remains and temples
- Accessible to the public, but some areas may be restricted

Abydos, used as a cemetery from prehistoric times onward, has yielded thousands of graves of various dates. Here, in a region known as the Umm el-Qa'ab, the kings of the 1st Dynasty, and some of the kings of the 2nd Dynasty, were buried in underground tombs topped by mud-brick superstructures with stone features. The royal burials were surrounded by warehouses to hold their copious grave goods, and by tombs provided for the servants and dogs who would serve their master after death. Nearby, each of the archaic kings built a massive rectangular mud-brick enclosure of unknown purpose.

In the Middle Kingdom (2023–1786 BC), the Umm el-Qa'ab became identified as the burial place of the god of the dead, Osiris. Developing into a major cult center, Abydos attracted large numbers of pilgrims who left offerings in the form of pots. An annual festival commemorating the death and rebirth of Osiris was celebrated until the end of the dynastic age.

The New Kingdom pharaohs Seti I (1306–1290 BC) and Ramesses II (1290–1224 BC) built stone temples at Abydos. Seti's beautifully decorated temple is dedicated to seven gods—Ptah, Re-Harakhty, Amen-Re, Osiris, Isis, Horus, and the dead and deified Seti himself—and included an unusual underground feature, the Osireion. Built in the form of a New Kingdom tomb with massive granite pillars supporting the roof, this appears to have been a cenotaph tomb intended for the king himself. Ramesses' smaller temple appears to lack this feature, although the area behind his temple has not been fully excavated.

False Tomb
The elaborate temple of Seti is supported by intricately carved columns. Seti's remains, however, are buried at Luxor. Such cenotaphs (false tombs) are a feature of the Abydos site.

Ready for War
A colorful wall relief in the temple of Ramesses II depicts the pharaoh in war dress. The temple was built to give Ramesses' spirit a close association with the god of death, Osiris.

List of Kings
The decoration in the temple of Ramesses II included this list of the kings of Egypt (left). It records the offerings that Ramesses made to his predecessors.

0
5000 BC
7500 BC
10,000 BC

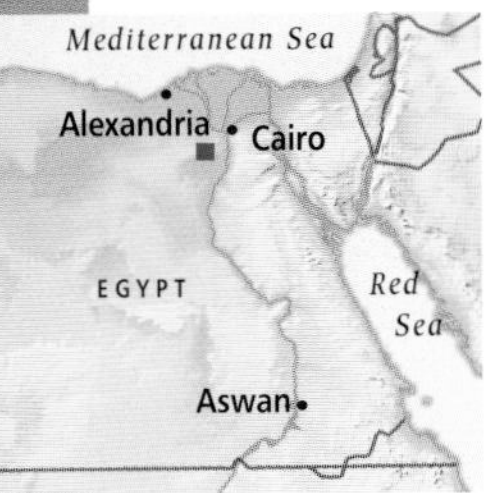

The Giza Pyramids

- Largest Egyptian stone-built monuments
- Dated to 4th Dynasty, 2551–2472 BC
- Known since ancient times
- Finds include pyramids, sphinx, solar boat, private tombs
- On public display but access to some areas may be restricted

The Great Pyramid, built by the pharaoh Khufu (Cheops), is the only surviving Wonder of the Ancient World. Constructed from approximately 2 million blocks of limestone, and standing some 480 feet (146 m) high with sides orientated almost exactly to true north, the pyramid dominates the Giza Plateau. For more than 4,000 years, it was the world's tallest building. The accuracy achieved by the ancient builders is remarkable: the base of the pyramid is almost completely level, while its sides make an almost perfect square, varying in length by less than 3 inches (7.5 cm).

Within the pyramid, passages lead both downward to an unfinished chamber, and upward to a limestone-clad room known today as the Queen's Chamber. Beyond this, high within the pyramid, is the red granite King's Chamber—the burial place of Khufu himself. Although its entrance was concealed and its passages were sealed with stone portcullises and a series of massive blocks, the pyramid had been robbed by the end of the Old Kingdom in 2150 BC.

Khufu's pyramid originally stood at the heart of a complex of religious buildings, but today the mortuary temple, causeway, and valley temple have vanished. The gleaming white limestone that once encased the pyramid survived until Medieval times, when it was stripped and reused in the building of Cairo.

Khufu's son, Khaefre, and his grandson, Menkaure, also built pyramid complexes at Giza. Their pyramids are on a smaller scale, although the pyramid of Khaefre, constructed on slightly higher ground, appears to be the largest of the three. Khaefre also built the sphinx—a creature with a lion's body and human head—that stands alongside his pyramid causeway.

Limestone Tombs
The craftsmanship of the pyramids is so exact that a playing card cannot be inserted between adjoining blocks of masonry. All three pyramids were originally encased in fine white limestone, but this outer layer was removed after AD 1222 in order to repair earthquake damage to nearby Cairo.

Inscrutable Monument
Carved from an enormous outcrop of rock near the pyramids, the Giza sphinx is 240 feet (72 m) long and 66 feet (20 m) high. Its face is thought to be a portrait of Khaefre, who commissioned the work.

0
2500 BC
5000 BC
7500 BC
10,000 BC

Deir el-Medina

- Unique Egyptian tomb-workers' village
- Dated to New Kingdom, 1550–1070 BC
- Revealed by the excavations of Bernard Bruyere in the 1920s
- Finds include workers' housing and numerous texts
- Site is open to the public, but access may be restricted

Ancient domestic sites are rare in Egypt as their mud-brick buildings have decayed over time. The state-owned, purpose-built village of Deir el-Medina is an important exception. Deir el-Medina was established at the beginning of the New Kingdom (1550 BC) to accommodate the workers engaged in building the hidden royal tombs in the nearby Valley of the Kings and Valley of the Queens. Here the workmen and their families lived in conditions of strict security designed to protect the royal graves from tomb robbers. The isolated walled village had only one gateway, which allowed guards to monitor those entering and leaving the site.

Within the mud-brick wall were terraces of long, narrow stone-built houses all with a similar design. A doorway led through a porch to a front chamber. Beyond this was the main living room lit by clerestory windows. A staircase led down to the cellar, while a doorway led to a storage room or bedroom. Finally came the open-roofed kitchen. Outside the village wall lay the tombs and chapels that the villagers had built for their own use.

The village flourished for some 500 years, serving as home to about 120 families, but was eventually abandoned at the end of the 20th Dynasty (1070 BC). Left behind were ostraca (inscribed pottery and stone fragments) and papyri, which allow us to reconstruct the villagers' lives. Many of these texts concern court cases, with accusations of corruption and disputes over property and donkeys being common.

Isolated Village
The village of Deir el-Medina was occupied for almost 500 years, yet it was located away from the Nile. All water and other essentials had to be transported to the village.

Ancient Notepads
Ostraca (above left) are fragments of pottery and stone that were used to record short semi-permanent texts. Their abundance at Deir el-Medina indicates an unusually high level of literacy among the village population.

Painted Tomb
Like the more elaborate tombs of the pharaohs that the workers built, the tombs of Deir el-Medina were decorated with vibrant wall paintings.

Cosmetic Chest
This painted wooden toiletries box, retrieved from a Deir el-Medina tomb, belonged to the wife of the royal architectural foreman Kha.

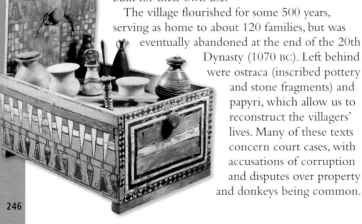

0
2500 BC
5000 BC
7500 BC
10,000 BC

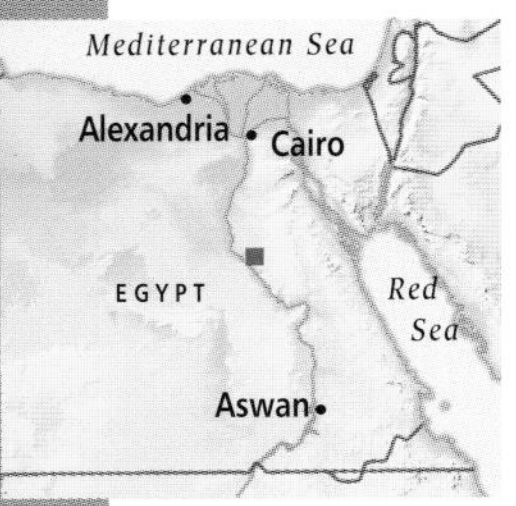

Amarna

- Capital city of Akhenaten, Egypt's "heretic king"
- Dated to 18th Dynasty, c. 1358–1340 BC
- Known since antiquity; first planned excavation in 1798–99
- Finds include tombs, bust of Nefertiti, Amarna Letters, stelae
- Site open to the public; bust of Nefertiti in Berlin Museum

When the "heretic king" Akhenaten dedicated himself and his country to a single god, the Aten (or sun's disk), he abandoned the traditional capitals of Thebes and Memphis, and established a new city on virgin land on the east bank of the Nile in Middle Egypt. The city was named Akhetaten, although today it is better known by its modern name of Amarna or Tell el-Amarna. A series of inscriptions (boundary stelae) defined the city's boundaries and set out the king's intentions: Amarna was to be Akhenaten's permanent home, and he was to be buried in the royal cemetery nearby.

The city, built in a mere four years, housed the royal family, the palace bureaucrats, the Aten priesthood, the royal guards, and numerous artisans. Nearby was a workman's village, designed to house the laborers who now started to construct the tombs of the elite in the nearby cliffs. Amarna was abandoned soon after Akhenaten's death and never reoccupied. Stone from the temples was stolen and reused in local building projects, the tombs were robbed and defaced, and the mud-brick buildings gradually crumbled.

Amarna, still under excavation, has yielded a series of unique archaeological finds. The Amarna Letters, copies of 18th Dynasty diplomatic correspondence written in cuneiform script, were discovered in the late 19th century by a local woman. In 1912 the ruined workshop of the royal sculptor Tuthmosis yielded the beautiful bust of Queen Nefertiti, consort to Akhenaten, which is today displayed in the Berlin Museum.

Worshiping the Sun
This stone stela recovered from Amarna shows Akhenaten and his family making an offering to the Aten. Akhenaten's religion lacked an ethical code, asking only that people be grateful to the sun for life and warmth. The religion failed to take permanent hold as it was too otherworldly to meet the needs of ordinary people.

The Beautiful One
Depicted in this famous painted limestone bust, Queen Nefertiti helped her husband transform Egypt's religious practices and was given unusual prominence in temple and palace reliefs. Her name means "the beautiful one is come."

0
2500 BC
5000 BC
7500 BC
10,000 BC

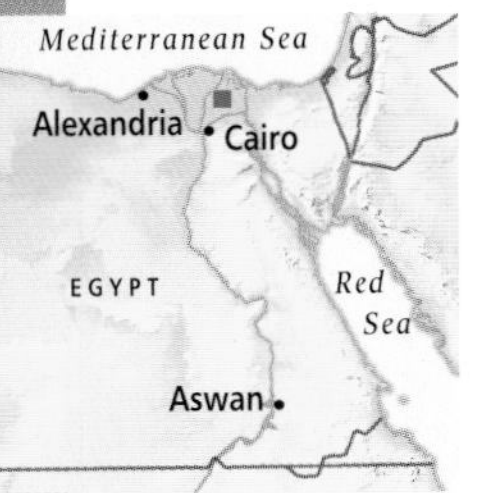

Tanis

- The largest archaeological site in the Nile Delta
- 21st and 22nd dynasties, c. 1069–712 BC
- Known since biblical times; site identified in 1722 at San el-Hagar
- Finds include temple, royal burials, statues
- The site is open to the public; artifacts in Cairo Museum

The 19th Dynasty Ramesses II had founded a magnificent capital city, Pi-Ramesse, in the eastern Nile Delta. By the end of the New Kingdom, however, the Pelusiac branch of the Nile was silting up and Pi-Ramesse was losing its water supply. The kings of the 21st Dynasty established a substitute capital at nearby Tanis, moving many of the more impressive monuments from Pi-Ramesse and incorporating them into their new city. Therefore, although none of the Tanis buildings predates the Third Intermediate Period, many of the statues and inscribed blocks are considerably older. Today, this site is represented by a large mound, or tell, which is still being excavated. Most of the archaeological work so far undertaken has concentrated on the temple site.

The Third Intermediate kings, rejecting both the pyramid form and the Valley of the Kings, had chosen to build their tombs within the precincts of the Tanis temple. Here, it was hoped, the royal burials would lie undisturbed, protected by the temple priests. In 1939 the French archaeologist Pierre Montet was excavating within the temple enclosure when he stumbled across the hidden royal tombs. A series of chambers yielded spectacular finds, including the silver falcon-headed coffin of Shoshenq II. Most impressive of all was the intact burial of Psusennes I: inside a pink granite sarcophagus lay a black granite mummiform sarcophagus holding a silver coffin. Within his coffin, Psusennes wore jewelry, amulets, and an inlaid golden face mask. His canopic jars—holding his lungs, liver, intestines, and stomach—stood beside his sarcophagi.

Tanis Unearthed
Much of Tanis remains to be excavated, but finds to date include numerous relief carvings. The city was well known from the Bible as Zoan, but it was not until 1722 that the connection was made with the prominent town-mound at San el-Hagar.

Royal Discovery
The royal tombs of Tanis were discovered in 1939 by the French archaeologist Pierre Montet (right), shown here inspecting the pink and black granite sarcophagi of Psusennes I.

Death Masks
Gold mummy masks covered the faces of Shoshenq II (above left) and Psusennes I (left). Shoshenq's coffin lay in the entrance chamber to the tomb of Psusennes.

0

2500 BC

5000 BC

7500 BC

10,000 BC

Nok Terracottas

- Oldest known pottery sculptures in sub-Saharan Africa
- Associated with iron-smelting sites dated to 600 BC to perhaps AD 300
- First Nok terracottas recovered during tin-mining operations in 1928
- Finds include baked clay sculptures and early iron-smelting site
- Pieces housed in various Nigerian museums and in private collections

In 1928 Colonel Dent Young, a miner at Nok in north-central Nigeria, spotted a 4 inch (10 cm) high terracotta sculpture of a human head being washed out of tin-bearing gravels and presented it to the Department of Mines Museum at the nearby town of Jos. In 1944 a near-life-size terracotta head was found at Jemaa, east of Nok, where it was being used as a scarecrow in a mineworker's vegetable plot. The Jemaa find was also taken to Jos. Here the heads came to the attention of archaeologist Bernard Fagg, who organized the rescue and description of the increasing quantities of "Nok Culture" material that was coming to light.

About 10 percent of the 200 or so known sculptures are small solid clay figures attached to pots or perhaps worn as pendants, but most are freestanding hollow human figurines 4 inches (10 cm) to 4 feet (120 cm) high. The head, often enlarged out of proportion to the body, is usually the part that has survived. A particular feature of the Nok sculptures is the treatment of the eyes, which are typically formed from a triangle or a segment of a circle, with a hollow hole for the pupil.

Much of what is now known about the Nok people is derived from their sculptures. The heads are clearly Negroid and depict intricate hairstyles (such as topknots and buns), beards, and mustaches, as well as ornaments and even physical deformities. Some of the sculptures seem to be connected to a residence, a possible shrine, or iron-smelting sites, but unfortunately most have been recovered from disturbed or unrecorded contexts and their function remains a mystery.

Terracotta Heads
Many Nok terracotta heads depict eyes as a triangle, with a hollow hole for the pupil (right), and wear elaborate hairstyles (below). Limb and torso fragments have also been found, so the heads may have formed part of complete figures.

Careful Reproduction
The Nok sculptors carefully reproduced physical features and deformities. Some scholars have suggested that the terracottas are associated with an agricultural fertility cult.

AD 500

0

1000 BC

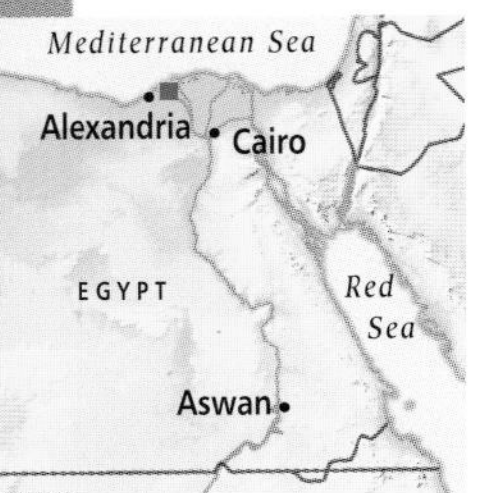

The Rosetta Stone

- Trilingual inscription used to decode hieroglyphics
- Dated to Year 9 of Ptolemy V in Ptolemaic Period, 196 BC
- Discovered in 1799 during the Napoleonic invasion of Egypt
- Find comprises black basalt slab uncovered during construction
- On public display in British Museum, London

The modern town of Rosetta (also known as Rashid) lies on the Mediterranean coast in the Nile Delta east of Alexandria. Here, in 1799 during the Napoleonic invasion, French engineers discovered a broken, inscribed basalt block. Following Nelson's victory over Napoleon at Aboukir Bay, the Rosetta Stone was seized and transported to London.

Linguists soon recognized the stone as a very important find. Its inscriptions represented the same text repeated in three different languages—a Middle Egyptian version written in hieroglyphs, a cursive Demotic version (the language spoken in Egypt during the Ptolemaic age), and a Greek version. All knowledge of the Egyptian hieroglyphic script had been lost centuries before when it was replaced by Arabic. Despite the abundance of hieroglyphs on Egyptian monuments, their meaning had eluded scholars. Since the Greek version on the Rosetta Stone could be read, the linguists realized that it might be possible to use this text as the key to deciphering the other two. Copies of the texts were circulated throughout Europe, and scholars set to work.

It was already known that the Egyptians wrote their royal names in a flattened ring, or cartouche. The French linguist Jean-François Champollion, identifying the cartouches in the Middle Egyptian inscription, was able to translate the name of Ptolemy by referring to the Greek inscription. This allowed him to start constructing an Egyptian alphabet. In 1822 Champollion reported that he had cracked the code—Egypt's ancient texts could now be read.

Royal Name
The names of Egyptian royalty were written in cartouches, flattened ovals. The cartouche on this earring represents the name of Tawosret, one of the few women to proclaim herself pharaoh of Egypt.

The Key to Egypt
The trilingual text on the Rosetta Stone marks the anniversary of the king and records his achievements. The basalt slab's real significance, however, is that it enabled scholars to decipher Egyptian hieroglyphs.

Ancient Scribe
The written language of the ancient Egyptians was in the hands of scribes, some of whom achieved great status. This sculpture is of Nespekasuti, the scribe of Karnah.

AD 500

0

500 BC

1000 BC

The Lydenburg Heads

- The oldest known examples of Iron Age art in southern Africa
- Dated to 7th century AD
- K.L. von Bezing collected first remains in 1962–64
- Finds comprise ceramic heads, artifacts, animal and human bones
- Heads on display in South African Museum, Cape Town

As a 10-year-old schoolboy, Dr K.L. von Bezing noticed pottery fragments lying about on what later proved to be an Early Iron Age village site in the town of Lydenburg, now in Mpumalanga Province in eastern South Africa. Some years later, between 1962 and 1964, he collected the fragments. When he started studying medicine at the University of Cape Town shortly afterward, he mentioned his collection to a member of the student archaeological society. The student then informed her lecturer, Ray Inskeep, who initiated the recording and study of the collected material as well as fresh investigations of the site.

Excavations conducted by T.M. Evers in 1976–78 established that the fragments probably originally lay in a pit. When pieced together, Von Bezing's fragments comprised two large and five smaller reddish ceramic heads, ranging in height from about 8 to 15 inches (20–38 cm). All very similar, they resemble upside-down elongated pots with incised decoration and the application of pieces of clay to form studs as well as features such as eyes, eyebrows, and ears. They bear traces of cream paint and specularite—a relatively rare and historically prized form of silvery sparkling hematite (a mineral)—and must have originally presented a glittering spectacle. The two larger heads could have been worn like helmets, while holes in the sides of the smaller ones suggest that they were attached to something. Fragments of similar material at contemporary South African Iron Age sites suggests that such heads were used over a wide area, possibly in initiation ceremonies or other rituals.

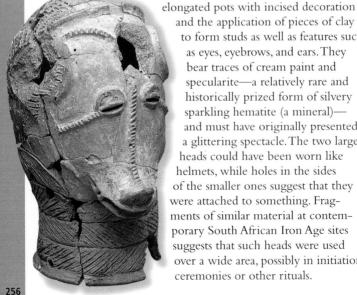

Ritual Art
The Lydenburg sculptures appear to have been used in rituals, such as initiation ceremonies, before being deliberately smashed and buried in deep pits.

Exaggerated Features
Resembling upside-down pots, the heads all feature two or three carved rings around the neck. This head (left) has exaggerated lips forming a snout, but the other six heads have lips formed from two crescents.

AD 1500

AD 1000

AD 500

0

Great Zimbabwe

- Most impressive stone-walled ancient capital in southern Africa
- Dated to 4th–19th centuries, capital of Shona state 1300–1450
- First European visitor was German geologist Carl Mauch in 1871
- Finds include stone walling and soapstone birds
- Site and site museum open to the public

The existence of stone structures deep in the southern African interior first became known to the Western world through the early 16th century Portuguese traders who visited the east African coast, but nearly four centuries passed before Great Zimbabwe was visited by a European. *Dzimbabwe* is the term used by Shona-speaking people for the court or house of a chief, usually consisting of stone-walled enclosures built on top of a hill. At least 150 zimbabwes are known, of which Great Zimbabwe is the biggest and most famous.

Early Iron Age people, who did not build in stone, occupied the site between about AD 300 and 1275. After this time, its first stone-walled enclosures were constructed and the site developed into a major center. In the 14th and early 15th centuries, Great Zimbabwe was home to about 18,000 people and the capital of an extensive Shona state that stretched beyond the boundaries of modern Zimbabwe. The king, certain members of his family, and important officials lived apart from commoners on top of a hill and became wealthy through control of trade with the east African coast. By 1450 the capital had moved elsewhere, although the site continued to be inhabited.

Probably no other archaeological site has inspired myths and political passions to the extent of Great Zimbabwe (see p. 41). The modern African country of Zimbabwe took its name from the site on independence from Great Britain in 1980, and a bird sculpture from the site is depicted on the nation's flag and coins. Despite nearly a century of archaeological and historical research, which indicates that the site was created by ancestors of the Shona people of Zimbabwe, some publications still refer to its "mystery" or cling to outdated romantic stories of exotic origins.

The Great Enclosure
The site has three main areas: the Hill Complex, which contained the residences of the royal family and officials; the Valley Ruins, the town where commoners lived; and the impressive Great Enclosure (shown here).

Massive Walls
Made up of an estimated 900,000 stone blocks, the massive outer walls of the Great Enclosure have a circumference of 820 feet (250 m) and a maximum height of 36 feet (11 m). The enclosure is thought to have been used as a premarital initiation school.

Zimbabwe Bird
Several soapstone figurines in the form of a bird have been found at the site. Each is about 12 inches (30 cm) tall and rests on a 3 foot (1 m) pillar. Interpreted as representing the role of royal ancestors, the birds have become a national symbol.

Sites and Treasures of

Europe

Since the 16th century, antiquarians and archaeologists have thoroughly investigated the remains of the past in Europe. Among their discoveries are the astounding art from the last Ice Age, the megalithic monuments of Malta and Britain, the classical architecture of Greece and Rome, and the ship burials of the Vikings.

"If I have to spend the rest of my life working in dirty, wet trenches, I doubt whether I shall ever again experience the shock and excitement I felt at my first glimpse of ink hieroglyphics on tiny scraps of wood."

Robin Birley (born 1935),
Director of Vindolanda excavation

Altamura Cave

- Oldest intact human skeleton in Europe
- Dated to Lower Paleolithic, c. 200,000–400,000 years old
- Discovered in cave in October 1993 by speleologists
- Finds comprise early human skeleton and animal bones
- Still in situ, but not accessible to the public

One of the most extraordinary paleontological discoveries in the world occurred in 1993, when speleologists penetrated an underground limestone cave at Altamura, Puglia, in southeast Italy. With great difficulty, the cave explorers descended almost 200 feet (60 m), where they found what appears to be an almost complete skeleton of an early human. They also discovered the bones of hyenas, deer, horses, and bovids in some galleries.

The human bones are in a little cavity, or apsidal niche, with the top of the skull turned down toward the floor. They are all thickly encrusted with cauliflower-like stalagmitic growths. This makes the features of the skull hard to make out, but the heavy brow-ridges suggest that the individual may be a link between *Homo erectus* and *Homo sapiens,* since some Neanderthal traits seem to be present along with more primitive features. If that is the case, its age could be placed, tentatively, at somewhere between 200,000 and 400,000 years old, making it the oldest virtually intact human skeleton known in Europe. Analysis is difficult since only some parts of the skeleton are visible, although initial studies have been carried out using optic fibers. Given the cave's inaccessibility, it will be extremely tricky to extract the bones from the site.

Hidden by Stalagmites
The full story of human evolution remains to be told, with new discoveries such as the early skeleton at Altamura, Italy, continuing to provide fresh evidence. The thick encrustation by stalagmites, however, has made the skeleton challenging to study.

A Missing Link
The skull features of the skeleton from the limestone cave in Altamura suggest that it may represent a link between *Homo sapiens* (above left) and *Homo erectus* (below left).

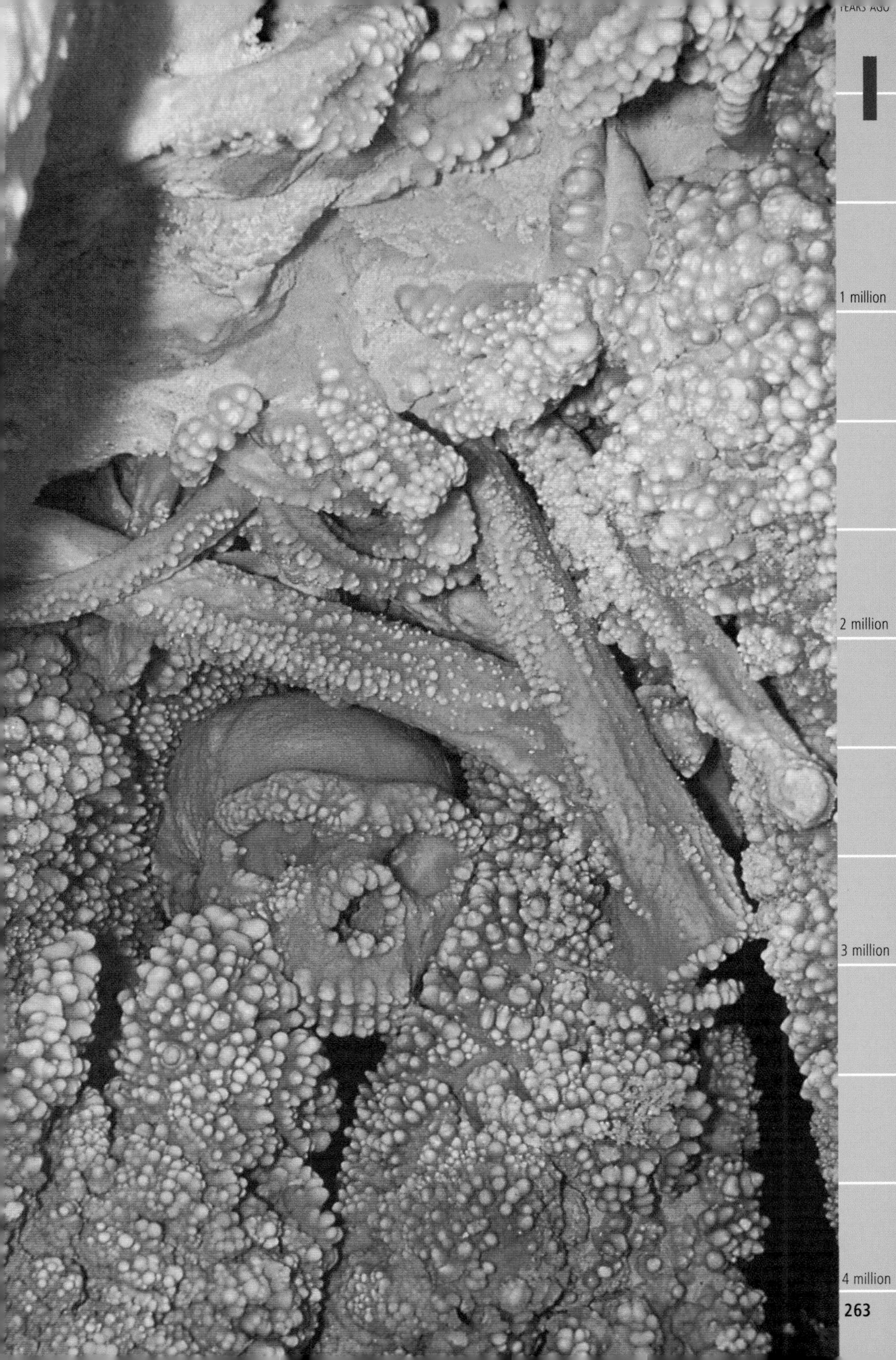
YEARS AGO
1 million
2 million
3 million
4 million

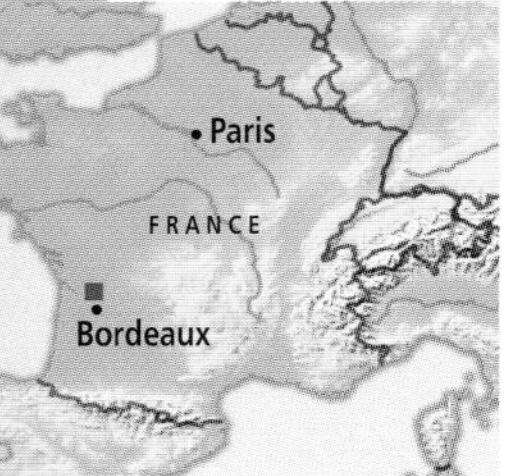

La Ferrassie

- Seven intentional burials by Neanderthals
- Dated to Late Pleistocene, 130,000–10,000 years ago
- First burial discovered in 1909 during excavations by Denis Peyrony
- Finds include Neanderthal burials, Paleolithic tools
- Fossil remains in Musée de l'Homme, Paris

The former rock-shelter of La Ferrassie is one of the most famous of all Neanderthal sites. Located near Les Eyzies in the Dordogne region of France, La Ferrassie was excavated by the eminent French prehistorian Denis Peyrony between 1896 and 1929. More recent investigations were conducted by H. Delporte during 1968–73. The collapsed rock-shelter contained a deep succession of loam and rubble deposits that date to the Late Pleistocene, and their analysis revealed much about changing climates during the period when Neanderthals and early modern humans occupied western Europe.

Between 1909 and 1921, Peyrony discovered the skeletal remains of six Neanderthals; Delporte later unearthed one more skeleton. The excavation of these remains—two adults and five children—helped to convince paleoanthropologists that the Neanderthals had intentionally buried their dead, although controversy continues to this day regarding the character of the burials. Study of the well-preserved extremities of these skeletons sheds light on the structure and function of Neanderthal hands and feet.

The Neanderthal remains were associated with a distinctive variant of the Middle Paleolithic stone-tool industry—known as the Ferrassie industry—that exhibits a high proportion of scrapers and heavy use of the Levallois prepared-core technique (see p. 142). La Ferrassie also contained a lengthy sequence of Upper Paleolithic levels above the Middle Paleolithic layers. These levels were inhabited by both Neanderthals and modern humans, and included tools from the Neanderthal Châtelperronian culture and the modern human Aurignacian culture.

Excavated Site
The first excavation at La Ferrassie was conducted by Denis Peyrony from 1896 to 1929. H. Delporte led further excavations of the site in 1968–73 (right).

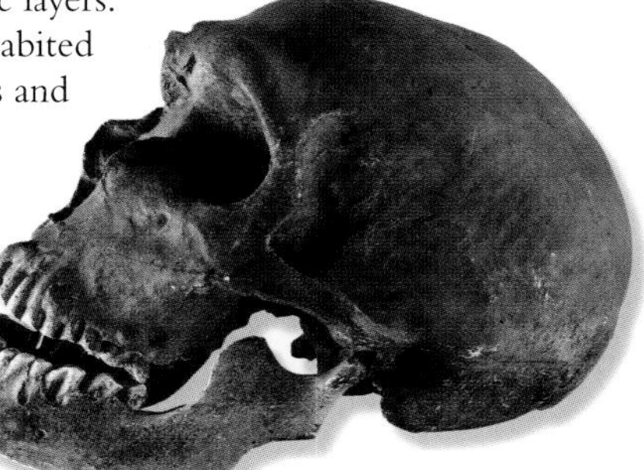

Neanderthal Skull
The skeletal remains found at La Ferrassie proved that Neanderthals deliberately buried their dead. While this indicates that they were able to connect past actions with an inert body, it does not necessarily provide any evidence of a belief in an afterlife.

YEARS AGO

1 million

2 million

3 million

4 million

Ice Age "Venus" Statuettes

- Early depictions of women in Eurasia
- Dated to Upper Paleolithic, *c.* 30,000–15,000 years ago
- Numerous discoveries from 1864 onward
- Public displays across Europe, especially Musée des Antiquités Nationales, Paris, and The Hermitage, St Petersburg

Well over a hundred small figurines of human females, made of stone, clay, and mammoth ivory, have been recovered from sites across Europe that date to the last Ice Age. Unfortunately nicknamed "Venuses" from the start, the statuettes include a handful with enormous breasts and buttocks, such as those from Lespugue and Willendorf, but these are by no means the norm. In fact, the carvings seem to represent women throughout their adult life, showing a wide range of physiological conditions, sometimes involving pregnancy and possibly even childbirth. This may explain why the breasts and abdomen are usually emphasized. The rarity of depicted vulvas, however, suggests that the intention was not overtly sexual. Most of the statuettes are highly stylized, with small heads and extremities. Only one or two depict faces or hair, or what may be clothing.

Some of the figurines were hidden, but others may have been meant for public exhibition. In western Europe, specimens were found carefully hidden under rocks in caves and rock-shelters. In eastern Europe, while many intact figurines were encountered in pits in hut floors, others were discovered in the layers of occupation debris that had built up on the floors. Rather than being seen as fertility idols, the eastern statuettes have often been interpreted by Russian scholars as mother- or ancestor-figures or as a mistress of the house.

An Ample Figure
The famous "Venus of Willendorf," found on the banks of the Danube in Austria, is carved from stone and stands about 4.5 inches (11 cm) tall. The artist has emphasized the pendulous breasts, protruding abdomen, and large buttocks.

A Simplified Approach
In contrast to the "Venus of Willendorf," this stylized figure from Dolní Věstonice in Moravia reduces the female form to a pair of breasts. These examples demonstrate the wide variety of styles evident in Ice Age sculpture.

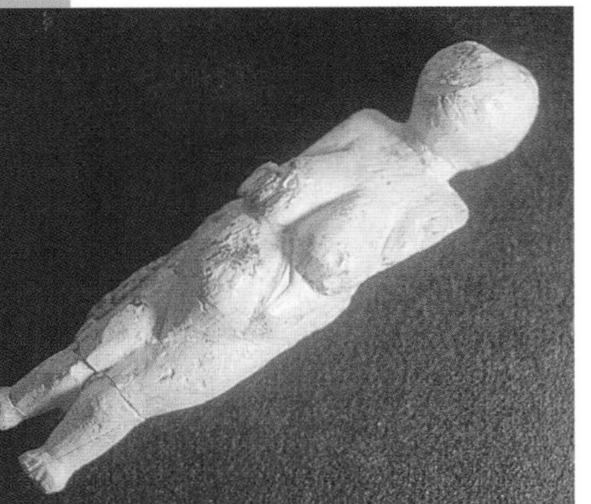

Russian Venus
This ivory figure was recovered from Kostenski, near Voronesh, in Russia. Kostenski has yielded more Venus figurines than any other site in Europe.

10,000
YEARS AGO

30,000

40,000

50,000

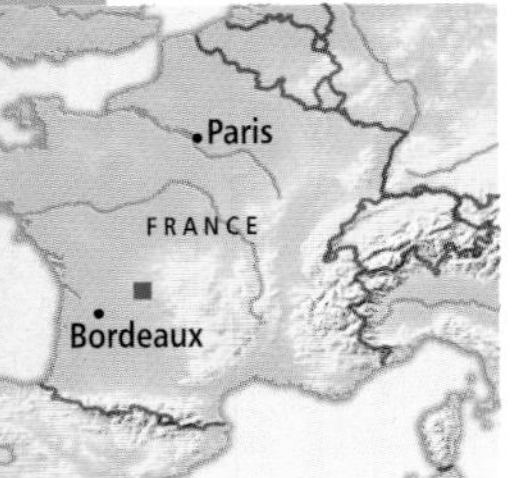

Lascaux Cave

- Best known and most spectacular of all Ice Age decorated caves
- Dated to Upper Paleolithic, c. 17,000–15,000 years ago
- Discovered by four boys in 1940 in Dordogne, France
- Closed to general public, but facsimile, Lascaux II, is open; a stone lamp from the site is in the Musée des Antiquités Nationales, Paris

The chance discovery of Lascaux cave during the Second World War is one of the most romantic stories in archaeology, featuring four teenage boys and a dog who explored a hole in a forest, only to find themselves inside a staggeringly beautiful painted cave. Although Lascaux is best known for its 600 magnificent paintings of aurochs (wild cattle), horses, deer, and "signs," it also contains almost 1,500 engravings, which are dominated by horses. The most famous feature is the great Hall of Bulls, which displays several aurochs figures, some of them 16 feet (5 m) long, the biggest figures known in Ice Age art; the hall also contains an enigmatic figure, baptised the "unicorn." A shaft features a painted scene of what seems to be a bird-headed man with a wounded bison and a rhinoceros.

Stone tools for engraving were discovered in the cave's engraved zones. Many lamps were also recovered, one of them a finely carved specimen in sandstone featuring engraved motifs. There were also 158 fragments of pigment, along with color-grinding equipment.

Much of the cave floor was lost when the site was adapted for tourism in the late 1940s, but it was probably never a habitation, being visited only briefly for artistic activity or ritual. Scaffolding was clearly used in some galleries to reach the upper walls and ceiling. Charcoal fragments from the cave floor have provided radiocarbon dates of around 17,000 years ago and 8,000 years ago.

The cave was closed to tourists in 1963 because of pollution—a "green sickness" of a proliferation of algae, and a "white sickness" of crystal growth. It was possible to reverse the effects of the green sickness and arrest the development of the white, but to ensure the survival of the cave's art, the number of visitors has been drastically restricted. As compensation, an impressive facsimile, Lascaux II, is now open nearby.

Hall of Bulls
Dominated by four enormous aurochs, drawn in black outline, the Hall of Bulls has been magnificently reproduced in the fascimile Lascaux II.

Bird-headed Man
In this scene, a wounded bison attacks a bird-headed man. The bird on a stick may be a spearthrower.

Chinese Horses
The painter of the so-called "Chinese horses" (below) suggested perspective by leaving the far-side limbs unconnected to the body.

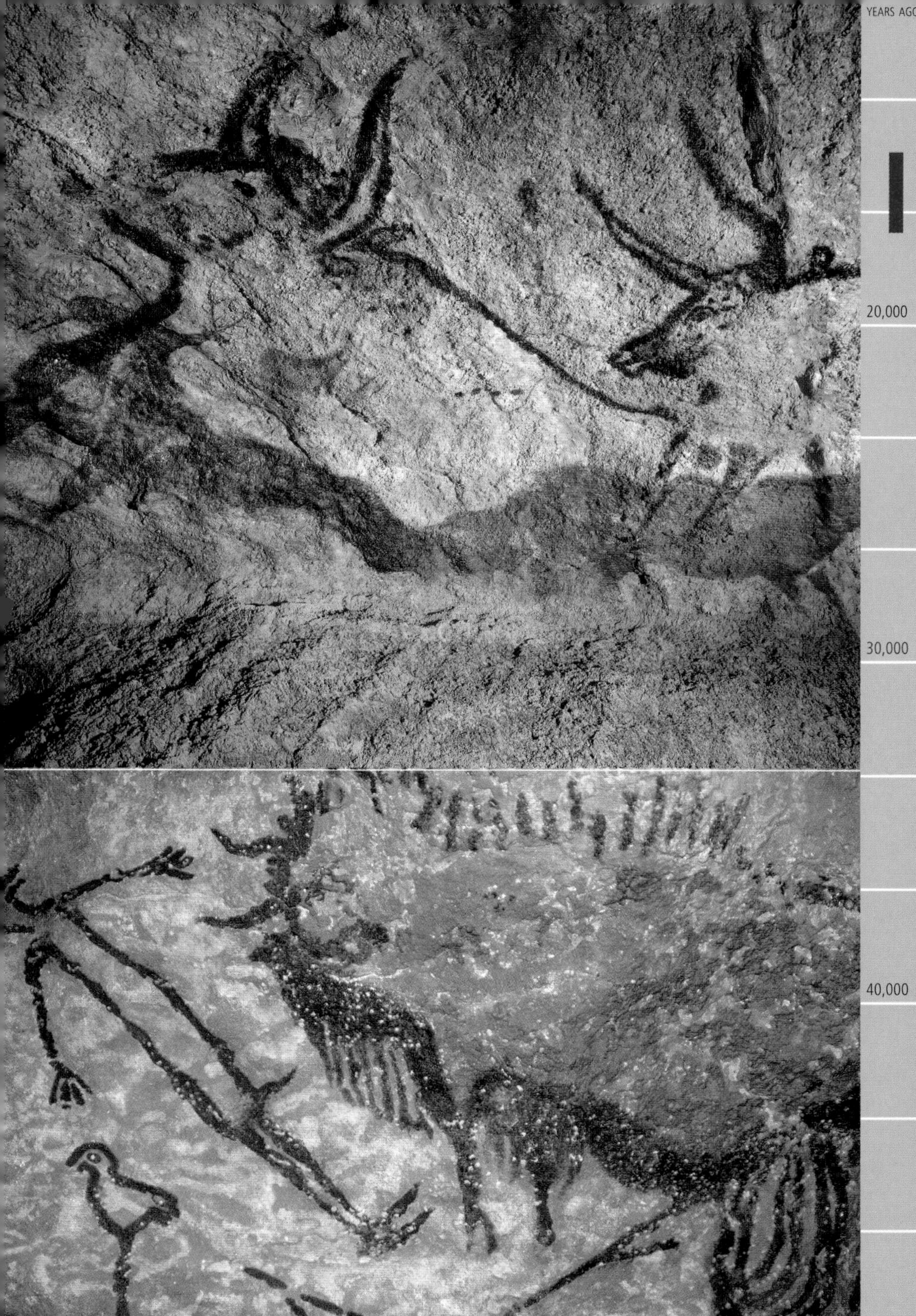

YEARS AGO
20,000
30,000
40,000
50,000

Mammoth-Bone Houses

- Only known "ruins" of Paleolithic Age
- Most dated to approximately 15,000–13,000 years ago
- Mammoth-bone houses first recognized in the 1960s
- Finds include mammoth bones and tusks, debris-filled pits, hearths
- Displays at Kostenki and in Palaeontology Museum, Kiev

The most ancient ruins on earth are the remains of houses constructed of mammoth bone by the Upper Paleolithic peoples of eastern Europe. These remarkable buried structures are found widely distributed across Poland, Ukraine, Belarus, and Russia, and most have been dated to roughly 15,000–13,000 years ago. The mammoth-bone houses probably provided essential shelter and warmth in a cold and largely treeless environment. They were circular or oval in plan with a centrally placed hearth (typically filled with bone fuel and ash) and measured between 20 and 30 feet (6–9 m) in diameter. The walls and roofing were composed of hundreds of mammoth bones and tusks that were probably covered with animal skins for insulation. Deep pits were dug into the ground around many of the houses for cold storage of bone fuel and/or meat.

At several sites, such as Mezhirich in the Ukraine and Yudinovo in Russia, as many as four separate mammoth-bone houses have been discovered. Archaeologists formerly speculated that the large quantities of bone used for the construction of these houses were obtained from mass kills of mammoth herds. However, examination of the bones, many of which display traces of weathering from exposure and gnawing by animals, indicates that they were probably gathered from natural concentrations of bone that had accumulated at stream confluences and at other locations on the eastern European landscape during the most recent Ice Age.

Mezhirich House
At Mezhirich, on the Dnepr River, in the Ukraine, four houses have been found, built from just under 70 tons (about 70 tonnes) of mammoth bones. The settlement may have supported between 30 and 60 people.

Mammoth Art
A mammoth skull painted with red ocher (left) was found in one of the Mezhirich houses.

Structural Design
Each hut had a solid base of large mammoth bones, a lighter superstructure, and a roof arch formed from mammoth tusks. The bones were carefully interlocked, often in symmetrical patterns.

YEARS AGO
20,000
30,000
40,000
50,000

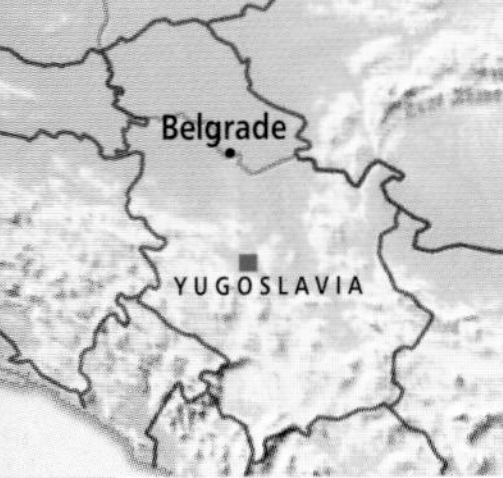

Lepenski Vir

- Settlement of sophisticated hunter-gatherers on Danube River
- Dated to c. 6700–5600 BC
- Found in 1965 during salvage excavations for dam
- Finds include trapezoidal houses and burials; sandstone sculptures
- Reconstructed site above dam; finds in National Museum, Belgrade

On the banks of the Danube River in Yugoslavia and neighboring Romania, a gorge known as the Iron Gates was the site of a number of hunter-gatherer settlements between about 7000 and 5600 BC. The most famous (although not one of the earliest) is Lepenski Vir, located on the Serbian bank of the river on a terrace overlooking a whirlpool. Lepenski Vir was discovered in 1965 during the construction of a hydroelectric dam and was then excavated for several seasons by Dragoslav Srejovic. The excavations revealed several successive habitations by hunter-gatherers, representing one of the most complex and sedentary Mesolithic communities in Europe.

Reconstructed Site
Cone-shaped huts punctuate the hillsides above the Danube at the settlement of Lepenski Vir, in Yugoslavia. The site was moved from its original position, on the banks of the river, to protect it from flooding caused by a nearby hydroelectric dam.

Remarkably uniform in shape and dimensions, the small houses of Lepenski Vir were positioned around a central open space. They had a sophisticated trapezoidal design and featured a central hearth formed by lining a pit with stone slabs. Graves of the inhabitants were found in and around the houses.

Associated with the houses, both inside and outside, are carved sandstone boulders, up to 24 inches (60 cm) high, that can be considered the world's first monumental sculpture. Some are engraved with abstract patterns of wavy lines, but the most striking are the representations of human heads found in front of several houses. The features of these sculptures, particularly the mouths, have a fishlike character, suggesting a complex naturalistic symbolism.

Carp, sturgeon, and catfish bones are found in many of the houses' hearths, while deer and boar were hunted on the adjacent slopes. For several centuries, the hunter-gatherers at Lepenski Vir traded with farmers living nearby. Eventually they gave up their foraging life and were absorbed into these neighboring farming communities.

Abstract Engraving
This sandstone boulder was found at the Lepenski Vir site. It is engraved with abstract patterns as well as a human face with a decidedly fishlike mouth.

2500 BC
5000 BC
7500 BC
10,000 B

Çatal Höyük

- First discovered example of early Neolithic sophistication
- Dated to c. 7000–5600 BC (but currently being reevaluated)
- Discovered in 1957; excavated in 1961–65 and since 1995
- Finds include early Neolithic wall paintings, shrines, figurines
- Site on display; finds in Museum of Anatolian Civilizations, Ankara

A large mound in the Konya plain in south-central Turkey, Çatal Höyük is among the most talked-about Neolithic sites in world prehistory, rivaled only by Jericho in the Near East. James Mellaart's excavations during the 1960s uncovered a settlement that confounded scholarly expectations of early Neolithic villages on almost all counts. The place was enormous, covering 32.5 acres (13 ha) and containing as many as 5,000 people, whereas the "typical" Neolithic village was supposed to be a fifth that size or smaller. Instead of the looser scatter of houses seen at other sites, Çatal Höyük's houses were so closely packed together that often the main entrance must have been through the roof. And inside, many houses displayed an exuberance of ritual and aesthetic activities entirely unparalleled at other early Neolithic sites—elaborate murals of geometric designs or naturalistic scenes; shrines featuring bull's horns fixed to the walls or short pedestals; female figurines, perhaps of the mother goddess, sometimes seated on elaborate chairs; and burials under floors containing a wealth of craft products and exotic goods.

Çatal Höyük's exceptional qualities stirred great excitement when Mellaart announced them, and have since caused much head-scratching. In fact, more recent work has turned up comparable features at other early Neolithic sites in the Near East, so Çatal Höyük is not the puzzling anomaly it once seemed. It remains, however, the most complete example of early Neolithic sophistication yet discovered.

Close Neighbors
Streets and lanes were uncommon in Çatal Höyük—the houses were built directly against one another in blocks, with access often through the roof. Its houses are remarkably standardized, each occupying a floor space of about 30 square yards (25 sq. m).

Wall Paintings
Elaborate murals decorated the walls of many houses and shrine rooms. They typically feature hunting scenes (right), landscapes, and abstract patterns.

Mother Goddess
The inhabitants of Çatal Höyük produced clay and carved stone mother-goddess figurines in every feminine aspect—youth, marriage, pregnancy, giving birth, and old age.

0
2500 BC
5000 BC
7500 BC
10 000 BC

Varna

- Rich Copper Age cemetery in Bulgaria
- Dated to Copper Age, 4500–4000 BC
- Accidental discovery during construction in 1972
- Finds include gold objects; copper axes and ornaments; shell beads
- Artifacts in Varna Museum of History, Varna

During the excavation of a trench in 1972, a large Copper Age cemetery was discovered near Varna, along the Black Sea coast of Bulgaria. In the years that followed, excavations by Ivan Ivanov resulted in the discovery of nearly 300 graves, some of which contained remarkable quantities of gold artifacts. The Varna finds provide a glimpse of the wealth and social structures of the society that lived in this area between 4500 and 4000 BC.

The graves at Varna are typically rectangular pits between 12 inches and 8 feet (30 cm–2.5 m) deep. About 20 percent of them did not contain bodies and are interpreted as cenotaphs (symbolic graves). In those that contained skeletons, the body had been placed in either an extended or a contracted position. A few of the graves lacked grave goods, but most had at least some objects, and a few held hundreds of items.

Gold objects have been found in about a fifth of the graves, including many of the cenotaphs. In some cases, a single grave contained more than 2 pounds (1 kg) of gold. One of the richest graves at Varna was Grave 43, which contained the skeleton of a man 40 to 50 years old and about 5 feet 9 inches (1.75 m) tall, along with 990 gold objects and many other artifacts made from copper, stone, clay, and shell. An unusual gold tube found by the man's hip has been interpreted as a penis sheath, while by his right arm was a copper ax and a "scepter," in which a wooden handle covered with beaten gold was topped with a stone macehead. Heavy gold rings adorned his arms and small gold beads and disks that had probably decorated his clothing were strewn around the skeleton. Clearly he was an individual of unusual status.

Rich Burial
This reconstruction of one of the rectangular grave pits at Varna shows the gold body ornamentation that was lavished upon prestigious individuals.

Scepter of Gold
The grave goods at Varna included this gold-sheathed "scepter." In addition to the spectacular gold artifacts, the burials contained many artifacts of copper, flint, and shell.

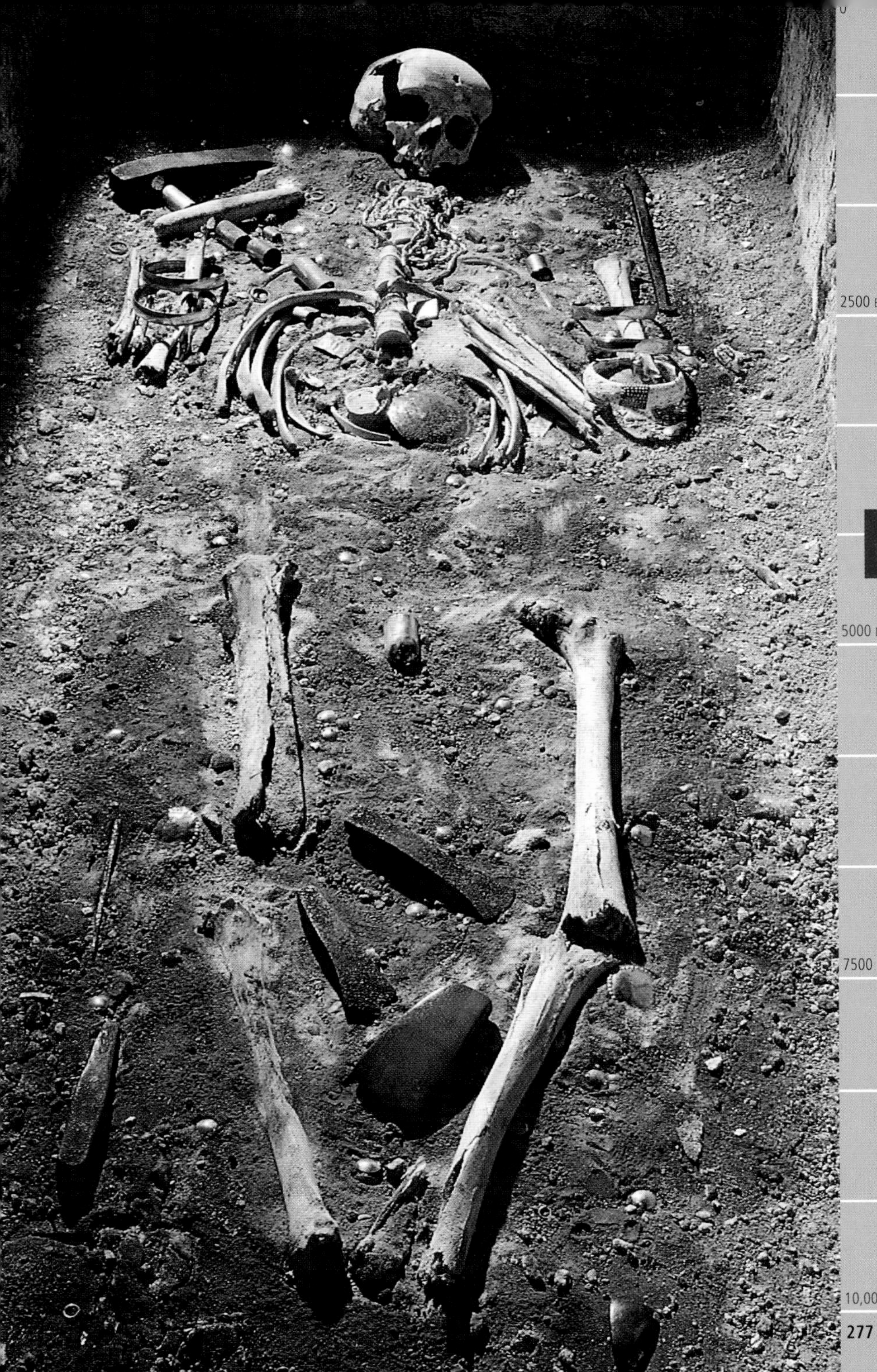

0
2500 BC
5000 BC
7500 BC
10,000 BC

Swiss Lake Dwellings

- Many waterlogged settlements built on piles
- Dated from Neolithic (c. 4,000 BC) to Late Bronze Age (c. 900 BC)
- First dwelling recognized in 1854, many others found since
- Finds include well-preserved organic remains
- Artifacts in many museums in Switzerland, Germany, and Austria

The winter of 1853–54 was cold and dry, causing water levels in lakes around the Alps to recede. At Obermeilen, near Zurich, this revealed a dark layer of sediment that contained animal bones and artifacts and from which wooden posts protruded. Ferdinand Keller, president of the Antiquarian Society of Zurich, investigated and realized that the posts were from prehistoric dwellings whose inhabitants had left the layer of refuse found on the lake bottom. Keller concluded that the houses had been built on platforms connected to the shore by gangplanks. Archaeologists and the public alike readily embraced the romantic idea of houses on platforms over water.

By the end of the 19th century, similar settlements had been found at many lakes around the Alps in Switzerland, Germany, Austria, France, and Italy. Many had been constructed during the Neolithic Age, and early archaeologists saw their plain, round-bottomed pottery and stone and antler tools as defining characteristics of early European farming communities. The waterlogged sediments contained cereal grains and peas along with many types of wild fruits and nuts. In addition, artifacts of wood, cloth, and twine—rarely preserved on dry sites—yielded a full picture of the equipment used. Some of the sites continued to be occupied during the Bronze Age, reflecting long-term settlement.

As more lake settlements were investigated, archaeologists began to doubt Keller's reconstruction of offshore platforms. It soon became clear that the houses had instead been built on the shorelines, with the posts keeping them from sinking into the muddy ground. We now know that the earliest were constructed before 4000 BC and that lakeshore settlement around the Alps persisted until after 1000 BC.

Hanging Pots
The Neolithic pottery found at the lakeside sites often features handles. These may well have been used to suspend the pots from the rafters as protection from moisture and vermin.

Ax Handles
The wooden handles (below) that held stone axheads usually perish on dry-land sites, but have been preserved by the damp conditions of the Alpine lake settlements.

Preserved Structure
The waterlogged nature of the Alpine sites has preserved the timbers of many Neolithic houses. A wooden floor and central hearth (right) can be easily made out at the Egolzwil site, near Zurich, Switzerland.

0

5000 BC

7500 BC

10,000 BC

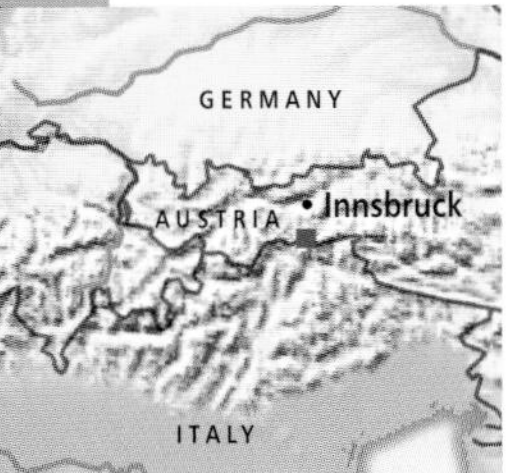

The Iceman

- Unusual preserved prehistoric body and associated clothing and tools
- Dated to Copper Age, 3300 BC
- Accidentally discovered by hikers, September 1991
- Finds include mummified body; clothing; bow, arrows, and backpack
- On display in South Tyrol Museum of Archaeology, Bolzano, Italy

On a spring day, tragedy overtook a hiker high in the Alps. Caught in a sudden late snowstorm or severely injured in a fall, the short man in his late forties perished in a small depression among rocky outcrops and was quickly covered by the snow and ice of a nearby glacier. There he lay for 5,300 years until a German couple discovered his corpse protruding from the ice and slush along the trail in September 1991. Although he was initially believed to be a recent victim of the mountains, finds near his body soon indicated that he had died many centuries earlier. The Iceman, or Ötzi as he is often called, soon became an archaeological celebrity who provided a rare glimpse of life in Copper Age Europe.

Preserved in the Ice
Four days after its discovery by hikers, the Iceman was removed by Rainer Henn, from Innsbruck's Institute of Forensic Medicine. Nobody suspected that they had just found the world's oldest fully preserved human body.

The first clue that the Iceman was ancient came from a copper ax and small flint dagger found near the body. A large quantity of items made from wood, leather, and grass—materials that did not occur naturally at this elevation—also accompanied the corpse. Radiocarbon dating of the body surprisingly showed that the corpse was about 5,300 years old, placing it in the Copper Age. The hiker was also carrying a yew bow, a leather quiver with 14 arrows, containers made from birch bark, and a backpack with a frame made from hazel and larch. His clothing included leather shoes stuffed with grass for insulation, leather leggings, and a fur wrap. Over this he wore a cape made from matted grass, while his head was kept warm with a bearskin cap.

Iceman Ax
The copper ax that was found with the Iceman bore traces of cooked starch grains on its blade. This has led researchers to suggest that he may have been eating porridge when he repaired the ax.

The Iceman had lived a hard life. Smoke from campfires had blackened his lungs, his teeth were worn, some of his ribs had been fractured, and his toes had been repeatedly frostbitten. He had inhaled arsenic, possibly from copper smelting. On his back and legs were mysterious tattoos. His last meal was a mixture of bread, vegetables, and meat.

0

2500 BC

5000 BC

7500 BC

10,000 BC

Skara Brae

- Well-preserved stone settlement of fishers and farmers on Orkney
- Dated to Late Neolithic, 3100–2500 BC
- Exposed by storm in 1850; excavated by V. Gordon Childe 1927–30
- Finds include stone houses with stone shelves and beds; artifacts
- Restored settlement is open to public

Just off the northern tip of Scotland lie the Orkney Islands, a desolate landscape where few trees grow. On the main island, a settlement was constructed 5,000 years ago at Skara Brae using the best local alternative to timber—slabs of flagstone. After several hundred years of occupation, Skara Brae was abandoned, perhaps because of its vulnerability to harsh weather. Drifting sand then buried the houses until they were exposed again by a storm in 1850. In 1927–30 Skara Brae was excavated by the renowned prehistorian V. Gordon Childe. Since then, other archaeologists have also investigated the site.

Houses by the Sea
With its proximity to the sea, Skara Brae was in an exposed position. To offer maximum protection from the elements, the houses were built into hollows and their walls were often more than 3 feet (1 m) thick. The single doorway to each house could be closed with a stone slab.

The central part of Skara Brae contains eight stone houses that had been built in the hollows of an old trash heap. Each consists of a large rectangular area, 15–20 feet (4.5–6 m) across, with a central hearth. In some houses, smaller alcoves open from this central chamber. The houses are connected by tunnel-like passages roofed with stone. Given the absence of timber, the houses may have been roofed with whale ribs covered by animal hides.

Stone fittings within the houses served as built-in furniture. Slabs of stone were fashioned into shelf units that probably held family belongings, while stone chests were filled with vegetation and furs to make beds. Stone pits in the floors had their seams filled with clay to make them watertight and may have stored shellfish.

Furniture of Stone
Wooden furniture would have disintegrated over time, but Skara Brae's stone furniture has survived, providing a clear idea of what a Neolithic house looked like.

The inhabitants of Skara Brae fished, kept cattle and sheep, hunted wild game, and cultivated grain on a small scale. They fashioned bone tools to prepare skins and furs, and made grooved pots for storing food. Other artifacts recovered from the site include antler and ivory pins, and beads made from stone and shell.

Spiral Sculpture
Among the artifacts discovered at Skara Brae was this stone sculpture, embellished with intricate spiral carvings.

Temple of Tarxien

- Early monumental temple complex on Malta
- Dated to Late Neolithic, c. 3000 BC
- Accidental discovery by farmer in 1914
- Finds include megalithic structures; altar; colossal female statue
- Restored temples open to the public

The Maltese archipelago in the central Mediterranean holds some of the most impressive prehistoric monuments in the world. Around 3000 BC, about a half-dozen temples and cemeteries were constructed using large slabs of limestone. Upright slabs formed complexes of interconnected courtyards with semicircular alcoves. Viewed from above, these courtyards have a characteristic symmetrical lobed plan.

The largest megalithic Maltese temple complex is found at Tarxien. It was discovered in 1914 by a farmer trying to remove the limestone blocks so he could cultivate his land. The Tarxien complex is divided into five major units, of which the South Temple and the Central Temple are the most important. The South Temple is entered through a passage in a limestone facade. Inside, the walls of its elliptical chambers are decorated with relief carving. The running spiral is the most common design, although two blocks have animal motifs. To one side was a fragment of a colossal statue of an obese woman. An altar stone had a hidden niche that contained a flint knife, which suggests that sacrifices were performed. From one of the apses of the Southern Temple, a passage leads into the Central Temple, which is 79 feet (24 m) long with six lobes—the largest part of the complex. Its limestone walls are decorated with friezes of animals.

Near Tarxien at Hal Saflieni is the Hypogeum, an enormous complex of artificial caves containing the remains of thousands of individuals. Running spirals were carved on the cave walls, just as they were above ground at Tarxien. Other temples on Malta include those at Hağar Qim and Mnajdra. The nearby island of Gozo features an impressive multilobed temple at Ggantija.

Colossal Goddess
All that remains of the enormous statue at Tarxien is a pair of massive legs and a skirt. The complete figure would have stood at least 6 feet (2 m) high. Similar statues occur in many Maltese temples.

Skillful Construction
Elaborate spiral carvings grace the temple walls. The architectural skill and massive scale of the Maltese temples indicate that the social organization of the Neolithic people must have been quite sophisticated.

Standing Statue
The temple of Hagar Qim contained a large, headless, standing statue carved from soft limestone. Such stone figures from Malta are often referred to as "mother goddesses," but some experts consider their sexuality ambiguous.

0

2500 BC

5000 BC

7500 BC

10,000 BC

Newgrange

- Large megalithic tomb with spectacular architecture
- Dated to Neolithic Age, c. 3000 BC
- Evident since construction; several excavations and modern restoration
- Finds include decorated orthostats, cruciform burial chamber
- Finds in Brú na Boinne Visitor Centre, Boyne Valley, Ireland

Along a bend in the Boyne River, north of Dublin in Ireland, lie three enormous megalithic tombs along with many smaller monuments. Knowth, Dowth, and Newgrange are the focal points of a vast mortuary and ceremonial complex that existed around 3000 BC. They are a type of megalithic monument called a passage tomb, in which the burial chamber is entered through a narrow entrance and corridor. Passage tombs are found throughout western Europe, but the Boyne Valley group are among the best known.

Megalithic Tomb
Sitting on a hilltop, the mound of Newgrange is visible from a distance, its quartz and granite retaining wall appearing bright white against the green grass (right). The tomb is entered through a narrow corridor (below right).

Newgrange is the most celebrated passage tomb in Ireland, famous not only for its size but also for its distinctive architecture and decoration. From the outside, it appears as a roughly circular stone-and-turf mound about 280 feet (85 m) in diameter and 36 feet (11 m) high. The perimeter of the mound is defined by 97 large blocks of stone, some decorated with engraved spirals, upon which a retaining wall of smaller stones was built. On the south side of the monument, where the entrance to the tomb is found, the retaining wall was made from white quartz and gray granite boulders, which give Newgrange its distinctive bright white facade.

The tomb chamber itself is entered through a passage constructed of upright stone slabs called orthostats, which average about 5 feet (1.5 m) high. The corridor leads to a chamber, also formed from orthostats, that has cells opening from its central part, giving it a cross-shaped plan. The roof of the chamber is constructed in a beehive shape from small flat stones.

Newgrange has been open to visitors since 1699, so the chamber was not investigated scientifically. Only a few cremated human bones have been found in crevices. Based on evidence from other passage tombs, Newgrange was a location of ritual and communal burial. The entrance is oriented so the rising sun at the winter solstice shines down the passage into the chamber.

Great Entrance Stone
This large stone (below) graces the entrance of Newgrange. Its surface is entirely covered with an engraved pattern of spirals, wavy lines, and lozenges.

0
2500 BC
5000 BC
7500 BC
10,000 BC

Stonehenge

- Celebrated henge monument and symbol of British prehistory
- Dated to Late Neolithic and Bronze Age, c. 2700–1500 BC
- Always evident on landscape; studied from 17th century onward
- Finds include sarsen uprights and lintels, trilithons; nearby barrows
- Visitors may view stones, but access to interior of circles is restricted

Located in the Salisbury Plain in Wiltshire, England, Stonehenge is the most famous prehistoric site in Europe, familiar to millions from its distinctive arrangement of upright stones and lintels. One of many circular monuments called henges that dot the landscape of the British Isles, it is among the most misunderstood prehistoric sites, adopted by many groups over time as having mystical powers.

Few visitors to the monument today comprehend the complexity of Stonehenge or the sequence of its construction. The earliest work occurred in the early 3rd millennium BC, when a circular ditch and bank were constructed. Later, around the interior edge of this enclosure, 56 small holes were dug, some containing human cremations. These are called the Aubrey Holes after John Aubrey, who discovered them in the 17th century. Toward the end of the 3rd millennium BC, two concentric circles of small bluestones were erected in the center of the monument. Bluestone is believed to come from the Preseli Hills of Wales, about 125 miles (200 km) away. A single bluestone, called the Heel Stone, was set up in the entrance to the enclosure.

The Stonehenge of today is the final construction stage that began around 2000 BC. The bluestone circles were taken down, and a single circle of about 30 sarsen (sandstone) stones was erected. Sarsen lintels were placed across the top of the uprights to form a continuous ring. Within this circle is a horseshoe arrangement of five sarsen trilithons (two upright stones that support a lintel). Finally, a circle of bluestones between the outer and interior sarsen constructions and a horseshoe of bluestones within the trilithon setting completed the monument.

Ritual Site
Stonehenge was almost certainly a place of gathering and ritual, although little is known about what actually occurred there. Recently, this Neolithic and Bronze Age monument has been adopted as a gathering place by believers in other mystical traditions.

Solar Alignment
Although Stonehenge is aligned such that the midsummer sunrise shines down the axis of the site, claims for it having been a prehistoric observatory or celestial computer remain the subject of debate.

0

5000 BC

7500 BC

10,000 BC

Bush Barrow

- Rich burial of an elite individual in Wiltshire, England
- Dated to Early Bronze Age, c. 2000 BC
- Opened by William Cunnington in 1808
- Finds include gold ornaments; bronze dagger and ax
- Artifacts in Devizes Museum, Devizes, Wiltshire

The Wiltshire landscape surrounding Stonehenge in southern Britain is dotted with hundreds of barrows, or burial mounds, that cover the graves of single individuals accompanied by artifacts. In the 18th century, it was realized that these were the burials of ancient Britons, and it became fashionable to dig into them to see what could be found. Such early attempts at archaeology were often little more than grave-robbing, but occasionally the practitioners had a serious interest in discovering information about the past. Two such antiquarians were William Cunnington, a wool merchant and amateur excavator, and Richard Colt Hoare, a London banker and Cunnington's financial backer. Together the pair investigated more than 400 barrows in Wiltshire.

In 1808 Cunnington opened a barrow in a cluster of mounds about half a mile (1 km) south of Stonehenge. Known as Bush Barrow, this grave contained the remains of a single male individual. Among the grave goods were several precious objects, including a gold belt-fastener, a gold diamond-shaped breastplate, two bronze daggers (one with a hilt studded with tiny gold nails), and a bronze ax. A stone with a shaft-hole drilled into it and several carved bone pieces are believed to have been the remains of a mace or scepter, although the wooden shaft has decayed.

Cunnington and Colt Hoare could only guess at the date and significance of their find. Today, we know that the person buried in Bush Barrow lived around 2000 BC, during the Early Bronze Age. The quality of the goods buried with him indicates that he was one of the leaders of the society that lived around Stonehenge, possibly a chief.

Other barrows nearby also contained the remains of elite individuals. Over many centuries, the accumulation of such mounds produced a landscape of monuments to individual ancestors. Such monuments would have been especially important to a society in which rank and prestige were determined by genealogy.

Gold Goods
The body buried in Bush Barrow was surrounded by precious metal objects. On his chest was a fine gold lozenge (top right), while a smaller lozenge (below right) lay by his right thigh. Near his head was a gold belt hook (far right).

Reconstructed Mace
A stone macehead and gold fittings from Bush Barrow have been used in this reconstruction of a ceremonial mace (below).

Buried Daggers
Bush Barrow contained three daggers—a small bronze dagger in the man's right hand, and two larger daggers (one bronze, the other copper) by his head.

0

2500 BC

5000 BC

7500 BC

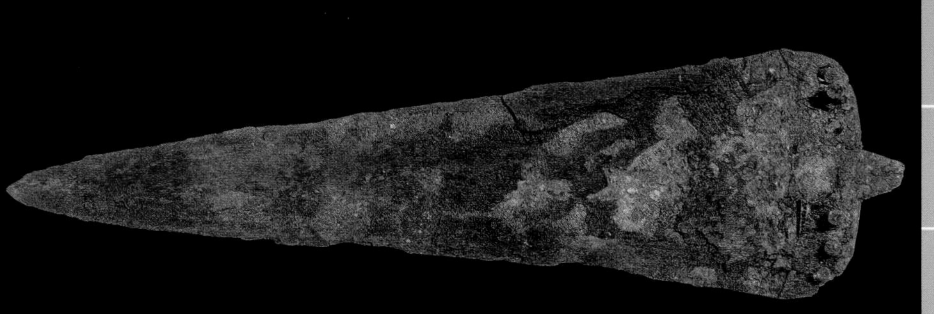

10,000 BC

Knossos

- Pre-eminent Bronze Age settlement and palace on Crete
- Palace built c. 1700 BC, destroyed 14th–13th century BC
- First excavated 1878; main excavations by Arthur Evans from 1900
- Finds include faience snake goddesses, wall paintings, clay tablets
- Palace on public display; some finds in Ashmolean Museum, Oxford

The longest-occupied settlement on the island of Crete, Knossos is the site of an important Bronze Age palace—the main center of the Minoan civilization that flourished on Crete during much of the 2nd millennium BC. Excavations by Arthur Evans from 1900 put Knossos firmly on the archaeological map.

The earliest palace was built in the 19th century BC, but the palace was destroyed on several occasions by earthquake and there are successive reconstruction phases. Three main phases have been identified: the earliest or Old Palace; the New Palace (rebuilt in the 17th century BC); and the final, "Mycenaean" palace (destroyed in the 14th or 13th century BC). Dominating a prosperous unfortified town, the Minoan palace was built around a central court. The main approach was from the west, leading to the ceremonial state entrance on the south side. The western wing comprised a series of narrow storage magazines, where grain, wine, and oil were kept in large clay jars (pithoi). In front of these, a series of basement shrines, including the famous Throne Room, looked out onto the court. The state apartments were located on the upper floor. The royal apartments were on the east side of the palace, and to their north were more storage rooms and work rooms.

The palace was richly decorated with wall paintings, the most famous being the bull-leaping scenes. Others include the saffron-gathering monkey, the griffins from the Throne Room, and the so-called "Priest King." The dolphins in the royal apartments probably decorated the floor. The portable wealth from Knossos includes faience snake goddesses, a bull's-head rhyton (libation vessel) of steatite, and an acrobat carved from ivory. The archives on clay tablets, in Linear A and Linear B (see p. 117), indicate that the palace had administrative functions.

Reconstructed Palace
The remains that occupy Knossos today belong to the palace that was rebuilt after an earthquake leveled most of the town in about 1700 BC. The new palace featured extensive colonnades and stairs between the different buildings.

Throne Room
The gypsum chair in the so-called Throne Room was almost certainly not the seat of the "ruler" of Knossos. Most archaeologists interpret this room as one of a series of small shrines flanking the west side of the central court.

Snake Goddess
The portable artifacts discovered at Knossos included a number of faience snake goddesses, which were made from earthenware decorated with colored glazes.

0
2500 BC
5000 BC
7500 BC
10,000 BC

Akrotiri

- Late Bronze Age town destroyed and preserved by volcanic eruption
- Dated to Late Bronze Age, with eruption occurring *c.* 1630 BC
- Site known since 19th century; excavations began in 1967
- Most important finds are the well-preserved wall paintings
- Town on public display; most finds in National Museum, Athens

The Late Bronze Age town of Akrotiri, on the island of Thera, was dramatically destroyed in a volcanic eruption in the late 17th century BC. Ironically, this same eruption has preserved the town perfectly, giving us a unique glimpse of life in a Bronze Age Aegean town. Although the date of the eruption has excited much controversy among archaeologists in recent years, the scientific evidence indicates that it occurred around 1630 BC. The site has been known since the late 19th century, with Spyridon Marinatos beginning excavations in 1967.

To date, only a small area of the town has been excavated, but at least 12 houses have been uncovered. The buildings stand up to three stories high and are well built, some incorporating stone-cut masonry. They are very rich in portable remains, especially imported Minoan and other pottery. Of particular interest are the negatives of furniture preserved in the volcanic ash, from which plaster casts have been made. Minoan standard lead weights and some occurrences of Linear A indicate close trading contacts with Minoan Crete.

The most interesting feature of Akrotiri is the unparalleled preservation of its wall paintings. The many landscape scenes include sea daffodils, ducks and reeds, a fantasy Nile scene, wild goats and crocus flowers, and the swallows and flowers from the Spring Fresco. The miniature fresco of a boat procession from the West House might illustrate life in this Bronze Age harbor town. The large-scale human figures include a fisherman and a "priestess," two boys boxing, and women and young girls collecting saffron to offer to a goddess.

Abandoned Town
The excavations at Akrotiri revealed freestanding two- and three-story houses. Water vessels and storage containers rest where they were left when the inhabitants abandoned the town to escape the devastating volcanic eruption.

Coastal Scene
This section of a wall painting from Akrotiri depicts a coastal town surrounded by rivers and mountains. Men and a woman from the town watch the departing ships, while above them, deer are being pursued by a lion.

Ordinary People
The wall paintings that decorated the houses of Akrotiri display the first depictions of ordinary people from this period, including a fisherman displaying his catch (left) and two young boxers.

2500 BC
5000 BC
7500 BC
10,000 BC

The Shaft Graves of Mycenae

- Staggeringly rich shaft graves from Bronze Age Greece
- Dated to 16th century BC
- Grave Circle A discovered in 1876; Circle B found in 1951
- Finds include gold face masks; elaborate gold jewelry; vases
- Grave circles on public display; finds in National Museum, Athens

Heinrich Schliemann's discovery in 1876 of a richly furnished grave circle inside the Lion Gate at Mycenae seemed to confirm Homer's description of the city as "rich in gold." A second, slightly earlier, grave circle was excavated outside the citadel walls in 1951 by the Greek Archaeological Service. Both circles date to the 16th century BC and display staggering wealth.

The earlier grave circle (B) contained 26 shaft graves, the oldest of which were relatively poorly equipped, but the richness of the grave goods intensified throughout its period of use. Circle A overlaps the final use of B, but housed just six massive shaft graves, containing a total of 19 burials. Two of the later graves from Circle B and all of the graves in Circle A were marked with massive carved stelae (upright stone slabs).

The most striking aspect of the shaft graves from Circle A is the sheer wealth deposited as grave gifts. Male burials were equipped with lavish ceremonial weapons, including a series of daggers finely decorated with scenes of hunting and landscapes. Females were adorned with lavish sheet-gold jewelry, including diadems, disks sewn onto the funerary shrouds, and bronze pins with rock-crystal heads. Several amber necklaces, imported from northern Europe, indicate the development of long-distance exchange in this period. All burials were provided with ceramic vessels, but the wealthiest graves had sheet-metal vases of gold and silver, including libation vessels that were possibly used in the funeral ceremony. Perhaps the most remarkable finds are the sheet-gold face masks, worn by the men of Circle A. Although the authenticity of the most famous of these masks—the so-called "Mask of Agamemnon"—has been called into question by certain scholars, there is no good reason to question the credentials of the others. Indeed, a prototype mask in electrum was found in one of the latest burials in Circle B.

Grave Circle A
In Homeric epic, Mycenae is the city of Agamemnon, the leader of the Greeks during the Trojan War, and is described as "rich in gold." In his excavations of Circle A (right), according to popular—but apocryphal—belief, Schliemann believed that he had found the mask of Agamemnon (see photograph, p. 32).

Treasury of Atreus
Mycenae also contains later *tholos* (beehive) graves. One of these is the Treasury of Atreus (right), built in the 14th century BC. The triangular space and the door surrounds were decorated with carved slabs and columns of marble.

Gold Grave Goods
The men of Circle A wore striking sheet-gold face masks. The sheer quantity of gold among the grave goods is astounding—there was at least 30 pounds (13 kg) of the metal in the three richest graves alone.

0
2500 BC
5000 BC
7500 BC
10,000 BC

Troy

- Prehistoric Aegean settlement; later became the city of King Priam
- Occupied from about 3000 BC; Troy VI dates to 14th–12th century BC
- First excavations in 1865; four excavations by Schliemann 1871–90
- Finds include Priam's Treasure, with a gold sauceboat and jewelry
- Citadel on public display; finds in Archaeological Museum, Istanbul

Troy is particularly important for its resonance as the city of King Priam sacked by the Greeks during the Trojan War—an event described in Homer's epic, the *Iliad*—but it also played a significant role in the development of Aegean prehistory as a discipline. More recently, Troy has made headlines because of the "rediscovery" of the so-called Priam's Treasure in the Pushkin Museum, Moscow.

The location of ancient Troy had been debated long before Heinrich Schliemann's first excavation in 1871–73 uncovered its remains. Nine cities of Troy have now been identified, the earliest dating to the Early Bronze Age (*c.* 3000–2600 BC), and the latest to the Roman period (334 BC–5th century AD). The Late Bronze Age city, Troy VI, is most commonly associated with the Trojan War, but in his hurry to get down to the early levels, Schliemann destroyed many of the relevant remains. In doing so, however, he brought to light evidence of a previously unknown civilization, which flourished in the northern Aegean during the 3rd millennium BC.

Priam's Treasure probably constitutes the most striking result of Heinrich Schliemann's excavations, particularly considering the romance of its 20th century history. Smuggled out of Turkey to Berlin by Schliemann, the gold disappeared at the end of the Second World War, resurfacing in Moscow only in 1993. The gold jewelry is particularly striking, featuring diadems and earrings with idol-shaped pendants, numerous gold hair-rings and beads, and pendants of gold, silver, carnelian, and amber. The treasure also includes a famous gold sauceboat, a gold pomegranate flask, various anthropomorphic vases, and four magnificent hammer-axes of polished stone.

Trojan History
When Schliemann began exploring the site of Troy, most scholars believed that Homer's epics were fictional. The excavations proved that the *Iliad* had some degree of historical basis.

Lower Layers
Workers take a break during the excavation of Troy XIII and Troy IX, which date to the Bronze Age.

Priam's Treasure
The gold that Schliemann smuggled out of Turkey included a sauceboat (below) , a flask, and several cups.

0

5000 BC

7500 BC

10,000 BC

The Ulu Burun Shipwreck

- Ancient Mediterranean shipwreck offering unique insight into trade
- Dated to Late Bronze Age, late 14th century BC
- Found by sponge-diver 1982; excavated by University of Texas since 1984
- Finds include raw materials, amphoras, pottery, gold jewelry
- Display of artifacts in Maritime Museum, Bodrum, Turkey

The development of maritime archaeology has had enormous implications for studies of ancient trade. Possibly one of the most important shipwrecks excavated is from Ulu Burun off the southern coast of Turkey. The wreck was discovered by a sponge-diver in 1982, and has been excavated since 1984 by a team of archaeologists led by George Bass. Radiocarbon dates place the ship in the late 14th century BC.

The shipwreck gives a unique insight into the bulk transportation of raw minerals in the East Mediterranean during the Late Bronze Age. Sailing toward the Aegean from Cyprus or the Levant, the boat was laden with large quantities of copper ingots in the form of oxhides. Similar ingots are widely distributed throughout the Mediterranean, as far west as Sardinia, and analyses suggest that the copper came from Cyprus. Other raw materials include ivory, Anatolian tin bun ingots, and glass ingots. The glass ingots show that glass was exported as a raw commodity rather than as a finished product; similar glass ingots have been found at the Mycenaean citadel of Midea.

Although many studies have emphasized the role played by Mycenaean pottery during the Late Bronze Age, this was found only in small quantities on the boat, and possibly comprised the personal belongings of the captain or crew. However, the boat was sailing back to the Aegean, and may have unloaded a cargo of Mycenaean pottery in the east. The shipwreck did contain large numbers of Levantine transport amphoras, mostly filled with terebinth resin, as well as small quantities of Cypriot pottery and nine Cypriot pithoi (storage jars). Such pottery is rather rare in the Aegean, although recent excavations in Crete have uncovered a Late Bronze Age emporium with some Cypriot imports. Other finds from the shipwreck include scrap metal, small quantities of Canaanite gold jewelry, and a unique wooden writing tablet.

Deep Excavation
The Ulu Burun wreck lay at a depth of 150 feet (50 m). To avoid the bends, divers could spend only 20 minutes at a time excavating. Here, a marine archaeologist inspects a Cypriot pithos, a storage jar that was filled with smaller pieces of Cypriot pottery.

Sunken Treasure
Among the wreck's cargo, which came from seven different Mediterranean civilizations, were the gold artifacts shown below. These include a medallion (top left), a goddess pendant (top right), and a falcon pendant (center).

Biskupin

- Waterlogged fortified settlement in Poland
- Dated to Iron Age, 700–600 BC
- Lowered lake levels led to chance find by schoolteacher in 1933
- Finds include wooden houses and streets; wide range of artifacts
- On-site museum and reconstruction of settlement open to public

In 1933 a Polish schoolteacher named Walenty Szwajcer noticed ancient timbers protruding from the peaty surface of a peninsula by Lake Biskupin, about 36 miles (60 km) northwest of the city of Poznań. He reported his discovery to the museum in Poznań, and Professor Józef Kostrzewski began excavations the following summer. Between 1934 and 1939, Kostrzewski exposed a remarkable waterlogged settlement, and the outlines of houses and streets gradually emerged from the tangled mass of wood.

The excavations revealed 13 rows of houses, with walls preserved at 3 feet (1 m) high. They consisted of an anteroom that opened into a central area with a stone hearth. Between the houses were streets made from logs. A rampart—strengthened with timber cribbing, earth, and stone—surrounded the settlement, while a wooden breakwater protected the shore.

Artifacts found in and around the houses dated Biskupin to about 700–600 BC. Many of the artifacts were made from perishable materials such as wood and cloth. They provided a glimpse of the entire range of implements used by people of this period, not just those of clay, stone, and metal that are normally preserved on dry sites.

Botanists and zoologists analyzed the numerous seeds and bones found among the timbers. They were able to conclude that millet, wheat, barley, rye, and beans were the main crops grown by the inhabitants of Biskupin. Pigs were the most important food animals, but cattle were also kept for milk and traction as well as for meat.

The Second World War interrupted Kostrzewski's excavations, but they resumed immediately after the war. A museum was established to house the finds, and some of the ramparts and houses have been reconstructed.

Reconstructed Town
In this reconstructed scene, the main street of Biskupin, flanked by two rows of houses, leads to the settlement's gate. Since reconstruction work began in 1968, the site has become a tourist attraction.

Wet Preservation
The excavations of 1934–39 revealed Biskupin's timber streets and the foundations of its ramparts, superbly preserved by the waterlogged nature of the site.

AD 500

0

500 BC

1000 BC

Hochdorf

- Rich burial of a Celtic chief
- Dated to Iron Age, Hallstatt Period, c. 600–500 BC
- Found by amateur archaeologist 1977, professional excavation 1978–79
- Finds include burial on bronze recliner; bronze, iron, and gold objects
- Display in Keltenmuseum Hochdorf, Eberdingen-Hochdorf

The century between 600 and 500 BC was a time of remarkable change in central Europe. Trade with Greek merchants in the colony at Massalia (the modern city of Marseille) reached up the Rhône River into eastern France and southern Germany. Luxury goods and wine were exchanged for furs, honey, grain, and amber. Control of this trade enabled Celtic chiefs to amass considerable wealth and power, which is reflected in their residences and burials.

One such burial was discovered in 1977 at Hochdorf, near Stuttgart in Germany, and was excavated over the following two years. Under a mound 200 feet (60 m) in diameter, excavations revealed a central burial shaft containing two nested timber chambers. The inner chamber contained the burial of a man almost 6 feet (1.8 m) tall in his thirties. He lay on a bronze settee that has no known parallel in central Europe. Its legs depicted bronze figures of eight women with upstretched arms, and it was upholstered with furs and textiles. Nearby was a bronze kettle manufactured in a Greek colony in Italy. Residue revealed that it had contained mead, drunk from a small gold bowl. Across the chamber, a wagon made of wood sheathed in iron rested on four massive 10-spoked wheels, but its light construction revealed that it was designed for ritual purposes only. Wagons are common elements in Celtic burials and were often used as platforms for still more grave goods. The walls of the burial chamber had been draped with cloth curtains, on which had been hung nine drinking horns.

The man in the Hochdorf burial wore a conical birchbark hat. His clothing and shoes were decorated with bands of hammered gold, while around his neck he wore a gold hoop. Numerous other metal objects were also found. Apparently the metal objects were manufactured nearby, for excavation of the mound revealed traces of gold, bronze, and iron working.

Intact Burial
The burial mound at Hochdorf has a height of 20 feet (6 m) and a diameter of 200 feet (60 m). One of a number of burials from the Hallstatt Period, it was unusual in that it had never been robbed.

Bronze Support
The chief lay on a bronze recliner that was lined with furs and textiles and supported by bronze figures of women with upstretched arms (below).

Drinking Horn
The tomb chamber contained the remains of nine drinking horns. This restored example (right) was made from bronze, iron, and gold foil.

AD 500

0

500 BC

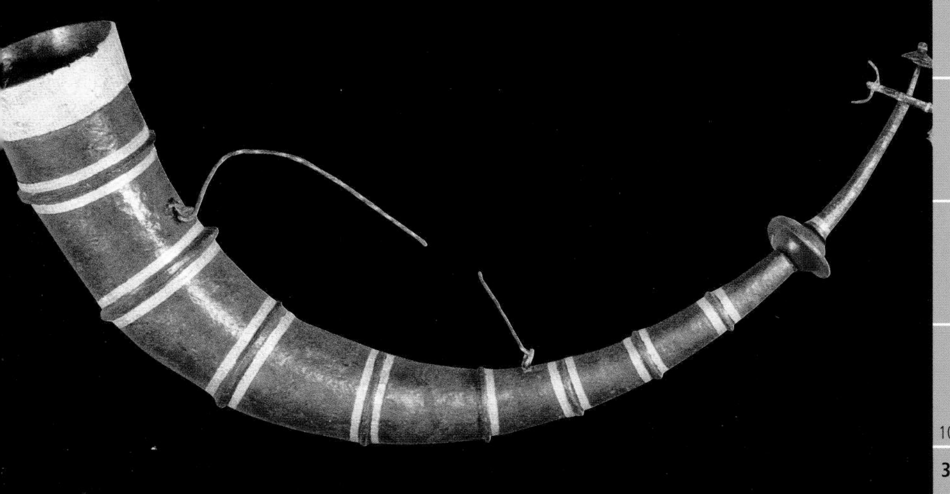

1000 BC

The Athenian Agora

- Heart of Athenian democracy
- Dated from Bronze Age to Modern, 2nd millennium BC onward
- Excavated by the American School of Classical Studies from 1930s
- Finds include stone sculpture, figure-decorated pottery, ballots
- On public display; finds in Agora Museum (on site)

The area to the north of the Athenian acropolis was known as the agora, the political and commercial heart of the city. While the space contains a number of Late Bronze Age tombs, in the late 7th century BC it seems to have become used for political gatherings; it is tempting to link this change with the political reforms of the lawgiver Solon, which extended power to a wider circle of citizens. In subsequent centuries, Athenian democracy flourished here, with the agora frequented by figures such as Socrates and Aristotle.

The site features the remains of three remarkable buildings: the Temple of Hephaestus, the best preserved classical temple in Greece; the Concert Hall of Agrippa, with the ruins of three colossal statues; and the Stoa of Attalos, a multipurpose center that has been reconstructed to house the Agora Museum.

Excavations have revealed the foundations of several other buildings, whose function was described by the travel writer Pausanias in the 2nd century AD. At the western edge of the space, nestling into a hillside, a series of buildings were constructed on a low terrace. At the southern end was the *bouleuterion,* where the council (*boule*) of 500 met. This gathering was formed by 50 members of each of the 10 tribes of Attica (the territory of Athens). The tribes were named after 10 mythical heroes of Attica, and images of these heroes were originally displayed on a long statue base, the remains of which have been discovered outside the *bouleuterion.* Each tribe governed the city for one-tenth of the year, its 50 representatives meeting and dining in the circular *tholos,* next to the *bouleuterion.* Other important buildings may have included a large law court (*heliaia*) in the southwest corner of the agora and a fountain house (*enneakrounos*).

Meeting Place
At the foot of the Athenian acropolis, the agora was centered on a broad open square that was used for political, judicial, religious, and commercial gatherings. Various public buildings bordered the square.

Preserved Temple
The Temple of Hephaestus sits on a hill behind the agora's public buildings. Built around 440 BC, it is the best preserved classical temple in Greece.

A Recorded Vote
When Athenians decided to ostracize a man, they recorded their votes on potsherds known as ostraca. This one names the leader Themistokles.

0

2500 BC

5000 BC

7500 BC

10,000 BC

Delphi

- Famous oracle in Greece
- Dated from Archaic to Roman, 7th century BC–4th century AD
- Excavated by the French School in Athens from the 1880s
- Finds include bronze sculpture, sculptured reliefs
- On public display; finds in Delphi Museum, Delphi

One of the most important sanctuaries of the Greek world was located at Delphi, on the slopes of Mount Parnassus in central Greece. Its popularity was based on the presence of an oracle that was consulted by leaders throughout the Mediterranean. At the heart of the sanctuary lay the Doric Temple of Apollo. After a devastating fire in the 6th century BC, the temple was rebuilt with marble figures placed in the triangular pediment at the eastern end; the Greek historian Herodotus records that the work was paid for by an Athenian family who had been in exile.

A sacred way led up to the temple. Along its route, various cities of the Greek world erected treasuries to house their dedications. One of the most prominent belonged to the Athenians; the travel writer Pausanias thought that it had been paid for by booty won from the Persians at the battle of Marathon in 490 BC. The Athenian treasury was decorated with relief slabs showing the exploits of the heroes Theseus and Hercules. Another treasury, built by the island of Siphnos, featured a continuous frieze depicting the battle between the gods and the giants.

Games were held at the sanctuary, with the champions celebrated by monuments. A bronze charioteer, part of a much larger group, marked the victory of Polyzalos of Gela in the 470s BC; the figure was buried after being toppled by an earthquake. The sanctuary also housed victory dedications. One of the most prominent, facing the east end of the Temple of Apollo, was a bronze tripod formed by twisted snakes and inscribed with the names of the Greek cities that had formed the alliance against the Persians in 480 BC. Although the base remains in Delphi, the snakes were eventually carried off to Constantinople, where they can still be viewed in the ancient hippodrome.

Temple and Theater
The Greeks believed that Delphi was the center of the world. Today, the ruins of the Temple of Apollo can be seen in front of the remains of the theater, which was used mainly for theatrical performances during the great festivals of the sanctuary.

Reconstructions
The Temple of Apollo was reconstructed twice—once in the 6th century BC after a fire, and again in the 4th century BC after an earthquake. The visible ruins are dated to the second reconstruction.

Marble Goddess
The temple was decorated with marble sculptures, such as this statue of Nike, the goddess of victory.

AD 500
0
1000 BC

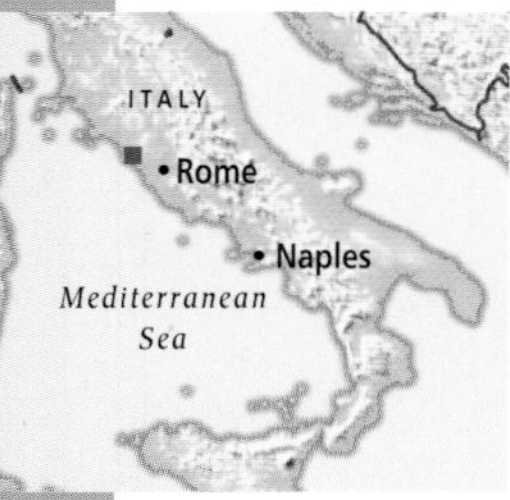

The Tombs of Tarquinia

- Highly decorated tomb paintings
- Dated to Iron Age, especially 600–300 BC
- Explored from the 19th century
- Finds include wall paintings, bronzework, Greek pottery
- On public display; finds in Museo Nazionale, Tarquinia

Among the finest Etruscan tombs are those found at Tarquinia in the hill of Monterozzi, a massive cemetery formed by chambers cut into the soft volcanic tufa. The walls of the most elaborate tombs were coated with a thin layer of plaster and then decorated in reds, blues, and greens. Some of the paintings hint at the Etruscan banquet. In the Tomb of the Triclinium, a flautist provides dancing music, while in the Tomb of the Lionesses, a massive garlanded krater (used for mixing water and wine) is flanked by a flautist and a harpist, and the painted roof suggests a banqueting tent. The images in other tombs refer to the mourning process. In the Tomb of the Augurs, two mourners, hands on head, flank painted doors. Elsewhere in the same tomb, two wrestlers appear to be involved in funeral games for the deceased; between them stand a stack of metal bowls that may represent the prize.

The tomb paintings seem to have been influenced by Greek art, and some scholars think they hint at the splendor of great Greek works, such as those that decorated the Painted Colonnade in the Athenian agora. The painting on a sarcophagus with scenes of Greeks fighting Amazons may well have been the creation of a Greek artist. Certainly, imported Athenian pottery has been found at Gravisca, the port of Tarquinia.

Tomb of the Leopards
The long walls of the Tomb of the Leopards are decorated with scenes of reclining banqueters. A serious conservation problem has arisen since the tombs were open to the public, with the paintings being attacked by moisture and fungus.

Fish and Fowl
Painted around 520 BC, the Fowling and Fishing Tomb contains Tarquinia's most famous wall paintings.

Banqueting Coffin
The Etruscan taste for banqueting that is evident in the tomb paintings is also reflected in this sarcophagus from Tarquinia. It shows the deceased reclining at a banquet.

The Parthenon

- Major temple from the city of Athens
- Dated to Classical period, 450–430 BC
- Extant from antiquity; reexamined in 19th century
- Finds include relief sculpture
- On public display; sculpture in British Museum, London

During the 5th century BC, the Athenian statesman Pericles built the Parthenon, the chief temple of the goddess Athena, on the hilltop of the Athenian acropolis. The ongoing cost of the temple's construction was listed in a series of accounts cut on marble stelae (slabs) on public view on the acropolis; parts of the text were recovered during excavations.

The marble temple was built in the Doric style, the oldest and simplest of the Greek architectural orders. The larger of the temple's two main rooms was approached from the east end and contained the colossal gold and ivory statue of Athena made by Pheidias, the most famous sculptor in ancient Greece. This statue, known from ancient descriptions as well as small-scale Roman copies, was destroyed when the Parthenon was sacked in Late Antiquity.

The outside of the building was decorated with a series of marble sculptures. In the triangular pediments at the west and east ends were three-dimensional sculptures showing, respectively, the battle between the gods Athena and Poseidon for the control of Attica (the territory of Athens), and the moment after the birth of Athena from the head of her father Zeus. Above the outer colonnade on each of the four sides of the temple were metopes (relief sculptures). These depicted the mythical battles between the Greeks and the Amazons (west), the gods and the giants (east), and the Lapiths and the Centaurs (south), as well as the Trojan War (north). A continuous frieze in low relief ran around the central building. It shows two processions, both starting at the southwest corner and moving toward the east end of the building.

Temple of Athena
The Parthenon dominates the acropolis, the religious center of Athens in the 5th century BC. The temple creates an impression of harmony and strength, in part due to such subtle refinements as a very slight inward inclination of the Doric columns.

Sculpted Decoration
The temple was lavishly decorated with naturalistic friezes and sculptures. Many of these were removed by Britain's Lord Elgin in 1801–1805 and sold to the British Museum (see p. 27).

AD 500
0
500 BC
1000 BC

The Imperial Fora of Rome

- The heart of the ancient city of Rome
- Dated from Iron Age to Modern, 8th century BC onward
- Exploration during the Renaissance; excavations during the 1930s
- Finds include architectural sculptured reliefs
- On public display; finds in Antiquarium of Forum Augustus, Rome

At the heart of the city of ancient Rome lay a series of fora, or public spaces, which contained administrative, legal, and religious buildings. This area included the navel of the city (*Umbilicus Urbis*), where tradition had it that Romulus had dug a hole when he founded the city.

To the south of the Capitoline, one of the hills of ancient Rome, stood the Roman Forum. During the days of the Roman republic, the forum was the scene of public meetings, law courts, and gladiatorial combats and was lined with shops and open-air markets. Under the empire, it became a center for religious and secular spectacles and ceremonies, and was completely rebuilt by the emperor Augustus. He named the new Curia (senate house) in honor of his adopted father, Julius Caesar. Caesar was further honored by the Temple of the Divine Julius, which dominated the southern end of the forum. In front of the temple was a platform for addressing the crowds, decorated with bronze rams from the ships of Augustus's rival, Mark Antony, who was defeated at the battle of Actium. Other structures include the Arch of Titus and the Temple of Castor and Pollux.

The Roman Forum's irregular layout contrasted with the two fora adjacent to it—the Forum of Julius, containing the Temple of Venus, which celebrated Caesar's ancestry from the goddess of love; and the Forum of Augustus, containing the Temple of Mars, vowed by Augustus at the battle of Philippi in 42 BC.

Subsequent emperors added to the range of public buildings in Rome. The emperor Trajan constructed a complex to the north of the Roman Forum. In addition to markets, he included a colossal column—Trajan's Column—that was decorated with a spiral frieze celebrating his conquests in the Dacian War.

Roman Forum
This view of the Roman Forum features three columns of the Temple of Castor and Pollux, with the Arch of Titus and the Colosseum in the background.

Vengeance Celebrated
Augustus built the Temple of Mars the Avenger (in the Forum of Augustus) after his victory at the Battle of Philippi, when he joined forces with Mark Antony to defeat Brutus and Cassius, the leading assassins of Julius Caesar.

First Emperor
Shown here on an aureus (gold coin), Augustus (63 BC–AD 14) was the first emperor of Rome. He reformed almost every aspect of Roman life and brought peace and prosperity to the empire.

AD 500

0

1000 BC

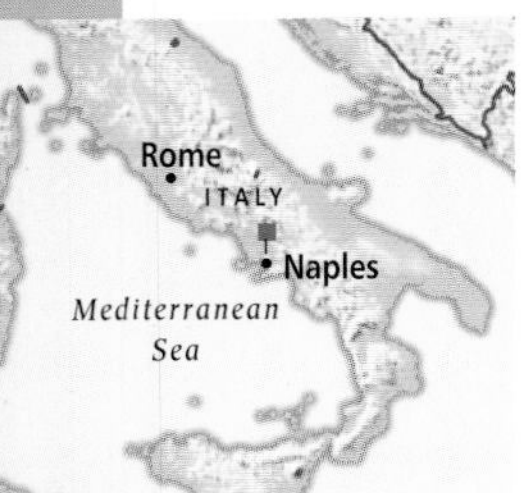

Pompeii

- Roman city buried by volcanic eruption
- Dated to Roman period, destroyed in AD 79
- Major exploration since 18th century
- Finds include wall paintings, silver plate, sculpture, personal objects
- On public display; finds in Archaeological Museum, Naples

The eruption of Mount Vesuvius on August 24, AD 79 buried the Roman city of Pompeii under a layer of pumice and ash—as deep as 16 feet (5 m) in some places. Although some residents may have escaped the destruction, early explorers found the remains of those who were not so lucky. Archaeologists realized that if the holes in the ash were filled with plaster, details of the bodies could be retrieved, offering a glimpse of those last tragic moments. Even the body of a dog, straining to escape from its chain, has been recovered.

House of the Vettii
The luxurious lifestyle enjoyed by ancient Rome's upper classes is exemplified by the House of the Vettii, one of the best preserved houses in Pompeii.

The importance of Pompeii (along with the neighboring town of Herculaneum, which was buried under volcanic mud) is that it provides an insight into life in a provincial city of Italy in the late 1st century AD. A number of houses have been excavated: their walls were decorated with elaborate, sometimes mythological paintings and their public rooms were filled with portrait sculptures and other works of art. One of the houses outside the walls, known as the Villa of the Mysteries, gained its name from an elaborate series of paintings that showed initiation into the secret rites of the god Bacchus (Dionysos).

A Thriving City
Nestled in the shadow of Mount Vesuvius, Pompeii was a prosperous city of 20,000 people. Its streets were laid out on a grid system and its buildings included a Roman forum and amphitheater, shops, temples, and homes.

The destruction also provided a snapshot of the commercial life of the city. The preservation of wine shops, bakeries still with loaves in their ovens, and the meat market is without parallel in the rest of the empire. Even political slogans were still painted on the walls of the streets. Public areas, such as the amphitheater (scene of a famous riot described by the historian Tacitus) and the forum (the center of civic administration), reflect the wealth of the city.

Plaster Corpse
The ash preserved the forms of long-vanished bodies, from which plaster molds could be made. This mold shows a struggling guard dog.

AD 500

0

500 BC

1000 BC

Vindolanda

- Roman frontier fort and civilian settlement
- Dated to Roman times, 1st century AD to 5th century AD
- Extensive excavations from the 1970s
- Finds include writing tablets, textiles, jewelry
- On public display; finds in Vindolanda Museum, Northumberland

During their occupation of northern England at the middle of the 1st century AD, the Romans built a small fort at Vindolanda on the line of the Roman road that cut between the rivers Tyne and Solway. This military site soon attracted civilians, and a small settlement grew up outside the walls.

The waterlogged nature of the site has preserved organic materials in larger quantities than on any other Roman site in Britain. Among the finds were a number of wooden boards. Archaeologists studied these under infrared light and realized that they were part of the archive of the fort. More than 1,600 texts have now been recovered. It seems that the Roman military unit was withdrawn from Britain in the spring or early summer of AD 105 to take part in the emperor Trajan's campaign in Dacia, in the Balkans. They started a bonfire but a sudden storm may have stopped the destruction. Letters include private correspondence from the wife of the commander at the fort—she even mentions a birthday celebration taking place in a nearby fort. Another letter gives details of a Roman soldier's requirements for underwear and woollen socks to help combat the cold of the frontier. Muster lists show how few men were in fact available due to illness, secondments, or other duties.

Recent excavations have uncovered the remains of a large wooden complex adjoining the fort. This may be the site of a temporary palace constructed during a visit by the emperor Hadrian when Hadrian's Wall was being built just to the north of Vindolanda.

Baths Suite
The Severan Commanding Officer's residence featured a baths suite. Originally part of an earlier structure built in the middle of the 2nd century AD, this section was incorporated into the Severan building in AD 197–211.

Tepidarium
These pillars once supported the flagged and concreted floor of the tepidarium, or hot room, in the military bath house (built early 3rd century).

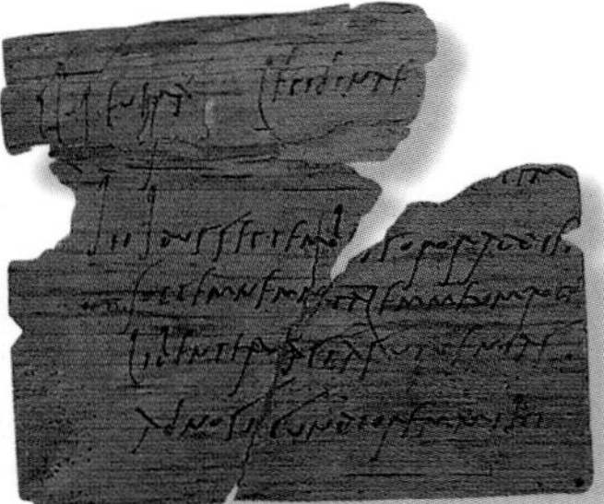

Party Invitation
One of the earliest known examples of writing in Latin by a woman, these fragments were recovered from Vindolanda. The text invites the commander's wife to a birthday party.

AD 500

0

500 BC

1000 BC

Sutton Hoo

- Richest Anglo-Saxon site in England
- Dated to Late Iron Age, AD 550–650
- Ship burial discovered in 1939
- Finds include gold and silver jewelry; metal bowls, coins, weapons
- Artifacts in British Museum, London

In 1938 Edith Pretty decided that the mounds on her estate near Ipswich in eastern England should be investigated, and hired Basil Brown, a local archaeologist. Brown and his assistants opened three of the smaller mounds, all of which had been robbed in antiquity, and found that they contained cremation burials from the Anglo-Saxon period. Despite the fact that the finds in these first mounds were not spectacular, Brown did manage to identify several iron objects as rivets used to hold together the planks of ships in the 1st millennium AD.

The following year, Brown began work again, this time exploring a large mound that he had previously ignored. Within a few days, he encountered a row of ship rivets at intervals in his trench. By meticulously finding the positions of the rivets one by one through careful excavation, and by following them down level by level, Brown established the outline of a decayed boat whose planks had not been preserved but whose sole traces were the rivets trapped by the matrix of soil. When he was through, Brown had uncovered the ghost of a buried vessel 88 feet (27 m) long with a burial chamber in the center.

A team of expert archaeologists was assembled to investigate the ship burial at Sutton Hoo. Over the next three weeks, a remarkable assortment of objects were uncovered, including metal weapons and armor, gold coins and jewelry, silver and bronze bowls, and other finely made objects—263 in all.

Some historians believe the ship was the burial of Raedwald, king of East Anglia from AD 599 to 625. Subsequent excavations have discovered burials under the other nearby mounds, indicating that this site was a cemetery for the Anglo-Saxon elite of the area. Some of the finds from Sutton Hoo resemble those from elite graves in Scandinavia, pointing toward connections across the North Sea.

Ghost Ship
The ship burial at Sutton Hoo was excavated in 1939. Although the boat itself had disintegrated, its outline could be traced by following the iron rivets, visible here in rows along the length of its sides.

Decorated Helmet
One of only four helmets dating to the Anglo-Saxon period ever found, this extraordinary iron helmet from Sutton Hoo features decorative bronze panels.

Belt Buckle
This magnificent solid-gold buckle would have been used to fasten a waist belt. Its surface is decorated with writhing snakes.

AD 2000

AD 1500

AD 1000

AD 500

0

Gokstad Ship

- Excellent example of Viking shipbuilding and royal burial
- Dated to Viking Age, c. AD 900
- Mound investigated in 1880
- Finds include Viking ship, wooden artifacts, textiles, animal bones
- Ship and artifacts in Vikingskiphuset, Oslo

The Gokstad ship is one of two remarkable Viking ships found in grave mounds near Oseberg on Oslofjord in Norway. In 1880 the inhabitants of this area dug into one of the local mounds in the hope of finding buried treasure. Instead of gold and silver they found a perfectly preserved Viking ship from about AD 900, 76 feet (23 m) long and 17 feet (5 m) wide. A layer of clay had trapped water around the ship, preventing decay of its oak planks. Moreover, its mast, spars, ropes, and 16 pairs of oars were also preserved.

A Hardy Vessel
Although it was excavated from a burial site, the Gokstad ship was an actual sea-going vessel, equipped with both oars and sails. The ship was slim and shallow with a deep keel, which would have made it easy to navigate even in shallow waters.

A central burial chamber held the skeleton of a tall, middle-aged Viking chief lying on a bed. Although the grave had been robbed of its weapons and valuables in antiquity, a few artifacts remained, including several small boats and a sled. Next to the skeleton lay a board game made from oak with gaming pieces made from horn. Fragments of textiles, some with gold thread, were part of the chief's clothing. Bones of at least a dozen horses, six dogs, and—surprisingly—a peacock were found in and around the ship. The peacock, native to south Asia, suggests connections between the Viking world and distant lands.

The Gokstad ship seized the imagination of the public. In 1893 a replica sailed from Norway to Newfoundland in 28 days, after which it was displayed at the Chicago World's Fair.

In 1904 another preserved Viking ship was found nearby at Oseberg. Shorter and older than the Gokstad ship, it contained a richly furnished grave of two women that included a four-wheeled cart, sleds, elaborate beds, riding equipment, tools, textiles, and at least 10 horses. The prow and the stern of the Oseberg ship were carved with Viking animal motifs. In contrast to the sea-worthy Gokstad ship, the Oseberg ship is believed to have been a "royal yacht" of sorts that would have been limited to cruising along the coast.

Animal Carvings
The beautifully carved stern of the Oseberg ship features animal motifs. Some scholars have suggested that the younger of the two women buried in the ship may have been the 9th century Queen Asa.

AD 1500
AD 1000
AD 500
0

Novgorod

- Early Medieval trading center and town in Russia
- Established in 9th century AD, flourished in 11th–15th centuries
- First excavations in 1929 directed by Artemii Artsikhovsky
- Finds include timber houses; artifacts; birch-bark manuscripts
- Artifacts in Novgorod United State Museum, Veliky Novgorod

Novgorod, one of the oldest towns in Russia, is located along the Volkhov River north of Lake Ilmen, about 100 miles (160 km) south of St Petersburg. Dating back to the 9th century AD, Novgorod flourished during Medieval times, and continues today as a modern town. The clay soil under the town blocks drainage, and the earliest layers have become waterlogged. This has preserved the Medieval timber buildings and streets, along with a remarkable array of artifacts made from perishable materials such as wood and leather.

Viking merchants who traded with the local Slavic communities during the 8th and 9th centuries AD established a series of trading settlements along the Volkhov, an important corridor between the Baltic area and the interior. One of the later settlements was Novgorod, which grew into a prosperous city during the 11th–15th centuries. Viking merchants were prominent among its inhabitants, but there was never a large-scale Scandinavian colonization. Instead, the Vikings began to adopt Slavic names and mix with the locals.

The plan of Novgorod consisted of a network of winding streets. As one layer of timber paving became waterlogged, another was laid directly upon it. At one location, 28 levels of timber paving are found, the earliest from AD 953 and the latest from 1462. Houses were generally log cabins organized into compounds of a dwelling, stables, workshops, and storage huts. In these compounds, artisans made leather goods, jewelry, glass, and pottery.

Some of the most unusual finds at Novgorod and nearby sites are birch-bark manuscripts called *beresty*, written using a stylus on soft bark between the 11th and 15th centuries. Such manuscripts indicate that many of the inhabitants of Novgorod were literate. Nearly a thousand have been found so far, and it is estimated that many more remain buried.

Written Records
The writing materials discovered at Novgorod include birch-bark manuscripts known as *beresty*, wax writing tablets known as *tseras*, and writing instruments. The documents deal with many different topics, including household, business, legal, and government affairs.

Medieval Shoes
The waterlogged Medieval layers of Novgorod have preserved many organic artifacts, such as these 14th century leather shoes.

AD 2000
AD 1500
AD 500
0

Sites and Treasures of Asia

From the Near East to Southeast Asia, great civilizations have left behind a rich archaeological record that includes the ziggurat of Ur, the Ishtar Gate of Babylon, the Frozen Princess in Siberia, the Terracotta Army of China's First Emperor, the Dead Sea Scrolls in Israel, and Java's temple of Borobudur.

"From the walls I had an uninterrupted view over a vast plain, stretching westward toward the Euphrates, and losing itself in the hazy distance. The ruins of ancient towns and villages rose on all sides; and, as the sun went down, I counted above one hundred mounds, throwing their dark and lengthening shadows across the plains."

Austen Henry Layard (1817–94),
English archaeologist and diplomat

Mount Carmel Caves

- Primary prehistoric site in the Levant
- Dated from Paleolithic, *c.* 600,000 years ago, to historical times
- First excavated by Dorothy Garrod 1929–34
- Finds include prehistoric human remains, stone and bone artifacts
- Caves on public display; finds in Israel Museum, Jerusalem

The importance of the caves in Mount Carmel, the limestone range near Haifa, was recognized after three of them—Tabun, El-Wad, and Skhul—were saved from being destroyed by quarrying in the 1920s. These three caves, along with a fourth (Kebara), were first excavated under the direction of the British prehistorian Dorothy Garrod from 1929 to 1934. Garrod and her successors discovered that the caves preserved different aspects of an almost continuous prehistoric sequence, spanning 600,000 years or more of human activity from the Lower Paleolithic through to historical times. The oldest stone artifacts are found in the deepest level of the huge cave of Tabun. The caves of Tabun, Skhul, and Kebara also contain human burials of the Middle Paleolithic period. In El-Wad and Kebara caves, artifacts of Upper Paleolithic times were followed by the burials and beautiful artifacts of the later Epipaleolithic Natufian people (*c.* 12,500–10,000 years ago).

The discovery that two species of Middle Paleolithic people occupied the caves remains fundamental in our interpretation of the course of human evolution. Early modern humans buried their dead, adults and children, in a small cemetery at Skhul cave about 100,000 years ago. They were apparently succeeded by Neanderthals, who left behind individual graves in Tabun and Kebara. All are central in the continuing puzzle concerning the origin and survival of modern humans and the extinction of the Neanderthals. The Natufians' fine bone and stone implements are evidence of their crucial contribution to the subsequent revolutionary transition from foraging to agriculture.

Digging Up the Caves First explored by Dorothy Garrod in 1929–34, the Mount Carmel caves continue to supply evidence of early people. Here, workers excavate the interior of Kebara Cave during a 1989 dig.

Paleolithic Skeletons The human remains found at the Mount Carmel sites have helped to establish a baseline for Paleolithic archaeology. A fossil skull and skeletal remains (left) were among the finds from Skhul Cave.

YEARS AGO
1 million
2 million
3 million
4 million

The City of Ur

- Important Sumerian city, later a commercial and religious center
- Dated to c. 5000–300 BC
- Identified in 1854; major excavations 1919, 1922–34
- Finds include Royal Cemetery, residential districts, cuneiform tablets
- Ur ziggurat restored in situ; artifacts in British Museum, London

Ur is southern Mesopotamia's most famous city—famous among the general public for its Royal Cemetery, and among archaeologists and ancient historians for many additional reasons. Tell al-Muqayyar, already long identified as Ur, did not receive proper examination until C.L. Woolley's excavations. During his dozen seasons of work, Woolley accomplished extraordinary results. At the deepest levels, he detected flimsy 'Ubaid huts dating to the city's beginnings around 5000 BC. He explored the ziggurat (stepped temple tower) and temple precinct, which had been constructed when Ur governed a small empire (Ur III, *c.* 2112–2004 BC); exposed several residential neighborhoods of the Old Babylonian period (2004–1595 BC); and uncovered important monuments of later periods as well.

Although Woolley's excavation technique may not be above reproach by today's standards, his work retains immense value precisely because he uncovered so much of the city and then published meticulous technical reports.

The highlight of the excavations is the Royal Cemetery—16 tombs dated around 2600–2500 BC within a cemetery of thousands of burials. The royal graves have a stone or brick chamber set at the bottom of a shaft, where the main burial was placed. A ramp from one side gave access to the chamber; here and next to the chamber lay the bodies of ladies-in-waiting and soldiers turned out in their finest garb. The wealth interred with the dead is stunning, and the artistry of the objects sets a standard that other Sumerian sites struggle to match.

Moon-God Temple
The best preserved of Mesopotamia's temple towers, the ziggurat at Ur was dedicated to the moon god. Three stairways of 100 steps each lead to the first of the structure's three terraces. The ruined walls of the city can be seen in the foreground.

Trapped Ram
Among the many magnificent works of Sumerian art found in the Royal Cemetery was this gold and lapis lazuli figure of a ram caught in a thicket (left).

Scenes of Celebration
The Standard of Ur (right) is a double-sided wooden panel inlaid with lapis lazuli and mother-of-pearl. This side of the panel depicts a ritual celebration scene, while the other side shows military action.

0
5000 BC
7500 BC
10,000 BC

Megiddo

- One of key sites for Bronze and Iron ages of the southern Levant
- Dated to c. 3500–500 BC, with traces of earlier occupation to 5500 BC
- Excavated by German, U.S., and Israeli teams over the past century
- Finds include Bronze Age temples and palaces; carved ivories
- Architecture on display in situ; objects in Israel Museum, Jerusalem

The southern Levant (Israel, Palestine, and Jordan) is the most intensively excavated part of western Asia. Megiddo and a handful of other sites hold pride of place among the hundreds that have been investigated. Excavations here have been so extensive that we can follow the changing character of the town throughout its existence. The history of Megiddo also describes the ebb and flow of town life in the region.

During the Early Bronze Age (3500–2000 BC), when towns developed and then disappeared again, Megiddo was a walled town with a magnificent temple. When towns redeveloped during the Middle and Late Bronze ages (2000–1200 BC), Megiddo featured a massive temple of Syrian design, adjacent to a palace. Later in the same period, the palace and other aristocratic houses moved to the city-gate area, perhaps to symbolize a separation of secular and religious authority. A famous hoard of carved ivories made in Egypt and the Levant appeared in the final edition of the palace. The Late Bronze Age palace was followed by an impoverished village. The site of Megiddo revived as a royal garrison town, with construction of a new city wall and elaborate triple-chamber gate and of large pillared buildings commonly identified as stables. Once considered the handiwork of Solomon (*c.* 950 BC), archaeologists now credit most or all of these structures to the later kings of Israel. When the Assyrians gained control of the site in the late 8th century BC, they rebuilt the town on a regular street grid as an administrative center.

On the Via Maris
For six millennia, Megiddo dominated the Via Maris, the major trading route in the Levant. The town's long and rich archaeological record makes it one of the most important sites in Biblical archaeology.

Gated Entrance
Stone gates interrupt the mighty fortifications that defended the city by the 9th century BC. The interior contained military and administrative buildings.

Gaming Board
The hoard of carved ivories discovered at Megiddo included this intricate gaming board. Every fifth hole was once inlaid with gold and blue paste.

0
5000 BC
7500 BC
10,000 BC

Tell Asmar

- Sumerian capital featuring religious architecture and art
- City first occupied by 3000 BC, abandoned after 1750 BC
- Excavated 1930–36 by Oriental Institute of Chicago
- Finds include temple with votive statues; houses of Akkadian Period
- Artifacts in Oriental Institute, Chicago; Iraqi National Museum, Baghdad

Tell Asmar is the site of the ancient Sumerian city of Eshnunna, located near the Diyala River at the northeastern edge of Babylonia. Around 1770 BC, Eshnunna's king rivaled Babylon's Hammurabi (see p. 340) in strength, but soon afterward Babylon won its first empire. Eshnunna fell into decline and was abandoned sometime after 1750 BC.

When archaeologists think of Tell Asmar, however, they first think of earlier times. In the 1930s, the Oriental Institute of Chicago, backed by John D. Rockefeller, undertook an ambitious project in the Diyala area, simultaneously excavating Tell Asmar and Tell Khafaje. The excavations were enormously important, for they recovered stratified pottery and objects that established a secure chronological framework for the Sumerian Early Dynastic and Akkadian periods (2900–2100 BC). For archaeologists, this accomplishment ranks with Leonard Woolley's discoveries at Ur (see p. 330).

The Chicago team also uncovered residential districts, workshops, graves, and temples. Among these was the temple of Abu, a deity of rainfall and the plow. The Abu Temple was remodeled several times throughout the 3rd millennium BC. During these episodes, the temple equipment appears to have been renewed, but rather than casually discarding the obsolete sacred objects, the priests buried them in pits dug beneath the temple floor. Archaeologists have unearthed buried collections of votive statues, which supplicants had placed in the temple to remind Abu of their pleas. The limestone figures, usually 12 to 24 inches (30–60 cm) tall, depict men and women standing with hands clasped before their chests in prayer, their large shell-inlaid eyes awestruck in the divine presence. Dated to 2700 BC, these statues are among the treasures of Sumerian art.

Votive Statues
An Iraqi excavator examines a hoard of Sumerian votive statues excavated in 1934. The well-subsidized U.S. expedition to Tell Asmar, with its elaborate research station, was in marked contrast to the austere English camps that had preceded it in the Near East.

Praying to Abu
Made from rock such as gypsum or limestone, the votive statues characteristically have a wide-eyed gaze and hands clasped at their chests in prayer. The male figures are dressed in flounced skirts and have long, square beards and long, flowing hair.

0
5000 BC
7500 BC
10,000 BC

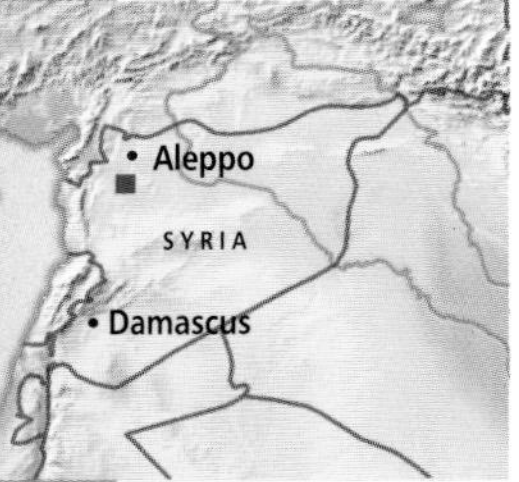

Ebla

- Discovery of early Syrian kingdom
- Dated to Bronze Age, 3000–1600 BC
- Excavations by Italian teams from 1964 to the present
- Finds include cuneiform archive, temples, palaces, royal burials
- Public can tour site; exhibits in Aleppo Museum, Idlib Museum

When in 1974 Paolo Matthiae announced his discovery of a large archive of clay cuneiform tablets at Tell Mardikh, archaeologists and historians of early Near Eastern civilizations had to reconsider their prejudices. For a long time, western Syria was the stepsister of Mesopotamian archaeology and had been denigrated as a mere recipient of civilization, a region whose inhabitants became literate only after 2000 BC. That view turned out to be ill-considered, but for decades few archaeologists chose to excavate the Bronze Age mounds west of the Euphrates River. But with Matthiae's discovery, 18,000 complete or fragmentary tablets unearthed from Palace G at Tell Mardikh have opened a window onto an unanticipated Syrian kingdom of 2400 BC.

The tablets, written in the local Semitic language, identify Tell Mardikh as the royal capital Ebla, and provide details about the extent of its kingdom, its diplomatic and commercial relations with Sumer and other neighbors, its internal economic affairs, and its religious practices. Although indeed indebted to the Sumerian tradition, Ebla's was a distinctly Syrian civilization.

An equally important Middle Bronze Age (*c.* 2000–1600 BC) city lies above the older capital, which meant that the Italian team could excavate only a portion of Palace G during the 1970s. Since then, they have patiently dug through the younger city, unearthing palaces, rich royal graves, temples, and fortifications, all important in their own right. But for many scholars this is preliminary work—the payoff for their patience will be uncovering the rest of Palace G and other parts of the old capital, and then exploring even older levels to find Ebla's roots.

Bronze Age Capital
During the Bronze Age, Ebla was a powerful kingdom and a major center on the trade route from the Euphrates to the Mediterranean. The settlement was deserted during the great upheavals that engulfed the Middle East about 1600 BC.

Palace G
In addition to the cuneiform archive, Ebla's Early Bronze Age mud-brick palace contained fragments of carved wooden furniture, Sumerian-style stone inlay and cylinder seals, imported Egyptian stone vessels, and 50 pounds (23 kg) of lapis lazuli.

Ebla Records
The cuneiform tablets, mostly the records of the palace official, describe a rich, powerful kingdom. The Ebla scribes borrowed some signs for whole words from Sumerian, but also devised signs to represent the syllables of their own language.

0

5000 BC

7500 BC

10,000 B

Mohenjo Daro

- Largest and most complex city of the Indus civilization
- City at its height 2600–1800 BC
- Excavations in 1924 of Buddhist stupa revealed ancient city
- Finds include architecture, seals, sculptures, domestic objects
- Site on display; finds in site museum and Karachi Museum, Pakistan

The great Indus city of Mohenjo Daro covered more than 620 acres (250 ha). The excavated central portion includes a high-walled citadel, where pillared halls and bathrooms surrounded a Great Bath, plausibly interpreted as a pool for ritual bathing. The houses in the planned lower town show a high standard of living. Built around a central courtyard from which a stairway led to upper floors and the roof, most houses had a brick-floored bathroom connected to the city's sophisticated network of drains; many also had toilets and most had a well, while public wells were available for those without.

The city lay at the crossroads of the Indus civilization, with the Indus River providing a highway between the mountains and the sea, and overland routes leading into the western hills and south into the fertile lands of the Saraswati River. Although the political organization of the Indus civilization is still uncertain, the location, size, and complexity of Mohenjo Daro suggest that it was the overall capital of the Indus state. Here every standard type of Indus artifact was manufactured, along with unusual objects such as inscribed stoneware bangles, which may have been badges of office. The unique Great Bath similarly sets this city apart.

Mohenjo Daro's antiquity cannot be established, because the lowest levels are waterlogged, but the city's decline around 1800 BC is clearly witnessed by squalid housing, the haphazard mixing of domestic and industrial activities, and the random disposal of dead bodies in abandoned buildings. The bodies show signs of serious diseases, which may in part explain the city's demise.

City Living
The planned lower town of Mohenjo Daro contained two-story houses for roughly 100,000 residents. The thick brick walls are separated by alleys.

Bullock Cart
The potters of the Indus Valley excelled at making small, delicate pieces, such as this terracotta model of a two-wheeled bullock cart with driver.

The Priest King
Dubbed "The Priest King," this 7 inch (18 cm) tall soapstone sculpture shows a bearded man wearing a decorated cloak over one shoulder, a diadem on his head, and an armband.

5000 BC
7500 BC
10,000 BC

Babylon

- Capital of Babylonia
- Dated from c. 2000 BC to early centuries AD
- Correctly identified in 1811; extensive excavations 1899–1917
- Finds include Nebuchadnezzar's imperial city
- Site on display, partially restored; artifacts in Berlin Museum

Babylon was the chief city of southern Mesopotamia from the time of the region's sixth king, Hammurabi (1792–1750 BC), to the end of Mesopotamian civilization in the 1st century AD. For these 2,000 years, the city remained the cultural and economic center of the region even during periods when it was not the political capital.

The city of Babylon lay in the northern reaches of the region to which it gave its name, on a now-dry branch of the Euphrates River. It was, however, a small and relatively unimportant place until Hammurabi established dominion over much of Mesopotamia, heralding the Old Babylonian kingdom (1792–1595 BC). Unfortunately, we know almost nothing about Hammurabi's Babylon, for these levels are still deeply buried under the debris of later versions of the city, especially Nebuchadnezzar's massive Babylon.

Nebuchadnezzar (604–562 BC) ruled the second great Babylonian empire, and became infamous for capturing Jerusalem and exiling the defeated Jews to Babylon. Robert Koldewey's excavations uncovered Nebuchadnezzar's city, which sprawled over 3.3 square miles (8.5 sq. km) on both sides of the river, surrounded by a massive wall and moat. Another walled city lay inside the first and formed the civic center of the empire. Here the famous Ishtar Gate opened onto the Processional Way, which ran south from the gate through the city. Nebuchadnezzar's palace sat just inside the gate. Further south, two adjacent plazas contained the temple of Marduk (the national god) and the great ziggurat, a stepped tower that has been identified with the biblical Tower of Babel.

Rediscovering Babylon
The location of Babylon had never been forgotten and peasants had recycled its building materials for centuries, but the first European to identify the site was Claudius Rich, in 1811. Excavations did not begin, however, until almost 90 years later.

Nebuchadnezzar's Gate
The vivid blue Ishtar Gate was decorated with rows of bulls (right) and dragons. Originally standing about 75 feet (23 m) high, the gate was removed brick by brick and reconstructed in the Pergamon Museum, Berlin.

The Lawmaker
Hammurabi (shown at left kneeling to a deity) unified much of Mesopotamia and established Babylon as its flourishing capital. He also left behind one of the oldest law codes, a sequence of 282 laws and penalties carved into a diorite pillar.

2500 BC
5000 BC
7500 BC
10,000 BC

The Land of Cities

- Oldest cities in the steppes of Eurasia
- Dated to Bronze Age, 18th–16th centuries BC
- Discovered in 1970s and 1980s during dam construction
- Finds include outstanding chariot burials, the earliest in the world
- Arkaim settlement on display as a museum-preserve

The location of the original homeland of the Indo-Europeans is one of the most contested issues in prehistory. When these peoples were a unified group, they called themselves *arya*—hence the term Aryans. From ancient Hindu and Iranian texts, it was known that they migrated to India and Iran from somewhere to the northwest in the late 2nd millennium BC. A hypothesis arose that the ancestors of these Aryans could have lived somewhere between the Volga River and the Ural Mountains, but until recently there was no archaeological evidence to support it.

In the 1970s at the Sintashta River in the southern Ural steppes, a complex of sites was discovered—a fortified settlement, five cemeteries, and a grandiose mortuary-temple construction—most of whose elements could be compared with and explained by the ancient written sources. Sintashta is especially famous for the cemetery in which warriors were buried with their chariots and horses. The lavish grave goods included ceramics, tools, weapons, horse harnesses, and jewelry.

Further research in the 1980s led to the discovery of a series of similar sites and the identification of the "Land of Cities" along the eastern slopes of the Urals. More than 20 fortified centers and related mortuary complexes are now known, as well as hundreds of smaller unfortified settlements. Arkaim is the best preserved and most thoroughly investigated complex among them.

In contrast to Sintashta, Arkaim yielded few artifacts, but the settlement is very well preserved. The excavation revealed that the settlement had been burned down, and the population had left the city before the fire, taking their possessions with them. All the wooden fenceposts and other constructions had burned, but the earthen walls of the settlement survived.

Arkaim from the Air
The Arkaim site, seen here in an aerial view, comprises a fortified settlement, with adjacent farming areas, burial mounds, and some unfortified settlements.

Stone Figurine
The Arkaim–Sintashta culture produced figurines such as this "man looking at the sky." Finds from Sintashta are displayed in the Museum of the University of Chelyabinsk.

5000 BC
7500 BC
10,000 BC

Stone statues of the Steppes

- Remarkable prehistoric stone figures
- Dated to Bronze Age (2nd millennium BC); Early Iron Age (mid-1st millennium BC); Early Middle Ages (late 1st to early 2nd millennium AD)
- Numerous discoveries from 18th century onward
- Some in situ, but most in museums in Russia, Ukraine, Mongolia

Beautiful, mysterious monuments, dubbed "steppe idols" by 18th century travelers, were placed in high locations all over the vast mountain steppes, from the Dniester in the west to the Altai and Mongolia in the east. Hundreds of them have survived, but many have no doubt been destroyed by time and people. Measuring 3 to 12 feet (1–4 m) tall, the statues were made of sandstone, granite, schist, basalt, and other kinds of stone. Their design often combines relief carving with engraving on the flat surfaces.

Among the oldest specimens are the fantastic statues of the Okunevo culture, which existed in the 2nd millennium BC in the Minusinsk Basin, southern Siberia. These usually have a saber-like shape with a face in the middle. Realistic human faces are very rare—normally they feature anthropomorphous masks decorated with lines, curves, a third eye, animal horns and ears, and a complicated headdress. Figures depicted with a large stomach and breasts probably represent pregnant women.

The so-called "deer-stones"—stone stelae decorated with pecked images—were erected in the Late Bronze Age and Early Iron Age over a vast territory from Mongolia to the Danube. Their appearance is connected with the beginning of the Epoch of Early Nomads in the Eurasian steppes. The stelae represent a warrior figure, but without clear human features. They are usually divided into three zones by two horizontal lines, depicting a necklace and belt. The upper part shows earrings, with three oblique lines in place of the face. The lower part has weaponry attached to the belt. The area between the necklace and the belt is completely covered with animal images, most often highly stylized figures of deer. The deer-stones can be compared with the clearly anthropomorphous Scythian statues of warriors.

Most of the Turkic statues of the 6th–9th centuries AD depict a man of mongoloid appearance, with mustache and beard, wearing a hat and jacket. A warrior's equipment usually hangs from his belt.

Mongolian Deer Stone
The Eurasian stone statues were not funerary monuments, as commonly believed, but were mainly made for ritual purposes. They remained objects of cult and reverence long afterwards.

Turkic Warrior
This Turkic warrior is shown in a static pose with his hands folded over a vessel.

AD 500

0

500 BC

1000 BC

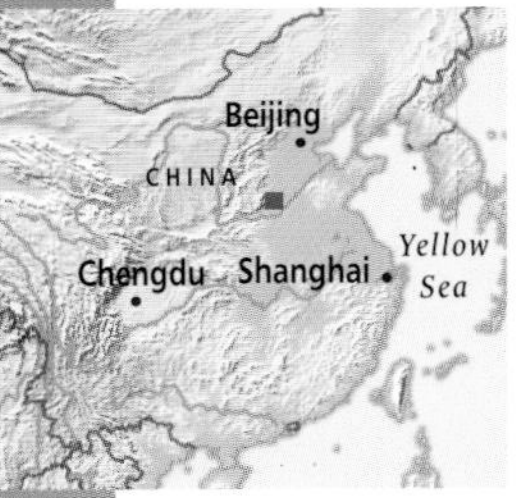

Anyang

- Royal capital with cemetery in China
- Dated to Shang Dynasty, 13th–11th centuries BC
- City walls and tombs discovered in 1928 in Xiaotun, Anyang, China
- Finds include bronze vessels, bells, weapons, jade objects, chariots
- Finds in Museum of History, Beijing; Museum of the Yin Ruins, Anyang

After 2000 BC the Shang Dynasty emerged in the North China plain, a complex Bronze Age civilization marked by written documents, metal-working, and a stable administration. In 1300 BC King Pankeng moved to the city of Yin, which remained the residence of the Shang royalty for more than 200 years, until it was destroyed by a disastrous flood. While written sources indicated the existence of this large Shang city, it was only in the early 20th century that traces of it were discovered. Oracle bones that had been used by the Shang kings for divination started appearing in druggists' shops and were traced to their source in Xiaotun, near Anyang.

Bronze Vessel
The bronzes unearthed at Anyang included ritual vessels used for consuming wine and for cooking meat. They were created in the workshops at the site. This vessel (right) features bird-shaped handles.

Archaeologists have excavated a rammed earth wall that divides the city into four sections: a royal palace, a section for craftsmen, residential areas, and a huge royal cemetery. The vast tombs of the royal family show the ability of the mighty rulers to mobilize human and material sources. Thousands of workers had to dig the shaft pits, construct the wooden burial chambers, and fill them with earth. To date, 11 royal tombs have been excavated. Many contained the remains of human sacrifices, beheaded followers who accompanied the king in death, as well as animals such as horses and dogs. The only tomb that had not been robbed was that of Lady Fu Hao (died 1250 BC), probably a consort of the Shang king, Wu Ding. Although this tomb did not belong to the main royal cemetery, it was nonetheless filled with extraordinary grave goods. Its 200 bronze vessels constitute the largest set of ritual vessels ever found in China. The tomb was also richly furnished with jade and stone objects and cowry shells, which were probably used for money. In 2000 another rammed earth wall was discovered and partly excavated north of Anyang. This new discovery predates the old capital and is now regarded as the largest walled Shang city yet found in China.

Oracle Bone
Originally used by for divination, the oracle bones from Anyang provide the earliest known examples of Chinese script, as well as information about rulers, battles, and religion.

Khorsabad

- Discovery of Assyrians, with royal Assyrian art and architecture
- Dated to late 8th century BC
- First excavated by French team in 1840s and 1850s
- Finds include wall reliefs, winged bulls, palace, cuneiform texts
- Displays in the Louvre, Paris, and the Oriental Institute, Chicago

Perhaps wanting to evade the byzantine rivalries inherent to any long-standing court of an imperial power, the kings of Assyria had a habit of founding new capitals: Assurnasirpal (883–859 BC) made his capital at Nimrud; Sennacherib (704–681 BC) moved his court to Nineveh; and Sargon (721–705 BC) built Dur-Sharrukin (Fortress of Sargon), also known as Khorsabad. Sargon laid out his city as an immense square, its walls enclosing an area of about 1 square mile (3 sq. km), and set two smaller walled compounds inside the city walls. The larger enclosure near the city's north corner contained the royal center. This comprised Sargon's palace, which was built upon a 30 foot (10 m) high platform; the temple of Nabu (god of writing) and other temples; a ziggurat; and the residences of high officials. A second palace occupied the other compound near the city's southern corner. When Sargon died before finishing his new city, Sennacherib moved the Assyrian capital to Nineveh.

Khorsabad was the scene of the first successful excavations in Mesopotamia when Frenchman Paul Botta began uncovering Sargon's palace in 1843. Botta's reports—which described the monumental statues of human-headed winged bulls guarding palace doorways, and the wall panels carved with scenes of Sargon's military accomplishments and his cultic observances—led to a wave of European enthusiasm for Mesopotamian archaeology. The wall reliefs of Assyrian palaces give a particularly vivid record of how these kings viewed their world. A team from the United States made further investigations of the palace area during the 1920s and 30s, discovering another winged bull and exploring other buildings in the palace compound.

Images of Assyria
Until the excavations of the 1940s, Assyrian culture was known only from the Bible. Among the elaborate wall reliefs in the Palace of Sargon was this one depicting the loading and transport of wood.

Winged Guardian
Massive statues of human-headed winged bulls guarded the doorways and gates of Khorsabad.

AD 500
0
500 BC
1000 BC

Persepolis

- Ceremonial capital of Achaemenid Persians
- Dated to 510–330 BC, with later occupation
- First European reports in 17th century; excavations in 20th century
- Finds include the architecture, art, cuneiform tablets
- Site on display in Iran; finds in National Museum, Tehran

Darius the Great (522–486 BC) was a usurper, belonging to a side branch of the Achaemenid family that created the Persian empire. After Darius seized power, he abandoned Parsagadae, the traditional Achaemenid center, and began constructing Persepolis. He built on a vast scale, and his successors were still adding to the capital a century later.

Persepolis is basically a large stone platform—25 acres (10 ha) in area and rising 40 feet (12 m) high—set up against a rising hill at the edge of a plain. A monumental double staircase led to a formal gateway, the entrance to the dense array of buildings on the platform. The apadana (a high pillared audience hall) of Darius was the most magnificent of these buildings—set upon its own platform overlooking the plain and built of finely polished stone and mud brick encased in cedar, its staircase is decorated with a famous relief portraying emissaries bearing tribute from all corners of the empire. In addition to other pillared halls, Persepolis contained harem quarters and a treasury. As Persepolis was the ceremonial center of the Persian dynasty, Darius and his successors were buried nearby in rock-cut tombs at Naqsh i-Rustam and elsewhere.

The end of Persepolis signaled the end of the Persian empire. Alexander the Great occupied Persepolis in 330 BC, burning the city after a drunken victory party. Copies of trilingual (Old Persian, Babylonian, and Elamite) cuneiform inscriptions from Persepolis and other Achaemenid monuments of southwestern Iran greatly helped archaeologists decipher the cuneiform script in the first half of the 19th century.

Enduring Ruins
Persepolis was never buried and forgotten, but remained exposed, appearing in the reports of many European travelers. The standing pillars that still dot the site represent the city's colonnaded halls.

A King on His Throne
The staircases and walls of the buildings featured carved reliefs of royalty, soldiers, officials, and envoys. This fine example shows Darius's son Xerxes, who tried but failed to add Greece to the Persian empire.

Princely Sculpture
The rich resources and sophisticated craftsmanship of the Achaemenid empire are demonstrated by finds such as this lapis lazuli head of a prince.

AD 500

0

1000 BC

Pazyryk Tombs

- Burials of nomadic elite with well-preserved organic artifacts
- Dated to Early Iron Age, 5th–3rd centuries BC
- First tomb excavated in 1929; most recent excavation in 1995
- Pazyryk finds in the Hermitage Museum, St Petersburg; Ukok finds in the Museum of the Institute of Archaeology, Novosibirsk, Russia

The cultures of the Scythian world are known for their kurgans—grandiose burial mounds that tower over the Eurasian steppes and foothills. One of these cultures, which developed 2,500 years ago in the Altai Mountains of southern Siberia, is called Pazyryk after the location of the first kurgan excavation. In 1929 the Soviet archaeologists Sergei Rudenko and Mikhail Gryaznov excavated a kurgan at an altitude of 5,250 feet (1,600 m) and found objects made of organic materials preserved by the frozen ground. Rudenko's excavation of another four kurgans in 1947–49 proved truly sensational. From the frozen tombs, he extracted carpets, clothes, and shoes; a chariot; mummified human bodies; horses in rich attire; musical instruments; various utensils; and numerous other artifacts of wood, leather, felt, and wool.

In the 1990s, in another area of the Altai Mountains—the Ukok Plateau at an altitude of 7,216 feet (2,200 m)—more frozen kurgans of the same culture were found and excavated by Natalia Polos'mak. One tomb belonged to the "Frozen Princess," a tattooed woman of about 25 years of age buried in a log coffin, with fine clothing and leather items and a remarkable tall wooden headdress. Another tomb was that of a man, the "Warrior" or "Horseman," also buried in a wooden coffin in a log-lined chamber. Aged about 25 to 30, a wound in his stomach suggests that he was killed in battle. He has two long braids of red hair and a tattoo of a deer on his shoulder.

The phenomenon of the frozen tombs arises from a unique combination of Pazyryk funerary rites and natural conditions. In the valleys of the Altai Mountains, there is no permafrost apart from that in the kurgans. The stone cairns above the timber burial chambers prevented the earth beneath from warming up in summer and intensified the freezing in winter. Water penetrated the burials, turned to ice, and froze the contents.

"Ice Maiden"
This preserved skull of a woman known as the Pazyryk "Ice Maiden" was found in central Asia in 1993.

"Sphinx" Wall-hanging
This iron-age wall-hanging is from barrow 5 at Pazyryk. It depicts a "sphinx"—a winged and antlered figure, half-human and half-lion.

Sculpted Deer
Among Pazyryk's organic artifacts was this wooden figure of a deer set on a globe-shaped base. The figure was probably once attached to a headdress.

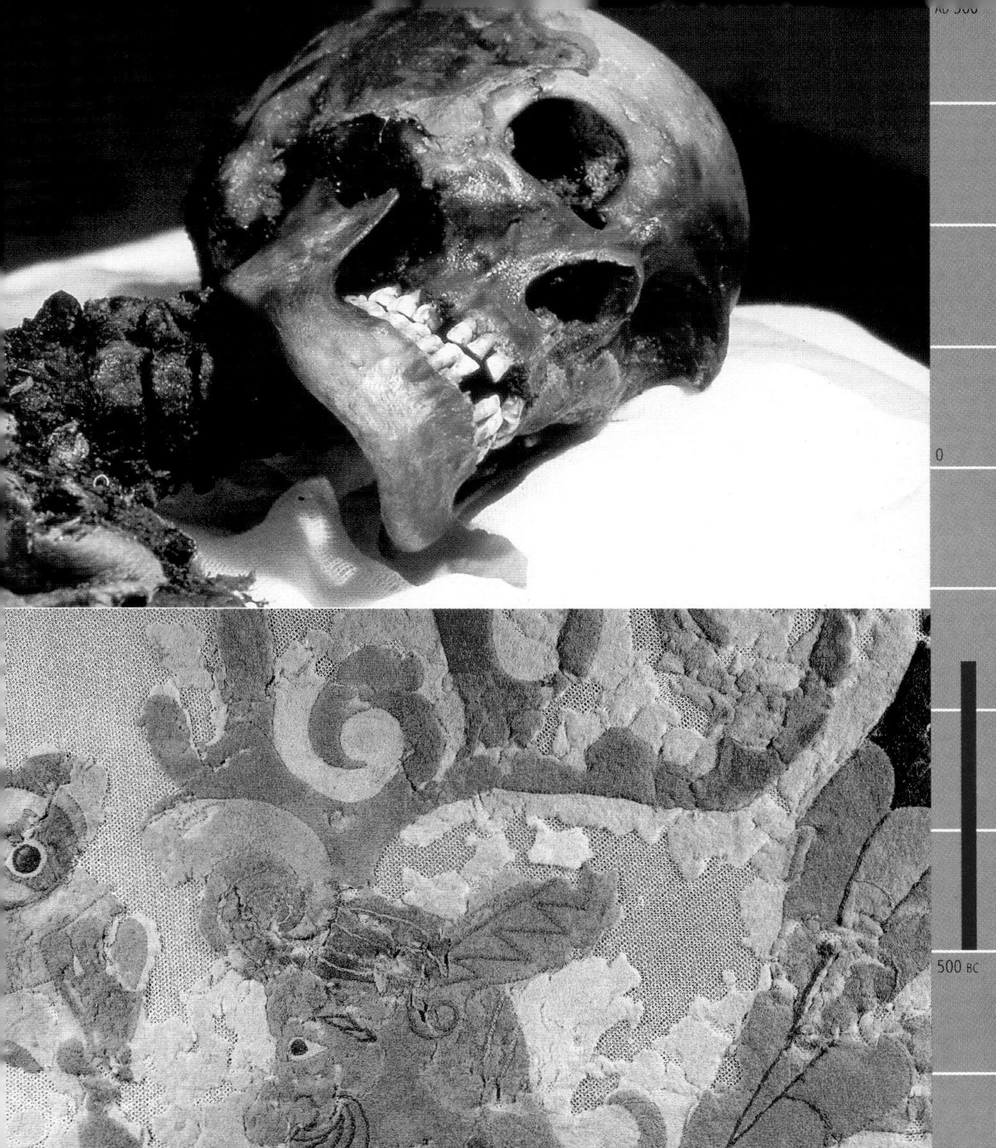

0

500 BC

1000 BC

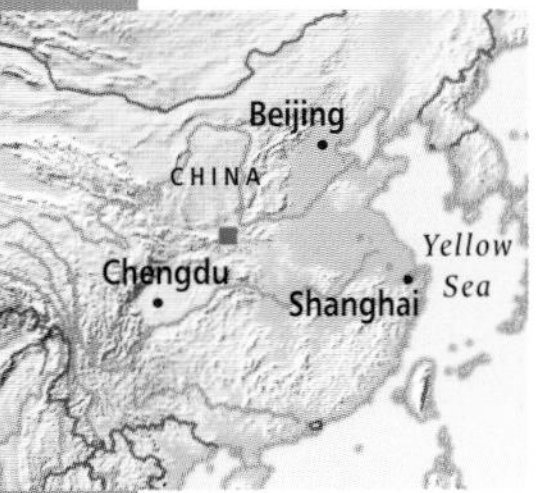

The Terracotta Army

- Tomb of the First Emperor of China
- Dated to Qin Dynasty, 210 BC
- Mound burial with side pits discovered in 1974 in Xi'an
- Finds include terracotta soldiers and bronze vessels, weapons
- Site on public display in Lintong, China

In 1974 a work brigade of farmers drilling a well discovered a subterranean chamber that archaeologists declared to be part of the tomb of the First Emperor of China, Qin Shihuangdi. Immediately after ascending the throne, the emperor ordered the construction of his huge mausoleum to begin. A force of 700,000 slave laborers, architects, and artisans worked on the project for 36 years, interrupted only by the emperor's sudden death in 210 BC.

While the tomb itself is still awaiting excavation, four of the side pits have been partly excavated. The biggest and most important pit contains the famous terracotta army of 7,000 armed soldiers and 600 horses. Standing in rows separated by rammed earth walls, the army was initially protected by a wooden crossbeam construction, but this burned down when rebels stole the weapons only 30 years after the emperor's death. Originally painted in bright colors, the life-size soldiers are made from molded interchangeable parts but finished by hand so that no two are identical. While the legs of each sculpture are solid, the rest of the body is hollow, allowing the different parts to be easily connected and transported. In 1976 a second pit with chariots and infantry, a third with the army headquarters, and a fourth completely empty pit were discovered. The excavated area is now covered by protective roofing and, while archaeological work continues, serves as an in situ museum. The emperor lies within a huge burial mound that is 154 feet (47 m) high, surrounded by two walls, and planted with pomegranate trees. While historical annals record the enormous wealth of grave goods in the tomb, it may well have been looted shortly after its completion.

A Representative Army
Declared a World Heritage site by UNESCO in 1987, the compound has become one of the world's major tourist attractions. The army includes generals, officers, infantrymen, archers, and cavalrymen.

Bronze Weapons
The warriors were originally accompanied by terracotta horses and chariots, and weapons. Bronze vessels were also found in the pits. A kneeling archer owned this bronze arrowhead.

An Individual Face
Each warrior's head is individually crafted, and there are 25 different styles of beard. The figures have revealed much about the hairstyles, clothing, armor, weaponry, and horse trappings of ancient China.

0

500 BC

1000 BC

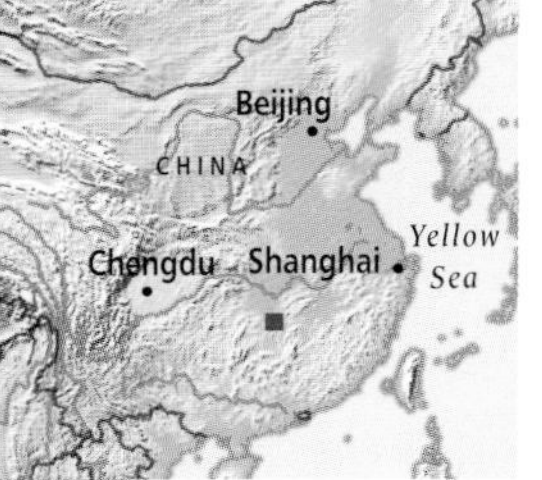

Mawangdui

- Richest Han dynastic family graveyard in China
- Dated to Han Dynasty, 186–168 BC
- Pit tomb discovered in 1972 in Changsha, Hunan province
- Finds include mummy, silk painting, lacquered coffins and vessels
- On public display at the Hunan Provincial Museum

The lavishly furnished tombs of aristocrats show that the fate of the dead was of immense concern during the Western Han Dynasty (206 BC–AD 9). In recent decades, especially in southern China, a number of tombs have been exposed during construction work, and in 1971 local workers discovered one of China's best-preserved tombs. A two-year excavation campaign revealed what is now known as Tomb 1 of the Marquise of Dai (died 168 BC). Subsequently, the tombs of her husband (died 186 BC), prime minister of the king of Changsha, and of their elder son were also discovered.

Tomb 1 was so exquisitely preserved because the solid wooden tomb chamber had been placed in a rectangular shaft filled with a thick water-resistant layer of charcoal and white clay. Within the wooden structure, five nested lacquered coffins held the mummified corpse of the marquise, wrapped in 20 silk garments. More than 1,000 artifacts, mostly lacquered, bronze, and ceramic vessels, had also been carefully wrapped in silk and placed in the smaller side compartments. The vessels were partly filled with food, such as fruit, meat, grain, and rice. Every item in the tomb was recorded on inventory bamboo slips. The painted silk banner that was draped over the coffins is an outstanding example of early Chinese figure painting.

Grave Goods
The lavish grave goods included lacquerware, such as this dish; bamboo boxes full of food, herbs, and clothing; and wooden figures. The tomb contained only few bronze artifacts and some ceramic vessels. No jade object had been placed inside.

Journey to Heaven
The painted silk banner that draped the coffins appears to illustrate the journey of the woman's soul. The bottom section shows the underworld. Above that is an earthly scene of the marquise and her attendants. The top section represents heaven, with the sun and the moon, and their symbol animals, raven and toad.

Exquisite Coffin
The marquise was buried in five nested coffins, each decorated with elaborate lacquerwork. After studying the well-preserved mummy, scientists determined that she had died at about 50 years of age.

AD 500

0

500 BC

1000 BC

Dead Sea Scrolls

- Ancient Hebrew scrolls including earliest known Old Testament books
- Dated to c. 150 BC–AD 135
- First scrolls accidentally discovered in 1947, others found later
- Finds include religious and secular texts
- Exhibits at the Khirbet Qumran settlement, in Israel/Palestine

The Dead Sea Scrolls are a legend of archaeological discovery, featuring a young shepherd boy who scrambled up a cliff to look for gold in a cave, only to find ancient Hebrew scrolls. More deliberate searches after 1947 turned up ancient manuscripts in dozens of caves in the rugged Judean Desert. The scrolls—comprising rolls of parchment, papyrus, and, in one case, copper—bear religious texts, administrative records, legal documents, and personal letters in Hebrew, Aramaic, Greek, and Nabataean, dated mainly to roughly 100 BC–AD 100.

Like many of the scrolls, those retrieved from 11 caves near Khirbet Qumran were hidden during the First Jewish Revolt against the Romans in AD 66–70. The Qumran scrolls are religious: canonical and apocryphal books of the Bible, commentaries on these books, hymns, rules for a righteous life, descriptions of the Temple and its activities, an account of apocalyptic battle, and horoscopes.

Excavation of Khirbet Qumran in the 1950s uncovered a walled settlement established during the 2nd century BC and destroyed by Roman legions during the First Jewish Revolt. Since 1947 most scholars have attributed both the scrolls and the settlement to the Essenes—a little-known fundamentalist sect of early Judaism. However, other scholars plausibly argue that the scrolls were removed from Jerusalem to be hidden before the Romans sacked the city in 68 BC, and that Khirbet Qumran was actually an ordinary fortified place. If this idea is correct, then mainstream Judaism still contained considerable diversity during the 1st century AD.

Hiding Spots
The cave-riddled cliffs that line the western shore of the Dead Sea have yielded dozens of ancient documents stored in pottery jars. The scrolls appear to have been deliberately hidden in the caves.

Subject Matter
Scrolls and scroll fragments found at Qumran and in many other caves in the Judean Desert belong to two main types. Some, like the Qumran scrolls, are religious, containing books of the Bible or biblical commentary. Others—administrative records and legal documents, letters and the like—have a secular character.

0
500 BC
1000 BC

Masada

- Herodian palace and fortress during the Jewish Revolt
- Dated from 1st century BC to 1st century AD
- Excavated during the 1960s
- Finds include Hebrew scroll, wall paintings
- Site on public display; finds in Israel Museum, Jerusalem

The high plateau of the citadel of Masada dominates the southern end of the Dead Sea. The dramatic location was made famous by the long siege of its Jewish occupants by a Roman army after the destruction of the city of Jerusalem in AD 70. When it was excavated in the 1960s, the site became a focus of national identity for the young state of Israel.

Visitors can still reach the plateau by climbing the steep Roman siege ramp on the west side—the wood used in its construction has been preserved by the dry air of the desert. The historian Josephus was a commander in the Jewish revolt until his capture. He recorded that just before the ramp was completed, the entire garrison—men, women, and children—committed suicide. The Roman siege works, consisting of a series of forts and a near continuous wall (except in the most craggy of spots), are a reminder of the organization of the Roman army even in such an inhospitable and arid setting.

On a series of terraces on the northern crag of the plateau, King Herod the Great had earlier built a complex palace, its levels connected by spiral staircases cut into the rock face and hidden from view. This palace was built using classical architecture and decorated with Roman-style wall paintings. Huge cisterns, fed by aqueducts that collected winter rain, were cut into the low part of the plateau. Herod had intended this to be a winter palace that could also serve as a refuge in time of trouble.

Natural Defenses
The rock of Masada is a natural fortress that rises from the Dead Sea. Once the site of King Herod's palace, it became the last stronghold of the Jews against the Romans in the 1st century AD.

Northern Palace
King Herod the Great built his northern palace on three terraces at the rock's tip. A second ornate palace was built on Masada's western edge, along with fortifications such as heavy walls and defensive towers.

Waterworks
Herod's complex featured two bathhouses—a small, private one in his northern palace, and a large, elaborate bathhouse made up of several rooms for guests and officials.

AD 500
0
500 BC
1000 BC

Borobudur

- Vast pyramidal Buddhist temple complex
- Constructed c. AD 775–830 by the Javanese Sailendra Dynasty
- First encountered by Europeans in 1814
- Some looting has occurred, but most freestanding and relief sculptures remain on display in situ

The great Buddhist shrine of Borobudur in central Java was begun around AD 775 and reached its present form around 830. The creation of the Sailendra Dynasty, who briefly controlled a kingdom extending into mainland Southeast Asia, the shrine was initially a stepped pyramid surmounted by a vast stupa (dome). Its base was decorated with bas-reliefs illustrating the lowest level of the Buddist cosmos—the world of the senses where the individual is ensnared by human desires. Later, a massive platform built to reinforce the structure encased and hid these reliefs. The huge stupa was also removed and the upper portion of the monument reconceived.

Five square tiers linked by staircases lead the worshiper up through galleries surmounted by small stupas, past niches containing statues of Buddhas. Relief scenes along the gallery walls illustrate the middle level in the Buddhist cosmos, along with scenes from the life of the Buddha and his former incarnations, and from the lifelong quest for knowledge of the Buddhist devotee Sudhana. Emerging from these closed-in and highly decorated levels, the worshiper reaches three circular terraces. Here, circles of fretwork stupas set around a central stupa enclose statues of Buddhas eternally meditating. Open to the air and without external distractions, this symbolizes the upper level of the cosmos, where one may gain enlightenment, finally free from earthly desires and perceptions. Borobudur is a complex and magnificent monument with many layers of meaning. Its construction would have been seen as a supreme way of acquiring spiritual merit, both for its sponsoring kings and for the ordinary individuals who worked on it.

Restored Monument
Until archaeological efforts began in the early 20th century, the temple was partly buried in jungle and its foundations were waterlogged. In 1973 UNESCO launched a massive restoration project that lasted 10 years and cost about $25 million.

Detailed Carving
Stories from the life of Buddha are illustrated on this relief panel. The soft, naturalistic carving style is unique to Borobudur.

Meditating Sculpture
Serene seated Buddhas (left) grace niches and stupas on the various levels of the Borobudur temple.

AD 2000
AD 1500
AD 1000
AD 500
0

Angkor Thom

- A huge Khmer city with complex of temples, palaces, and terraces
- Mostly dated to late 12th century AD
- Always known in Cambodia, but first seen by Europeans in 16th century, and made known by French publications in 1860s
- Carvings in many museums, especially the Musée Guimet, Paris

Cambodia's great city of Angkor Thom, 900 hectares (9 sq. km) in area, was founded by the ruler Jayavarman VII, and probably remained the Khmer capital until the 17th century. The walls of the city form a square of 1.8 miles (3 km) per side and are pierced by four great monumental gates. Each gate is 75 feet (23 m) high, features a tower carved with four faces pointing north, south, east, and west, and is approached by an impressive avenue lined with carved gods and demons carrying a giant serpent across the moat.

The complex within the city walls includes many temples from various centuries, with the four entrance roads converging at the Bayon. One of the greatest monuments of the whole Angkor complex, the Bayon probably started out as a Hindu monument, but was converted to a Buddhist sanctuary before its completion sometime between the late 12th and early 13th centuries. It is renowned for its 54 towers, each with four smiling faces of an Avalokitesvara (a future Buddha), and its remarkable bas-reliefs depicting scenes of daily life and of events in Khmer history such as great naval battles. To the north of the Bayon stands the great carved Elephant Terrace, 10 feet (3 m) high and 300 yards (300 m) long, as well as numerous smaller temples.

Temple Ruins
Angkor Thom features the ruins of the Bayon and many other temples but few residential structures. The city's population probably lived in wooden and thatch houses that have since vanished.

Carved Warriors
The magnificent bas-relief carvings of the Bayon display great vigor in their depiction of historical events, such as battles (right), and scenes from everyday life.

Buddhist Deity
Gracing one of the Bayon's 54 towers, this sculpture depicts an Avalokitesvara, the Buddhist deity who protects against shipwreck, fire, robbers, assassins, and wild beasts.

AD 2000
AD 1500
AD 1000
AD 500
0

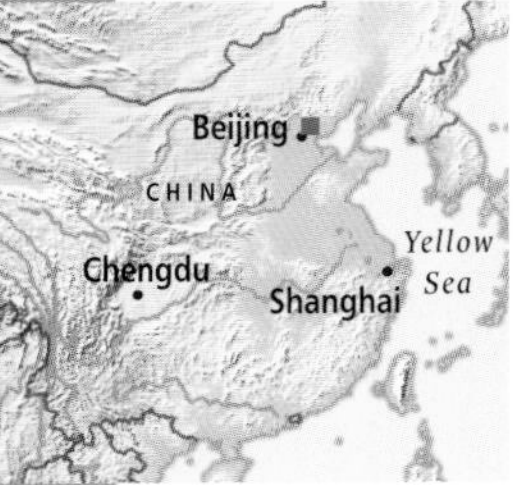

Ming Tombs

- Largest imperial cemetery in China
- Dated to Ming Dynasty, AD 1409–1584
- Royal Ming tombs excavated from 1956 to present day
- Finds include gold crown, gold and silver jewelry, jade, porcelain
- Three tombs open to the public

In the long tradition of rich burials for the Chinese emperors, the mausoleums of the Ming royalty (1368–1644) are outstanding. Thirteen Ming emperors are buried over an area of 15 square miles (40 sq. km) in the hilly terrain outside Beijing. Construction of the tombs started in 1409 and ended with the fall of the Ming dynasty. Each tomb is located at the foot of a separate hill and is linked to the other tombs by a road called the Spirit Path. A richly decorated stone archway at the head of the path is one of the best preserved specimens of its kind in China. Inside the gate, the path is lined with 18 pairs of enormous stone statues of humans and animals.

At each tomb, a sacrificial hall and stela pavilion lead to the burial mound, which contains an underground palace for the deceased. To date, only three tombs have been excavated. Dingling, the tomb of the 13th emperor and his two empresses, was completed in six years (1584–90). Because the aboveground architecture had been destroyed in 1644, it was only by chance that archaeologists could locate the tomb's entrance in 1956. The underground palace consists of five chambers: the antechamber with three marble thrones, two side chambers for the empresses, and the main chamber, which contained three wooden coffins as well as 26 chests filled with precious grave goods. In 1987 the Ming tombs were declared a UNESCO World Heritage site.

An Imperial Tomb
At the Dingling Tomb, ritual buildings lead the way to the underground burial chambers of the emperor Wanli (reigned 1573–1619) and his two empresses. Wanli paid the enormous sum of 250 tons (227 tonnes) of silver for the tomb's construction.

Underground Palace
The central chamber of the Dingling Tomb contains marble thrones and fine Ming vessels. More than 3,000 artifacts have been recovered from the tomb, the most precious being the golden crowns of the emperor and his queen.

The Spirit Path
Grand stone statues line the Spirit Path that leads to the tombs. The human figures represent different kinds of officials, while the animals include elephants, lions, camels, horses, unicorns, and griffins.

AD 2000
AD 1000
AD 500
0

Sites and Treasures of Oceania

From the world's oldest cremation to the pottery of the Lapita culture, the immense stone statues of Easter Island, and the remains of one of New Zealand's earliest settlements, the archaeological discoveries of Oceania have helped to establish the antiquity of Australia's settlement and the pattern of colonization throughout the Pacific.

"In Easter Island ... the shadows of the departed builders still possess the land ... the whole air vibrates with a vast purpose and energy which has been and is no more."

Katherine Routledge (1866–1935), English ethnographer

Lake Mungo

- Site of Mungo Lady, world's oldest cremation
- Cremation dated to about 23,000 BC
- Mungo Lady discovered in 1969 by Jim Bowler
- Nearby finds include many living sites and burials
- Interpretive displays at Lake Mungo Visitor's Centre

In 1969 environmental scientist Jim Bowler, from the Australian National University, was studying ancient climates in the Willandra Lakes area of far west New South Wales and came across burnt bones eroding from dunes at Lake Mungo. He thought the bones might belong to a kangaroo, but they proved to be the remains of a young woman, perhaps 19 years old. She had been cremated on the shores of Lake Mungo about 25,000 years ago. Her bones were then gathered and smashed, and finally interred in a small pit. Bowler had found the world's oldest evidence of ritual cremation.

Mungo Lady was a startling find at a time when archaeologists had only recently demonstrated Ice Age occupation of Australia. In 1974 a second remarkable burial was found nearby. The body of a 50-year-old man had been laid in a shallow grave and covered with red ocher. At the time, archaeologists thought this burial was about 30,000 years old, but recent studies of the bones and the surrounding sediments suggest that it is actually much older, perhaps dating to about 60,000 BC.

The discoveries at Lake Mungo firmly established the dispersal of fully modern humans into Australia and provided rare insights into ancient beliefs. Surveys and excavations have continued there ever since, and human remains, the bones of extinct animals, and living sites continue to be discovered. These finds provide a detailed picture of Aboriginal adaptation to changing environments over the last 40,000 years and more. The remains of Mungo Lady were returned to the custody of local Aboriginal people in 1992.

Dry Lake
A crescent-shaped dune known as the Walls of China borders the shore of dried-up Lake Mungo, in western New South Wales.

Shellfish Supper
Piles of discarded shells from freshwater shellfish testify to a time when a wet Lake Mungo provided a rich food supply to the area's Aboriginal people.

YEARS AGO
20,000
30,000
40,000
50,000

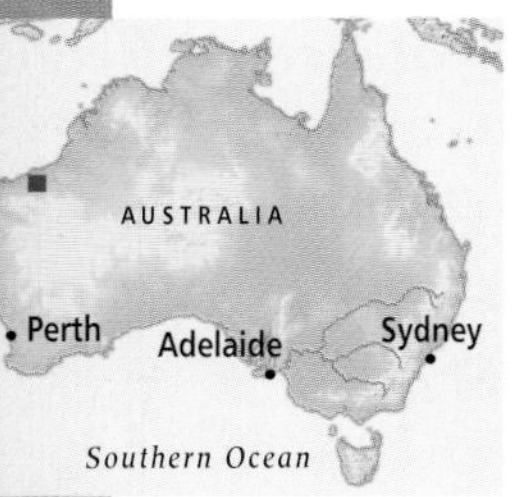

Pilbara Petroglyphs

- Spectacular collection of images pecked and engraved into rocks
- Undated, but definitely prehistoric
- Spear Hill Complex discovered in 1982 by Howard McNickle
- Small display on Pilbara rock art, with casts and original petroglyphs, in the Western Australian Museum, Perth

Pilbara is by far the richest petroglyph area of Australia, with hundreds of thousands or maybe millions of figures. What was christened the Spear Hill Complex by its discoverer, Howard McNickle, comprises an area of great granite rocks, outcrops, and hills. In all, he numbered 28 sites—with Spear Hill itself as Site 1—but some of these are enormous and could easily be subdivided.

Although a few rock paintings can be seen in shelters and overhangs, the vast majority of figures are petroglyphs—images made by pecking away the rock's dark surface, or patina, to expose the lighter, almost golden rock beneath. The contrast in color produces some very striking images, visible from a great distance. There are some very elaborate panels featuring stylized human figures; speared animals (often kangaroos) and birds (mostly emus); flying creatures; hunting scenes; tracks of humans, animals, and birds; and many geometric and abstract patterns. The sexual organs are sometimes exaggerated on the human figures, and one or two of them are drawn in an X-ray style, with something of their internal anatomy being shown.

Most of the images were placed on and around vertical rock faces, but some occur on fragile horizontal rock "pavements" that crack if walked upon, making their study a very delicate matter. Unfortunately, there is virtually no traditional information available to explain the meaning or significance of this gallery of images, since no knowledge relating to them has been handed down to the present-day Pilbara Aboriginal people. Although all the petroglyphs remain undated, archaeologists have determined that they are undoubtedly prehistoric, and some—especially those where a dark patination has re-formed—are probably of great antiquity.

Speared Animals
One of the petroglyphs at Site 19 at Spear Hill shows an emu and a kangaroo, apparently speared. More than half of the animals depicted at Spear Hill have spears in them or are being wounded by boomerangs, which underlines the paramount importance of hunting in this culture.

Split Rock
A huge boulder at Site 5 in the Spear Hill Complex features petroglyphs of human-like figures. A natural cause, such as lightning, split the rock at some time after the art was produced.

10,000
YEARS AGO
?
20,000
30,000
40,000
50,000

Lake Condah

- Well-preserved complex of inland fish traps and Aboriginal dwellings
- Age uncertain: probably about 2000 BC to 19th century AD
- Victoria Archaeological Survey began recording in 1977
- Finds include pre-contact and historic Aboriginal sites
- Display at Aboriginal Keeping Place, Hamilton, Victoria

Lake Condah, in Victoria, Australia, is part of a large wetland complex, formed about 25,000 BC by lava flows from the eruption of Mount Eccles. Local Aboriginal people later took advantage of the rich resources of the wetlands, and seem to have lived at least semipermanently by the lake. The rocky volcanic landscape meant that they often built partly in stone rather than in wood or bark, so their structures are unusually well preserved.

The most remarkable remains at Lake Condah are those of the stone channels, weirs, and traps that formed a large, complex system for catching eels and other fish. The local Aborigines built the channels and weirs to manage and direct water flow and must have had a detailed practical understanding of seasonal changes in lake levels. Eels and other fish could be kept in ponds and then trapped through gaps in the weirs. The age of the system is unknown, although some traps visible today would have been well above the water level 4,000 years ago. This suggests the traps were built more recently, although older ones may be buried under lake sediments. The system probably grew in size and complexity through many generations. It was abandoned soon after Europeans first settled in Victoria in the 1840s. Led by Peter Coutts, the Victoria Archaeological Survey began studying the complex in 1977.

There are hundreds of other stone structures situated around Lake Condah. A hut foundation was excavated in 1981. Other structures may be windbreaks or hunting blinds.

Circular Structure
Among the hundreds of finds around Lake Condah is this circular stone structure, shown here under excavation in 1981.

Channel and Pond
Rising floodwaters pass through a narrow channel into this shallow pond, which was once part of a fish-trap system.

Fish Trap
Woven funnel baskets (left) were strategically placed along the low walls of V-shaped or barrier-type fish traps. Flood waters carrying fish were forced through the narrow opening into the basket, where the fish would be trapped.

0
2500 BC
5000 BC
7500 BC
10,000 BC

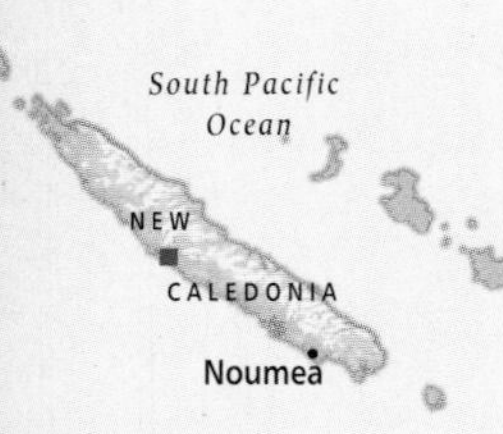

Lapita

- Type site of the Lapita cultural complex
- Dated to 1st millennium BC
- Discovered in 1910 by geologist Maurice Piroutet
- Finds include beachfront midden containing shell, bone, and pottery
- Artifacts in National Museum, Noumea

In 1910 French geologist Maurice Piroutet discovered pottery sherds with distinctive stamped decoration at the Fouè Peninsula on the west coast of the main island of New Caledonia. In 1952 the U.S. archaeologists Gifford and Shutler excavated the site, which they named Lapita. They recognized the similarities between pottery from Lapita and from other sites throughout the Pacific, from Watom Island (off New Britain) to Tonga. As a result, they were able to identify the enigmatic Lapita style associated with the first human settlers of Melanesia, much of Polynesia, and parts of Micronesia. The Lapita sites were linked by long-distance trading networks.

During their excavations, Gifford and Shutler found midden deposits dating to about 850 BC. These contained animal bone, shell, and pottery and occurred along a south-facing beach covering an area at least 400 by 30 yards (400 x 30 m). The beach location is typical of Lapita sites—others have evidence of structures built on piles over the water.

Small-scale surveys over the next few decades revealed more of the site and its stratigraphy. Large-scale modern excavations were finally carried out as salvage missions in 1994 and 1995, when the best preserved part of the site was about to be disturbed by the construction of an aquaculture complex. The extremely rich archaeological deposit that was uncovered included a pit containing an extraordinary collection of sherds and two virtually complete pots. Altogether, more than 15 pots have been reconstructed. This is the first time such complete vessels have been found on any Lapita site.

Lapita Design
These three sherds of Lapita pottery (left, right, and below right) were excavated from the site of Kamgot, on Babase Island about 37 miles (60 km) off the coast of New Ireland, Papua New Guinea. They have been dated to about 1300–1200 BC, the time of the area's earliest Lapita settlements. The stamped decoration is typical of the elaborate designs found on Lapita pottery throughout the Pacific.

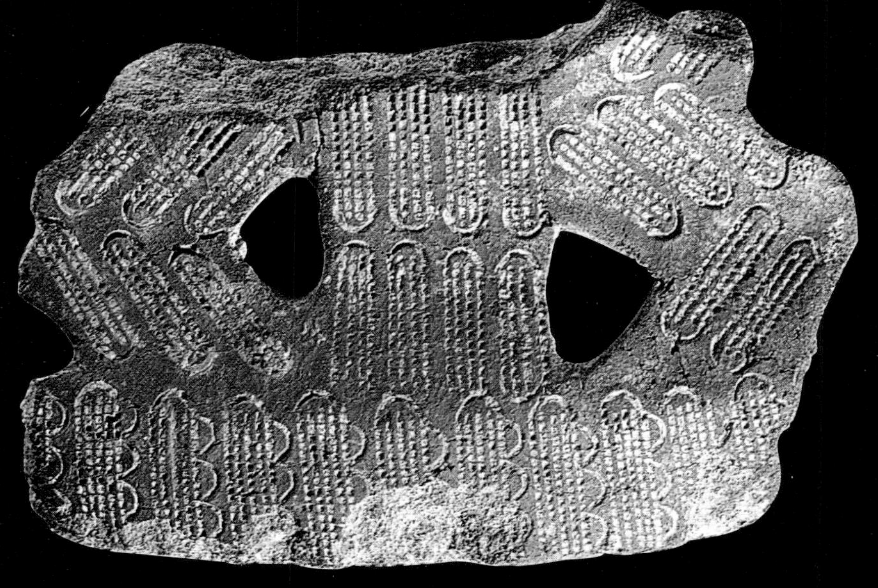

AD 500

0

500 BC

Easter Island Statues

- One of the most spectacular Stone Age cultures in the world
- Dated to c. AD 1000–1500
- First known discovery by Westerners made on Easter Sunday, 1722
- Most statues still in situ, with many re-erected on platforms; single statues in museums in Chile, London, Brussels, Paris

The first known Western visitors to what was baptised Easter Island, in 1722, were astounded—as were all subsequent visitors—by the huge stone statues that ringed the volcanic island. The island is small, with an area of only 66 square miles (171 sq. km), and the prehistoric inhabitants had erected stone platforms (ahu) around its perimeter, eventually setting up statues of ancestor figures (moai) on them. The numbers varied, but Tongariki, the biggest such platform, held no less than 15 giant statues.

Many moai probably remain undiscovered, buried in the sediments that envelop the sides of the Rano Raraku crater where they were quarried, but it is reckoned that between 800 and 1,000 were made. The statues were carved from a soft volcanic rock known as tuff. They are all variations on a theme, ending at the abdomen and featuring elongated heads, arms held tightly at the sides, and long fingers meeting at a stylized loincloth. The ears are sometimes lengthened and perforated. The moai range in height from 6 to 30 feet (2 to 10 m) and weigh up to 82 tons (75 tonnes). They were carved at the quarry with hard basalt picks, thousands of which have been found at the site along with hundreds of statues in every stage of production.

More than 230 finished statues were transported to the ahu and set up on the platforms, always facing the villages protectively, with their backs to the sea. Sometimes, heavy cylindrical "topknots" of scoria, a red lava rock from a quarry at Puna Pau, were raised onto their heads. Eyes of white coral with a pupil of obsidian (black volcanic glass) were inserted into the sockets for certain ceremonies. Later strife on the island—caused primarily by food shortages triggered by the islanders' destruction of the original bird population and tree-cover—led to all the statues being toppled by the middle of the 19th century.

Standing Guard
Many of the statues have now been restored and returned to their ahu. Thought to represent ancestral chiefs, the moai face inland to overlook and protect the villages.

Work in Progress
In and around the quarry of Ranu Raraku, about 400 unfinished statues in every stage of manufacture were mysteriously abandoned by their makers.

Decorated Giant
The most prestigious statues were given eyes of white coral with obsidian pupils and great cylindrical topknots of red scoria.

AD 2000

AD 1500

AD 1000

AD 500

0

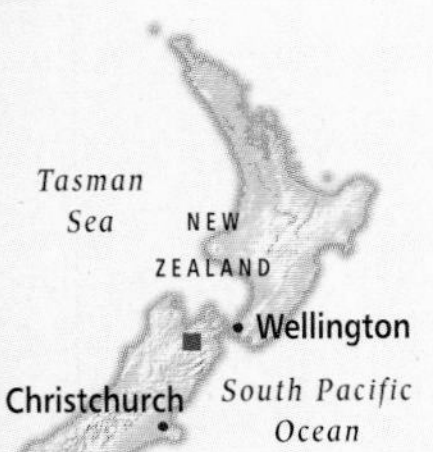

Wairau Bar

- Burial site and settlement; one of the oldest sites in New Zealand
- Dated to late 13th century AD
- Discovered in 1930s by Jim Eyles
- Finds include more than 40 burials, rich grave goods, occupation areas
- Collections in the Canterbury Museum, New Zealand

Wairau Bar is one of the oldest and richest sites in New Zealand. Located at the north end of the South Island, it was discovered in the 1930s by Jim Eyles. Roger Duff's major excavations there in the 1940s produced a series of rich burials and evidence of habitation. Several other archaeologists have excavated parts of the site since then.

Excavating the Site
Wairau Bar on the South Island of New Zealand was discovered by Jim Eyles in 1938. Since its first major excavation, in the 1940s, several archaeologists, including this 1964 team, have investigated the early site.

Duff defined his "Moa-hunter" Period of New Zealand archaeology on the basis of his finds at Wairau Bar (the now-extinct moa were very large flightless birds). Although his terminology is no longer used, the material culture from the site still defines the Archaic Phase in New Zealand. The artifacts resemble those from sites elsewhere in eastern Polynesia.

There are three distinct burial areas at Wairau Bar, with more than 40 graves. Grave goods include moa eggs and joints, stone adzes (cutting tools), and necklaces and pendants fashioned from whale ivory and moa bone. Features such as postholes and ovens indicate the main settlement. Large numbers of moa bones were found at the site. These have been conservatively estimated to represent the remains of 8,733 moa. Other species found include fur seal, dolphin, dog, and the extinct swan, as well as fish and shellfish.

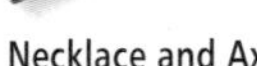

Necklace and Ax
The artifacts recovered from Wairau Bar include a chunky necklace made from reel-shaped pieces of moa-bone units and a sperm-whale tooth (left) and a huge argillite axhead (below left).

Wairau Bar was occupied in the late 13th century AD, just decades after the first humans arrived in New Zealand. New dating evidence suggests that the occupation was very brief, perhaps even as short as 20 years. This, along with other early sites with similar features, suggests that the earliest colonists in New Zealand targeted large game and moved their settlements frequently, whenever local resources were depleted.

AD 2000
AD 1500
AD 1000
AD 500
0

Sites and Treasures of

The Americas

The rich past of the New World is revealed through the abandoned cliff dwellings of the Anasazi and the extensive Great Serpent burial mound in North America; the Maya pyramids and the Aztec temples in Central America; and the Inca ruins of Machu Picchu and the remarkable Nasca lines in South America.

"Beneath the trees were the ruins of an Inka temple, flanking and partly enclosing the gigantic granite boulder, one end of which overhung a small pool of running water … There was not a hut to be seen; scarcely a sound to be heard. It was an ideal place for practicing the mystic ceremonies of an ancient cult."

Hiram Bingham (1878–1956),
U.S. historian who rediscovered Machu Picchu

Monte Verde

- One of the earliest occupation sites in the New World
- Dated to at least 14,700 years ago, possibly up to 33,000 years ago
- Discovered by a team from the Southern University of Chile in 1976
- Nothing to see now at the excavation site; the finds are at the Universidad Austral de Chile, Valdivia

For many years, a myth held sway in archaeology that the New World was first entered and occupied only about 11,000 or 12,000 years ago by groups of hunters who exploited mammoths and other big game with impressive stone-tipped weapons. The site of Monte Verde in Chile, excavated in the 1970s and 1980s by a team led by U.S. archaeologist Tom Dillehay, has played a major role in shattering that myth by revealing the existence of people in southern Chile at an earlier date (perhaps up to 33,000 years ago) who were not living off big game.

Bones from large Ice Age animals, some bearing traces of butchery, were first found in a creek at Monte Verde in 1975 by a local family. Ironically, it was these big game bones that led archaeologists to investigate the site further. They discovered that peat had preserved a remarkable range of organic materials, including wooden tools, the remains of nearly 70 species of plants (including chewed leaves), and bits of meat and hide. These finds produce a picture of an advanced community of hunter-gatherers, living by a stream in a dozen timber structures, and carrying out domestic tasks and eating a very varied diet that relied far more on plants and small game than on large animals. Their diet included seeds, nuts, fruits, berries, and tubers. The houses contained small clay-lined pits for holding hot coals that were probably used for both cooking and heating. One remarkable structure, shaped something like a wishbone and set apart from the houses, was associated with plants with medicinal qualities, which suggests a special or possibly ritual function.

Traces of Shelter
Architectural foundations at the Monte Verde site indicate that 12 or so semirectangular huts once stood here. Pole frames were also excavated, some with fragments of skins still clinging to them.

Shattering myths
These remains of a mastodon and a paleo-llama, found at the Monte Verde site, have been dated at 12,000–13,000 BC. It was finds like these that changed theories about human habitation of the New World.

The Earliest Tools
The stone tools recovered from Monte Verde date back to at least 14,700 years ago, providing evidence of a hunting-gathering culture that preceded the big-game hunters of the Clovis culture by 2,000 years or more.

20,000

30,000

40,000

50,000

Head-Smashed-In

- One of the oldest and best preserved buffalo kill sites
- Dated from 5,700 years ago to the 19th century
- First excavated in 1938 by Junius Bird
- Finds include many bone deposits, projectile points, and other artifacts
- Displays in the Head-Smashed-In Interpretive Center at the site

For thousands of years, the Plains Indians of North America hunted the bison, or buffalo, and obtained from this animal most of the fundamentals of survival, using its meat, hide, bone, and sinew. Early on, Indians decided to take advantage of the bison's herding instincts and devised so-called catastrophic kills, in which sometimes hundreds of animals would be stampeded to their death. Indians drove the bison into arroyos (gullies), into specially constructed corrals or pounds, and, perhaps most spectacularly, over cliffs. The cliff stampedes are called buffalo jumps.

Buffalo Jump
The Plains Indians utilized the natural features of the Head-Smashed-In site, forcing herds of bison to stampede over the cliffs. This sort of communal kill required great planning and patience and involved hundreds of hunters.

One of the most intensively studied and best preserved buffalo jumps is the Head-Smashed-In site on the eastern edge of the Porcupine Hills of southern Alberta, Canada. Like most others, it was used in autumn when the bison were in their prime. The first component of the site is a series of natural gathering basins, where small groups of animals were slowly herded. The animals were then stampeded between drive lanes—long lines of stone cairns extending back almost 10 miles (16 km) to the gathering basin. These lanes funneled the herd into a small jump area, a section of cliff steep enough to either kill or incapacitate the animals. At the bottom of the cliff is a series of bone beds, many feet in thickness, the remains of the kill itself. Adjacent to the jump area is the camp-site and processing area. Here, Indians camped, butchered the carcasses, and processed the meat for transportation.

Bison Remains
The Head-Smashed-In Interpretive Center displays some of the thousands of bison skulls that have been excavated from the site.

0
7500 BC
10,000 BC

Olmec Colossal Heads

- The earliest sculpted monuments known from Mesoamerica
- Dated to Formative Period, *c.* 1200–400 BC
- First Olmec heads discovered in the 1920s by Matthew Stirling
- Many Olmec sculptures were removed during construction work and are now on display in an archaeological park in Villahermosa, Tabasco

Olmec colossal heads are huge monolithic sculptures carved from volcanic rock, and varying in height from 5 to 11 feet (1.5–3.4 m), and in weight from 6 to 50 tons (5.5–45.5 tonnes). They represent what is at once the most enigmatic and the least common archaeological remnant of Olmec culture. Only 16 heads are known in total, with ten from San Lorenzo (*c.* 900 BC–AD 1200), four from La Venta (*c.* 900–400 BC), and two from Tres Zapotes (*c.* 100 BC–AD 500).

Geologists have determined that all of the heads were quarried from basalt sources in the Tuxtla Mountains, located some 62 miles (100 km) from La Venta. This is a convincing argument for complex sociopolitical organization. Olmec rulers must have been able to command hundreds, if not thousands, of laborers to quarry, transport, and carve these gigantic stones.

While clearly belonging to one and the same tradition, the heads betray at least three strong regional styles. They all have flat noses and thick lips, but each is clearly the portrait of an individual. Moreover, the heads all wear leather helmets of the type common in a Mesoamerican ballgame which was played largely by nobles and kings, and which was tied closely to mesoamerican concepts of kingly conduct. James Porter has observed that some of the heads are themselves recarved from the monolithic thrones of various Olmec rulers, suggesting that the gigantic heads possibly represent those same rulers in death.

Colossal Head
Believed to be portraits of Olmec rulers, the massive heads are the most distinctive works of art produced by the early Mesoamerican culture.

Crying Baby
The Olmec style is evident in many smaller sculptures, including this hollow figurine of a crying baby. The style eventually spread throughout Mesoamerica, probably due to intensive Olmec influence in the form of trade and conquest.

0

2500 BC

5000 BC

7500 BC

10,000 BC

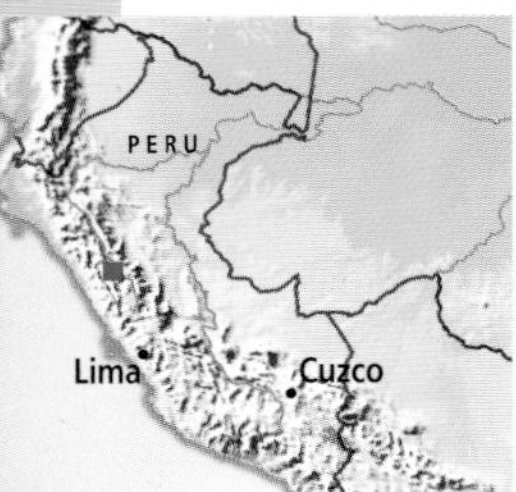

Chavín

- Center of an art style and religious cult that spread through the Andes
- Dated to c. 900–200 BC; major occupation c. 400 BC
- Scientific discovery made in 1920s by Julio C. Tello
- Finds include stone temples, stone sculptures, distinctive artifacts
- Site may be visited; artifacts in Museo de la Nación, Lima

Chavín de Huantar is a major archaeological site known for its architecture, underground passageways, large stone carvings, and iconography, as well as for its early age. Its significance lies in the wide influence of Chavín art and iconography, which spread throughout much of the central Andes during the 1st millennium BC. Located in the Andean highlands between two rivers along a major trade route from the coast to the eastern tropical forests, Chavín appears to have controlled early trade between the two regions. The architecture of the site is clearly influenced by the structure of earlier sites on the coast of Peru, but the iconography, which includes jaguars, monkeys, and serpents, appears more closely linked to the jungles to the east.

The site of Chavín de Huantar covers approximately 12 acres (42 ha) and features a temple complex of roughly 12 acres (5 ha), as well as a domestic area that may have housed as many as 3,000 inhabitants. The temple complex consists of the U-shaped Old Temple and the central pyramid, or New Temple. The Old Temple, made of carved stone blocks, contains numerous interior rooms or galleries connected by a complex of passages, stairways, and drains. Inside the galleries, carved stone monoliths depict various gods, with a 15 foot (4.5 m) monolith known as the Lanzón showing what may have been the central deity, the Smiling God.

Smiling God
Inside the Old Temple at Chavín de Huantar, a stone monolith is carved with an image of the Smiling God, which may have been the central deity.

Cat Pendant
This gold pendant from Chavín shows a seated cat. The two halves of the pendant and the head and ears were made separately and then welded together.

Musical Shaman
This hollow ceramic figure depicts a flute player wearing a jaguar headdress. The facial tattoos indicate that he is a shaman, who would have used music to induce hallucinations and summon spirits.

AD 500

0

1000 BC

The Lines of Nasca

- Most visible monument of ancient Nasca civilization
- Dated to c. AD 100–700
- Probably known to locals long ago; observed from air in 1920s
- Finds comprise giant figures and lines etched on the desert plain
- Lines can be seen from small aircraft and an observation tower

One of the most remarkable archaeological phenomena anywhere is the Nasca lines, especially the figures made on the Nasca plain between the Nasca and the Ingenio rivers. The figures, including a monkey, a spider, spirals, whales, birds, and a figure known as the needle and thread (probably a weaving implement), are confined to the Nasca plain, while the lines and geometric shapes are found in a much wider area.

Discovered in the pioneering days of commercial flights, the lines received considerable early publicity, but were quickly threatened by development and road building—the Pan American Highway cuts through more than one figure. The lines might never have been preserved had it not been for one woman who passionately protected, studied, and promoted them. Maria Reiche (1903–98) was a German who came to Peru in 1932 to serve as a governess. She became fascinated with the lines, mapping them in detail and developing a theory that they had been used for astronomical observation. Working for years with virtually no funding, often battling to keep vehicles from driving across them, she finally succeeded in drawing enough attention to the lines that they became a major tourist attraction. The Peruvian government eventually declared the Nasca plain completely off limits, even to foot traffic.

Because of their enormous size, the lines are best seen by air, although they are also visible from hills and high places. This has led to intense speculation as to the function of the Nasca lines, as well as why they were built and by whom. Archaeologists have determined that the figures were made by the Nasca culture (see p. 216)—they are stylistically similar to figures seen on Nasca pottery, and direct dating methods have confirmed that they were made during Nasca times.

Nasca Geoglyphs
The figures visible on the Nasca plain include a dog (right) and a hummingbird (below right). Part of a long tradition of geoglyphs (large figures made on the ground), the Nasca lines may have served some kind of astronomical or calendric function, and could have been used for ceremonies or processions.

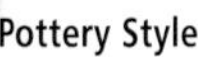

Pottery Style
The style of the lines resembles the figures on Nasca pottery. This large ceramic drum shows three double-headed serpents holding chili peppers.

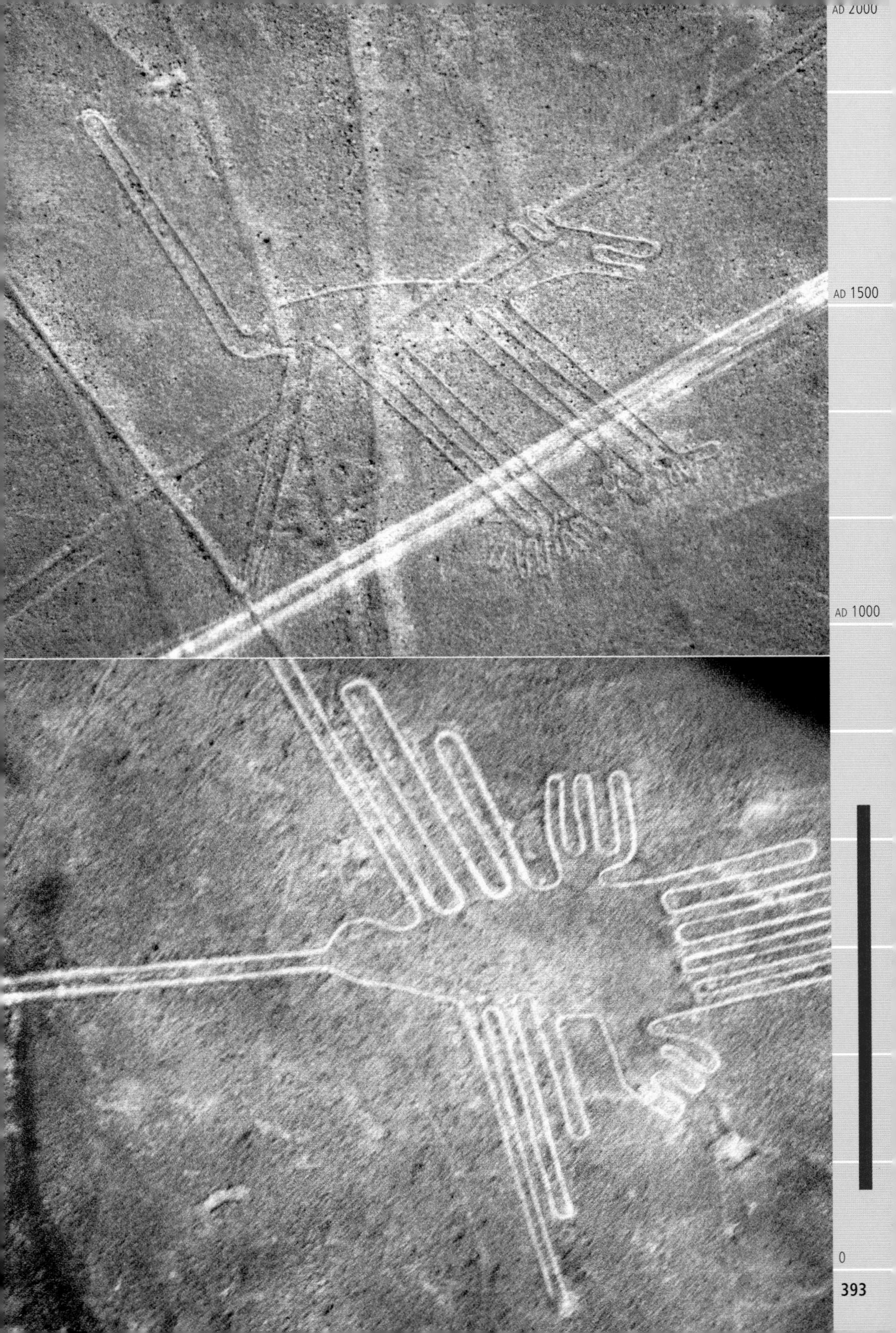
AD 2000
AD 1500
AD 1000
0

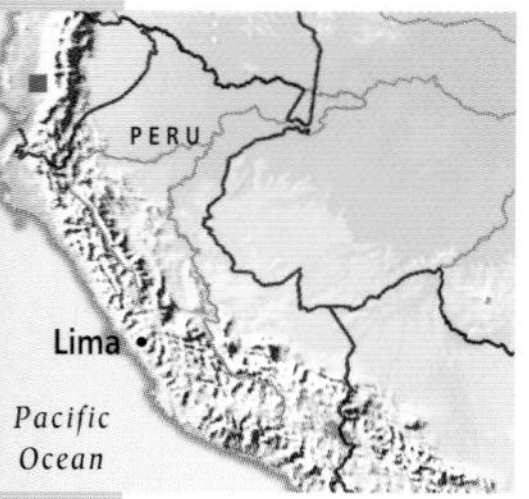

Sipán

- Site of the richest ancient tomb ever found in the Americas
- Dated to Moche culture, AD 100–700
- Site has long been known; major tombs discovered in 1988
- Finds include elaborate ritual regalia
- Site open to public; some finds in site museum

On the night of February 16, 1987, archaeologist Walter Alva was awakened by a call from the local police and asked to identify some remarkable Moche artifacts that had just been seized from a band of looters who were fighting among themselves. Some of these men told Alva that the extraordinary artifacts had come from Sipán. With the help of the police, Alva was able to begin studying the site (only after some tense standoffs with local residents, who wanted to keep looting), and what he eventually found became one of the most important archaeological discoveries of recent years—a series of tombs that were larger and richer than any seen before in the Americas. Alva's meticulous and painstaking excavations of the tombs allowed the exact reconstruction of the burials and the detailed study of the artifacts and the technology, and eventually revealed who had been buried in the tombs.

Ritual Regalia
The astonishing array of grave goods buried with the "Sénor (Lord) of Sipán" included feather headdresses, a gold headdress, metal-decorated clothing, royal banners, shell-bead pectorals, gold and silver jewelry, and pottery.

Decades of archaeological research on Peru's north coast had shown that the Moche civilization (see p. 216) had developed intensive irrigation agriculture, ruled vast areas of the coast and inland valleys, built large mud-brick pyramids, and created sophisticated pottery, metalwork, and other crafts, many using exotic goods brought from as far away as the eastern jungles of the Andes. Specialists had identified many important figures in the paintings seen on Moche pottery and architectural friezes, but had never imagined that the figures shown in various rituals were real. The excavations at Sipán showed that they were indeed real, and that real people—those buried in the central tombs of the Sipán pyramid—had dressed as the figures seen in the paintings, and had most likely participated in the very rituals depicted. This groundbreaking work led to similar finds at other sites, revolutionizing the study of the Moche, one of the most remarkable early civilizations of the Americas.

Noble Burials
The burials of two men and three women surrounded the Sénor of Sipán's coffin. One of the men was buried with a dog.

AD 2000
AD 1500
AD 1000
0

Teotihuacán

- Largest urban center in Mesoamerica during Classic Period
- Dated from c. 400 BC to c. AD 700
- Always known as ritual site; excavated by numerous teams since 1890s
- Key ruins include Pyramids of the Moon, Sun, and Feathered Serpent
- Site is open to the public, with several museums on site

Teotihuacán was the largest urban center of Mesoamerica during the Classic Period (AD 200–700), with a population of 150,000, and was in fact one of the largest cities in the world at that time. It was first settled in the Late Formative Period (600–200 BC), and during the Terminal Formative (200 BC–AD 200) it underwent a major urban renewal program to conform to a grid pattern around the Avenue of the Dead.

The Avenue of the Dead stretches more than 1 mile (2 km), oriented at 16 degrees to the east of north, a significant alignment for astronomical reasons. At the northern end of the avenue is the Pyramid of the Moon, at the head of a broad plaza featuring civic-administrative buildings including the Palace of the Feathered Butterfly. Midway along the Avenue is the even larger Pyramid of the Sun. Near the southern extreme is the Citadel, an enclosed plaza surrounded by temple platforms. Within the plaza is the Temple of the Feathered Serpent, and behind this structure were two large residential areas that may have been the primary residence of the city's rulers.

Teotihuacán established a far-flung but poorly understood empire, with its obsidian tools, ceramics, and architectural styles found in many parts of central Mexico and as far southeast as the Maya capitals of Tikal, Copán, and Kaminaljuyu. Yet Teotihuacán came to a dramatic end about AD 700 when its center was burned and abandoned. Occupation continued on the periphery of the city, suggesting that the destruction may have resulted from conflict between the populace and an over-taxing bureaucracy. The collapse of Teotihuacán, however, remains one of the great mysteries of Mesoamerican archaeology.

Avenue of the Dead
Lined with important government buildings, temples, and residential areas, the Avenue of the Dead terminates at the Temple of the Moon.

Panther Mural
Vivid murals, such as the Panther Fresco (below right), decorate some of Teotihuacán's buildings.

Elaborate Facade
A carved stone facade (below) of feathered serpents, seashells, and grotesque heads encircles the pyramidal Temple of the Feathered Serpent.

0
500 BC
1000 BC

Mesa Verde

- The best preserved set of archaeological sites in the United States
- Dated from AD 400 to 1300
- First recognized by Euroamericans in the late 19th century
- Finds include well-preserved organic and inorganic artifacts
- Ruins open to the public; artifacts on display in site museum

Mesa Verde (Spanish for "green table") is located in southwest Colorado where a series of mesas (flat-topped mountains) is dissected by deep canyons. On the mesa tops and in deep overhangs on the canyon walls are hundreds of well-preserved archaeological sites belonging to the Anasazi (ancestral Pueblo) tradition. The most spectacular of the sites, such as Cliff Palace, Spruce Tree House, and Balcony House, date to the 13th century and comprise well-constructed masonry structures, several stories in height. These included houses and storage rooms, as well as circular structures known as kivas, which were used for ceremonial activities.

The dry environment of the Southwest has preserved many organic artifacts, such as pots full of corn, and sandals made from yucca plants. The Anasazi were heavily reliant on the farming of corn, beans, and squash, although they also hunted and gathered a wide variety of natural resources. They are famous for their beautifully decorated pottery.

Together with the rest of the Four Corners region, Mesa Verde was abandoned by the Anasazi toward the end of the 13th century, probably because of drought, although incursions by other Indian groups may also have prompted the move. Its inhabitants traveled to the south and west and became the ancestors of today's Pueblo Indians.

Cliff Dwellers
In about the 13th century, the Anasazi shifted their dwelling sites from the mesa tops to the canyon walls (right). Cliff Palace, the largest of Mesa Verde's cliff dwellings, contained more than 200 rooms.

Basketmakers
The Anasazi were direct descendants of the earlier Basketmaker peoples, who left behind skillful weavings such as this fiber apron (left).

Preserved Artifacts
As well as inorganic objects such as jewelry, the dry environment of Mesa Verde has preserved organic artifacts such as baskets. These pieces (below left) were found in Balcony House.

Chaco Canyon
Another major Anasazi center in the Four Corners region was Chaco Canyon. It contained 13 villages, the largest of which was Pueblo Bonito (right).

AD 2000

AD 1500

0

Tiwanaku

- Major city-state at the center of a series of colonies and outposts
- Center of a state from around AD 500 to 1000
- Known since prehispanic times; visited by the Inca
- Finds include monumental carved stone architecture, stone sculptures
- Site open to the public; artifacts in site museum

The ruins of Tiwanaku gave the 16th century Spanish conquerers an early clue that great civilizations had existed in the Andes before the Inca. Located in Bolivia's high plains at the southern end of Lake Titicaca Basin, Tiwanaku was first built as one of a number of towns with small temples around the shores of the lake. These towns, which relied on herding, hunting, fishing, and some agriculture, shared control of the region until around the year AD 400. At that time, Tiwanaku began to take over, incorporating the other towns into the tightly controlled core region of what became the Tiwanaku state. For the next several hundred years, Tiwanaku would exert profound influence on the south-central Andes, through a mixed strategy of colonization, indirect control, and trading relationships that stretched from the western coast to the eastern jungles of what is now Bolivia, Chile, and Peru.

The core of the ancient city is made up of a series of huge monumental structures. The largest is the Akapana pyramid, a stone-faced terraced mound about 650 feet (200 m) long and 55 feet (17 m) high that contains a central sunken courtyard. Other major constructions include the Kalasaya, a huge raised platform 425 feet (130 m) long, and the T-shaped stepped mound known as the Pumapunku. Perhaps the most famous monuments are the Gateways of the Sun and the Moon, which feature detailed carvings of important deities. With its stone-block architecture and sophisticated engineering, Tiwanaku had a clear influence on the development of later Inca architecture.

Sacred Site
Sculptured heads protrude from a stone wall at Tiwanaku. Such elaborate stone carvings of deities and supernatural creatures, along with the city's ceremonial plazas and pyramids, attracted pilgrims to the site for centuries.

Stone Gateway
The Gateway of the Sun, located on the Kalasaya mound, is carved from a single block of stone.

Colossus
Tiwanaku features a number of monumental stone carvings. This is one of two huge anthropomorphous figures still standing on the Kalasaya mound.

AD 2000
AD 1500
AD 1000
AD 500
0

Temple of the Inscriptions

- Temple containing first and richest Late Classic Maya tomb discovered
- Dated to Late Classic Period, AD 650–700
- Discovered by Mexican archaeologist Alberto Ruz in 1952
- Finds include stucco reliefs, limestone sarcophagus, jade artifacts
- Tomb replica and artifacts are in the Museo Nacional, Mexico City

Palenque's towering Temple of the Inscriptions commands a sweeping view of forest-covered hillocks and northern alluvial plains. It was named for three prominent hieroglyphic panels found inside its upper sanctuary, still the longest inscription to have survived intact from Classic Maya times (*c.* AD 250–900).

For many years, archaeologists thought that the temple foundations were solid, and therefore concealed no hidden treasures. But in 1949 Alberto Ruz discovered a long, rubble-choked stairway leading deep into its interior. Four long, painstaking years later, he discovered a spectacular tomb housing an enormous limestone sarcophagus. This was the final resting place of K'inich Janaahb' Pakal I, greatest of Palenque's kings.

Pakal was born on March 26, AD 603 into a city devastated by warfare. With most of the ruling lineage lost in battle, he became king at the tender age of twelve. In time, however, he was able to stabilize affairs in his ruined capital, and his 68-year reign saw great expansion in the kingdom and the construction of many of the pyramids and palaces that can be seen today.

Pakal died at the age of 80 on August 28, AD 683. His body was painted with cinnabar, adorned with a mosaic jade mask, and interred in his sarcophagus just three days later. Its carved lid bears an elaborate depiction of the king at the moment of rebirth, predicting his resurrection and return.

Stepped Temple
The largest single building at Palenque, the Temple of the Inscriptions rises in nine levels to a height of 79 feet (24 m). Its name comes from three panels of hieroglyphs discovered in its upper sanctuary.

Jade Treasure
Pakal's jade funerary mask (left) was composed of seven parts. Other jade artifacts in the tomb included a diadem, ear ornaments, necklaces, pectorals, wristlets, rings, statuettes, and a belt.

The Name of Pakal
In the Temple of the Inscriptions, Maya hieroglyphs represented the name K'inich Janaahb' Pakal, which roughly translates as "The Great Sun, Waterlily Shield." Pakal ruled Palenque for 68 years, from AD 615 to 683.

AD 2000
AD 1500
AD 1000
AD 500
0

The Cavern of Naj Tunich

- The largest Late Classic pilgrimage center in the Maya lowlands
- Dated to Late Classic Period, largely 8th century AD
- Discovered by Bernabé Pop in 1979 while on a hunting expedition
- Finds include hieroglyphic texts, figural art, masonry tombs, ceramics
- Site is now guarded to protect it from vandalism

The cavern of Naj Tunich—which means "house of stone" in the local Mopan Maya language—is situated at an elevation of about 2,000 feet (600 m), and bites deeply into the limestone hills of southeastern Petén, Guatemala. Accidentally discovered by a local hunter in 1979, the cave was first studied in the early 1980s, and its artifacts, art, and hieroglyphic inscriptions have since been thoroughly documented.

Cave of Life and Death
The mouth of Naj Tunich leads to a series of chambers and galleries decorated by Maya artists. Such caves related to both life and death—in times of drought, they acted as natural wells, while in Maya mythology, they are portals to the underworld.

Caves were associated with the underworld in Maya religious thought, and were therefore the locales of pilgrimage and intensive ritual conducted for ancestors and gods. The intricate painted hieroglyphs and figural art that decorate the walls at Naj Tunich document nobles, sages, and scribes of the local city-states of Ixtutz, Ixkun, and Sacul making pilgrimages to this important shrine.

The cave walls also feature occasional texts recording events of historical import, such as Ixkun's war upon Caracol on August 14, AD 780, or the visit of a lord from distant Calakmul, a great capital some 125 miles (200 km) to the north-northwest. Most of the paintings are associated with large hearths and torches, signaling the encampments of the artists themselves, but some are associated with altars, votive offerings, and the remains of many small fires for the offering of incense.

Numerous pits and four-sided masonry enclosures just within the mouth of the cave were used as tombs. The location of these tombs deep inside the natural mouths of mountains resembled the burials of other Maya nobles within funerary pyramids.

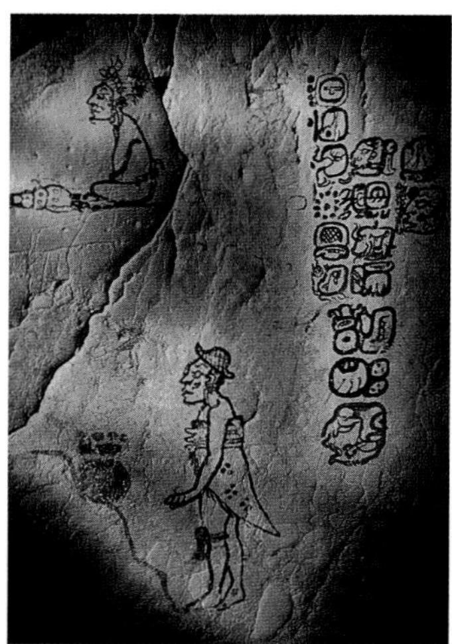

Images from the Underworld
Drawings 21–23 (dated October 14, AD 789 by the hieroglyphic text to the right) depict a musician, his conch shell trumpet before him, quietly contemplating the darkness (top). Meanwhile a size-nine ball rolls down steps to a waiting ballplayer (bottom).

AD 2000
AD 1500
AD 1000
AD 500
0

Cahokia Mounds

- The largest and most complex earthen mound site in North America
- Dated to AD 700–1500
- First EuroAmerican interest in the site was in the early 19th century
- Finds include pottery, stone projectile points, bone tools, grave goods
- Artifacts on display in Interpretive Center at site

Located just east of St Louis, near the confluence of the Mississippi and Missouri rivers, Cahokia comprises more than 100 earthen mounds, used variously as platforms for buildings, as burials, and as boundary markers. The largest, Monk's Mound, covers 14 acres (5.7 ha) and has four terraces rising 100 feet (30 m) above the surrounding land. On top of the mound was a chiefly building, some 50 feet (15 m) high. The nearby site of Woodhenge is a circle of postholes, originally containing upright posts that were used for astronomical predictions.

Named after a local Indian tribe, Cahokia was as close to a city as anything in pre-Columbian North America. Its food supply came from agriculture, no doubt supplemented by hunting, fishing, and gathering. The center of a political network, its trading ties covered thousands of square miles. Almost certainly, its inhabitants were organized into a class society, and a high degree of centralized control would have been needed to organize the removal of the 50 million cubic feet (1.4 million cubic meters) of earth that was used to create the mounds.

Cahokia is just one of the more spectacular mound complexes found throughout the American Midwest and Southeast. Other large complexes include Etowah in Georgia and Moundville in Alabama. These large earthen mound complexes are in fact the culmination of a building tradition that goes back to before the time of Christ. Along the valleys of the Illinois, Ohio, and Mississippi rivers and their tributaries are thousands of smaller earthen mounds that were used as burial markers for important people in ancient Native American society. The Great Serpent Mound, located in Ohio, is an effigy of a serpent with a burial mound in its open mouth. It measures more than 1,330 feet (410 m) long and an average of 3 feet (1 m) high. It may have been built as early as 700 BC, although recent analyses suggest a date of AD 1000.

Monk's Mound
The largest artificial earthen mound in North America, the Monk's Mound complex originally featured a chiefly building and was surrounded by a palisade of upright timbers.

Giant Snake
Created by the Adena/Hopewell culture, the long earthen snake of Great Serpent Mound appears to hold an egg in its mouth.

Cahokia House
A model thatched hut is displayed at the Cahokia Mounds State Historic Site. The houses of Cahokia were arranged in rows and around open plazas.

AD 2000
AD 1500
AD 500
0

L'Anse aux Meadows

- Oldest European settlement in the New World
- Dated to AD 1000
- Discovered in 1960 by Helge and Anne Stine Ingstad
- Finds include a variety of Norse domestic artifacts
- Interpretive Center, reconstructed site, and artifacts on display

Although the majority of people seem to think of Christopher Columbus as the first European to visit the New World, in fact, the Vikings of Scandinavia provide the first good evidence for such contact. Sporadic remains of their visits have been found as far west as northern Quebec, but the most spectacular and best documented example is the remains of the Norse village of L'Anse aux Meadows, located on Epaves Bay, on the northern coast of Newfoundland. This site represents the oldest European settlement in the New World, and is all that remains of the famous exploration voyages of Leif Erikson, son of Erik the Red, and his colonization of a land referred to in the Norse sagas as Vinland. The sagas tell of Erik the Red's AD 986 journey to Greenland, where he established a settlement of a few thousand Vikings. Leif Erikson then continued moving west, finally reaching the coasts of Baffin Island and Labrador, and then sailing south to a land he called Vinland.

The location of the site was probably chosen to allow exploration of the adjacent coast, both north and south, for further settlement and colonization. Drastically different from contemporary Indian settlements in the area, the site contains the remains of eight turf houses, a smithy, a charcoal kiln, and middens (rubbish dumps). There is also evidence of workshops for carpentry and weaving. The typical Norse artifacts recovered include a spindle whorl, a hollowed stone oil lamp, a bone needle, a bronze pin, and iron rivets. Occupation was brief, perhaps as short as 30 years, probably because of the hostility of the locals and the land's unsuitability for agriculture.

Viking Homes
Replicas of the Vikings' sod houses form the centerpiece of the L'Anse aux Meadows National Historic Site on the northern tip of Newfoundland.

Turf Structures
The Viking huts (right) had walls of piled turf and roofs of turf supported by a wood frame. The largest structure, with five rooms and a workshed, probably housed several families.

Norse Brooches
These brooches made from bronze (left and below left) and copper (above left and below) and plated with silver and gold were recovered from L'Anse aux Meadows.

AD 2000

AD 1500

AD 500

0

The Templo Mayor

- Central feature of Aztec ceremonial center of Tenochtitlán
- Dated to c. AD 1350–1521, destroyed by Spanish after conquest
- Rediscovered in 1978 and excavated by Eduardo Matos Moctezuma
- Finds include twin temples; Coyolxauqui stone; offerings
- Site and museum in Mexico City open to the public

The Templo Mayor, or Great Temple, was the central feature of the Aztec ceremonial center in Tenochtitlán. Ethnohistoric sources record descriptions of the Templo Mayor as it existed at the time of the Spanish conquest in 1519. It featured two temples atop a single pyramidal base: on the right was the temple dedicated to Huitzilopochtli, the Aztec deity of warfare, and on the left was the temple of Tlaloc, the storm god whose rains were the foundation of the Aztecs' agricultural lifestyle.

Archaeological remains of the Templo Mayor were discovered in downtown Mexico City in 1978, when excavations for a utility line unearthed the colossal Coyolxauqui stone. In Aztec legend, Coyolxauqui, the moon goddess, was the jealous sister of Huitzilopochtli and was dismembered by him when she attempted to slay their mother, Coatlicue. The legend continues that Coyolxauqui's body was rolled down to the base of Serpent Mountain. The Coyolxauqui stone depicts the dismembered body of the moon goddess, leading Mexican archaeologist Eduardo Matos Moctezuma to recognize the Templo Mayor as a symbolic reenactment of Serpent Mountain.

The subsequent excavations at the Templo Mayor have uncovered at least six stages of the Aztec pyramid, indicating that it was sequentially enlarged and renewed through ritual acts. More than a hundred offerings have been found, revealing wonderful details of the cosmological vision of the Aztecs, who used exotic materials to create meaning-laden caches of sacred objects. The history and artifacts of the Templo Mayor are wonderfully presented to the public both through the site museum and through a well-illustrated website.

Aztec Center
Excavations in Mexico City have revealed the remains of the Templo Mayor, which dominated a vast walled ritual complex in the Aztec capital of Tenochtitlán.

Sacrificed Goddess
The Coyolxauqui stone depicts the naked body of the moon goddess, with her limbs and head severed. The basalt carving has a diameter of more than 10 feet (3 m).

AD 2000
AD 1000
AD 500
0

Machu Picchu

- Superb example of the architecture and landscape design of the Inca
- Dated to Inca times, possibly built in mid-15th century
- Rediscovered in 1911 by Hiram Bingham, a U.S. explorer
- Finds include architecture, burials, and artifacts
- On public display (the most visited archaeological monument in Peru)

Machu Picchu is the most famous archaeological site in the Andes. Located at the low end of the Urubamba Valley (known as the Sacred Valley of the Incas), several hours' journey from the Inca capital at Cuzco, this extraordinary site was built high above the river in the saddle between the two jungle peaks of Machu Picchu and Huayna Picchu. With its beautiful, impressive architecture, breathtaking location, and dramatic views, Machu Picchu stands out even from other well-planned and finely built Inca sites.

Inca Architecture
The site of Machu Picchu contains some of the finest Inca architecture known, with shrines and temples, waterworks and baths, and royal living quarters. The peak of Huayna Picchu rises in the background.

Machu Picchu was established by the Inca emperor Pachacuti as a royal estate or possibly as a spiritual retreat. The location of the site suggests its religious significance—Machu Picchu is situated among a number of mountain peaks that were sacred to the Inca. The city was built to take advantage of countless views of sacred sites, as well as to facilitate astronomical and solar observations.

Located about four days' walk from Cuzco, Machu Picchu appears to have had only a small permanent population, even though the city could hold about a thousand inhabitants. Apparently, the site was looked after by a small group of retainers, and only truly came to life when the emperor visited with his entourage. After Pachacuti's death, his descendants continued to maintain the city for some time, but it gradually fell into disuse, and had been abandoned by the time the Spaniards arrived in Peru. Because of this, the site is barely mentioned in early Spanish chronicles, and it remained unknown until early in the 20th century. Today, the site is one of Peru's top tourist spots.

Bedrock Art
This striking sculpture was carved into the bedrock in a small grotto beneath a structure known as the *torréon* (tower).

AD 2000
AD 1500
AD 1000
AD 500
0

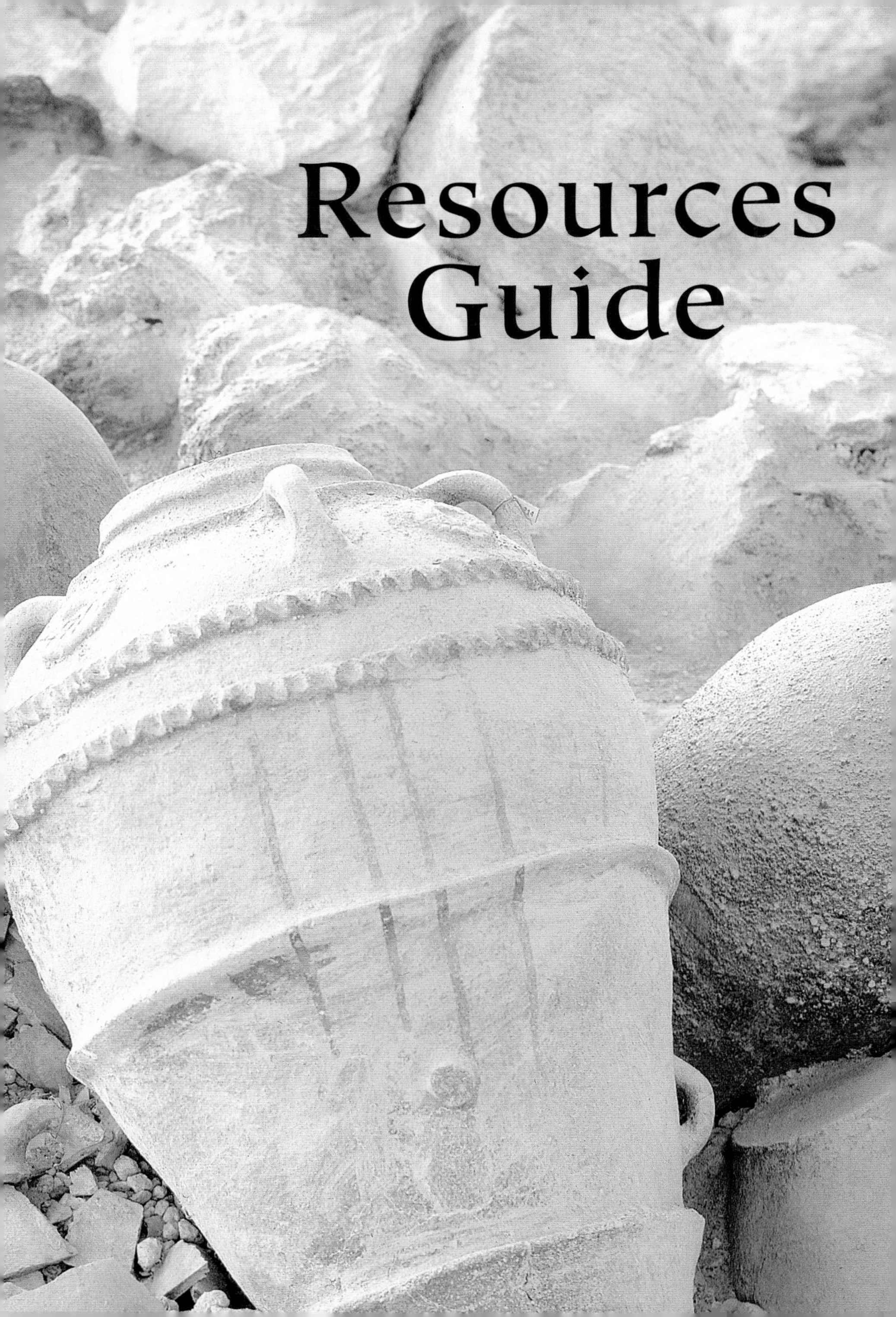

Resources Guide

Resources Guide

BOOKS

The History of Archaeology

The Story of Archaeology: 100 Great Discoveries, by Paul G. Bahn (Barnes and Noble/ Weidenfeld and Nicolson, 1995). The history of archaeology told through its greatest discoveries. [Beginning].

The Cambridge Illustrated History of Archaeology, edited by Paul G. Bahn (Cambridge University Press, 1996). A beautifully illustrated and comprehensive account of archaeology's history. [Intermediate].

The Discovery of the Past: the Origins of Archaeology, by Alain Schnapp (British Museum Press, 1996). An illustrated introduction to early European archaeology. [Intermediate–Advanced].

A History of American Archaeology, by Gordon R. Willey and Jeremy A. Sabloff (W.H. Freeman, 1993). A comprehensive review of the history of American archaeology. [Intermediate–Advanced].

A History of Archaeological Thought, by Bruce G. Trigger (Cambridge University Press, 1990). The most comprehensive and scholarly review of the development of academic archaeology. [Advanced].

The Land of Prehistory: a Critical History of American Archaeology, by Alice Beck Kehoe (Routledge, 1998). A withering yet very sound attack on the political and ideological structure of academic archaeology in America. [Advanced].

Archaeological Methods and Theory

The Amateur Archaeologist, by Stephen Wass (Routledge, 1992). This book shows the novice how to get involved in archaeological projects and how modern archaeology is conducted. [Beginning].

Discovering Our Past: a Brief Introduction to Archaeology, by Wendy Ashmore and Robert J. Sharer (Mayfield, 2000). A clear and succinct introduction to modern archaeology. [Beginning].

The Practical Archaeologist: How We Know What We Know About the Past, by Jane McIntosh (Checkmark, 1999). A clearly written and illustrated introduction to archaeology. [Beginning].

Frauds, Myths, and Mysteries: Science and Pseudoscience in Archaeology, by Kenneth Feder (Mayfield, 1998). An exposé of some of archaeology's most famous hoaxes. [Beginning].

Archaeology: a Very Short Introduction, by Paul G. Bahn (Oxford University Press, 1996). A humorous but accurate introduction to modern archaeology. [Beginning].

Archaeology: Theory, Methods and Practice, by Colin Renfrew and Paul G. Bahn (Thames and Hudson, 2000). A comprehensive description, relying on excellent examples drawn from around the world, of all the major methods and theories currently used in archaeological interpretation. [Intermediate–Advanced].

The Oxford Companion to Archaeology, edited by Brian M. Fagan (Oxford University Press, 1996). Over 700 entries cover the whole gamut of archaeology, its history, theories, and techniques. [Intermediate–Advanced].

Historical Archaeology, by Charles E. Orser and Brian M. Fagan (Addison-Wesley, 1995). A review of the world of contemporary historic archaeology. [Intermediate].

Encyclopedia of Underwater and Maritime Archaeology, edited by James P. Delgado (Yale University Press, 1998). Richly illustrated and comprehensive guide to underwater archaeology, covering prehistory to the modern period. [Beginning–Intermediate].

Engendering Archaeology: Women and Prehistory, edited by Joan M. Gero and Margaret W. Conkey (Blackwell, 1991). A series of essays that explores the potential for and problems involved in identifying gender relations in the archaeological past. [Advanced].

Environmental Archaeology: Principles and Practice, by Dena Dincauze (Cambridge University Press, 2000). An in-depth look at the techniques used to reconstruct past environments. [Advanced].

Loot, Legitimacy and Ownership: the Ethical Crisis in Archaeology, by Colin Renfrew (Duckworth, 2000). A look at the trade in illicit antiquities and how that practice severely reduces scientific knowledge of the past. [Intermediate].

Native Americans and Archaeologists: Stepping

Stones to Common Ground, edited by Nina Swidler, Kurt E. Dongoske and Roger Anyon (Altamira, 1997). This series of essays looks at the potential for Native Americans and archaeologists to come together in creating an archaeological past that is mutually respectful. [Intermediate–Advanced].

The Archaeology Education Handbook, by Karolyn E. Smardz and Shelley J. Smith (Altamira, 2000). This book is designed to help archaeologists teach children about the discipline. [Intermediate].

Human Evolution

Making Silent Stones Speak: Human Evolution and the Dawn of Technology, by Kathy D. Schick and Nicholas Toth (Simon and Schuster, 1993). A detailed review of how stone tool technology evolved. [Beginning–Intermediate].

The Human Career: Human Biological and Cultural Evolution, by Richard G. Klein (University of Chicago Press, 1999). A detailed well-illustrated review of human evolution. [Advanced].

In Search of the Neanderthals, by Christopher Stringer and Clive Gamble (Thames and Hudson, 1993). An up-to-date review of what we know about these ancestors. [Intermediate].

Neanderthal, by Douglas Palmer (Channel Four Books, 2000). [Intermediate].

The World

People of the Earth: an Introduction to World Prehistory, by Brian M. Fagan (Addison-Wesley, 1997). A comprehensive review of world prehistory. [Intermediate].

The Origins of Human Society, by Peter Bogucki (Blackwell, 1999). An introduction to the development of human society from its origins in Africa to the appearance of modern societies. [Beginning–Intermediate].

Europe

Oxford Illustrated Prehistory of Europe, edited by Barry Cunliffe (Oxford University Press, 1994). An Illustrated introduction to European archaeology. [Intermediate].

Exploring Prehistoric Europe, by Christopher Scarre (Oxford University Press, 1998). An exploration of prehistorical sites in Europe. [Beginning].

Journey Through the Ice Age, by Paul G. Bahn and Jean Vertut (University of California Press, 1997). A beautifully illustrated book on the art of Paleolithic Europe. [Beginning–Intermediate].

Ancient Marbles to American Shores: Classical Archaeology in the United States, by Stephen L. Dyson (University of Pennsylvania Press, 1998). This book covers the development of classical archaeology in the United States. [Intermediate–Advanced].

The Archaeology of Greece, by William R. Biers (Cornell University Press, 1996). A detailed synthesis of ancient Greece from the Bronze Age to the post-Classical period. [Intermediate].

Roman Italy, by T.W. Potter (University of California Press, 1990). A detailed survey of the archaeology of Italy from the Etruscans to the fall of the Roman Empire. [Intermediate].

The Archaeology of Britain, by Ian Ralston (Routledge, 1998). This is a comprehensive review of British archaeology. [Intermediate].

Africa

Human Beginnings in South Africa: Uncovering the Secrets of the Stone Age, by H.J. Deacon and J. Deacon (David Philip, 1999). A very readable and authoritative account of human origins. [Intermediate].

From Lucy to Language, by Donald Johanson and B. Edgar (Witwatersrand University Press, 1996). A review of the evidence for the earliest human ancestors. [Intermediate].

African Archaeology, by David W. Phillipson (Cambridge University Press, 1995). A detailed and comprehensive review of the continent's archaeology. [Intermediate].

The Archaeology of Africa: Food, Metals and Towns, edited by Thurston Shaw, P. Sinclair, B. Andah, and A. Okpoko (Routledge, 1995). A review of African archaeology intended for the specialist. [Advanced].

Cultural Atlas of Ancient Egypt, by John Baines and Jaromir Malek (Checkmark, 2000). A comprehensive and well illustrated introduction to ancient Egypt. [Beginning–Intermediate].

The Pyramids of Egypt, by I.E.S. Edwards (Penguin, 1961). The standard introduction to ancient Egypt [Beginning].

The Americas

Ancient North America: the Archaeology of a Continent, by Brian M. Fagan (Thames and Hudson, 2000). A detailed and very thorough review of North American archaeology. [Intermediate–Advanced].

Exploring Ancient Native America, by David Hurst Thomas (Routledge, 1999). A succinct review of American archaeology. [Beginning–Intermediate].

The Settlement of the Americas: a New Prehistory, by Thomas D. Dillehay (Basic Books, 2000). A provocative look at the evidence for the earliest peopling of the Americas. [Intermediate–Advanced].

Red Earth, White Lies: Native Americans and the Myth of Scientific Fact, by Vine Deloria (Fulcrum, 1997). A critique on how archaeological science has falsely portrayed the past of Native Americans. [Intermediate].

The Maya, by Michael D. Coe (Thames and Hudson, 1999). An introduction to the archaeology of this central American civilization. [Beginning–Intermediate].

Mexico: From the Olmecs to the Aztecs, by Michael D. Coe (Thames and Hudson, 1994). This books covers the archaeology of the rise of civilizations in Central America. [Beginning–Intermediate].

The Aztecs, by Richard F. Townsend (Thames and Hudson, 1993). An introduction to the last and most powerful indigenous empire of Central America before European conquest. [Intermediate].

The Ancient Kingdoms of Peru, by Nigel Davies (Penguin, 1998). A review of the archaeological evidence for the pre-Columbian civilizations of Peru. [Beginning–Intermediate].

The Incas and their Ancestors: the Archaeology of Peru, by Michael E. Moseley (Thames and Hudson, 1993). A synopsis of the archaeology of the civilizations of Peru. [Advanced].

The Cities of Ancient Mexico: Reconstructing a Lost World, by Jeremy A. Sabloff (Thames and Hudson, 1997). An illustrated introduction to the major sites of ancient Mexico, complete with a site gazetteer. [Beginning–Intermediate].

Asia

The Rise of Civilization in East Asia, by Gina Lee Barnes, (Thames and Hudson, 1999). A synthesis of the rise of civilization in the Far East. [Advanced].

The Rise of Civilization in India and Pakistan, by Bridget and Raymond Allchin (Cambridge University Press, 1982). A scholarly look at how civilization arose in the subcontinent. [Advanced].

The Cambridge Illustrated History of China, by Patricia Buckley Ebrey (Cambridge University Press, 1996). A comprehensive synthesis of Chinese civilization. [Intermediate].

China: a New History, by John King Fairbanks and Merle Goldman (Harvard University Press, 1998). A scholarly and comprehensive analysis of China and its people. [Intermediate].

The Pacific

Prehistory of Australia, by John Mulvaney and Johan Kamminga (Smithsonian Institution Press, 1999). A review of the archaeology of that continent beginning 40,000 years ago. [Intermediate].

Polynesians: Prehistory of an Island People by Peter Bellwood (Thames and Hudson, 1978). A good introduction to the aboriginal peoples of the Pacific. [Beginning].

On the Road of the Winds: an Archaeological History of the Pacific Islands before European Contact, by Patrick Vinton Kirch (University of California Press, 2000). A detailed introduction to the archaeology of an often ignored area. [Intermediate].

PERIODICALS

Archaeology is so popular that many local and regional societies put out their own journals and newsletters. Add to these the hundreds of professional journals (regional, national, and international) and the dozens of commercially produced magazines, and you can see why you are spoiled for choice when it comes to archaeology! We have found the following website to be a good introduction to the hundreds of journals available: http://www.anthro.org. The following journals are only a sample of what is available:

Aerial Archaeology Newsletter
African Archaeology Review
African-American Archaeology Newsletter
American Archaeology
American Journal of Archaeology
Andean Past
Antiquity
Archaeology
Archaeology in Oceania
Archaeology Ireland
Australian Archaeology
Biblical Archaeology Review
Canadian Journal of Archaeology
Current Archaeology
Discovering Archaeology
Egypt Revealed
European Journal of Archaeology
Journal of Egyptian Archaeology
Journal of Caribbean Archaeology
Journal of Roman Archaeology

The Mammoth Trumpet
Medieval Archaeology
Scientific American
Society for Historical Archaeology Newsletter
Southeast Asian Archaeology
World Archaeology

ORGANIZATIONS

Many communities have some sort of society or organization that caters to the amateur archaeologist. These societies hold regular meetings, have trips to local archaeological sites, and sometimes work with professional archaeologists. These organizations often advertise their meetings in the local newspaper, and this is a good place to make your first contact. Museums and archaeology and anthropology departments at universities can also be very helpful in directing you to amateur archaeological societies. The following organizations will help get you started on the right road.

Archaeological Institute of America
656 Beacon Street,
Boston, MA 02215-2010, USA
aia@bu.edu

Council for British Archaeology
Bowes Morrell House,
111 Walmgate,
York Y01 2UA, UK

Institute of Nautical Archaeology
P.O. Drawer HG, College Station, TX 77841-5137, USA
nautical@tamvm1.tamu.edu

International Union of Prehistoric and Protohistoric Sciences
University Museum, 33rd and Spruce Streets, Philadelphia, PA 19104-6324, USA

Society for American Archaeology
900 Second Street NE, Suite 12
Washington DC 20002, USA
www.saa.org

Australian Archaeological Association
School of Archaeology,
University of Sydney,
NSW 2006, Australia
www.archaeology.usyd.edu.au

New Zealand Archaeological Association
P.O. 6337,
Dunedin North, New Zealand
www.nzarchaeology.org

WEB SITES

The World Wide Web is a limitless resource for archaeologists—professional and amateur. The following sites are useful portals for many specific web sites.

General web sites
These are very useful portals that take you to many diverse web sites on archaeology. Excellent places to start.
http://www.archaeology.about.com
http://www.serve.com/archaeology/
http://bubl.ac.uk/link/a/archaeologyresearch.htm
http://ads.ahds.ac.uk/

Yahoo archaeology
This contains links to hundreds of other archaeology web sites.
http://dir.yahoo.com/Social_Science/Anthropology_and_Archaeology/

Archnet
This has links to web sites all over the world, organized into the following regions: Africa, the Arctic, Asia, Australia and Pacific, Central America, Europe, Near East, North America, South America.
http://archnet.asu.edu/

Classics Search from Swansea
A series of related web sites that provide access and addresses to many detailed web sites and archaeological organizations.
http://www.swan.ac.uk/classics/www/index.htm

Australian Archaeology
These web sites have links to other Australian and Pacific archaeology web sites.
http://artalpha.anu.edu.au/web/arc/resources/regions.htm
http://artalpha.anu.edu.au/web/arc/arcworld.htm
http://www.archaeology.usyd.edu.au

Canadian Archaeological Association
This is the official web site for Canada's primary professional organization and has useful links to other Canadian archaeological web sites.
http://www.canadianarchaeology.com

Society for American Archaeology
This is the official web site for the USA's primary professional organization. It has useful information on public affairs.
http://www.saa.org

European Archaeology
These web pages provide links to various web sites on European archaeology.
http://odur.let.rug.nl/arge/
http://home.worldnet.fr/~clist/Anthro/Texts/archeuro.html
http://www.academicinfo.net/archyeurope.html
http://www.e-a-a.org/

Council for British Archaeology
This web site proclaims itself as the "gateway to British archaeology online" and has many useful links.
http://www.britarch.ac.uk

Archaeology Africa
Specially designed for students and teachers, this web site gives links to many other web sites on African archaeology.
http://www.archafrica.uct.ac.za

Glossary

Absolute dating: applying a calendrical date to a site, artifact or feature. It is also called chronometric dating.

Acropolis: literally "high city," a natural hill that formed the center of ancient Greek cities.

AD: Anno Domini (in the year of the Lord). Refers to dates after the birth of Christ.

Agora: originally the market place, later a public meeting place, in ancient Greek cities.

Anthropology: the study of humans, concentrating on culture, defined as non-genetic human behavior. Normally broken down into cultural anthropology (contemporary cultures); archaeology (cultures of the past); linguistic anthropology (languages and their cultural roles); physical anthropology (the evolution of humans and the relationship between biology and culture).

Archaeological record: the sum total of all artifacts, features and other objects produced by humans, which are found at an archaeological site.

Archaeology: the branch of anthropology that studies past human behavior through the physical remains of the past.

Artifact: any portable object manufactured or used by humans.

Asia Minor: peninsula of western Asia between the Mediterranean and the Black seas. It includes a large segment of modern-day Turkey

Assemblage: a collection of artifacts used at a particular time and place, and thought to represent an ancient activity or set of activities.

Australopithecine: term for the earliest hominids, who appeared in Africa approximately 5 million years ago.

Barrow: an artificial earthen mound raised over Neolithic and Bronze Age burials.

Bas-relief: sculpture in which the figures project slightly from the background.

BC: refers to dates before the birth of Christ.

Bipedal: having the ability to walk habitually on two legs. Characteristic of humans.

BP: refers to dates before the present, conventionally defined as 1950.

Bronze Age: period of the human past when bronze was the dominant material used for tools. Its date varies from place to place.

c. (Circa): approximately, when referring to a date. Literally, it means "around."

Cartouche: an inscribed or painted outline around hieroglyphic figures indicating that they be read as a unit.

Caryatid: in ancient Greece, a column carved in the form of a female.

Cenotaph: a monument commemorating a dead person or group of dead people, whose bodies are elsewhere.

Citadel: a fortress, often on a natural prominence, that served as the central defensive point of a town or city.

City-state: an independent and sovereign city and its surrounding tributary territories. It is most typically used in referring to specific political entities of ancient Greece and Mesopotamia.

Civilization: a particular form of state-level social and political organization identified by such features as cities, a class system, writing, and monumental architecture.

Colonnade: a row of columns that supported a roof, most usually in Greek architecture.

Context: a comprehensive description of an artifact's or feature's matrix (the sediment in which it lies), its provenience (three-dimensional location), and its association (its spatial relationship to other artifacts and features).

Copper Age: period of the human past when copper was the dominant material used for tools. Its date varies from place to place.

Cuneiform: an ancient writing system of Mesopotamia, so called because the individual characters are wedge-shaped (*cuneus* is Latin for wedge).

Diadem: a crown or headband, often covered with precious jewels or metals, worn as a symbol of authority.

DNA: deoxyribonucleic acid. It is found in chromosomes and is responsible for the transference of genetic information in all living entities. It consists of two nucleotide strands that are wrapped around each other.

Doric style: one of the three major orders of ancient Greek architecture.

Dynasty: a ruling royal family or clan that holds power over several generations.

Experimental archaeology: the replication of ancient technologies in order to better understand ancient production processes and the use of specific artifacts.

Faience: an opaque glaze made of crushed quartz that was applied to ceramic surfaces.

Far East: the countries of East Asia, such as China and Japan.

Feature: a non-portable artifact on an archaeological site, such as a hearth or wall.

Find: an individual artifact, often one of some significance.

Findspot: the location of a find, measured and recorded three-dimensionally.

Four Corners region: that part of the United States surrounding the point where the states of Utah, Colorado, New Mexico, and Arizona all converge.

Geoglyph: a large-scale drawing carved or fashioned into the ground or landscape such as the Nasca Lines of Peru.

Hellenistic: referring to Greek culture after the time of Alexander the Great (356-323 BC).

Hieroglyph: literally sacred writing, an early form of writing in which the characters represent objects rather than sounds or syllables.

Historic period: a period when writing systems existed. The historic period in any particular region begins when writing systems emerge or when literate cultures come into contact with the region's pre-literate inhabitants.

Hominid: any member, fossil or living, of the family of hominidae. Humans and their ancestors belong to this family.

Hominin: similar to or having human characteristics.

***Homo erectus*:** a fossil human form that lived from approximately 2 million years ago to 200,000 years ago. *Homo erectus* is found over a large part of the Old World.

***Homo habilis*:** the earliest representative of the genus *Homo*, this form of human appeared in Africa about two million years ago.

***Homo sapiens*:** genus and species to which modern humans as well as earlier extinct forms belong. The first appearance of *Homo sapiens* may be as early as 400,000 years ago. The term is Latin for wise man.

Hunter-gatherer: a food-procurement system based on the gathering of wild plants and the hunting of wild animals. Hunter-gatherer groups tend to be small in size and mobile in order to take advantage of the seasonal availability of the resources they procure.

Indo-European languages: a huge family of related languages that stretches from northern India to Europe.

In situ: in place. A description of artifacts in sites that are recovered by the archaeologist in their original location.

Iron Age: period of the human past when iron was the dominant material used for tools. Its date varies from place to place.

Krater: ancient Greek vessel used for mixing water and wine.

Last Ice Age: is called the Würm, Weichsel or Wisconsin glaciation depending where on earth it took place. This period, which lasted from about 115,000 to 12,000 years ago, is characterized by massive glaciers that covered large portions of the northern hemisphere.

Levant: the lands next to the east coast of the Mediterranean.

Lintel: a horizontal stone or wooden piece that supports the weight above a door or window.

Lithic: a piece of portable stone that is the result of human manufacture, whether it be a stone tool or a piece of waste material.

Megalith: a large, often undressed, stone used in building construction.

Mesoamerica: a term for Central America that includes such countries as Mexico, Honduras and Nicaragua.

Mesolithic: a period of European prehistory after the Paleolithic but before the advent of Neolithic farmers, when hunter–gatherers were adapting to a warming environment.

Metope: a flat slab of stone, sometimes carved, that was part of the frieze in Doric architecture.

Mya (million years ago): in the study of evolution, events are dated by how far before the present they occurred.

Neanderthal: an extinct form of *Homo sapiens* that appeared in the Old World before 100,000 years ago and lived until about 30,000 years ago.

Near East: the term for Southwest Asia: Turkey, Iraq, Syria, Lebanon, Israel and Jordan, amongst others.

Neolithic: the period of Old World prehistory characterized by the appearance of farming, settled communities and pottery. It follows the Mesolithic and appears at different times in different places.

New World: a generic term for the Americas.

Old World: a generic term for Europe, Asia, and Africa.

Ostraka: in classical Greek cities, people voted on whether individuals should be exiled by writing their names on ostraka, fragments of pottery.

Paleolithic: a vast period that covers most of human existence, from our origins 5 million years ago to about 12,000 years ago. This period sees the emergence of biologically modern humans, as well as significant developments in the human cultural repertoire.

Pantheon: 1) the collective gods and goddesses of a particular religion; 2) 2nd century AD circular temple in Rome.

Pediment: the triangular space, sometimes covered with sculpture, at the end of a Greek temple, formed by the angle of the roof.

Pectoral: pertaining to the chest.

Petroglyph: an image that has been pecked or engraved onto a rock wall.

Potsherd: a fragment of a ceramic vessel.

Pre-Columbian: the period of history in the Americas prior to first contact by Christopher Columbus (AD 1492). Often used synonymously with prehispanic.

Prehispanic: the period of history in the Americas prior to the invasion by Spain in the 16th century.

Prehistory: that period of the human past that predates the emergence of writing systems.

Portcullis: a metal grating that could be dropped in front of the doorway of a medieval castle for defence.

Radiocarbon dating: an absolute dating method developed by Willard Libby in 1949. It takes advantage of the fact that all organic materials contain measurable amounts of radioactive carbon (Carbon 14). At death the radiocarbon begins to disintegrate at a known rate. By measuring the amount of radioactive carbon left, scientists can determine how long ago the organism died. Latest versions of the technique can date objects up to 70,000 years old.

Relative dating: any system of dating that is not based on a calendrical system. Often artifacts or sites are described as earlier or later than other artifacts or sites.

Rhyton: an ancient Greek drinking or pouring horn or vessel, shaped usually in the form of an animal's head.

Semitic languages: a group of languages that includes Akkadian, Arabic, Aramaic, Ethiopian, Hebrew, and Phoenician.

Settlements: the term is used most often in Egypt and Mesopotamia.

Steatite: soapstone, a relatively soft stone that was valued for carving.

Stela(e): an upright stone slab, serving a commemorative or similar function, on which was carved an inscription or other design.

Steppe: a large, relatively flat and treeless, grassland plain.

Stone Age: a generic term for that period of the human past in which stone, bone and wood were the primary raw materials from which tools were made. It covers the Paleolithic, Mesolithic, and Neolithic periods.

Stratigraphy: (the interpretation of) the vertical layering in an archaeological site or a geological deposit that allows scientists to relatively date the artifacts or fossils in the layers (or strata).

Stratified excavation: excavating an archaeological site according to the natural or cultural strata in the site.

Stupa: a pile of earth or other material commemorating Buddha, a sacred event or a sacred place.

Tell: a mound made from the accumulated building debris of collapsed ancient settlements. The term is used most often in Egypt and Mesopotamia.

Trilithon: a megalithic structure composed of two upright stone pillars, topped by a horizontal slab.

Typology: the classification of artifacts into groups or types, based on their sharing similar characteristics or attributes.

Ya (years ago): in archaeological dating, dates are measured from 1950, the period when radiocarbon dating became a practical tool in the archaeologist's arsenal.

Ziggurat: in ancient Mesopotamia, a monumental pyramidal structure composed of brick or stone stories of decreasing size built on top of each other.

Index

Contributors and Acknowledgments

CONSULTANT EDITOR

Dr Paul Bahn
Born and raised in Hull, England, Dr Bahn studied archaeology at the University of Cambridge, and wrote his Ph.D. thesis (1979) on the prehistory of the French Pyrenees. He held post-doctoral fellowships, at Liverpool and London, plus a J. Paul Getty post-doctoral fellowship in the History of Art and the Humanities. Dr Bahn moved into freelance work in the mid-1980s, and since then has devoted himself to writing, editing and translating books on archaeology, plus occasional forays into journalism and as much travel as possible. Dr Bahn's main research interest is prehistoric art, especially rock art of the world, and most notably Paleolithic art.
(Ice Age art, Easter Island)

CONTRIBUTORS

Dr Caroline Bird
AUSTRALIA
(Australasia, gender archaeology)

Dr Peter Bogucki
Associate Dean
School of Engineering and Applied Science
Princeton University
UNITED STATES OF AMERICA
(General and historical material, European prehistory)

Jane Callander
Graduate Student
University College London
(Institute of Archaeology)
University of London
UNITED KINGDOM
(Mount Carmel)

Dr Philip Duke
Professor of Anthropology
Fort Lewis College
UNITED STATES OF AMERICA
(General and historical material, and North America)

Dr Christopher Edens
Resident Director
American Institute for Yemeni Studies, Sana'a, YEMEN
(Near East and western Asia)

Dave Evans
Archaeology Manager
Humber Archaeology Partnership
UNITED KINGDOM
(General material and excavation techniques)

Dr David W.J. Gill
Senior Lecturer and Sub-Dean of the Faculty of Arts and Social Studies
University of Wales Swansea
UNITED KINGDOM
(Classical world)

Dr John F. Hoffecker
Research Associate
Institute of Arctic and Alpine Research
University of Colorado at Boulder
UNITED STATES OF AMERICA
(Paleolithic Age)

Dr Geoffrey G. McCafferty
Associate Professor
Department of Archaeology
University of Calgary
Alberta, CANADA
(Mesoamerica)

Dr Jane McIntosh
UNITED KINGDOM
(India, Southeast Asia)

Elena Miklashevich,
Department of Archaeology
Kemerovo State University
RUSSIA *(Siberia, central Asia)*

Dr Margarete M. Prüch
Research Fellow
Deutsches Archäologisches Institut, GERMANY
(Far East)

Dr Louise Steel
Department of Archaeology
University of Wales Swansea
UNITED KINGDOM *(Aegean)*

Dr Anne I. Thackeray
Research Associate
Department of Archaeology
University of the Witwatersrand
SOUTH AFRICA
(Human evolution, Africa)

Dr Joyce Tyldesley
Honorary Research Fellow
School of Archaeology, Classics and Oriental Studies
Liverpool University
UNITED KINGDOM *(Egypt)*

Dr Karen Wise
Associate Deputy Director (Research and Collections) and Associate Curator (Anthropology)
Los Angeles County Museum of Natural History
UNITED STATES OF AMERICA
(South America)

Marc Zender
Doctoral Candidate
Department of Archaeology,
University of Calgary
Alberta, CANADA
(Maya)

Weldon Owen Pty Limited would like to thank the following people for their assistance in the production of this book: Dr Ron Clarke of the University of Witwatersrand; Robin and Barbara Birley of the Vindolanda Trust; Puddingburn Publishing Services (index); Peta Gorman and Marney Richardson.

PHOTOGRAPH CREDITS

AAP/AAP Image 358b; Aboriginal Affairs Victoria 374b, 375b, 375t; AdLibitum/Stuart Bowey 10tl, 67t, 78b; Ancient Art & Architecture Collection Ltd. 134t, 140t, 214t, 277, 298b, 336b; Anthroarcheart 214b, 362b, 363b, 393b, 393t, 396b, 397b, 397t; APL/Adam Woolfitt/CORBIS 21c, 53c, 82t, 110t, 151c, 273, 282b, 283b, 285b, 286b, 288b; APL/Ali Meyer/CORBIS 267c; APL/Alison Wright/CORBIS 413; APL/Amos Nachoum/CORBIS 72b; APL/Angelo Hornak/CORBIS 194tr; APL/Araldo de Luca/CORBIS 112t, 174t, 178, 179b, 284b; APL/Archivo Iconografico, S.A./CORBIS 21b, 30t, 54l, 124t, 127t, 142b, 144b, 149t, 160t, 179t, 180b, 180t, 185c, 194tl, 250b, 254b, 266c, 276b, 311t, 314b, 338b, 352b, 353b; APL/Asian Art & Archaeology, Inc./CORBIS 34c, 155c, 347, 356b, 356c, 357c; APL/Bettmann/CORBIS 2c, 14–15c, 20b, 26t, 28bl, 28br, 31c, 35bl, 44b, 51t, 54t, 77br, 80t, 102l, 109, 149c, 232b, 268b, 331b; APL/Bowers Museum of Cultural Art/CORBIS 43c; APL/Brian Vikander/ CORBIS 91, 237, 365t; APL/Buddy Mays/CORBIS 12b, 289; APL/Carmen Redondo/CORBIS 315b; APL/Charles & Josette Lenars/CORBIS 45c, 99t, 115b, 145t, 198b, 208, 210b, 220b, 269b, 310b, 311b, 337b, 353t, 363t, 391; APL/Chris Lisle/CORBIS 163t; APL/Christel Gerstenberg/CORBIS 221t; APL/Christie's Images/ CORBIS 32b; APL/Christine Osborne/CORBIS 40b, 203b; APL/Christopher Cormack/CORBIS 35br; APL/CORBIS 56b, 66c, 86bl, 154t, 196t, 197c, 218b, 224–225, 292b, 293b, 293t, 319b, 319t, 349c, 394b, 395c; APL/ CORBIS/George Rinhart 222t; APL/Cordaiy Photo Library Ltd/CORBIS 222b; APL/Craig Lovell/CORBIS 73; APL/ Danny Lehman/ CORBIS 123b, 153t; APL/Dave G. Houser/CORBIS 96b, 223, 371, 412b; APL/David Lees/CORBIS 48t, 81b, 331t; APL/David Muench/CORBIS 121b; APL/David Paterson/CORBIS 283t; APL/David Ball 244b; APL/Dean Conger/ CORBIS 41t, 111, 135b, 251t, 367b; APL/Dewitt Jones/CORBIS 121t; APL/Diego Lezama Orezzoli/CORBIS 98c, 195, 339; APL/Ed Young/CORBIS 97t; APL/Elio Ciol/CORBIS 337t; APL/Eye Ubiquitous/ CORBIS 23b; APL/Francis G. Mayer/CORBIS 352b; APL/Frank Lane Picture Agency/CORBIS 176; APL/Gail Mooney/CORBIS 168r, 177b, 295t; APL/Galen Rowell/CORBIS Cover; APL/Gianni Dagli Orti/CORBIS 8–9c, 12t, 22b, 22t, 25r, 26b, 30b, 51b, 70t, 114, 116t, 128–129, 143c, 148t, 150t, 163c, 168l, 169b, 175t, 179c, 217, 246b, 246c, 249c, 269t, 275b, 287b, 287t, 294b, 295b, 297b, 297t, 306c, 308b, 334b, 340b, 400b, 410b, 414–415; APL/Greg Probst/CORBIS 409b; APL/Hanan Isachar/CORBIS 333t, 359; APL/Historical Picture Archive/ CORBIS 56r; APL/Hulton-Deutsch Collection /CORBIS 18–19c, 33t, 75b, 77bl, 251b, 31t; APL/James L. Amos/ CORBIS 119, 379b; APL/Jim Zuckerman/CORBIS 97c; APL/John Slater/CORBIS 198t, 354b; APL/Jonathan Blair/ CORBIS BCt, 36–37c, 36–37c, 39t, 58b, 63l, 64t, 74t, 75t, 78t, 79t, 98–99b; APL/Keren Su/CORBIS 92–93; APL/ Kevin R. Morris/CORBIS 326–327, 364b; APL/Kevin Schafer/CORBIS 309t, 401b; APL/Kimbell Art Museum/ CORBIS 210t; APL/Larry Lee/ CORBIS 172t; APL/Liz Hymans/CORBIS 399b; APL/Lowell Georgia/CORBIS 38t, 108t, 354c; APL/Luca I. Tettoni/ CORBIS 4–5c; APL/Ludovic Maisant/CORBIS 58t; APL/Macduff Everton/CORBIS 42, 403; APL/Marilyn Bridges/ CORBIS 43t; APL/Michael Nicholson/CORBIS 113c, 309b, 341b; APL/Michael S. Lewis/ CORBIS 407t; APL/ Michael S. Yamashita/CORBIS 193t, 315t; APL/Michael St. Maur Sheil/CORBIS 151b, 259b; APL/Mimmo Jodice/ CORBIS 16–17c, 170t, 260–261; APL/MIT Collection/CORBIS 259t; APL/Natalie Fobes/CORBIS 76t; APL/Nathan Benn/CORBIS 216, 361b; APL/Nik Wheeler/CORBIS 158b, 165t, 206c, 341t, 345, 411; APL/O. Alamany & E. Vicens/CORBIS 112b; APL/Paul A. Souders/CORBIS 386b, 387; APL/Paul Almasy/CORBIS 285t; APL/Penny Tweedie/CORBIS 205b; APL/Pierre Colombel/CORBIS 152b; APL/Ralph A. Clevenger/CORBIS 64r; APL/Ralph White/CORBIS 83b, 83t; APL/Raymond Gehman/CORBIS 45t; APL/Richard A. Cooke/CORBIS 121c, 398b, 406b, 407b; APL/Richard T. Nowitz/CORBIS 20t, 21t, 63t, 96t, 323, 333b, 360b; APL/Robert Harding/ CORBIS 338c; APL/Robert Holmes/CORBIS 228–229; APL/Roger Ressmeyer/CORBIS 124b, 317b; APL/Roger Wood/CORBIS spine, 55b, 117t, 243b, 243t, 250c, 353b; APL/Roman Soumar/CORBIS 90; APL/Sakamoto Photo Research Laboratory/CORBIS 200t; APL/Sally A. Morgan/CORBIS 141; APL/Sean Sexton Collection/CORBIS 316b; APL/ Steve Kaufman/CORBIS 201t; APL/Steve Raymer/CORBIS 70b; APL/Ted Spiegel/CORBIS 52t, 312b, 361t; APL/ The Purcell Team/CORBIS 366b, 367t; APL/Todd Gipstein/CORBIS 46b; APL/Tom Bean/CORBIS 382–383; APL/ Underwood & Underwood/CORBIS 84b; APL/Vanni Archive/CORBIS 32t, 47t, 113r, 165c, 166t, 172b, 248b, 296c, 313c; APL/Wild Country/CORBIS 115t, 399t; APL/Wolfgang Kaehler/CORBIS 34t, 53t, 221b, 299b, 307b, 307t, 355c, 365b, 401t, 409t; APL/Yann Arthus-Bertrand/CORBIS 45b, 245c, 299t; Arkaim Museum 343c; Arlene Mellaart 275t; Australian National Maritime Museum 138b; Bibliotheque Nationale de France 23c, 25t; Bill Curtsinger/National Geographic Image Collection 300b, 301; British Museum, London 17b, 24t, 27b, 33c, 71t, 86br, 87b, 87c, 87cr, 87tl, 94b, 94t, 98tl, 102b, 103cr, 103tl, 103tr,142t, 173c, 182b, 182t, 183b, 184t, 185b, 242b, 254tr, 255c, 320cl, 320cr, 321c, 348b, 104tl, 105b, 106b, 106t, 107b, 107t, 146t, 147t, 189b, 318b; Canterbury Museum, New Zealand 380bl, 380br, 381; David Evans 79b; David Phillipson 191b; Dean

Peter Bogucki/Princeton University 302b, 303; Elena Miklashevich 202t, 325c, 342b, 344b; Getty Images/Tony Stone 25b; Glen Summerhayes 376b, 377b, 377t; Hellenic Ministry of Culture, Greece 46tl; Hinterleitner/ Gamma/Picture Media 280b, 281; http://www.smm.org/catal/ 65c; Humber Archaeology 38b, 72t,104tr; J. Callander 329; Jerry Edmanson/photolibrary.com 29c; Landesdenkmalamt, Baden-Wurtemburg, Stuttgart/ Germany 304b, 305b, 305t; Mercy Hurst Archaeological Institute 139t; Mortimer Wheeler 85t; Museo Archeologico Statale Altamura 263; N.J. Saunders 220t; National Museum of Denmark 50b; National Museum of Kenya 239; Neil Newitt/Courtesy of The Age 49b; Novgorod Museum 324b; Oriental Institute of the University of Chicago 332b, 335; Pablo Arias 144t; Parks Canada Agency 408b; Paul Bahn 95b, 95t, 145b, 258b, 266b, 271, 372b, 373c; Peter Luck/South Australian Museum 204t; photolibrary.com 27t, 50t, 52b, 130b, 378b, 379t; photolibrary.com/A.G.E. FOTOSTOCK 6c, 368–369; photolibrary.com/Hiroshi Higuchi 44t; photolibrary.com/James King-Holmes/SPL 89; photolibrary.com/John Elk 197b; photolibrary.com/John Reader/ SPL 1c, 68–69, 84t, 126–127, 130t, 132t, 133t, 136t, 230, 231, 234b, 235, 238, 262b, 262c, 328b; photolibrary.com/Munoz-Yague/Eurelios/SPL 100b, 188b, 188t, 189t; photolibrary.com/Robert Frerck 209; photolibrary.com/Sheila Terry/SPL 88b; photolibrary.com/Sipa Press 62t, 64b; photolibrary.com/SNS/SIPA PRESS 100t; photolibrary.com/SPL 103b, 353t; photolibrary.com/Stephen Studd 166–167; photolibrary.com/The Bridgeman Art Library 118t, 177c; photolibrary.com/Tom McHugh 233; photolibrary.com/Volker Steger/SPL 137t; Prof. Hilary John Deacon 241b, 241t; Reg Morrison 370b; Robert Harding Picture Library/Robert Frerck 385b; Scala 272b; South African Museum 240b, 256b, 257; Steven Fischer 207b; Steven Snape 247t ; Swiss National Museum, Zurich 278b, 279b, 279t; Sylvain Grandadam/photolibrary.com 57c; The Art Archive 117cl, 135t, 264b, 290b, 291b, 330b; Tim Denham/Australian National University 155b; Tom Dillehay 384b, 385t; University College London Library 125t; University of Leicester 265; Werner Forman Archive 13b, 17c, 28t, 40t, 48c, 55t, 80b, 88t, 101, 108b, 110b, 116b, 118b, 120t, 127b, 152t, 156–157, 158t, 160c, 161b, 162b, 164t, 181, 186, 187t, 190t, 192b, 200b, 206b, 210c, 212, 213b, 213c, 236b, 247b, 252b, 252c, 253, 274b, 317t, 322b, 346b, 388b, 389, 390b, 390c, 392b, 398c, 402l; Werner Forman Archive/ British Museum London 39c; Werner Forman Archive/Museum Fur Volkerkunde, Berlin 218c, 218t; Western Australian Museum 204c; Wilbur E. Garrett/National Geographic Image Collection 404b, 405; Wiltshire Heritage Museum, Devizes 291t; York Archaeological Trust 60b, 60t, 61, 67b

MAPS Stuart McVicar, Lorenzo Lucia and Laurie Whiddon
ILLUSTRATIONS John Richards, except page 402 Mike Gorman.

CAPTIONS

Pages 14–15: An archaeologist works on the Mycenae excavations of 1952–54.

Pages 16–17: This statue is a Roman copy of the Hellenistic sculpture "Farnese Bull."

Pages 18–19: Howard Carter opens the screens around King Tut's sarcophagus.

Pages 36–37: A scuba diver tags artifacts before they are brought to the surface during a 1977 underwater excavation in Turkey.

Pages 66–67: This gold mummy mask, dating to about 850 BC, covered the face of King Shoshenq II at Tanis, Egypt.

Pages 68–69: Paleoanthropologist Alun Hughes sits above the excavations of the early hominid site of Sterkfontein, South Africa.

Pages 92–93: Terracotta warriors guard the tomb of China's First Emperor.

Pages 126–27: These two fossil skulls belonged to australo-pithecines, apelike upright-walking human ancestors.

Pages 128–29: A bull and a horse are featured in this replica of a Lascaux cave painting.

Pages 156–57: The Maya Codex Cospi depicts planetary gods.

Pages 224–25: The smallest of the three great pyramids at Giza is the pyramid of Menkaure. The three small pyramids beside it belong to Menkaure's queens.

Pages 228–29: Sunlight streams between the columns of the Temple of Seti, Abydos, Egypt.

Pages 260–61: This fresco painting, dated to about 50 BC, was unearthed at the Villa of the Mysteries, at Pompeii, Italy.

Pages 326–27: Elaborate relief sculptures decorate the Buddhist Bayon temple at Angkor Thom, Cambodia. The temple is dated to the late 12th century AD.

Pages 368–69: Easter Island is famous for its giant stone statues known as moai.

Pages 382–83: The Anasazi ruins of Cliff Palace, at Mesa Verde in Colorado, USA, date to the 13th century AD.

Pages 414–15: The excavations of Akrotiri, on the Greek island of Thera (modern Santorini), provided rich finds of Bronze Age pottery.